CAMPING AND WOODCRAFT

VOLUME I: CAMPING

THE DELUXE MASTERPIECE ON OUTDOORS
LIVING AND WILDERNESS TRAVEL

THE EXPANDED 1916 VERSION
IN TWO VOLUMES

BY **HORACE KEPHART**

LEGACY EDITION

THE LIBRARY OF AMERICAN OUTDOORS CLASSICS
BOOK 19

FEATURING
REMASTERED CLASSIC WORKS OF THE HIGHEST QUALITY
FROM **THE TIMELESS MASTERS AND TEACHERS**
OF CAMPING, OUTDOORS SKILLS, WOODCRAFT,
AND TRADITIONAL HANDCRAFTS

Doublebit Press
Eugene, OR

New content, introduction, and annotations
Copyright © 2020 by Doublebit Press. All rights reserved.

Doublebit Press is an imprint of Eagle Nest Press
www.doublebitpress.com | Eugene, OR, USA

Original content under the public domain.
First published in 1916 by Horace Kephart.

This title, along with other Doublebit Press books including the Library of American Outdoors Classics, are available at a volume discount for youth groups, outdoors clubs, or reading groups.

Doublebit Press Legacy Edition ISBNs

Volume I - Camping
Hardcover: 978-1-64389-081-4
Paperback: 978-1-64389-082-1

Volume II – Woodcraft
Hardcover: 978-1-64389-083-8
Paperback: 978-1-64389-084-5

Disclaimer: Because of its age and historic context, this text could contain content on present-day inappropriate outdoors activities, outdated medical information, unsafe chemical and mechanical processes, or culturally and racially insensitive content. Doublebit Press, or its employees, authors, and other affiliates, assume no liability for any actions performed by readers or any damages that might be related to information contained in this book. This text has been published for historical study and for personal literary enrichment toward the goal of the preservation of American outdoors history and heritage.

First Doublebit Press Legacy Edition Printing, 2020

Printed in the United States of America
when purchased at retail in the USA

INTRODUCTION
To The Doublebit Press Legacy Edition

Horace Kephart can probably be called the Dean of outdoors writing at the turn of the 20th Century. Although Nessmuk (George W. Sears) is the original old camper and woodsman who penned about the skills of the outdoorser, it was Kephart who voraciously collected tidbits and tips about outdoors life and used this information as he prolifically wrote about the outdoors.

Kephart commonly published in outdoors and sportsmen's magazines of the day and was a household name among people who avidly visited the fresh air of the forests and rivers. One day, Kephart finally collected his writings and compiled the book you hold in your hands, which is really one of the original how-to manuals of the outdoors and camp life. This present version, however, is a significantly expanded work of his original *Book of Camping And Woodcraft*, which was published in 1906. In this version, Kephart added hundreds of pages of new insights and illustrations to guide the traveler of the wilderness and to help folks to make the most of the time outdoors.

Inside these pages are decades, if not centuries of knowledge of the camping tradition, cookery and kitchen tips, and as much backwoods and bushcraft knowledge of the woods and wilderness that Kephart could find in the day. Many of the tips included within have been long lost to time, as more modern camping equipment and conveniences have become popular. However, the information contained within these pages is timeless and more important today than ever! The master woodsfolk of the 21st Century digital age stand to benefit from learning the old ways of the woods masters and camping traditionalists!

Kephart's two-volume work *Camping and Woodcraft* served as the standard for outdoors adventure for many decades after it was published. A true outdoorsperson has both versions of Kephart's *Camping and Woodcraft* series represented on their cabin shelves, in their camping kit, or proudly displayed in their home collection for study. Each version has overlapping, but unique information. This later 1916-17 version of *Camping and Woodcraft* is this most common version of Kephart's work over the 20th Century, and was later bound into a single, large volume (1921).

A TIMELINE OF HORACE KEPHART'S CAMPING & WOODCRAFT BOOKS
1906 – *The Book of Camping and Woodcraft* (first work)
1916-17 – *Camping* (significantly expanded work, first volume)
1916-17 – *Woodcraft* (significantly expanded work, second volume)
1921 – *Camping and Woodcraft* (two volumes in one, few revisions)

About the Library of American Outdoors Classics

The old experts of the woods and mountains taught timeless principles and skills for decades. Through their books, the old experts offered rich descriptions of the outdoor world and encouraged learning through personal experiences in nature. Over the last 125 years, camping, outdoors recreation, and woods activities have substantially changed. Many things have gotten simpler as gear has improved, and life outside or on the trail now brings with it many of the same comforts enjoyed in town. In addition, some activities of the olden days are now no longer in vogue, or are even outright considered inappropriate or illegal, such as high-impact camping practices like chopping down live trees. However, despite many of the positive changes in outdoors methods that have occurred over the years, *there are many other skills and much knowledge that have been forgotten* from the golden era of American outdoors recreation.

By publishing the Library of American Outdoors Classics, it is our goal at Doublebit Press to do what we can to preserve and share the works from forgotten teachers that form the cornerstone of the history of the American outdoors. Through remastered reprint editions of timeless classics of outdoor recreation, perhaps we can regain some of this lost knowledge for future generations.

Because there were fewer options for finding outdoors gear in the early 1900's, experts in *"woodcraft"* skills (not to be confused with today's use of the word to mean woodworking or making things of wood) had to have a deep knowledge of the basic building blocks of outdoor living. This involved not only surviving in the outdoors, but to also have a comfortable and enjoyable time. As Nessmuk puts it in his book *Woodcraft,* "We do not go to the woods to rough it; we go to smooth it — we get it rough enough in town. But let us live the simple, natural life in the woods, and leave all frills behind." Nessmuk did not advocate for folks to go outside and have a terrible time. That would be contrary to the whole point of getting outside. Instead, he advocated for a "simpler" life by leaving some of the creature comforts of the city behind, but also entering the outdoors in a smart and practiced way that made the experience a much more satisfying vacation from home. The goal is to be comfortable so you can focus on having a good time outside and take in everything exposure to nature can offer. However, to be comfortable, one has to know the ins and outs of camping and outdoors life. Despite all the advances in campcraft and outdoors recreation, the old masters of the woods would all likely argue that this will only come from practicing the basics.

Because there was no market yet for specialty outdoors recreational gear (and thus, few outfitters), most outdoors gear came from military surplus piles or was custom made. As such, the old masters of woodcraft often made their own gear suited to their tastes. Through much experience in the woods and field, the great outdoors experts had to know why things worked the way they did by understanding the great web of cause and effect in nature. They had to learn from experience why certain gear worked better in different conditions or know how to solve problems off-the-cuff when things got hairy. They used the basic blocks of camping and outdoors knowledge to fine-tune their gear. They gained experience whenever they could and tried things different ways so they could gain mastery over the fundamentals and see challenges from many angles.

Today, much of the outdoor experience has been greatly simplified by neatly arranged campsites at public campgrounds and gear that has been meticulously improved and tested in both the lab and the field. Many modern conveniences are only a brief trek away, with many parks, campgrounds, and even forests having easy-access roads, convenience stores, and even cell phone signal. In some ways, it is much easier to camp and go outdoors today, and that is a good thing! We should not be miserable when we go outside — lovers of the outdoors know the essential restorative capability that the woods can have on the body, mind, and soul. Although things have gotten easier on us in the 21st Century when it comes to the outdoors, it certainly does not mean that we should forget the foundations of outdoors lore, though. All modern camping skills, outdoors equipment, and cool gizmos that make our lives easier are all founded on principles of the outdoors that the old masters knew well and taught to those who would listen.

Every woods master had their own curriculum or thought some things were more important than others. This includes the present author — certain things appear in this book that other masters leave out of theirs. The old masters also taught common things in slightly different ways or did things differently than others. That's what makes each of the experts different and worth reading. There's no universal way of doing something, especially now. Learning to go about something differently helps with mastery or learn a new skill altogether. Again, to use the metaphor from the above paragraphs, outdoors skills mastery consists of learning the basic building blocks of outdoors living, woods and nature lore, and the art of packing properly for trips. Each master goes about describing these building blocks differently or shows a different aspect of them.

Therefore, we have decided to publish this Legacy Edition in our Library of American Outdoors Classics series. This book is an important contribution to the early American recreational outdoors literature and has important historical and collector value toward preserving the American outdoors tradition. The knowledge it holds is an invaluable reference for practicing skills and hand craft methods. Its chapters thoroughly discuss some of the essential building blocks of knowledge that are fundamental but may have been forgotten as equipment gets fancier and technology gets smarter. In short, this book was chosen for Legacy Edition printing because much of the basic skills and knowledge it contains has been forgotten or put to the wayside in trade for more modern conveniences and methods.

Although the editors at Doublebit Press are thrilled to have comfortable experiences in the woods and love our high-tech and light-weight equipment, we are also realizing that the basic skills taught by the old masters are more essential than ever as our culture becomes more and more hooked on digital stuff. We don't want to risk forgetting the important steps, skills, or building blocks involved with thriving in the outdoors. The Legacy Edition series represents the essential contributions to the American outdoors tradition by the great experts of outdoors life and traditional hand crafting.

With technology playing a major role in everyday life, sometimes we need to take a step back in time to find those basic building blocks used for gaining mastery – the things that we have luckily not completely lost and has been recorded in books over the last two centuries. These skills aren't forgotten, they've just been shelved. *It's time to unshelve them once again and reclaim the lost knowledge of self-sufficiency.*

Based on this commitment to preserving our outdoors and handcraft heritage, we have taken great pride in publishing this book as a complete original work. We hope it is worthy of both study and collection by outdoors folk in the modern era of outdoors and traditional skills life.

Unlike many other photocopy reproductions of classic books that are common on the market, this Legacy Edition does not simply place poor photography of old texts on our pages and use error-prone optical scanning or computer-generated text. We want our work to speak for itself, and reflect the quality demanded by our customers who spend their hard-earned money. With this in mind, each Legacy Edition book that has been chosen for publication is carefully remastered from original print books, *with the Doublebit Legacy Edition printed and laid out in the exact way that it was presented at its original publication.* We provide a beautiful, memorable experience that is as true to the original text as best as possible, but with the aid of modern technology to make as beautiful a reading experience as possible for books that are typically over a century old.

Because of its age and because it is presented in its original form, the book may contain misspellings, inking errors, and other print blemishes that were common for the age. However, these are exactly the things that we feel give the book its character, which we preserved in this Legacy Edition. During digitization, we ensured that each illustration in the text was clean and sharp with the least amount of loss from being copied and digitized as possible. Full-page plate illustrations are presented as they were found, often including the extra blank page that was often behind a plate. For the covers, we use the original cover design to give the book its original feel. We are sure you'll appreciate the fine touches and attention to detail that your Legacy Edition has to offer.

For outdoors enthusiasts who demand the best from their equipment, this Doublebit Press Legacy Edition reprint was made with you in mind. Both important and minor details have equally both been accounted for by our publishing staff, down to the cover, font, layout, and images. It is the goal of Doublebit Legacy Edition series to preserve outdoors heritage, but also be cherished as collectible pieces, worthy of collection in any outdoorsperson's library and that can be passed to future generations.

Every book selected to be in this series offers unique views and instruction on important skills, advice, tips, tidbits, anecdotes, stories, and experiences that will enrichen the repertoire of any person who enjoys escaping the city and finding their way to the trails of the wilds. To learn the most basic building blocks of outdoors life leads to mastery of all its aspects.

Studying This Book

The pages within this book present an overwhelming amount of information, facts, and directions to memorize that are often outdated and at the least, out of practice by modern standards. That doesn't mean that these pages have nothing to teach! It's just going to likely be new stuff for many readers.

Our one suggestion is *don't try to memorize everything,* especially when you're thumbing through the book or even reading it cover-to-cover. Writings from the late 1800's to early 1900's can be dense and out of style for someone not used to reading these types of books. Instead, gain some basic familiarity with each topic by thumbing through the pages, looking at the illustrations, and seeing the section headers. Then, choose a few topics or skills for deeper study.

Before camping or other outdoors trips can even begin, some planning and reflection is useful, which may be best done in town before you go out to the field. First, it might be helpful to read through the book with plans in mind. The book can provide useful material for close study and reflection when in town before you head out to the field to practice.

Secondly, once you've come up with a practice plan, you will of course want to start doing tasks and skills in the field. Doublebit Legacy books and the Library of American Outdoors Classics represents many field skills to master that have long sense been out of practice, but hopefully not forgotten! These include making and trying different kinds of tents or shelters, cooking (including any fish and game caught by you in the field), making many types of fires, setting up camp to suit your personal needs, beating the bugs and elements, understanding the terrain and weather, making furniture, brushing up on your nature lore, emergency survival, and testing your personal outfit and tools.

Any of the old tutors of woodcraft will tell you in their classic books that you can only truly learn how to go camping and do woodcraft by *actually doing it*. Home study indeed does you well by using the many guidebooks that have been published over the previous 125 years. However, hundreds more lessons will become immediately available to you the moment you start with some of the old-style tasks. This old style of outdoorsing is indeed outdated in many ways, but the approach still has much to teach modern campers who have become accustomed to carved out campsites, cabin and RV camping, and high-tech equipment.

Before the days of outfitters, outdoors adventurers made their gear, which was tailored to their individual needs. Many experiments were done in the field to tweak their gear to get that ever-changing point of "perfect." Aside from experiencing wonderful lessons in history, getting outside and doing some of the activities this book will give you an appreciation for modern advances in outdoors and handcraft method and tools of the trade, as well as a deeper understanding of the foundations of outdoors and hand-craft life in the event that your gear fails you or you otherwise find yourself in situations where knowing the principles will get you unstuck fast.

If we were to tally up each of the individual tips in the Doublebit Library of American Outdoors Classics, they would easily number in the thousands. The old masters represent centuries of previous knowledge that have been all but lost to 21st Century, technology-driven folks. To this point, although experience and *actually doing stuff* are the best forms of learning, taking a mindful approach to study of these works also benefit your development as a competent outdoorsperson and handcrafter.

You may also find it invaluable to take these volumes with you on your camping or other outdoors trips. In addition to having reading material on a variety of topics in the field for down time, you'll also find a thousand things to try in these pages if you're bored. Although skills may be best studied when in the field through experience and reflection, you may also study woods skills at home as well. Gaining familiarity through reading, videos, and other media are a great start toward building your ability toward gaining mastery in the field.

So, without blabbering on further, we hope you enjoy your Doublebit Legacy Edition. May your trails be clear and your experiences be memorable!

- The Doublebit Press Editors

CAMPING
AND
WOODCRAFT

A HANDBOOK FOR VACATION CAMPERS
AND FOR
TRAVELERS IN THE WILDERNESS

BY
HORACE KEPHART
Author of "Our Southern Highlanders," "Sporting
Firearms," "Camp Cookery," etc.

VOL. I

CAMPING

NEW YORK
OUTING PUBLISHING COMPANY
1916

Copyright, 1916, by
OUTING PUBLISHING COMPANY

To
THE SHADE OF NESSMUK
IN THE
HAPPY HUNTING GROUND

PREFACE

The present work is based upon my *Book of Camping and Woodcraft,* which appeared in 1906. All of the original material here retained has been revised, and so much new matter has been added that this is virtually a new work, filling two volumes instead of one.

My first book was intended as a pocket manual for those who travel where there are no roads and who perforce must go light. I took little thought of the fast-growing multitude who go to more accessible places and camp out just for the pleasure and healthfulness of open-air life. It had seemed to me that outfitting a party for fixed camp within reach of wagons was so simple that nobody would want advice about it. But I have learned that such matters are not so easy to the multitude as I had assumed; and there are, to be sure, "wrinkles," plenty of them, in equipping and managing stationary camps that save trouble, annoyance, or expense. Consequently I am adding several chapters expressly for that class of campers, and I treat the matter of outfitting much more fully than before.

It is not to be supposed that experienced travelers will agree with me all around in matters of equipment. Every old camper has his own notions about such things, and all of us are apt to be a bit dogmatic. As Richard Harding Davis says, "The same article that one declares is the most essential to his comfort, health, and happiness is the very first thing that another will throw into the trail. A man's outfit is a matter which seems to touch his private honor. I have heard veterans sitting

PREFACE

around a camp-fire proclaim the superiority of their kits with a jealousy, loyalty, and enthusiasm they would not exhibit for the flesh of their flesh and the bone of their bone. On a campaign you may attack a man's courage, the flag he serves, the newspaper for which he works, his intelligence, or his camp manners, and he will ignore you; but if you criticise his patent water-bottle he will fall upon you with both fists."

Yet all of us who spend much time in the woods are keen to learn about the other fellow's "kinks." And field equipment is a most excellent hobby to amuse one during the shut-in season. I know nothing else that so restores the buoyant optimism of youth as overhauling one's kit and planning trips for the next vacation. Solomon himself knew the heart of man no better than that fine old sportsman who said to me "It isn't the fellow who's catching lots of fish and shooting plenty of game that's having the good time: it's the chap who's *getting ready to do it.*"

I must thank the public for the favor it showed my *Book of Camping and Woodcraft,* which passed, with slight revision, through seven editions in ten years. For a long time I have wished to expand the work and bring it up to date. As there is a well-defined boundary between the two subjects of camping and woodcraft, it has seemed best to devote a separate volume to each. The first of these is here offered, to be followed as soon as practicable by the other, which will deal chiefly with such shifts and expedients as are learned or practised in the wilderness itself, where we have nothing to choose from but the raw materials that lie around us.

Acknowledgments are due to the D. T. Abercrombie Co., New York, the Abercrombie & Fitch Co., New York, and the New York Sporting Goods Co., for permission to reproduce certain illustrations of tents and other equipment.

This book had its origin in a series of articles

PREFACE

under the same title that I contributed, in 1904–1906, to the magazine *Field and Stream*. Other sections have been published, in whole or in part, in *Sports Afield, Recreation, Forest and Stream,* and *Outing*. A great deal of the work here appears for the first time.

Many of these pages were written in the wilderness, where there were abundant facilities for testing the value of suggestions that were outside the range of my previous experience. In this connection I must acknowledge indebtedness to a scrap-book full of notes and clippings from sportsmen's journals which was one of the most valued tomes in the rather select "library" that graced half a soap-box in one corner of my cabin.

I owe much both to the spirit and the letter of that classic in the literature of outdoor life, the little book on *Woodcraft*, by the late George R. Sears, who is best known by his Indian-given title of "Nessmuk." To me, in a peculiar sense, it has been *remedium utriusque fortunæ;* and it is but fitting that I should dedicate to the memory of its author this pendant to his work.

HORACE KEPHART.

Bryson City, N. C.,
February, 1916.

CONTENTS

CHAPTER		PAGE
I	VACATION TIME	17
II	OUTFITTING	23
III	TENTS FOR FIXED CAMPS	29
IV	FURNITURE, TOOLS, AND UTENSILS FOR FIXED CAMPS	53
V	TENTS FOR SHIFTING CAMPS	68
VI	TYPES OF LIGHT TENTS	76
VII	LIGHT CAMP EQUIPMENT	109
VIII	CAMP BEDDING	124
IX	CLOTHING	138
X	PERSONAL KITS	164
XI	PROVISIONS	178
XII	CAMP MAKING	208
XIII	THE CAMP-FIRE	225
XIV	PESTS OF THE WOODS	241
XV	DRESSING AND KEEPING GAME AND FISH	264
XVI	CAMP COOKERY — MEATS	290
XVII	CAMP COOKERY — GAME	305
XVIII	CAMP COOKERY — FISH AND SHELLFISH	321
XIX	CAMP COOKERY — CURED MEATS, ETC.— EGGS	332
XX	CAMP COOKERY — BREADSTUFFS AND CEREALS	342
XXI	CAMP COOKERY — VEGETABLES — SOUPS	363
XXII	BEVERAGES AND DESSERTS	378
XXIII	COOK'S MISCELLANY	386
	INDEX	395

ILLUSTRATIONS

	PAGE
Wall Tent, with Fly	29
Extension Fly	36
Tropical Tent	37
Bobbinet Window	39
Mosquito Curtain	39
Asbestos Pipe Guard	40
Locating Corner of the Tent	42
Tent Stake and Guy Rope	43
U. S. Army Wall Tent with Fly (Officers' Tent)	45
Storm Set	45
Wall Tent on Shears with Guy Frame	46
Lashing for Shear Legs	47
Shear Legs Spread	47
Magnus Hitch (not apt to slip along a pole)	47
Wall Tent with Side Bars	48
Trenching Tent	49
Tent Floor	50
Guys Weighted with Log	51
Guy Rope Fastened to Fagot to Be Buried in Ground	51
Narrow Cot	54
Compact Cot	54
Telescoping Cot	54
Cot with Mosquito Screen	54
Folding Chair	56
Folding Arm Chair	56
Roll-up Table	56
Roll-up Table Top	56
Table with Shelf	57
Compact Table	57
Folding Shelves	57
Wall Pocket	57
Small Camp Stove	61
Stove Packed	61

ILLUSTRATIONS

	PAGE
Stove for Large Wood	61
Field Range	62
Field Range (packed)	62
Dutch Oven	64
U. S. A. Conical Tent	78
Sibley Tent Stoves	79
Miner's Tent	82
Frazer Tent	83
Marquee	83
George Tent	84
Layout of George Tent	85
Royce Tent	87
Royce Tent	89
Royce Tent	90
Wedge Tent, Outside Ridge Rope	92
Pegging Bottom of Tent	93
Side Parrels	93
Whymper Alpine Tent	95
Hudson Bay Tent	95
Ross Alpine Tent	96
Separable Shelter Tent	96
Shelter half with Wall	97
Tarpaulin Tent	98
Baker Tent	99
Camp-fire Tent	100
Canoe Tent with Pole	102
Canoe Tent with Ridge	102
Compac Tent	104
Snow Tent	105
Explorer's Tent	106
Little Giant Scale	115
Cooking Pot	119
Pot Chain	119
Coffee Pot	119
Miner's Coffee Pot	119
Cup	120
Miller Frying Pan	120
Reflector (angular back)	121
Reflector (flat back)	121
Reflector (folded in case)	121

ILLUSTRATIONS

	PAGE
Sheet Steel Oven	122
D. T. Abercrombie Sleeping Bag	130
Fiala Sleeping Bag	131
U. S. A. Regulation Sleeping Bag	136
Shattuck Camp Roll	136
Comfort Sleeping Pocket	137
Combination Bed Roll, Stretcher Bed and Bed Tick	137
Combination as Stretcher Bed	137
Combination as Hammock	137
Combination as Bed Roll	137
Neckerchief Folded for Hood	143
Neckerchief Hood Adjusted	143
U. S. Army Canvas Legging	145
Canvas Strap Puttee	145
Woolen Spiral Puttee	145
True Bow Knot	151
Reef Knot Formed	151
Reef Knot Drawn Tight	151
U. S. Army Shoe	152
Sole of Army Shoe, Showing Proper Method of Placing Hobnails	152
Soled Moccasin (made over last)	159
Dunnage Bag	164
Kit or Provision Pack	164
Screw Hook Fastening for Box Lid	164
Hatchet	166
Sheath Knife	167
Compass with Course Arrow	169
Map Case	171
U. S. A. Dispatch Case	171
To Fold Triangular Bandage	175
Rare Natural Crotch	219
Common Crotch	219
To Make a Crutch	219
Spring Box	221
Latrine	223
Indian Deer Pack	268
The Place to Use Your Knife	270

CAMPING AND WOODCRAFT

CHAPTER I

VACATION TIME

"So priketh hem Nature in hir coráges,—
Thanne longen folk to goon on pilgrimages,
And palmeres for to seken straunge strondes."
— *Canterbury Tales.*

To many a city man there comes a time when the great town wearies him. He hates its sights and smells and clangor. Every duty is a task and every caller is a bore. There come visions of green fields and far-rolling hills, of tall forests and cool, swift-flowing streams. He yearns for the thrill of the chase, for the keen-eyed silent stalking; or, rod in hand, he would seek that mysterious pool where the father of all trout lurks for his lure.

To be free, unbeholden, irresponsible for the nonce! Free to go or come at one's own sweet will, to tarry where he lists, to do this, or do that, or do nothing, as the humor veers; and for the hours,

"It shall be what o'clock I say it is!"

Thus basking and sporting in the great clean out-of-doors, one could, for the blessed interval,

"Forget six counties overhung with smoke,
Forget the snorting steam and piston-stroke,
Forget the spreading of the hideous town."

This instinct for a free life in the open is as natural and wholesome as the gratification of hunger and thirst and love. It is Nature's recall to the simple mode of existence that she intended us for.

Our modern life in cities is an abrupt and violent change from what the race has been bred to these many thousands of years. We come from a line of forebears who, back to a far-distant past, were hunters in the forest, herdsmen on the plains, shepherds in the hills, tillers of the soil, or fishermen or sailors at sea; and however adaptive the human mind may be, these human bodies of ours still stubbornly insist on obeying the same laws that Father Adam's did.

There are soothsayers who forecast that, in the course of evolution, we shall conform to what are now abnormal and mischievous conditions; that man is the most adaptive of all creatures, accommodating himself to greater extremes of temperature and so forth than any other of the higher animals; that moreover he is constantly inventing machines and processes to better his condition, so that we may reasonably expect him to make even the crowded city a wholesome place of residence, though people dwell tier above tier, and our old-fashioned domestic life be quite out of the question.

It may be so. We can fix no bounds to Nature's conforming power. She has produced certain vertebrates, such as the mud-turtle and the hellbender, so eminently adaptive to circumstances that they are equally at home whether immersed in air, water, or mud. And there is the Chinaman, who, being of a breed that has been crowded and coerced for thousands of years, seems to have done away with nerves. " He will stand all day in one position without seeming in the least distressed; he thrives amidst the most unsanitary surroundings; overcrowding and bad air are nothing to him; he does not demand quiet when he would sleep, nor even when he is sick; he can starve to death with supreme complacency." A

VACATION TIME

missionary says: "It would be easy to raise in China an army of a million men — nay, of ten millions — tested by competitive examination as to their capacity to go to sleep across three wheelbarrows, with head downwards like a spider, mouth wide open, and a fly inside."

Some of our own people seem to get no satisfaction out of anything but chasing after dollars without let-up from year to year, save when they are asleep, or in church, or both. We recall a certain rich man who boasted that in the eighty-eight years of his career he had not once taken a vacation or wanted one. Naturally his way was the right way, and he proceeded to show it. "What right," asked he, "has a clerk to demand or expect pay for two weeks' time for which he renders no equivalent? Is it not absurd to suppose that a man who can work eleven and a half months cannot as well work the whole year? The doctors may recommend a change of air when he's sick; but why be sick? Sickness is an irreparable loss of time." I am not misquoting this very rich man: his signed pronouncement lies before me — the sorriest thing that ever I saw in print.

Seriously, is it good for men and women and children to swarm together in cities and stay there, keep staying there, till their instincts are so far perverted that they lose all taste for their natural element, the wide world out-of-doors? In any case, although evolution be a very great and good law, yet is it not a trifle slow? How about you and me? Can we wait a few thousand years for fulfilment of the wise men's prophecy? We are neither coolies, nor mudturtles, nor those other things with the awful name.

Granting, then, that one deserves relief now and then from the hurry and worry that would age him before his prime, why not go in for a complete change while you are about it? Why not exorcise the devil of business and everything that suggests it? The best vacation an over-civilized man can have is to go where he can hunt, capture, and cook his own meat, erect his own shelter, do his own chores, and so, in some measure, pick up again those lost arts of wildcraft that were our heritage through ages past, but of which not one modern man in a hundred knows anything at all. In cities our tasks are so highly specialized, and so many things are done for us by other specialists, that we tend to become a one-handed and one-idead race. The self-dependent life of the wilderness nomad brings bodily habits and mental processes back to normal, by exercise of muscles and lobes that otherwise might atrophy from want of use.

If one would realize in its perfection his dream of peace and freedom from every worldly care, let him keep away from summer resorts and even from farms; let him camp out; and let it be the real thing. There are "camps" so-called that are not camps at all. A rustic cottage furnished with tables and chairs and beds brought from town, with rugs on the floor and pictures on the walls, with a stove in the kitchen and crockery in the pantry, an ice-house hard by, and daily delivery of groceries, farm products, and mails, may be a pleasant place in which to spend the summer with one's family and friends; but it is not a camp. Neither is a wilderness clubhouse, built on a game preserve, looked after by a caretaker, and supplied during the season with servants and the appurtenances of a good hotel.

A camp proper is a nomad's biding-place. He may occupy it for a season, or only for a single night, according as the site and its surroundings please or do not please the wanderer's whim. If the fish do not bite, or the game has moved away, or unpleasant neighbors should intrude, or if anything else goes wrong, it is but an hour's work for him to pull up stakes and be off, seeking that particularly good place which generally lies beyond the horizon's rim.

Your thoroughbred camper likes not the atten-

VACATION TIME

tions of a landlord, nor will he suffer himself to be rooted to the soil by cares of ownership or lease. It is not possession of the land, but of the landscape, that he enjoys; and as for that, all the wild parts of the earth are his, by a title that carries with it no obligation but that he shall not desecrate nor lay them waste.

Houses, to such a one, in summer, are little better than cages; fences and walls are his abomination; plowed fields are only so many patches of torn and tormented earth. The sleek comeliness of pastures is too prim and artificial, domestic cattle have a meek and ignoble bearing, fields of grain are monotonous to his eyes, which turn for relief to some abandoned old-field, overgrown with thicket, that still harbors some of the shy children of the wild. It is not the clearing but the unfenced wilderness that is the camper's real home. He is brother to that good old friend of mine who, in gentle satire of our formal gardens and close-cropped lawns, was wont to say, "I love the unimproved works of God." He likes to wander in the forest tasting the raw sweets and pungencies that uncloyed palates craved in the childhood of our race. To him

> "The shelter of a rock
> Is sweeter than the roofs of all the world."

The charm of nomadic life is its freedom from care, its unrestrained liberty of action, and the proud self-reliance of one who is absolutely his own master, free to follow his bent in his own way, and who cheerfully in turn, suffers the penalties that Nature visits upon him for every slip of mind or bungling of his hand. Carrying with him, as he does, in a few small bundles, all that he needs to provide food and shelter in any land, habited or uninhabited, the camper is lord of himself and of his surroundings.

"Free is the bird in the air,
　And the fish where the river flows;
Free is the deer in the wood,
　And the gipsy wherever he goes.
　　Hurrah!
　And the gipsy wherever he goes."

There is a dash of the gipsy in every one of us who is worth his salt.

CHAPTER II
OUTFITTING

"By St. Nicholas
I have a sudden passion for the wild wood —
We should be free as air in the wild wood —
What say you? Shall we go? Your hands, your hands:"
— *Robin Hood.*

In some of our large cities there are professional outfitters to whom one can go and say: "So many of us wish to spend such a month in such a region, hunting and fishing: equip us." The dealer will name a price; you pay it, and leave the rest to him. When the time comes he will have the outfit ready and packed. It will include everything needed for the trip, well selected and of the best materials. When your party reaches the jumping-off place it will be met by professional guides and packers, who will take you to the best hunting grounds and fishing waters, and will do all the hard work of paddling, packing over portages, making camp, chopping wood, cooking, and cleaning up, besides showing you where the game and fish are "using," and how to get them. In this way a party of city men who know nothing of woodcraft can spend a season in the woods very comfortably, though getting little practical knowledge of the wilderness. This is touring, not campaigning. It is expensive; but it may be worth the price to such as can afford it, and who like that sort of thing.

But, aside from the expense of this kind of camping, it seems to me that whoever takes to the woods and waters for recreation should learn how to shift for himself in an emergency. He may employ guides and a cook — all that; but the day of disaster may come, the outfit may be destroyed, or the city man may find himself some day alone, lost in the forest, and compelled to meet the forces of Nature in a struggle for his life. Then it may go hard with him indeed if he be not only master of himself, but of that woodcraft which holds the key to Nature's storehouse. A camper should know for himself how to outfit, how to select and make a camp, how to wield an axe and make proper fires, how to cook, wash, mend, how to travel without losing his course, or what to do when he has lost it; how to trail, hunt, shoot, fish, dress game, manage boat or canoe, and how to extemporize such makeshifts as may be needed in wilderness faring. And he should know these things as he does the way to his mouth. Then is he truly a woodsman, sure to do promptly the right thing at the right time, whatever befalls. Such a man has an honest pride in his own resourcefulness, a sense of reserve force, a doughty self-reliance that is good to feel. His is the confidence of the lone sailorman, who whistles as he puts his tiny bark out to sea.

And there are many of us who, through some miscue of the Fates, are not rich enough to give *carte blanche* orders over the counter. We would like silk tents, air mattresses, fiber packing cases, and all that sort of thing; but we would soon " go broke " if we started in at that rate. I am saying nothing about guns, rods, reels, and such-like, because they are the things that every well conducted sportsman goes broke on, anyway, as a matter of course. I am speaking only of such purchases as might be thought extravagant. And it is conceivable that some folks might call it extravagant to pay thirty-five dollars for a thing to sleep in when you lie out of doors on the ground from choice, or thirty dollars for pots and pans to cook with when you are " playing hobo," as the unregenerate call our sylvan sport. To

OUTFITTING

practise shrewd economies in such things helps out if you are caught slipping in through the back gate with a brand-new gun, when everybody knows that you already possess more guns than you can find legitimate use for.

If one begins, as he should, six months in advance, to plan and prepare for his next summer or fall vacation, he can, by gradual and surreptitious hoarding, get together a commendable camping equipment, and nobody will notice the outlay. The best way is to make many of the things yourself. This gives your pastime an air of thrift, and propitiates the Lares and Penates by keeping you home o' nights. And there is a world of solid comfort in having everything fixed just to suit you. The only way to have it so is to do the work yourself. One can wear ready-made clothing, he can exist in ready-furnished rooms, but a ready-made camping outfit is a delusion and a snare. It is sure to be loaded with gimcracks that you have no use for, and to lack something that you will be miserable without.

It is great fun, in the long winter evenings, to sort over your beloved duffel, to make and fit up the little boxes and hold-alls in which everything has its proper place, to contrive new wrinkles that nobody but yourself has the gigantic brain to conceive, to concoct mysterious dopes that fill the house with unsanctimonious smells, to fish around for materials, in odd corners where you have no business, and, generally, to set the female members of the household buzzing around in curiosity, disapproval, and sundry other states of mind.

To be sure, even though a man rigs up his own outfit, he never gets it quite to suit him. Every season sees the downfall of some cherished scheme, the failure of some fond contrivance. Every winter sees you again fussing over your kit, altering this, substituting that, and flogging your wits with the same old problem of how to save weight and bulk without sacrifice of utility. All thoroughbred campers do this as regularly as the birds come back in spring, and their kind has been doing it since the world began. It is good for us. If some misguided genius should invent a camping equipment that nobody could find fault with, half our pleasure in life would be swept away.

This is not saying that outfitters' catalogues should be ignored. Get them, by all means, and study them with care. Do this at home, comparing one catalogue with another, that you may know just what you want and what you don't want, before you go out to make purchases. Then you will not be such easy prey to the plausible clerk, and your selection will bear the stamp of your individuality.

The joys and sorrows of camp life, and the proportion of each to the other, depend very much upon how one chooses his companions — granting that he has any choice in the matter at all. It may be noticed that old-timers are apt to be a bit distant when a novice betrays any eagerness to share in their pilgrimages. There is no churlishness in this; rather it is commendable caution. Not every good fellow in town makes a pleasant comrade in the woods. So it is that experienced campers are chary of admitting new members to their lodges. To be one of them you must be of the right stuff, ready to endure trial and privation without a murmur, and — what is harder for most men — to put up with petty inconveniences without grumbling.

For there is a seamy side to camp life, as to everything else. Even in the best of camps things do happen sometimes that are enough to make a saint swear silently through his teeth. But no one is fit for such life who cannot turn ordinary ill-luck into a joke, and bear downright calamity like a gentleman.

Yet there are other qualities in a good camp-mate that are rarer than fortitude and endurance. Chief of these is a love of Nature for her own sake — not the "put on" kind that expresses itself in gushy

OUTFITTING

sentimentalism, but that pure, intense, though ordinarily mute affection which finds pleasure in her companionship and needs none other. As Olive Shreiner says: "It is not he who praises Nature, but he who lies continually on her breast *and is satisfied,* who is actually united to her." Donald G. Mitchell once remarked that nobody should go to the country with the expectation of deriving much pleasure from it, as country, who has not a keen eye for the things of the country, for scenery, or for trees, or flowers, or some kind of culture; to which a New York editor replied that "Of this not one city man in a thousand has a particle in his composition." No doubt a gross exaggeration; but the proportion of city men who do thoroughly enjoy the hardy sports and adventures of the wilderness is certainly much larger than those who could be entertained on a farm; yet the elect of these, the ones who can find plenty to interest them in the woods when fishing and hunting fail, are not to be found on every street corner.

If your party be made up of men inexperienced in the woods, hire a guide, and, if there be more than three of you, take along a cook as well. Treat your guide as one of yourselves. A good one deserves such consideration; a poor one is not worth having at all. But if you cannot afford this expense, then leave the real wilderness out of account for the present; go to some pleasant woodland, within hail of civilization, and start an experimental camp, spending a good part of your time in learning how to wield an axe, how to build proper fires, how to cook good meals out-of-doors, and so forth. Be sure to get the privilege beforehand of cutting what wood you will need. It is worth paying some wood-geld that you may learn how to fell and hew. Here, with fair fishing and some small game hunting, you can have a jolly good time, and will be fitted for something more ambitious the next season.

In any case, be sure to get together a company of

good-hearted, manly fellows, who will take things as they come, do their fair share of the camp chores, and agree to have no arguments before breakfast. There are plenty of such men, steel-true and blade-straight. Then will your trip be a lasting pleasure, to be lived over time and again in after years. There are no friendships like those that are made under canvas and in the open field.

In the following pages I treat the matter of outfitting in detail, not that elaborate outfits are usually desirable — for they are not — but because in town there is so much to pick and choose from. There are many patterns of this, that, and the other article of equipment, some good for one kind of camping, some for another. I try to explain their "points," that the reader may choose intelligently according to his needs.

CHAPTER III
TENTS FOR FIXED CAMPS

When camp is made in a certain locality with no intention of moving it until the party is ready to go home, it usually is called a "permanent camp." This is a misuse of terms; for a camp of any kind is only a temporary biding place. "The camp and not the soil," says Gibbon, "is the native country of the genuine Tartar." When speaking of a camp fixed in one place for a considerable time, I shall call it a fixed camp or stationary camp. It differs from a shifting camp, so far as outfitting is concerned, in permitting the use of heavy and bulky equipment and more of the comforts of home.

WALL TENTS.— For fixed camps, situated where there are wagon roads or other adequate ways of transportation, the best cloth shelter is a wall tent, rectangular or square, of strong and rather heavy material.

Fig. 1.— Wall Tent, with Fly

It is a trade custom to list tents according to an arbitrary scale of ground dimensions, in even feet, although the cloth seldom works out exactly so; for ground dimensions are governed by the number of widths of cloth used and the number of inches to the width, allowing for seams. To slit the cloth lengthwise would destroy its strongest part, the selvage, besides being a waste of material. Moreover, cloth stretches or shrinks in handling.

In the following table are given the trade sizes, actual ground dimensions (these may vary), standard heights of wall and center, and weights of unproofed tents (without flies, poles, or stakes) in sizes commonly used by campers. These sizes apply only to tents made of standard 29-inch duck. If 36-inch stuff, or some other width, is used, proportional allowances must be made.

STANDARD WALL TENTS.
29-INCH DUCK.

Trade sizes.	Actual width and length.	Height wall.	Height center
9 x 9 ft.	9⅓ x 9⅓ ft.	3 ft.	7½ ft.
9 x 12 ft.	9⅓ x 11½ ft.	3 ft.	7½ ft.
12 x 12 ft.	11½ x 11½ ft.	3½ ft.	8 ft.
12 x 14 ft.	11½ x 14½ ft.	3½ ft.	8 ft.
12 x 16 ft.	11½ x 16¼ ft.	3½ ft.	8 ft.
14 x 14 ft.	14 x 14 ft.	4 ft.	9 ft.
14 x 16 ft.	14 x 16¼ ft.	4 ft.	9 ft.

Trade sizes	Weights of tents.			Poles and Stakes.
	8 oz.	10 oz.	12 oz.	
9 x 9 ft.	24 lbs.	30 lbs.	36 lbs.	28 lbs.
9 x 12 ft.	29½ lbs.	35 lbs.	42 lbs.	30 lbs.
12 x 12 ft.	36 lbs.	41½ lbs.	50 lbs.	35 lbs.
12 x 14 ft.	40 lbs.	49 lbs.	59 lbs.	39 lbs.
12 x 16 ft.	44 lbs.	57½ lbs.	63 lbs.	40 lbs.
14 x 14 ft.	44½ lbs.	58 lbs.	68 lbs.	41 lbs.
14 x 16 ft.	51½ lbs.	63 lbs.	76 lbs.	45 lbs.

Weight of poles and stakes varies a good deal, according to size and density of wood.

Flies of same length as tent, and same kind of duck, weigh about half as much as the tent itself.

As a rule, not more than four persons should occupy one tent. Two in a tent will get along better; for camp life is very intimate in any case.

TENTS FOR FIXED CAMPS 31

A group of small tents around a common campfire is quite as sociable as if the party were all bunked together — except when sociability is *not* wanted, as when some wish to sleep and others want to play cards. Even a camper does not care to reduce his individuality to a least common multiple.

Two small tents need not be made of so heavy material as a large one of cubic capacity equal to both of them. They are easier to erect and manage. They are more adaptable to various camp sites. Their short poles are handier to transport (for that matter, jointed ones may be bought, up to a limit of twelve feet total length). And small tents are stancher in a gale than big ones.

Roominess is not to be estimated by ground dimensions alone. It depends much upon height of center and walls. If a tent is to be used right on the ground, not elevated over a floor with baseboards, it should be made higher in center and walls than the standard proportions given in the table. This is not expensive: the charge is only five per cent. of the cost of regular tent for each six inches of added height.

To my notion the best all-round size of wall tent for two people, if weight and bulk and cost are of any consequence, is the so-called 9 x 9 or a 9 x 12, built with 3½-foot walls, instead of 3-foot, and 8-foot center, instead of 7½-foot. For four persons a 12 x 14 is commonly used; but a 14 x 14 with 4-foot walls and 9-foot center has double the head-room of the standard 12 x 14, and 2½ feet more space between cots, if these are set lengthwise of the tent, two on a side.

Before selecting a tent, consider the number of people to occupy it, and their dunnage, and the furniture. Then draw diagrams of floor and end elevation, of various sizes, fitting in the cots, etc., according to scale; so you can get just what you want — no more, no less.

TENT MATERIALS.— The conventional tent is

made of plain cotton duck. A single roof of such material will shed rain, if the stuff is closely woven, but only so long as it is stretched at a proper angle, rather taut, and nothing touches it from the inside. If so much as a finger-tip should be rubbed against the under side of the roof, a leak would spring there, due to capillary action. It is of little use to draw the finger from the drip spot down to the tent wall, for, although this runs the water off for a time, fresh dripping will start on each side of the line.

Nor is it possible to avoid slackness in a roof of plain canvas during a wet spell of weather. Cloth that is not water-proofed will shrink a great deal as soon as it gets wet; hence the guy ropes must be let out, and the roof allowed to sag, before the rain comes; otherwise the shrinkage of the canvas will loosen your tent stakes, or even pull them all up together, when down goes your house about your ears!

For these reasons, a tent should either be water-proofed, or should have a supplementary roof called a fly. These matters will be considered later.

Cotton duck comes in three general grades, known as single filling, double filling, and army duck.

Single filling duck is made of coarse yarn, loosely woven, and of an inferior grade of cotton. It is suitable only for cheap tents that are not intended for continuous use, and generally is a bad "bargain" even then. It is weaker than the same weight of the other grades and is poor stuff to shed water.

Double filling duck is of closer texture, better fiber, and is equal to all but the hardest service. For average summer camping it is good enough.

Army duck is the best grade made, of selected cotton free from sizing, both warp and filling doubled and twisted, closely woven, and free from imperfections — if it comes up to army standard. It will outwear any other tent material of the same weight, except flax (which I have not seen used in this country), and sheds water much better than cheaper grades.

Khaki generally means simply duck or twill that has been colored to the familiar leaf brown of hunting togs. It may be had in almost any grade, the best, of course, being army tent khaki.

The strength and durability of duck depends largely upon its weight per square foot. Standard tent duck comes in weights of 8 ounces, 10 ounces, 12 ounces, and upwards, to the running yard of material 29 inches wide (army duck, 28½ inches). But other duck is made in 36-inch width, or wider. The 36-inch stuff is about one-fourth lighter per running yard than 29-inch duck; in other words, its "8-ounce" weight is really about 6-ounce, its "10-ounce" is 7½-ounce, its "12-ounce" is 9-ounce stuff, as compared with standard goods. *Bear this in mind* when comparing qualities and prices of tents by different makers. Some tent makers specify in their catalogues which width is used; others do not. In case of doubt, get samples of cloth before purchasing.

Since guys and beckets (loops for the pegs) generally are fitted only where there are seams, it follows that a tent made of wide duck is not so stanch as one of standard widths. All things considered, 8-ounce army duck (28½-inch) and 10-ounce double filling standard (29-inch) are superior to 12-ounce double filling of 36-inch width.

For fixed camps, nothing less than 10-ounce standard duck for tents, and 8-ounce for flies, should be used; 12-ounce for tents, and 10-ounce for flies, is preferable, unless the tent be quite small and portability is a factor to be considered.

TRICKS OF THE TRADE.— Not all of them, by any means; but a few tricks for the novice to look out for if he is not sure of his tent maker.

Prices fluctuate, of course, with the cotton market, at least in the better grades of duck. And yet, in the same season we may notice considerable difference in prices for what is ostensibly the same thing. There is a legitimate margin of variation in tent prices according to local cost of production; but when " bargains " are offered, keep your weather eye open. There are many different qualities of duck in grades that nominally are alike — all the way from honest clear cotton to weighted stuff that is almost shoddy.

A tent may be stunted in height to deceive the purchaser, since most buyers consider only the ground dimensions. A flattened roof and low walls mean less head-room and greater danger of leakage. Very cheap tents may have worthless jute ropes, instead of hemp or sisal, and their poles and stakes may be defective.

Low prices generally go with inferior workmanship. Look out for single seams, chain stitching, insufficient stay-pieces or reinforcements where the chief strains come, and machine-clamped brass grommets, that tear out easily, instead of galvanized iron rings sewed in by hand.

High prices, on the contrary, may mean refinements that ordinary campers do not need. Between the two extremes there is wide room for choice. For example, at the time of this writing, you can get a new 9 x 9 wall tent of single filling duck (29-inch), complete with fly, poles, stakes, and ropes, for as little as $11.50. For the best grade of U. S. Army 9 x 9 officers' tent you would pay $51.50. Of course, the army tent is of far better material than the cheap one, and it is higher at center and walls, but a good part of the difference in price is due to hand sewing and hand workmanship throughout, in the officers' model, even to finishing every becket and door-string with a Matthew Walker knot.

WATERPROOF TENTS.— A waterproof tent needs no fly to shed rain; but it should have eaves to carry drip free from the walls, if there are any. It costs less than a plain tent of equal quality with fly,

TENTS FOR FIXED CAMPS 35

weighs less, bulks less when packed, does not mildew, does not have to be dried out every time before moving, and is easier to set up and manage than one with a fly.

A prime advantage of the processed cloth is that it does not shrink when rained on. This means a lot of trouble saved. With a tent of ordinary canvas it is necessary to slacken guys before a rain, and at night before turning in, lest the stakes be pulled loose. Of course, if long guy ropes are used they will shrink, and must be eased before a rain, even though the tent itself be waterproof.

Waterproof materials, and home methods of waterproofing tents, are discussed in Chapter V. For heavy tents, such as we are now considering, my own preference is either "green waterproof" (Willesden) duck or a cravenetted khaki. Both of these are perfectly rainproof, in heavy and closely woven stuffs; they are soft, and are not affected by heat or cold.

Colored tents, either khaki or green, are restful to the eyes, blend pleasantly with their surroundings, and are not so likely as white ones to attract the attention of unwelcome visitors, from insects to tramps. They do not soil so easily as white canvas, and do not make shadow pictures of the inmates by lantern light. Khaki or green is cooler under the summer sun than white. It moderates the glare for those who would sleep late or take a siesta (some cannot sleep well in a white tent under a full moon), and it does not light up so brilliantly as white canvas when the lightning flashes.

TENT FLIES.— A fly is an auxiliary roof of canvas, to shed rain and to make the tent cooler.

Most tent flies are set tight on top of the regular ridge pole. A better plan, when the camp is not to be shifted for a good while, is to use two ridge poles, and so have a space between the fly and the ridge for air to circulate through. In small tents, it is handier to have a stout band on the ridge of the tent itself, with strings by which it can be suspended from an outside ridge pole that is cut in the woods, this pole being set up on shears at each end. This leaves the doorway unobstructed. Such a rig permits the use of any sized fly, with only one ridge pole (Fig. 11).

Many like to have the fly large enough to form a 7- or 8-foot canopy in front of the tent; but there are disadvantages in this rig: it cuts off side entrance, and it makes the fly a sport of the winds. A gust can get tremendous purchase under a pro-

Fig. 2.— Extension Fly

truding roof and is likely to send it sailing. Even in moderate winds there will be a great slatting and banging, just when one wants to drop off to sleep. Generally it is best to have a spare fly, as I have mentioned for the dining place, and erect a frame in front of the tent over which this cloth can be stretched for an awning (Fig. 2). In this case the awning can be rigged as high as one wishes, and will not be in the way of entering the tent from one side..

A fly large enough to project three or four feet for shelter over the doorway is not objectionable; in fact it is a good thing, especially if made long enough to come almost to the ground at the sides.

TENTS FOR FIXED CAMPS 37

Figure 3 shows one of Edgington's tropical tents with such a fly (similar ones are made in this country). Note the liberal air-space between fly and tent. The shelter outside the tent walls is useful

Fig. 3.— Tropical Tent

for baggage, dry wood, dogs, etc. Such a fly weighs and costs about as much as the tent itself. For security in a wind, the "storm set" should be used (Fig. 10).

SOD-CLOTH.— If a tent is not to be floored and fitted with a base-board, it should have a sod-cloth. This is a strip of 8-ounce canvas, about 9 inches wide, that is sewed all along the bottom edge of the tent walls, both sides and ends (Fig. 16). When the tent has been set up, this sod-cloth is turned in on the floor and weighted down with poles or stones. Its function is to keep out insects and draughts that otherwise would enter through the numerous gaps that are left between tent pegs. The bottom edge of a tent is the worst possible place to get ventilation from; one might as well seek to ventilate a house through cracks in the floor. Banking the tent inside with leaves and earth is a poor substitute for a sod-cloth. It will not stay tight for an hour, and the earth rots the canvas.

GROUND-SHEET.— In a small tent that often is shifted from place to place, a ground-sheet to cover the floor and lap over the sod-cloth is a good thing to keep the interior dry and secure against insects; but in a fixed camp such a carpet is a nuisance. It gets filthy, and it stays so. Bare earth is soon trodden down hard so that it is easy to sweep and keep clean. I have lived for months in an unfloored cabin, and my partner and I had no trouble to keep the earthen floor neat to the eye and more sanitary than any carpet. If you want a floor in a tent, build a real one of dressed boards brought along for the purpose.

VENTILATION.— "Nessmuk" used to rail at wall tents and wedge tents because they were so fusty and damp and cheerless. So they are when improperly built and carelessly managed. One's main reason for camping out should be to get plenty of fresh air and sunshine. It is not enough to have good air in daytime. One-third of our time is spent in bed. And yet it is common practice to close the tent tight at night, especially if there are any mosquitoes about. Consider. Who would spend summer nights at home with no window open? Well, a tent closed up is less permeable to air than the average house with windows down.

The notion that night air in the woods is malarial or otherwise unwholesome is idiotic. It is the best air there is. Still, you can't buy a wall tent in America that has proper means of ventilation, unless you have it built to order. Army tents have ventilators, so-called, that are nothing but a hole at each peak, four inches wide and eight inches long. A tent window, to be of any account, should be not less than 12 x 18 inches.

Our best tent makers will fit one or more windows in a tent wherever the owner wants them, at from $1.00 to $2.50 each. The opening is covered with fine-mesh bobbinet, taped around the edges and crosswise, with a canvas storm flap that can be raised or lowered from the inside (Fig. 4). A more elaborate kind, that may be detached and rolled up when the tent is folded, is made of copper mosquito

TENTS FOR FIXED CAMPS

bar, and has a celluloid window that can be slipped in when it rains.

In a tent of ordinary size, one such window at the rear, with the doorway left wide open in fair weather, will make the place a cheerful and wholesome abode instead of a fusty den.

MOSQUITO BAR.— The doorway may be screened by a sort of drop-curtain of bobbinet or cheesecloth; ordinary mosquito netting is too easily torn, and its mesh is too open to exclude the smaller mosquitoes and gnats. Bobbinet is expensive. The tent-

Fig. 4.— Bobbinet Window   Fig. 5.— Mosquito Curtain

maker will attach a cheesecloth front to a tent 9 to 14 feet wide for about $2.85.

REAR DOOR.— For about the same price as a window, and serving as well for ventilation, the tent-maker will put an extra door in the rear end of the tent, with cheesecloth screen. This is a better arrangement for hot weather, and often convenient when there is a driving rain or a contrary wind; but it reduces the space for wall-pockets, shelves, etc.

DOOR WEIGHTS.— To do away with pegs at the entrance, that you are apt to stumble over, tie a short and rather heavy pole to the bottom of each flap. This holds the door open when desired, and closes it securely against dogs, "varmints," and the elements.

STOVE-PIPE HOLE.— A simple tin protector for this opening is an annoyance at night, for it scrapes and skreeks when the canvas slats in the wind. Tent-makers supply pipe shields of asbestos that are quite safe, noiseless, and roll up nicely with the tent when it is stored or *en route*. A flap covers the opening when no stove is in use (Fig. 6).

Fig. 6.— Asbestos Pipe Guard

TENT POLES AND PINS.— Poles should be of ash, white pine, or spruce, straight-grained and free from defects. At each end there should be a galvanized iron band to keep the pole from splitting.

A wall tent requires stakes (unless a frame is built for the guys) about two feet long, and becket pins about sixteen inches. Shorter ones will not hold in loose or sandy soil. Wooden ones do very well for stationary camps.

CARE OF TENTS.— Never except when unavoidable should a tent be rolled up when wet. Even if it be only damp from dew, an unprocessed tent will soon mildew if packed away in that state. The parts that require most drying are where the material is doubled, as at the seams and along the edges: the bottom edge especially, and the sod-cloth, are sure to rot if not thoroughly dried before stowing away.

To protect the tent in transport, it should be carried in a stout bag; otherwise it is likely to be punctured.

Tent pins are to be carried in a bag of their own, not only to save them from being lost, but also because their inevitable dampness when camp is struck would rot the tent if they were rolled up with it.

TO MEND A TEAR IN CANVAS.— Cross-stitch it flat, using a sail needle and twine, and taking a narrow hold on each side with one stitch, then a wider hold with the next one, and so on alternately.

TENTS FOR FIXED CAMPS

Then it will not tear again so easily as if narrow stitches were taken all along, nor will it be likely to ruck. Temporary repairs can be made with adhesive plaster.

SECOND-HAND TENTS.— Second-hand army tents that are in good, serviceable condition, having been condemned for stains or other trifling defects, may be bought cheaply from dealers who get them at government auctions. These army tents are always well designed and well made. Second-hand tents, however, should not be bought without inspection; they may be mildewed or otherwise unserviceable.

TENT RENTAL.— Some tent-makers and outfitters have tents for rent. From a list at hand I copy the following charges for wall tents: 10 x 12, $2.00 first week, and half this for each succeeding week; 12 x 14, $2.00 *do.;* 14 x 16, $3.00 *do.;* flies, half these prices. In some places a whole camp equipment can be rented.

PITCHING WALL TENTS.— A tent should stand squared and taut and trim. This not only that one's eyes may dwell with pride upon his camp, but because a tent that is wrinkled and set askew will not shed a downpour nor stand stanchly against a gale.

In erecting any square or rectangular tent, the first thing is to locate the corners, and from them to determine where the corner guy stakes are to be driven. Soldiers do this by measuring with the upright poles, but as the height of a common tent may not bear the right relation to its spread, for this purpose, a knotted string may be better.

Set up the tent in your yard at home and adjust poles and guys until the angles of the wall are true and the canvas is drawn smooth all around. To square the corners, observe that a triangle the sides of which are 3, 4 and 5 ft., or multiples of these, forms a right angle.

Then take a stout fish-line, fasten a small peg at one end, and drive this peg close into one corner of the tent (*A*, Fig. 7). Draw the line straight (gently, so as not to stretch it) to center of upright pole (*B*) (if there be one) in the doorway; tie a knot in it there, and then go on to the corner *C*, where it is knotted again. Drive a small peg at *C*, pass the string around it, and on to the corner *D*, where another knot is tied and peg driven. Then draw the line diagonally back to *A*, and knot it. Cut the line at the last knot, reel it up on its peg, and keep it stowed with the tent for future use.

When the camp ground is reached, it is but the work of a moment to peg out, with the knotted

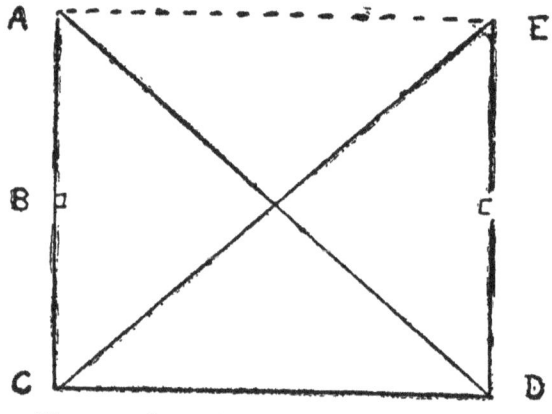

Fig. 7.— Locating Corners of the Tent

string, first the triangle *ACD* and then, reversing, *EDC*. You then have located exactly the positions of the four corners for your tent, and marked where the uprights shall be set, and the tent is sure to stand "square."

A wall tent is set up with inside or outside poles, and its wall and fly are guyed out either to stakes or to horizontal poles set up on posts. We will consider these methods in turn.

WALL TENT ON INSIDE POLES, STAKED.— This is the usual way of setting up a wall tent, with or without a fly; but it is not the best, except when it is necessary or expedient to carry shop-made poles and stakes with the outfit, as in the case of an army,

TENTS FOR FIXED CAMPS 43

or of a party traveling by wagon and frequently moving camp.

Having chosen the best frontage, lay out the corners and end centers with cord and small pegs, as described. Then drive the corner guy stakes diagonally outward from tent corners, slanting them as shown in Fig. 8. If fly guys are to be looped over them, as well as wall guys, the stakes should be long enough to project well and still take firm hold in the ground. (When striking a tent, do not work

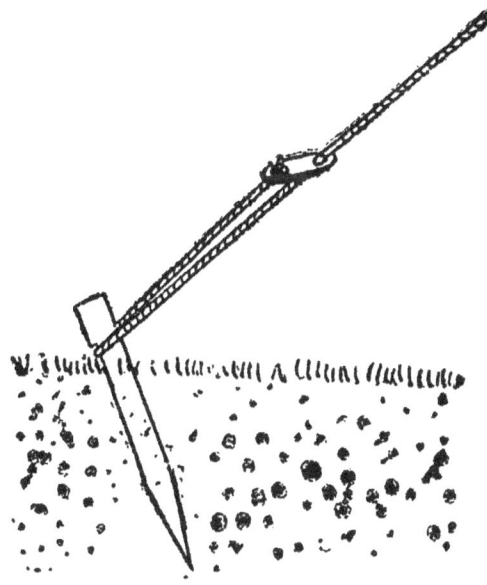

Fig. 8.— Tent Stake and Guy Rope

the stakes forward and backward to loosen them, but slip a looped rope over the notch and pull at angle that stake was driven.) Corner stakes are driven several feet away from tent, depending on slope of roof, and two or three feet outward, fore and aft, to make the guys draw diagonally.

Now unroll the tent and drag it away by the ridge until it is laid out flat over the ground selected.

Insert ridge pole (rounded side up) inside the tent, with its holes for the spindles (iron pins in end of uprights) meeting the grommets or large eyelets at ends of tent ridge. Place uprights at front and rear, at right angles to ridge, spindles inserted in ridge pole and passing out through peak grommets.

If a fly is to be used, lay it out flat over the tent, spindles passing through grommets as in the tent.

If end guys are to be run out fore and aft, or the storm set is used (Fig. 10), slip the loops of the long guys over the spindles.

A man at each end now takes hold of an upright, and the two raise tent and fly together. Then one or two men hold the tent in position while one or two others guy out the corners (beginning on the windward side) so that the tent will stand by itself. See that the uprights stand truly perpendicular.

Tie up the door and peg down the corners of the tent wall.

Guy out the sides to stakes, tightening or slackening the ropes alternately with their slides until the tent stands true and the guys draw evenly.

Stretch the fly similarly, making sure that it touches the tent nowhere except at the ridge. It should clear the eaves by at least 6 inches, preferably 9 or 10 inches. This requires an extra set of stakes driven outside the wall stakes, or a single set of long stakes with double notches (army tents). In the latter case there is not enough clearance for hot weather, unless the fly ropes are propped up on crotched sticks (see further under ACTION OF WIND ON TENTS). A better method, without any stakes, is described later.

Finish pegging down the tent wall; or, if there is a sod cloth, weight it down with flat rocks or poles, which is a better rig, not only to exclude draughts and insects, but also because then the tent wall can readily be clewed up to the eaves, in fine weather, to sun and air the interior.

The tent now stands square and taut all around (Fig. 9), secure against all but heavy end winds. To brace it against end strain you could run a pair of long guys out fore and aft; but such a rig is a

TENTS FOR FIXED CAMPS 45

never-ending source of wrath and objurgation. It is forever in the way, prevents having the camp-fire in front where you want it, and is sure to be run into or tripped over by anyone who goes out of the tent at night.

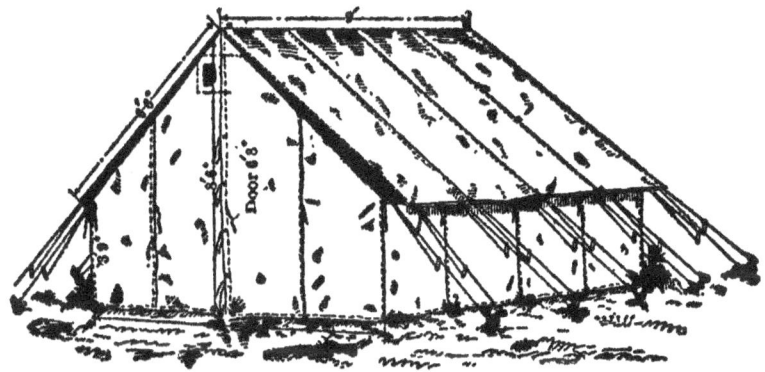

Fig. 9.— U. S. Army Wall Tent with Fly. (Officers' Tent)

STORM SET.— Better end braces are rigged with a pair of long guy ropes each of which has a loop in the middle to go over the upright spindle and a regulating lashing at each end. These may be made fast to corner stakes set diagonally outward from

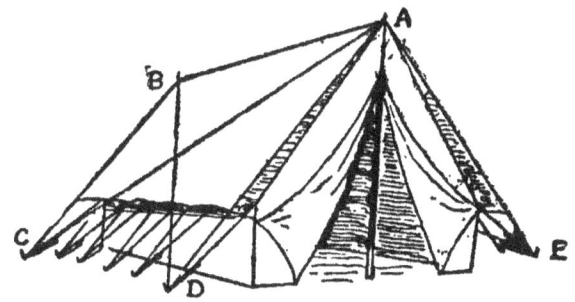

Fig. 10.— Storm Set

the tent corners, as with army hospital tents; but a better plan is what I call the storm set (Fig. 10), in which the ropes are carried backward to the opposite corners. The storm set leaves both ends of the tent free from obstruction, takes less room, does not tend to pull apart a jointed ridge pole, if such is used, keeps the fly from "ballooning" when wind gets under it, and is the most secure of all end braces because the strain each way is met by ropes pulling, over a triangle of wide base, directly back against the wind.

In the illustration, the loop at middle of one guy is slipped over the spindle A, one end is drawn back to C and the other to the stake opposite C. Similarly the other guy runs from B to D and E.

WALL TENT WITH GUY FRAMES.— Tent stakes are troublesome things at best. Generally when you go to driving them you find stones or roots in the way. They do not hold well except in favorable

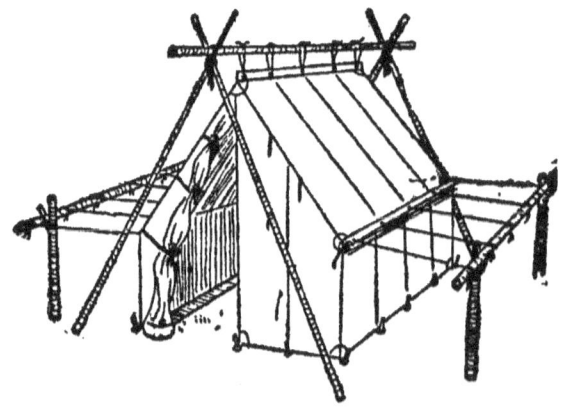

Fig. 11.— Wall Tent on Shears with Guy Frame

soil and in dry weather. When guy ropes get wet they shrink and engage in a tug of war that loosens the stakes.

If poles grow near the camp site it is more satisfactory to drive four heavy crotched corner stakes and lay a stiff pole across each pair of them at about the height of the tent wall and parallel to its sides, to which the guy ropes are made fast (see Fig. 11).

If a fly is used, lash a rather heavy pole to each edge and drop these poles over the guy rods. Their weight automatically keeps the fly taut at all times, wet or dry.

TENT ON SHEARS.— Tent poles are bothersome

TENTS FOR FIXED CAMPS 47

on the train and in a wagon, and impossible in a canoe or on a pack train unless they are jointed. Socketed poles become useless, or hard to refit, if a ferrule is stepped on or otherwise dented. An upright pole in the doorway must be dodged every time you go in or out. A pair of shear legs at each end of the tent, to support the ridge pole, is a stancher " set."

Cut four straight poles a couple of feet longer than the distance from peak to corner of tent, and a stiff stick for ridge pole about two feet longer than

Fig. 12.— Lashing for Shear Legs. (For Tent Shears it is not Necessary to Take so many Turns)

Fig. 14.— Magnus Hitch. (Not Apt to Slip Along a Pole)

Fig. 13.— Shear Legs Spread

the tent. To bind the shear poles, lay a pair of them side by side; with a small rope take several turns around both poles near their upper ends, not too tightly, then pass the ends of the rope one up and the other down, to form a cross-lashing, and tie them with a reef knot (Fig. 12). When the butts of the shear legs are drawn apart the crossing of the tips puts a strain on the knot and effectually secures them (Fig. 13).

Having spread out the tent and inserted the ridge pole (or tied it outside), raise tent with the shears, and spread their legs until the tent just touches the ground when ready to be pegged down (Fig. 11). One man can raise a rather heavy tent in this way by working first at one end and then at the other.

In the case of a wall tent with fly, erect side frames for the guys (Fig. 11); but if no fly is used, all that is needed is to lash side poles to the shears and tie the eaves fast to them: this is the best rig for a small waterproof tent that is to be moved often (Fig. 15).

Sometimes the rear end of the ridge pole can be lashed to a convenient sapling, or rested in the fork of a limb. Some campers plant a single crotched post at the rear, but usually it is easier to set up shears than to find a suitable crotch and plant it

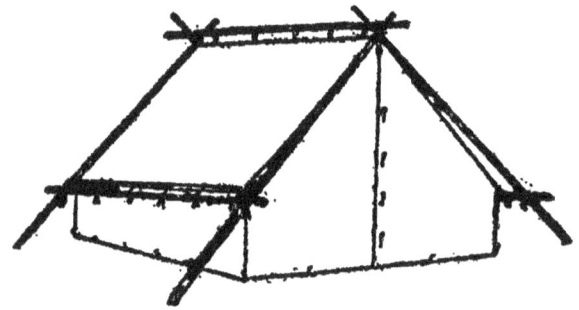

Fig. 15.— Wall Tent with Side Bars

firmly. It is one advantage of shear legs that they can be erected without difficulty anywhere, although the ground may be rocky or frozen.

This rig has several other merits. It leaves the doorway unobstructed. The legs do not sink so much in soft soil or sand as single uprights; if they should sink, they can be raised in a trice by drawing the butts closer together. Similarly, when the tent shrinks, from wetting, the strain can be eased by simply lifting one shear leg and pushing it a little farther outward. When the canvas sags, draw the legs closer to their mates, and you stretch the tent as taut as a drum-head.

An inside ridge pole is best for a large, heavy

TENTS FOR FIXED CAMPS

tent; but it must be straight and smooth, or it will wear the canvas and make it leak. Small or medium-size tents are best made with a strongly reinforced outer ridge with cords by which the tent is tied to an *outside* ridge pole (Fig. 11). In this case the pole need not be so straight nor so carefully trimmed.

An outside ridge pole is excellent to keep a tent fly clear all around from the tent roof, permitting a free circulation of air between the two, which keeps the tent cool in summer.

TRENCHING THE TENT.— This should always be done if camp is not to be moved frequently. Do not dig the ditch V-shaped, but cut straight down, just outside the tent pegs and slope the trench inward toward this dam (Fig. 16). Cast the dirt away; never bank it against the tent, for it would quickly rot the canvas. Give the ditch a uniform slope toward the lowest ground around the tent. In the shallowest places it need not be over three inches deep. A trench that does not drain well is worse than none.

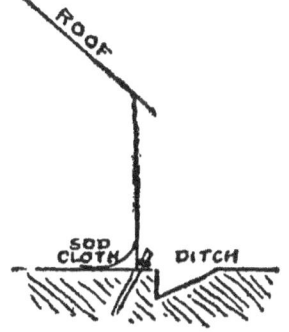

Fig. 16.— Trenching Tent

TENT FLOORS.— In fixed camp, especially if it is in a sandy place, the tent should have a board floor. Lay down the requisite number of 2" x 4" scantling as floor-joists, setting them on flat rocks or posts if necessary. (It is well to let the front and rear joists project far enough for a guy-rope frame to be nailed to them.) Plank them over with dressed lumber. The edges should be dressed to match; tongued and grooved flooring is best.

If you have enough lumber, run a base-board around the sides and rear. Inside the base-boards, at each corner, set up a 2" x 4" joist to height of tent wall, and connect these corner posts at top by narrow boards, on the outside, corresponding to the base-boards (Fig. 17).

Such a frame helps to hold the tent in shape. The upper boards are convenient for hanging up wall-pockets, guns, etc., where they are handy but out of the way.

Loop the tent-pin beckets over nails in the base-boards: then the walls can be clewed up in warm weather.

Before laying a floor the tent first should be set up without it and accurate measurements taken (or the measuring string previously mentioned may be used). If the floor is too small there will be en-

Fig. 17.—Tent Floor, with Wall Rail, Base-board, and End Joists Projecting that Corner Stakes May Be Nailed to Them

trance for draughts and insects; if it projects, the canvas will not fit over it, and rainwater will run in.

A portable tent floor may be made in sections that bolt together. The sections should not be too large to lie flat in a wagon box (for standard roads, wagon boxes are usually 42 inches wide; for narrow tracks, 38 inches; length of box usually 10½ ft.). Dimensions and number of sections will depend, of course, upon size of tent.

TENTS ON ROCKY OR SANDY GROUND.— If the ground is too rocky to drive stakes in it, or is hard frozen, erect the tent on shears and guy it out to rocks or growing bushes.

Tent stakes do not hold well in sand or in ground that has been soaked by rain. It is customary, in such cases, to attach the guys to a double row of

TENTS FOR FIXED CAMPS

stakes, one behind the other, or interlocking at right angles (one stake driven at a sharp angle toward the tent, the other outward so that its notch engages the head of the other stake, the two forming an inverted V, thus Λ).

An easier and more secure way is to lay a heavy pole over the guy ropes close to the stakes (Fig. 18), and, if need be, weight it down with rocks, earth, or sand.

In a very sandy place, where no log is to be found, dig a small pit for each guy, tie the rope around a fagot or to a bag of sand (Fig. 19), bury this, and stamp the sand over it.

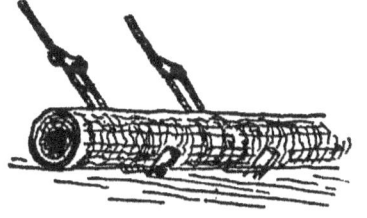

Fig. 18.— Guys Weighted with Log

Fig. 19.— Guy Rope Fastened to Fagot to Be Buried in Ground.

ACTION OF WIND ON TENTS.— Unless one encamps in an open country the wind will seldom strike his tent steadily in a direction parallel with the ground. Rather it goes eddying and curling like driven smoke: hence the flapping and slatting of the fly-sheet.

During a squall a violent blow may fall straight down upon the roof as though bent on snapping the poles; then, rebounding, it will try to carry the tent away and aloft, as though your shelter were an open umbrella. This action is often marked in ravines and in a glade surrounded by tall trees, but it may occur anywhere. The stanchest tents for a very windy situation are those of conical or pyramidal form, set up on or under tripods.

A fly-sheet is a perfect wind trap, especially if it projects in the form of a porch, or is set well away from the ridge of the tent. This is one reason why I prefer a waterproofed tent without fly (except for hot climates). If a porch is wanted, rig a sheet of canvas over a separate frame in front of the tent; then, if it blows away, it will not wreck the tent too.

The flies of army tents, and of other patterns built for hard and varied service, are guyed to double-notched wall stakes, and so set rather close to the roof (see Fig. 9).

CHAPTER IV
FURNITURE, TOOLS, AND UTENSILS FOR FIXED CAMPS

When you go a-camping, make yourself as comfortable as you can. It is neither heroic nor sensible to put peas in your boots to mortify the flesh. There is no comfort in toting a lot of baggage over bad trails, but when there is a wagon to carry folding cots and camp chairs, take them along.

Pack your provisions, and some of the other things, in boxes that will serve for cupboards and cold-storage in camp. Put some ready-cut shelf boards in them, and leather for hinges. Make sure beforehand that you can get enough lumber at your destination to make a dining table and benches.

Straw beds on the ground soon get fusty, and they attract vermin. Fixed bunks in a tent harbor dirt and dampness.

Cots.— For a bed in fixed camp, or wherever transportation is adequate, choose a folding cot. It is easy to keep presentable. It makes a comfortable lounge or settee, as well as a good bed. It can be picked up bodily and carried out every morning to sun and air, leaving the tent floor free for sweeping.

Wire-bottomed cots are too cumbersome for general camping. Canvas stretcher-beds with frames that fold compactly are the right things. I have chosen four models for illustration.

Length.	Width.	Height.	Closed.	Weight.
78 in.	27 in.	14 in.	38 x 5 x 4 in.	17 lbs.
78 in.	27 in.	13 in.	29 x 8 x 4 in.	17 lbs.
78 in.	30 in.	20 in.	34 x 7 x 5 in.	15 lbs.
78 in.	36 in.	18 in.	38 x 6 x 6 in.	20 lbs.

Fig. 20.— Narrow Cot

Fig. 21.— Compact Cot

Fig. 22.— Telescoping Cot

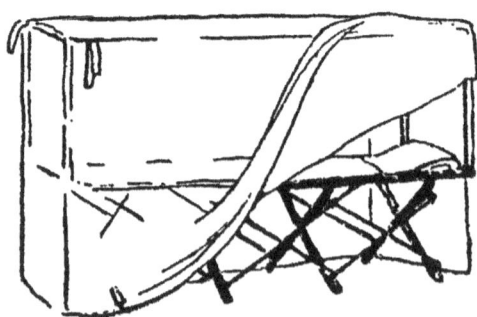

Fig. 23.— Cot with Mosquito Screen

FURNITURE FOR FIXED CAMPS

The first and fourth of these cots differ only in size and weight. The second folds so compactly that it can be stowed in a short chest or steamer trunk. The third opens like a lazy-tongs, can be set up in less than a minute, and is unusually high and roomy for its weight.

The wider the cot, the more comfortable it will be, especially in cold weather. On a very narrow cot the sleeper's body raises the covering free from the bed on both sides, leaving gaps through which cold air draws upward between mattress and blanket, chilling the sleeper, no matter how much covering he may pile on. Sleeping-bags obviate this.

The cotton pad mattresses made for camp cots are needlessly bulky and heavy, hard to lie on, and hard to keep dry in the moist forest air. Much better is a folded comforter stuffed with wool instead of cotton. It can be kept dry and sweet by hanging it out in the sun like a blanket. Wool stays fluffy and springy, but cotton batting mats down and gets lumpy, besides retaining moisture.

To be secure against insect pests is as essential to peace and comfort in camp as a dry roof overhead, if not more so.

If the tent itself is not thoroughly screened against flies and mosquitoes, then by all means get from the outfitter a cot frame and netting (Fig. 23), or, as a makeshift, rig for yourself a pyramidal head-screen of netting or cheesecloth, to be hung by a string above the bed, with the edges of three sides tucked under the mattress after you turn in.

CAMP CHAIRS.— Folding stools without backs are by no means comfortable. Far better is a chair in which you can recline and rest the whole body. The pattern shown in Fig. 24 folds as easily as an umbrella, to a size 3 ft. long by 3 in. square, and, when opened, adjusts itself perfectly to the body. It weighs 4½ pounds. A larger size, high enough to rest the head, weighs 6¼ pounds.

The armchair, Fig. 25, knocks down into six parts

which are carried in a bag, forming a package 29 x 6 in., that weighs 8 pounds. This is the Indian "Rhorkee" chair, a favorite with old campaigners the world over. With the addition of a foot-rest of

Fig. 24.— Folding Chair   Fig. 25.—
Folding Arm Chair

some sort it makes a fairly comfortable bed. Caspar Whitney and Richard Harding Davis consider it the best camp chair made. Several of our sporting goods houses carry it in stock.

CAMP TABLES.— A small table in the tent is an-

Fig. 26.— Roll-up Table   Fig. 27.—
Roll-up Table Top

other convenience that pays for its transportation. The model shown in Fig. 26, with roll top, comes in two sizes, 36 x 27 and 36 x 36 inches. It folds into a package about 6 inches in diameter, and weighs

FURNITURE FOR FIXED CAMPS 57

16 pounds. The top separately, weighing only 6 pounds, and costing but $1.25, can be set up on forked stakes, as illustrated in Fig. 27.

The table shown in Fig. 29 folds into a package only 27 inches long, and weighs 15 pounds.

Fig. 28.— Table with Shelf   Fig. 29.— Compact Table

A stronger and more rigid table than either of these has legs that cross in four directions (Fig. 28). It may be bought either plain (16 pounds) or with a folding shelf underneath (23 pounds). The top is 36 x 27 inches; size folded, 36 x 7 x 5 inches. By an interlocking device, two or more of these tables may be fastened together, for mess purposes.

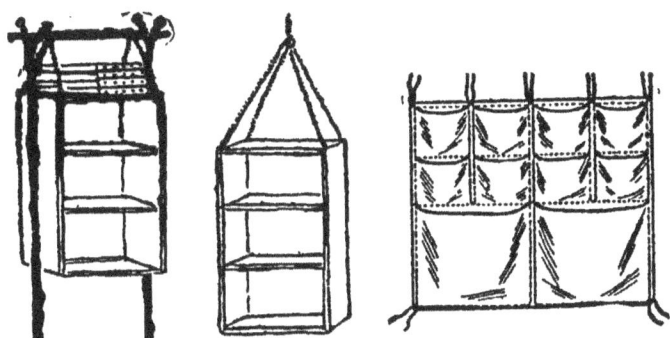

Fig. 30.— Folding Shelves   Fig. 31.— Wall Pocket

If boards are not procurable near the camp site, a portable dining table for a party of four to six is quickly rigged by setting up two roll table tops (Fig. 27) side by side.

SHELVES AND WALL POCKETS.— To keep a tent from being littered with small articles that are always in the way except when you want them and can't find them, shelves or wall pockets, or both, are well-nigh indispensable. These may be purchased ready-made.

The camp cupboard here illustrated (Fig. 30) has four shelves, each 10 x 30 inches, folds into a parcel 4 x 10 x 30 inches, and weighs 7 pounds. Other sizes are manufactured.

The wall pocket (Fig. 31) is 30 x 36 inches, and weighs 1½ pounds. Such things can easily be made at home to suit individual requirements.

CLOTHES HANGERS.— There are various kinds of tent-pole hooks for suspending clothing, a lantern, and accoutrements. Such a contrivance is to be clamped to the rear upright, or to the center pole, depending on the kind of tent. Some are made of leather or webbing so as to be adjustable to poles of any size.

In any tent with a ridge pole two screw-eyes should be put in at opposite ends from which to suspend by cords a straight stick to hang clothes on. This is especially handy for wet clothes on rainy days.

MEDICAL KIT.— About the best thing of this sort, for average campers who do not have to go very light, is the " Household (B) " first aid box fitted up by the American National Red Cross, Washington, D. C. The case is of heavy tin, 10 x 9½ x 3½ inches, white enameled inside and out, and contains the following articles:

1 2-oz. bottle Alcohol.
1 2-oz. bottle Aromatic Spirits of Ammonia.
1 2-oz. bottle Syrup of Ipecac.
1 2-oz. bottle Jamaica Ginger.
1 2-oz. bottle Liniment.
1 2-dram vial Olive Oil.

1 2-dram vial Oil of Cloves.
1 Bottle Soda Mint Tablets.
1 Bottle Cascara Sagrada Tablets.
2 Iodine Containers.
1 Package A. R. C. Finger Dressings (6)

FURNITURE FOR FIXED CAMPS 59

1 Package A. R. C. Small Dressings (3)
2 A. R. C. First Aid Outfits.
6 Assorted Bandages.
1 1-yard package Picric Acid Gauze.
1 Spool Adhesive Plaster.
1 Pair Scissors.
1 Paper Safety Pins.
6 Wooden Tongue Depressors.
1 Medicine Dropper.
1 Package Paper Cups.
1 Tourniquet.
1 Clinical Thermometer.
1 2-oz. Package Absorbent Cotton.

Brief directions telling how to use these are pasted inside the lid, but one should order at the same time a copy of the excellent little *American Red Cross Abridged Text-book on First Aid* (General Edition) by Major Charles Lynch, Medical Corps, U. S. A. For prices see the Red Cross catalogue, which is sent free on application to the address given above.

TOOLS.— An axe and a hatchet are indispensable (see Chapters VII and X). If much wood is to be cut, and there are poor axemen in the party, a crosscut saw is the tool for them. The long pattern for two men is much the easiest to cut with, but mean to transport; a one-man cross-cut with 3-ft. blade and auxiliary handle for the left hand will do very well.

A hand saw is necessary if you are to make a dining table, tent floor, and so on. Make the cook swear on his cook-book that he will not use that saw on meat bones (provide him with a cheap kitchen saw).

A spade or miner's shovel will be needed for trenching, and for excavating the refuse pit, latrine, and perhaps a cold-storage hole and a camp oven.

For small tools, see Chapter VII.

Take an assortment of nails and tacks, a spool of annealed wire, a ball of strong twine, and a bundle of braided cotton sash cord (for clothes line, emergency guys to tent, etc.).

If you have a dog, string some heavy wire between two trees as a " trolley," and chain him to it at night, so he can move back and forth.

Here is a good wrinkle that I found in a sportsmen's magazine: If there are children in camp, "put a small cow-bell in the lunch basket or berry pail of the youngsters before you let them go into strange woods. It will reassure both them and you, and may be the means of preventing a tragedy. Trust them to shake it up if they get lost!"

LANTERNS.— If a powerful light is wanted in camp, a gas lantern of the type advertised in sportsmen's journals is a good thing, or an acetylene lantern that is made so that the flame can be regulated. Ordinarily a common kerosene lantern will serve very well.

CAMP STOVES.— If there is a separate commissary tent, the cooking can be done on a common blue-flame oil or gasolene stove, set up on a perfectly level stand. Such a stove is useless out of doors unless fitted with a wind-shield. Do no cooking in the living tent: it attracts flies and vermin.

The best cooking stoves for campers are those specially designed for the purpose, and burning wood. There are many patterns, of varying merit. Do not buy a folding stove for ordinary camping: they are bothersome and flimsy.

I leave out of account stoves without ovens (I can see no good reason for a stove at all unless it has an oven). There are shown here three different types of sheet steel camp stoves, each good in its way.

The first one (Figs. 32, 33) is very compact, yet large enough to cook for four persons, or six in a pinch. When packed and locked in its metal crate, it measures $10\frac{1}{2} \times 18 \times 21\frac{1}{2}$ inches, and can be checked as baggage. Inside the fire-box ($8 \times 10 \times 17$ inches) are packed three sections of adjustable 4-inch pipe, and two automatic locking bars. Inside the oven ($7\frac{1}{2} \times 10\frac{1}{2} \times 17$ inches) there is stowed a 5-gallon water reservoir, and with it a set of sheet iron and tin cooking utensils and table service for six persons. When the stove is in use, the reservoir hooks on to the left side of the stove, next to the fire box, and increases the stove top to 17×28 inches.

FURNITURE FOR FIXED CAMPS 61

This is a most useful addition, since plenty of hot water is needed for cooking and in washing up.

The fire box takes in 16-inch wood. The oven is large enough for a 9 x 15-inch bread pan and will roast a good-sized fowl.

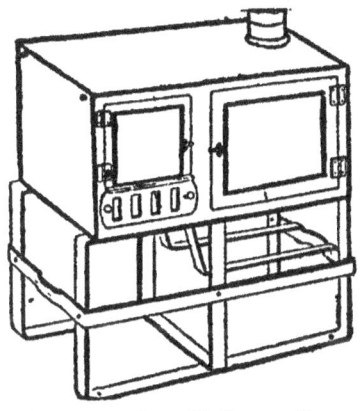
Fig. 32.— Small Camp Stove

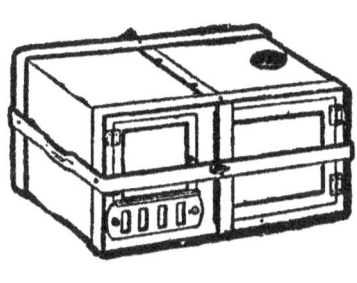
Fig. 33.— Stove Packed

When the stove is set up, it is mounted on its steel crate and the locking bars are attached under the oven to form a warming rack. It is not intended for tent heating.

This stove weighs 25 pounds, and the reservoir and utensils about 15 pounds more. To make the pots and pans nest in the oven, they are made square or rectangular. For fixed camps it is best to select your own utensils, and carry the larger ones in a separate box.

The second stove (Fig. 34) is made with fire box extending its entire length. It will take in a billet 28 inches long, which will keep a fire all night, and will be ready for cooking five minutes after the dampers are opened in the morning. When packed for transportation, the stove measures 30 x 14 x 12 inches, and weighs

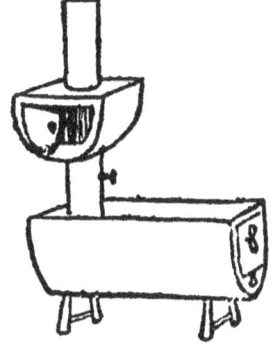
Fig. 34.— Stove for Large Wood

29 pounds (43½ pounds complete with grub box and utensils). When set up, the 14 x 30-inch top is free for utensils; the oven, above it, takes a 10 x 14-inch pan for baking or roasting. Oven, legs, and pipe stow inside the body of the stove, leaving space for a 12 x 13 x 9½-inch galvanized box that holds cooking utensils and is used in camp as a dish-pan or as a vermin-proof box for provisions.

A cook-stove with sheet-iron top needs no plates. If you get one with plates, be sure they are far

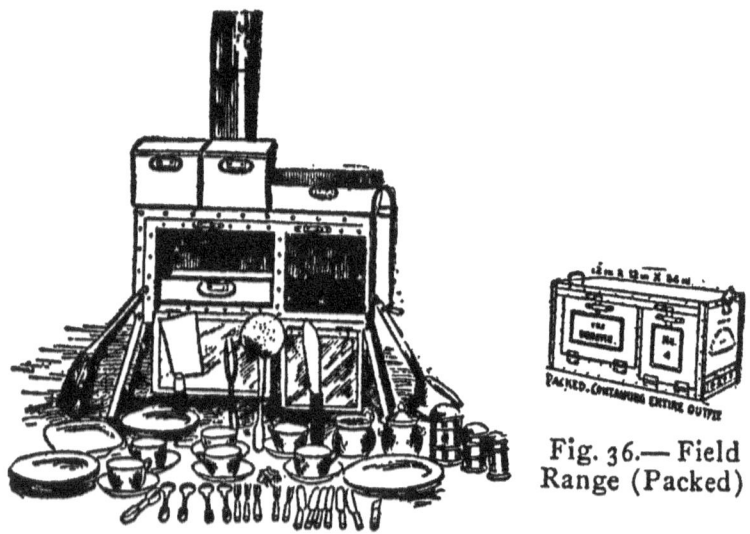

Fig. 36.— Field Range (Packed)

Fig. 35.— Field Range

enough apart so that the vessels do not interfere with each other.

The third type of stove (Figs. 35, 36) is one regularly used by our Geological Survey, Forestry Bureau, and is similar to the Army range, but smaller. The No. 4 size, to cook for 6 to 15 men, packs, with utensils, in a space 12 x 13 x 22 inches. The oven is 8 x 12 x 12 inches. The range weighs 52 pounds, the utensils 20 pounds, and a dining service for six persons, in enamel and white or plated metal, 13 pounds. For continuous field service this is a quite practical range.

FURNITURE FOR FIXED CAMPS 63

Personally, I never use a camp stove, preferring to cook in the open.

As for a heating stove in a tent, my experience tallies with that of Dr. Breck: "Either it bakes you with a temperature of ninety degrees, or it takes the first opportunity to go out directly you close your eyes, and you awake trembling with cold, the thermometer registering somewhere 'round zero." Someone else has called the tent stove "a portable hell." But there are those who like it, for cold-weather camping; and I admit that if the tent is not less than 10 x 14, and the stove's fire-box is big enough to take in a thick billet two feet long, so that it will keep a smouldering all-night fire without your everlastingly pottering around it, there are times and places where a stove in the tent may be a good thing.

If you do set up a stove, be sure to fix a spark-arrester over the top of the pipe. This need not be anything more costly than a piece of wire netting.

If the stove must be set rather close to the tent wall, take along a sheet of asbestos as a shield. One of the pads used for dining-tables will do very well. Such things can be bought at department stores, or of mail-order houses.

When starting a fire in an "air-tight," use little fuel at first, or you will smother the flame in its own smoke. If the stove has no legs, make a board frame like the sides of a low box, or a crib of notched logs, and fill in with gravel.

CAMP GRATES AND FIRE IRONS.— A stove is merely a convenience and an economizer of fuel. Quite as good meals can be cooked over an open fire. Even when it rains, a bonfire can be built to one side and hard coals shoveled from it to a spot sheltered by canvas where the cooking is done. But it pays to take along either a folding grate or a pair of fire irons to hold the frying-pan, etc., level and close over the coals. Then you will need no long stick attached to the frying-pan handle, nor must the cook give all his attention to that one utensil when frying or making pancakes.

Of folding grates there are many and ingenious patterns. I never use any of them; for they are likely to warp from heat or to rust in service, and become unmanageable. Simpler, cheaper, and quite as useful, are a pair of "fire-irons," which are simply two pieces of flat *steel* 24 x 1½ x ⅛ inches, weighing 2½ pounds to the pair, that any blacksmith will cut for you in a minute. Lay them across a couple of logs or flat rocks that are placed on either side of the fire. You can space them apart to suit vessels of different sizes. They will stand any amount of abuse; if they get bent, you can quickly hammer them back into shape.

OVENS.— When there is no stove in the outfit, you will need some kind of camp oven. For a fixed camp a good kind is the old-fashioned Dutch oven (Fig. 37). How to use it is explained in Chapter XX. For a party of four to six it should be of full 13-inch diameter, which will weigh about 17 pounds. Lighter ones, but much more expensive, are made of aluminum with iron tops. Aluminum will not stand the high heat necessary for the top, but does very well for the body of the vessel, if thick enough.

Fig. 37.—Dutch Oven

Such ovens are favorites in the South and the Far West. They are better than reflectors (see Chapter VII) for any baking or roasting that requires considerable time (inimitable for pot-roasts and baked beans), but rather unhandy for biscuits, though all right for biscuit-loaf.

OTHER UTENSILS.— For stationary camps, or for traveling by wagon, the most satisfactory material for pots and table service is enameled ware. It is easier to clean than any other metal, and it is not

FURNITURE FOR FIXED CAMPS

corroded, like tin, by fruits or vegetables steeped, cooked or left over in it. The tendency of enameled ware to chip and flake in cold weather can be tamed by warming gradually before exposing to fierce heat.

Pressed tinware of heavy gauge is good enough for most purposes, though hard to clean when greasy. It is unfit to cook tart fruit in, and it makes tea "taste." Thin soldered tinware is treacherous, dents and rusts easily, and lasts but a short time.

Aluminum is needlessly expensive for the class of camping we are now considering.

Where compactness need not be studied, frying-pans with stationary handles are more practical than the folding kind.

A complete cooking, washing, and table set, for six persons, is listed below. It is heavy (about 58 pounds, with oven and fire irons, or 38 pounds without them), but cheap (about $13.50 with, or $10.50 without oven and irons) and should last a long time.

UTENSILS FOR 6 PERSONS IN FIXED CAMP.

Dutch Oven, cast iron, 13¼ x 6 in. (omitted if there is a stove).
2 Fire Irons, flat steel, 24 x 1½ x ⅛ in. (omitted if there is a stove).
Dish Pan, enameled, 16 x 5 in.
Wash Basin, enameled, 13¾ in.
2 Milk Pans, enameled, 10½ in. (for mixing and serving).
Water Pail, enameled, 10 qt.
3 Covered Pails, enameled, 3, 4½ and 6 qt., nesting.
Double Boiler, enameled, 3½ qt.
Coffee Pot, enameled, 3¼ qt.
Tea Pot, enameled, 2 qt.
Graduated Measure, enameled, 1 qt.
2 Frying-pans, steel, 10⅛ in.
2 Pot Covers, tin, 10½ in.
Broiler, wire, 9 x 14 in.
3 Pot Chains.
Tea Ball, aluminum.
Dipper, enameled, 1 qt.
Basting Spoon, enameled.
Skimmer, enameled.
Soup Ladle, enameled.

Cake Turner, steel.
Butcher Knife, steel.
Flesh Fork, steel.
Kitchen Saw, steel.
Spring Balance, 24 lb.
Pot Cleaner, wire.
Can Opener and Corkscrew.
Salt Shaker.
Pepper Shaker.
10 Dinner Plates, white enameled, 8½ in.
6 Cups, white enameled, 1 pint (handles cut to nest).
6 Cereal Bowls, white enameled.
6 Knives, steel.
6 Forks, white metal.
6 Teaspoons, white metal.
6 Dessert Spoons, white metal.
2 yds. Table Oilcloth.
2 yds. Turkish Toweling (dish towels and clouts).
100 Paper Napkins.
1 bar Sapolio.
1 bar Fels Naphtha Soap.

A milk-can should be added if the camp is near a farm-house.

FIRELESS COOKERS.— A great deal of the bother of cooking can be saved by using a fireless cooker, in which all of the slow processes are performed (roasting, baking, stewing, boiling, and making porridge). In this case only a few simple utensils are required, a wood stove is dispensed with, and there is no need of anyone staying in camp to watch the fire and the cooking. The soapstone radiators can be heated over an alcohol or blue-flame stove. Hot meals can be had at all hours, even when the party is traveling.

A rough-and-ready fireless cooker, which can also be used as a cold-storage box, was described some years ago in *Outing*.—

"When preparing your outfit this summer, pack some of your belongings in a soap or cracker box that has a fairly close-fitting lid. Take along an old white quilt or a blanket that can be folded into a pad to fit the box, or make a crude pad out of unbleached muslin with cotton batting, about one inch thick. Include in your outfit a granite cooking pail commensurate in capacity with the

FURNITURE FOR FIXED CAMPS 67

size of your party. In setting up camp, the soap box is to be lined with three or four thicknesses of newspaper (this can be done easily with the aid of a few tacks) and filled with clean hay or straw, packed firmly; and a close little nest hollowed out to fit the cooking pail.

This camp fireless cooker has been tested and has proved a pleasant luxury as well as a convenience in camp life. It makes possible cooked cereals, rice, evaporated fruits and slow-cooking vegetables, where otherwise they would be excluded from the menu. If there are children in the party, these things are particularly desirable. Keep the soap box in a sheltered place. Let the food in the cooking pail begin to boil briskly over the camp fire, then remove it, seeing that the cover is tightly closed (it should be a cover that shuts *in*), and place it in its hay nest. Tuck over it the cotton pad and three or four thicknesses of newspaper and shut down the lid of the box. Breakfast cereals may remain in the cooker over night. Meat, or slow-cooking foods should boil on the camp fire for fifteen minutes before being placed in the cooker.

This will also be found a heat-saving and labor-saving device for those housewives who remain at home — and it costs almost nothing.

It is not necessary to have ice for keeping milk cool and sweet in hot weather. The fireless-cooker, which conserves heat at the boiling point for many hours, will also conserve cold, or, more properly, keep heat out. A box lined with paper, packed with clean hay, straw or shavings and securely covered, is all that is needed. The bottle of milk, received ice-cold from the dairyman's wagon and placed directly in this device, will keep sweet as long as may be desired."

CHAPTER V
TENTS FOR SHIFTING CAMPS

Tents were devised long before the dawn of history, and they still are used as portable dwellings by men of all races and in all climes. Every year sees countless campers busy with new contrivances in canvas or other tent materials, seeking improvements — and still the prehistoric patterns hold their own. Wherever caravans or armies march, or people travel by wagon, or summer vacationists take to a gipsy life, we see wall tents of house shape, or conical ones, of heavy canvas.

But for a small party traveling in rough country, with pack animals, or in light water-craft, or perchance afoot, such cumbersome affairs are out of the question.

Wherever transportation is difficult it is imperative that the tent should be light, compact to carry, and, if you are to make camp and break camp every day or two, it must be so rigged that it can be set up easily and quickly by one or two men.

The tent should shed heavy rains and stand securely in a gale. It should keep out insects and cold draughts, yet let in plenty of pure air. If cold weather is to be encountered, either the tent should be fitted with a very portable stove, or it should be open in front and so shaped as to reflect the heat of a log fire down upon the occupants, yet not smother them with smoke. All of which is easily said, but harder to combine in fact. Hence the multitude of tent patterns.

In designing a light tent we begin by cutting

TENTS FOR SHIFTING CAMPS 69

down the size to what will "sleep" the occupants and their personal duffle. Since the party is to be out of doors all day, save in uncommonly bad weather, a small tent will suffice. Then we dispense with a fly, and make the tent of waterproof material, not only to shed rain but also because plain canvas is very heavy when wet. If the journey is through a well wooded country, no poles or stakes are carried: they are to be cut on the spot. If, however, saplings are scarce in the land, then the tent is made to set up with only one pole, and this pole may be jointed; no guy stakes are used, and the pegs are light things made of steel, as few as practicable.

Tents that are to be carried on pack animals need to be of strong, heavy duck, or else carried in stout bags; otherwise they will be ruined by the sawing of lash ropes and snagging or rubbing against trees and rocks. For such work the best of army duck is none too good.

MATERIALS FOR LIGHT TENTS.— Otherwise the most suitable material is very closely woven stuff made from Sea Island or Egyptian cotton, which has a long and strong fiber. A thin cloth of this kind is stout enough for most purposes, yet very light, and a tent made from it rolls up into a much smaller bundle than one of duck. It comes in various weights and fineness of texture. The standard grade of "balloon silk" runs about $3\frac{1}{2}$ oz. to the *square* yard in plain goods, and $5\frac{1}{2}$ oz. when waterproofed with paraffine. This trade name, by the way, is an absurdity: the stuff has no thread of silk in it, and the only ballooning it ever does is when a wind gets under it.

Cheaper goods, of coarser weave, and intermediate in weight between this and duck, do well enough for easy trips, if waterproofed.

WATERPROOF OR RAINPROOF CLOTHS.— These may be classed under two heads: (*A*) cloth filled with paraffine or other water-shedding substance; (*B*) cloth chemically treated so that each fiber or thread is itself repellant of water, but the interstices are left open.

In the first instance it is not practicable to treat the cloth before making it up; the whole tent should be soaked in a waterproofing mixture, or the "wax" ironed in, thus insuring that the seams are tight. Paraffine is used either plain (in which case it is liable to crack or flake in cold weather) or combined with some elastic substance. The "mineral wax" called ozocerite or cerasine (often used as a substitute for beeswax, and sold by dealers in crude drugs) is not so brittle as paraffine, adheres better, and, like paraffine, has no deleterious action on cloth, being chemically neutral. I have not known of it being used by tent-makers, but believe they should try it. Crude ozocerite is nearly black; when refined it is of a yellow color (cerasine) and resembles beeswax but is not so sticky. It makes a tough compound with rubber.

The plain wax process renders cloth quite waterproof, but adds considerable weight, makes the stuff rather stiff, and increases its liability to catch afire when exposed close to a stove or camp-fire.

Cloth of class *B* is subdivided in two groups:

(1) Cravenetted goods, like duxbak and gabardine, are processed in the yarn, or by chemical treatment applied to the raw strands themselves before they are twisted into thread. Such cloth is not so waterproof as waxed or oiled stuff, yet tents made of it can be depended upon to shed rain. It is as pliable as plain cloth, not perceptibly heavier, and is not affected by changes of temperature.

(2) Willesden canvas (or twill, etc., as the case may be), also known in England as "green rot-proof," is cotton stuff soaked in an ammoniacal solution of copper that dissolves enough cellulose in the cloth to coat each fiber with a more or less impermeable "skin" of its own substance, and turns the material a light shade of green. It is not so waterproof as waxed cloth, yet sheds rain very well if the mate-

TENTS FOR SHIFTING CAMPS 71

rial is closely woven. What is known in this country as "green waterproof" has gone through the cupro-ammonium process and then is lightly waxed besides, making it quite waterproof but more pliable and slower burning than plain waxed stuff.

The mills produce many grades of light cloth suitable for tenting. Each tent-maker chooses for himself, and generally does his own waterproofing. In comparing samples, count the number of threads to the inch with a magnifying glass, then note weight per square yard, and strength.

Cloth proofed with linseed or other drying oil is not strong enough for tenting (for its weight); it is sticky in hot weather, stiff in cold, and dangerously inflammable.

FEATHERWEIGHT TENT MATERIALS.— Pedestrian and cycle campers sometimes go in for the utmost possible lightness and compactness of outfit that will serve their purposes. For tents they use the most finely woven cotton, linen, or silk, not waterproofed, but depending upon extreme closeness of texture to shed rain. The cloth may "spray" a little in the first heavy downpour, but it will not leak so long as nothing rubs it from within.

I have a sample of very close-woven silky cotton stuff from which a Puget Sound tent-maker turns out "A" tents complete of the following weights: $3\frac{1}{2} \times 7 \times 4$ ft. high, 2 lbs.; $4\frac{1}{2} \times 7\frac{1}{2} \times 5$ ft., $2\frac{3}{4}$ lbs.; $7\frac{1}{2} \times 7\frac{1}{2} \times 7$ ft., 5 lbs.

Lightest of all rain-proof materials, strongest for its weight, and, of course, most expensive, is silk. It can be woven more closely than any other textile and so needs no waterproofing (oiled silk, such as surgeons use, weighs more than "balloon silk"). Genuine silk is the toughest of all fibers; but it does not stand much friction, hence should be reinforced at all friction surfaces, and rolled up when packed away, not folded in creases. It is unsuitable for any but special tents made for pedestrians. A London maker, T. H. Holding, sells a tentlette (if I may coin a term) of Japanese silk, in wedge shape, 6 x 5 x 4 ft. 6 in. high, that weighs under 12 ounces; and it is a practical little affair of its kind. Of one of these he reports: "It has stood some of the heaviest rains, in fact records for thirty hours at a stretch, without letting in wet, and I say this of an 11-oz. silk one."

WATERPROOFING CLOTH AT HOME.— If one has home facilities, there is no reason why he should not make a good job of waterproofing for himself.

PARAFFINE PROCESS.— The cheapest, simplest, and, in some respects, the most satisfactory way is to get a cake or two of paraffine or cerasine, lay the tent on a table, rub the outer side with the wax until it has a good coating evenly distributed, then iron the cloth with a medium-hot flatiron, which melts the wax and runs it into every pore of the cloth. The more closely woven the cloth, the less wax and less total weight.

Some prefer to treat the tent with a solution of paraffine. In this case, cut the wax into shavings so it will dissolve readily. Put 2 lbs. of the wax in 2 gallons of turpentine (for a 7 x 9 tent or thereabouts). Place the vessel in a tub of hot water until solution is completed. Meantime set up the tent true and taut. Then paint it with the hot solution, working rapidly, and using a stiff brush. Do this on a sunny morning and let tent stand until quite dry. The turpentine adds a certain elasticity to the wax; benzine does not.

For tents to be used in cold weather before an open fire, the following process is better:

ALUM AND SUGAR OF LEAD.— First soak the tent overnight in water to rid it of sizing, and hang up to dry. Then get enough *soft* water to make the solutions (rainwater is best; some city waters will do, others are too hard). Have two tubs or wash-boilers big enough for the purpose. In one, dissolve alum in hot soft water, in the proportion of ¼ lb. to the gallon. In the other, with the same amount of hot water, dissolve sugar of lead (lead acetate — *a poison*) in the same proportion. Let the solutions stand until clear; then add the sugar of lead solution to the alum liquor. Let stand about four hours, or until all the lead sulphate has precipitated. Then pour off the clear liquor from the dregs into the other tub, thoroughly work the tent in it with the hands

TENTS FOR SHIFTING CAMPS 73

until every part is quite penetrated, and let soak overnight. In the morning, rinse well, stretch, and hang up to dry.

A closely woven cloth should be used.

This treatment fixes acetate of alumina in the fibers of the cloth. The final rinsing is to cleanse the fabric from the useless white powder of sulphate of lead that is deposited on it. Failures are usually due to using hard water, or a less proportion of alum than here recommended, or to not dissolving the chemicals separately and decanting off the clear liquor. When directions are followed, the cloth will be rain-proof and practically spark-proof, but not damp-proof if you use it as a ground-sheet to lie on, or if exposed to friction. After a good deal of use, the tent will need treating over again, as the mineral deposit gradually washes out.

Remember that cotton goods shrink considerably when first soaked.

ALUM AND SOAP.— Shave up about a pound of laundry soap and dissolve it in 2 gallons of hot water. Soak the cloth in it, dry out thoroughly, and then soak in an alum solution as above, and dry again.

I have had no success with the alum and lime method mentioned by " Nessmuk."

Good waterproofing compounds can be purchased ready-made from some tent-makers.

The following recipes, although not suitable for tents, are useful for other articles of equipment, and are included here while on the subject of waterproofing cloth:

OILED CLOTH.— For ground-sheets to use under bedding: get some of the best grade of *boiled* linseed oil of a reputable paint dealer. One quart will cover five or six square yards of heavy sheeting. Pour it into a pan big enough to dip your hand into. Lay out the cloth and rub the oil into it between your palms, using just enough oil at a time to soak the cloth through, filling the pores, but leaving no surplus. Then stretch it in a barn or garret, or other dry shady place, for one week. Finish drying by hanging in the sunlight three or four days, first one side up, then the other.

FLEXIBLE CELLULOID COATING.—A flexible enamel such as is used on fly lines for fishing is also useful for finishing seams in articles sewed up from waterproofed cloth.

Get some old photographic films, soak them in hot water, and scrub off the gelatine surface with a small stiff brush.

When they are dry, gradually add them to acetone until the solution is of the consistency of varnish. If a drop of it dries transparent and firm, it is fit. In this state it makes a strong cement or hard rod varnish that will not crack or peel. To make it flexible, proceed as follows:

Add common benzine to the amount of one-fourth the acetone. Shake well. Let the mixture stand and settle. Draw off the clear varnish from the water at the bottom, and test as before. If it does not dry clear and firm, add a little more benzine.

Now add castor oil to the amount of two-thirds the weight of the dry celluloid films that have been used, shake well, and give it time to thoroughly mix. Test: if not tough enough, add a little more oil. If too soft, add a little celluloid solution.

This does not evaporate so fast as a solution of celluloid in amyl acetate ("banana oil"). The castor oil gives it its flexibility.

DYEING CLOTH.— Use Diamond dye of a kind recommended by the makers for *cotton* goods. Follow directions on package. Dye the tent a deeper shade than what you want in service, for it will fade considerably in sun and rain. The dyeing must be done before waterproofing.

CONSTRUCTION OF LIGHT TENTS.— In a tent of thin material it is important that the widths be narrow, to keep the shelter taut when set up, and that the seams be reinforced with tape, to relieve the cloth itself from overstrain. Eaves, bottom, and corners should be strengthened with double cloth.

If there is a ridge, have it reinforced, with tapes attached whereby to suspend the tent from an *outside* ridge pole when desired.

There should be a sod-cloth all around, unless the tent has a sewed-in floor.

A tent that is to be used in "fly time" is certainly incomplete without a curtain of cheesecloth or bobbinet to exclude insects. This is best made to attach or detach at will, if the tent is also to be used late in the season with an all-night fire in front of it.

All tents that are made to close up at night or in

TENTS FOR SHIFTING CAMPS 75

bad weather should be fitted with screened windows for ventilation. The smaller the tent, the greater the need of this.

Guy-rope slides, if there are any, should be of galvanized wire. Grommets (galvanized iron rings worked in by hand) are much better than brass eyelets which are likely to pull out.

Ropes and beckets are to be small but strong; braided sash cord is best for a ridge rope.

Tent pins of steel are more durable and less cumbersome than wooden ones. In well forested countries none need be carried, but four steel corner pins help in setting up the tent quickly.

CHAPTER VI
TYPES OF LIGHT TENTS

Local conditions, means of transportation, and size of party, are to be considered in choosing among the many tent models that have been designed for campers who travel light. All depends on where you go, when you go, how you go, and what you want to do. The perfect all-round tent is a myth, like the perfect all-round gun. Of one thing, though, be sure: that whatever rig you choose shall be stanch against wind. The utmost pinnacle of comfort is reached when one lies at night under canvas, with a storm roaring toward him through the forest, and chortles over the certainty that no wind can blow *his* tent down. And it takes just one second of parting guys and ripping cloth to tumble him off his perch and cast him headlong into the very depths of woe.

LIGHT WALL TENTS.— A wall tent is the favorite cloth shelter of soldiers, engineers, explorers, naturalists, trappers, loggers, and other practical men who live away from civilization a great deal of the time. For one thing, it gives the most head-room for a given amount of material; and that counts, especially in continuous bad weather, or when one comes in wet all over and wants to hang up his clothes to dry. It is the best form of tent if a stove is carried; and that may be necessary in a thinly wooded country, late in the season. The vertical ends permit large ventilators or windows that may be kept open in almost any weather. There is no waste space, as in tents without walls.

Wall tents for flying camps should be much lighter, of course, than those mentioned in Chapter

III. In wooded country they are to be set up with shears, as previously described; or, if the ground favors, and a quick set is desired, run a ridge rope from tree to tree, or from a tree to a stake, stretch the guys, and do not bother to pin down the bottom but simply weight the sod-cloth.

Light waterproof wall tents may be had in great variety of sizes and materials, from which the following are selected as examples (width, depth, height, and wall, in order given):

BALLOON SILK (WHITE).

7⅓ x 7⅓ x 7 –2   10½ lbs.
8¾ x 8¾ x 7½–3   14¾ lbs.
10¼ x 10¼ x 8½–3½ 20   lbs.

TANALITE (TAN), EMERALITE (GREEN).

7   x 7   x 7 –2   10 lbs.
8½ x 8½ x 7½–3   14 lbs.
10   x 10   x 8½–3½ 19 lbs.

TANO (TAN), NILO (GREEN).

7½ x 7½ x 7–2   9 lbs.
7½ x 9   x 7–2½ 11 lbs.
9   x 12   x 7–2½ 13 lbs.

KIRO (OLIVE DRAB).

7   x 7   x 7–2½ 12½ lbs.
9½ x 11¾ x 8–3   20¾ lbs.
11¾ x 14   x 9–3½ 27   lbs.

EXTRA LIGHT GREEN.

6½ x 6½ x 6 –2   7   lbs.
8   x 8   x 7 –2½ 10   lbs.
9½ x 9½ x 7½–3   13½ lbs.

GREEN EGYPTIAN.

7⅓ x 7⅓ x 7–2   9½ lbs.
9¾ x 9¾ x 8–3¼ 16½ lbs.
9¾ x 12⅓ x 8–3¼ 19   lbs.

GREEN STANDARD.

7⅙ x 7⅙ x 7 –2   12   lbs.
9½ x 9½ x 8 –3¼ 19½ lbs.
11¾ x 11¾ x 9½–3½ 27½ lbs.

All of the above-named tents have tape ridges that can be tied to outside poles, and are fitted with sod-cloths.

Smaller, and larger, and intermediate sizes are made; but if a lighter shelter is wanted it is generally best to choose some other shape than a wall tent; and, if a larger one, then use heavier material that will stand up better and endure more strain.

Directions for setting up wall tents are given in Chapter III (see especially Figs. 11, 15).

CONICAL TENTS.— A tent may be "light" absolutely (so many pounds all told) or relatively (so

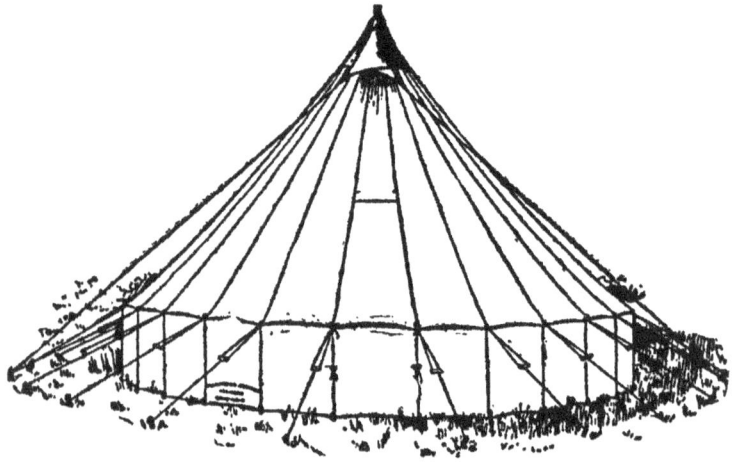

Fig. 38.— U. S. A. Conical Tent

many pounds per man sheltered). Conical tents of military pattern, such as the old Sibley, the present U. S. A., and the Bell tent of the British service, belong to the latter class.

The U. S. Army conical wall tent (Fig. 38) is 16 ft. 5 in. in diameter, 10 ft. high, and has a 3-ft. wall. It is erected by a single pole, the butt of which fits into a folding steel tripod, thus shortening the pole and giving it better bearing. At the top is an opening shielded by flaps. It is heated by a bottomless cone-shaped stove of 2-ft. diameter at the base (Fig. 39) with 5-in. pipe. This stove con-

TYPES OF LIGHT TENTS

sumes little fuel. It is fed with sticks stood on end (dry "cow chips" will do), and the draught is regulated by banking earth around the bottom. Such a tent is roomy and comfortable for eight men in any weather. It will shelter a dozen or more at a pinch.

A conical tent is best for a party traveling on the plains, where violent windstorms or cloud-bursts or blizzards may suddenly be encountered, and where there is little or no timber. A cone sheds winds and rain better than any other shape, as it has a steep pitch and equal bracing in all directions. On the other hand, it is not fit for rough grounds;

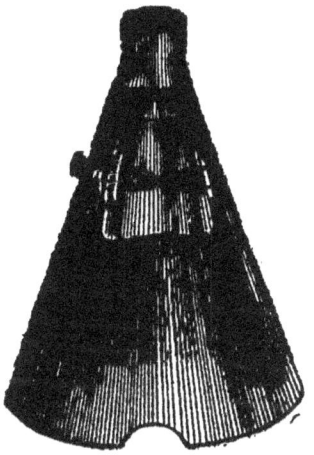

Fig. 39.—Sibley Tent Stove

unless the site is smooth and level the tent bottom will gape in some places and sag in others. A conical tent cannot be set up properly without a full set of pegs, and it requires many of them.

Smaller and lighter conical tents are made for various tastes; but no tent of this shape should be of less diameter than 13 feet with wall, or 14 feet without one; for the occupants are supposed to lie like spokes of a wheel, and their feet must not come too near the center pole.

The army conical wall tent is usually pitched by eight men, of whom the director is designated as No. 8. They work as follows:

Upon the hood lines of the tent are placed three marks; the first about 8 feet 3 inches, the second about 11 feet 3 inches, the third about 14 feet 2 inches from the hood ring; the first marks the distance from the center to the wall pins, the second to the guy pins, and the distance between the second and third is the distance between guy pins. These distances vary slightly for different tents and should be verified by actual experiment before per-

80 CAMPING AND WOODCRAFT

manently marking the ropes. To locate the position of guy pins after the first, the hood ring being held on the center pin, with the left hand hold the outer mark on the pin last set, with the right hand grasp the rope at the center mark and move the hand to the right so as to have both sections of the rope taut; the center mark is then over the position desired; the inner mark is over the position of the corresponding wall pin.

To pitch the tent, No. 1 places the tent pole on the ground, socket end against the door pin, pole perpendicular to the company street. No. 2 drives the center pin at the other extremity of the pole. No. 3 drives a wall pin on each side of and 1 foot from the door pin. No. 4 places the open tripod flat on the ground with its center near the center pin. The whole detachment then places the tent, fully opened, on the ground it is to occupy, the center at the center pin, the door at the door pin.

No. 8 holds the hood ring on the center pin, and superintends from that position. No. 1 stretches the hood rope over the right (facing the tent) wall pin and No. 2 drives the first guy pin at the middle mark. No. 1 marks the position of the guy pins in succession and No. 2 drives a pin lightly in each position as soon as marked. At the same time No. 5 inserts small pins in succession through the wall loops and places the pins in position against the inner mark on the hood rope, where they are partly driven by No. 6. No. 4 distributes large pins ahead of Nos. 1 and 2; No. 7, small pins ahead of Nos. 5 and 6; No. 3 follows Nos. 1 and 2 and drives the guy pins home. No. 7, after distributing his pins, takes an ax and drives home the pins behind Nos. 5 and 6. No. 4, after distributing his pins, follows No. 3 and loops the guy ropes over the pins.

Nos. 1, 2, and 3, the pins being driven, slip under the tent and place the pin of the pole through the tent and hood rings while No. 8 places the hood in position. Nos. 1, 2, and 3 then raise the pole to a vertical position and insert the end in the socket of the tripod; they then raise the tripod to its proper height, keeping the center of the tripod over the center pin; while they hold the pole vertical. Nos. 4, 5, 6, and 7 adjust four guy ropes, one in each quadrant of the tent, to hold the pole in its vertical position, and then the remaining guy ropes. As soon as these are adjusted the men inside drive a pin at each foot of the tripod if necessary to hold it in place.

The tent may also be pitched by four men. No. 4 holds the hood ring and superintends. After the tent is in position on the ground it is to occupy, the pins are distributed by Nos. 2 and 3. Number 3 takes the place of

TYPES OF LIGHT TENTS 81

Nos. 5 and 6 in placing the wall loop pins. After all the pins are placed they are driven home, all assisting.

This takes a long time to describe, but the thing is done in a jiffy.

TEEPEES.— The teepee (pronounced *tee*-pee) of the plains Indians was an admirable shelter for the country they roamed over. Being of conical shape, and erected on a set of inside poles meeting at the top and with their butts radiating in every direction, it was proof against anything but a tornado. A very small fire in the center sufficed to keep it warm, and the smoke was wafted out of a hole at the top by an ingenious arrangement of flaps set according to the direction of the wind, in combination with an inner curtain around the bottom of the teepee, a little higher than a man's head, with its lower edge confined like a sod-cloth. The draught, entering freely through the gaps between tent pegs, emerged at top of curtain, and was drawn " a-fluking " upward by the warm current of air from the fire.* It has been said that no white man can manage a fire in a teepee without smoking the occupants out. This is an error: I have done it myself; but I had the best of dry wood in plenty, and I gave that fire more attention than it deserved.

The beauty of the teepee is that there is no center pole in the way. However, it needs at least nine lodge poles, and they should be slender, stiff, and straight. This rules it out of consideration by campers generally. Remember, too, that the real Indian teepee was made of skins, impermeable to wind and proof against sparks. Under modern conditions, if you must have a fire in your tent, use a stove.

PYRAMIDAL TENTS.— For a party of only two or three, traveling light, in a region where trees and saplings are scarce, as on the plains, or the coast, or in the mountains above timber-line, and where storms

---

* For details and illustrations see Edward Cave's *The Boy's Camp Book*, pp. 31-33.

may be violent, there is nothing better than a pyramidal or "miner's" tent (Fig. 40). It requires only one pole, and but few pegs. It has more available ground space than a conical tent of equal cubic capacity. It is economical of cloth. Next to the cone, it is the most stable form of tent, and it sheds rain and snow better than any other. One man, without assistance, can set it up in a trice. It sets well on uneven ground, and is easy to trench.

Pyramidal tents may be had with walls; but they are not nearly so easy to erect as one without a wall,

Fig. 40.— Miner's Tent

and many more pegs must be carried. This shape is at its best in the plain miner's form of a size suitable for two or three men: namely, a 7 x 7 x 7 or a 9½ x 9½ x 8½ ft., weighing, in different materials, from 5¼ to 14 lbs. A jointed pole of ash will weigh about 4½ lbs. in 7-ft., or 5 lbs. in 8½ ft. length, and a dozen 9-inch steel tent pins about 2 lbs.

Since the only head-room in such a tent is directly under the peak, a center pole is constantly in the way. If a little extra weight is not prohibited, it is better to carry a pair of jointed shear poles that set up inside the tent, one on either side, like two legs of a tripod. Of course, if poles can be found near camp, the tent may be erected on outside shears or tripod. For this purpose, or for suspending from

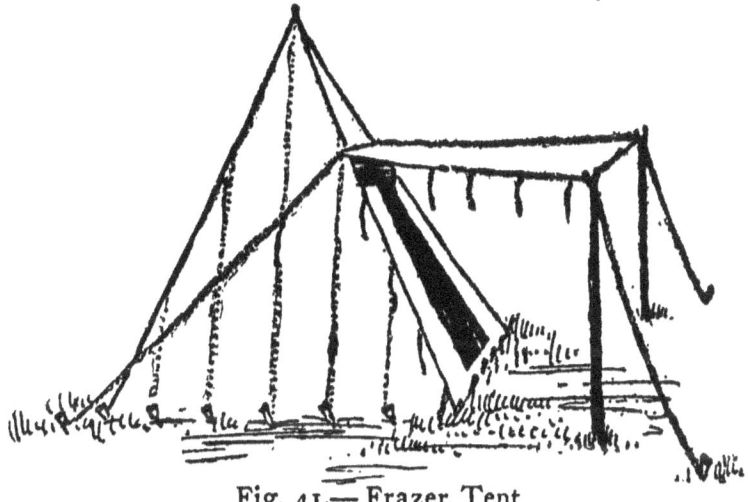

Fig. 41.—Frazer Tent

a limb, it should have a strong canvas loop sewed to the peak.

If the tent is to be used on a sandy coast or desert,

Fig. 42.—Marquee

or where insects are very bad, it is best made with a ground-cloth sewed fast to the bottom, or with a separate one that fits over a rather wide sod-cloth.

The Frazer tent (Fig. 41) has a small awning to shield the doorway, and a cloth " sill " that holds the bottom together. There is a window at the rear. Only a small screen is required at the doorway to keep out insects, yet the ventilation is good. It is not a cold-weather tent, as it cannot be thrown wide open, like a plain miner's tent, to receive the rays of a camp-fire.

Some canoeists in "civilized waters" prefer the marquee (Fig. 42), because it has more head-room than a pyramidal tent. It has spreaders attached to the center pole, like ribs of an umbrella, to extend the eaves, and guy ropes to stiffen them against wind; but in spite of these braces it is not very stable.

SEMI-PYRAMIDAL TENTS.— The lightest of enclosed tents that allow a man to stand upright under shelter is one shaped like a pyramid cut vertically in

Fig. 43.—George Tent

half. Since the pole, if one is used, stands in front, it is less in the way than the center pole of a pyramidal tent, but a guy or two must be run out for-

TYPES OF LIGHT TENTS

ward to brace it. A better rig, when poles can be cut on the spot, is an outside tripod (as an example see Fig. 66). If a small tree *happens* to stand conveniently on the camp site, the tent peak can be suspended from it.

A good example of this model is the George tent (Figs. 43, 44). For two men, its dimensions are 7 x 7 x 7 ft. In waterproofed "balloon silk" it weighs about 5¼ lbs., including pegs, and rolls up into a parcel 12 x 5 in., convenient for the knapsack. To pitch it: Peg down at 1 and 2 (Fig. 44),

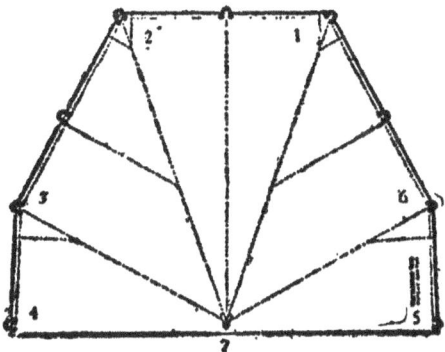

Fig. 44.—Layout of George Tent

carry 3 and 6 at right angles to 1 and 2, pull taut, peg down, insert pole, and raise; or suspend as above. This is done in one minute, if no poles have to be cut. A cheesecloth front is needed in fly time. In cold weather the front is left open, and the sloping back and sides reflect camp-fire heat down upon the sleepers.

Semi-pyramidal tents must be well guyed to stand up in a contrary wind. They are best suited to canoeists and forest cruisers.

MODIFIED PYRAMID TENT.—A shelter tent adaptable to varied conditions, and a very good model for "go light" trips, was recently described in *Outing* by its designer, R. S. Royce. His article is here reprinted in full, by permission of the publishers.

86 CAMPING AND WOODCRAFT

THE ROYCE TENT.

"Several seasons ago, desiring a very light tent for side trips, or, in fact, anywhere that a comfortable shelter was needed under conditions which would not permit of using a wall tent, one was designed which so well met all requirements and aroused so much interest among the outing brotherhood as to warrant presenting a detailed description of it.

Keeping away from the idea of a mere shelter to crawl under, and insisting on having something really comfortable in the event of several stormy days or nights, and with a spirit of comradeship that finds more fun in an outing shared by one or two friends, rather than alone, a tent was designed to afford room for two or three and high enough to sit, dress, or stand in.

This sounds like something too big for the ruck-sack, or a minor corner of a pack-basket, without crowding the other essentials of going light. However, it was accomplished at a weight of four pounds, making a package about 6 inches in diameter and 12 inches long for carrying; erected, it covers 56 square feet, as a closed half pyramid 7 feet 9 inches high and 7½ feet square (Fig. 45). But this is not all, for it is extensible to a pyramid 7½ x 13 feet, still 7 feet 9 inches high, but open at one end to the peak (Fig. 47); or it may be extended at the front of the half pyramid in a triangle the width of the tent, 7½ x 2½ feet, closing completely and increasing the length of the tent to 10 feet (Fig. 46). The objection is immediately presented that this is too large a tent for going even moderately light, but one may reasonably ask how much smaller package or lighter can you take, and get room for standing, sitting, and sleeping?

Considering this, first, as a half pyramid tent, 7½ x 7½ and 7¾ feet high; no form gives so much ground space with headroom from so little material as a pyramid; none sheds water better, nor resists wind so well, and none is simpler or quicker to erect.

The objections to a pyramid, of scant headroom and lost space on ground by rapidly sloping roofs; of presence of pole in the center, and of possible rain leak anywhere on the entrance side from peak to ground, are largely overcome by carrying the peak to 7¾ feet, giving more headroom and nearer perpendicular roofs; and by making the peak over the center of one side, instead of in the middle of the tent, giving a perpendicular entrance opening and no pole in the ground space. This gives better than a 45-degree pitch to the back roof and about 65-degree pitch to the side roofs; sheds rain well,

TYPES OF LIGHT TENTS 87

without necessary recourse to waterproofing, and allows of erection not only over a single upright pole, or suspension from overhanging branch, but also permits of setting up near any upright tree to which the peak-line may be extended diagonally upward in a general line with the slope of the back roof, thus generally eliminating the tent-pole problem.

Now, some of the arguments for this half pyramid be-

Fig. 45.— Front Upright

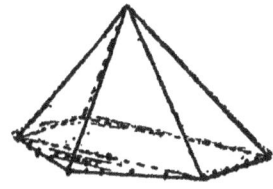
Fig. 46.— Wings Advanced 2½ feet

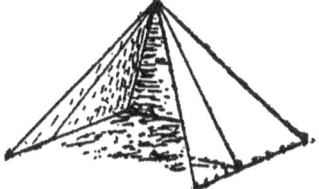
Fig. 47.— Wings Extended sheltering 7½ x 13 feet

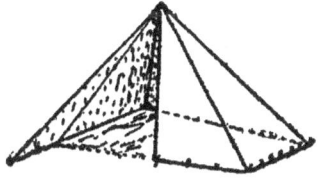
Fig. 48.— One Wing Closed, One Open for Wind-break

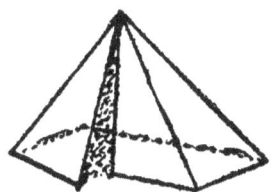
Fig. 49.— One Wing Partly Extended

ROYCE TENT

ing given, another exists in the use of it with the front open (flaps turned away back on the side roofs), when it proves to be as truly a baker tent as the one usually described as such, and heats well with a fire in front.

The peculiar feature of this design is in the extra size and the form of the flaps, which make possible the triangular extension of the front for 2½ feet and still closing completely; and the further extension of the flaps, in plane with the side roofs, leaving an open-ended true pyramid 7½ x 13 feet, at an increase of only 2¼₁₀₀ yards of material and not over one-quarter pound weight, over that required for the simple half pyramid 7½ feet square, barely closed.

This is worth while for most of us, for it permits of considerable extra room at practically no expense of weight or material, and allows of use in a variety of ways otherwise impossible: viz., the flaps extended completely, in plane with the side, leave an unroofed triangle, within which a fire may be built, allowing the camper to sit under either flap, and, protected, manipulate his frying pan, etc.; or one may be so extended and the other closed, affording a wind and rain protection with good ventilation, or one may be closed and the other extended 2½ feet (as for triangular front), leaving an open doorway without disclosing to view the interior, on account of the extra wide flaps (Fig. 48).

Another peculiarity is that in the event of finding only a short tent-pole and no tree to tie to, the tent may be set up with any height pole, under 7½ feet, and dress taut and trim, and, incidentally, cover a larger ground space, but, of course, at cost of less pitch to the roofs. The front being open clear to the peak, and all lines converging there, it is very easily cleared of insects by brush or smudge.

Of course, any pyramid tent, without perpendicular side walls, is free from the need of stakes, as only short pegs are necessary; when a quick shelter is needed, the peakline over a branch or to a tree and pegs at the four corners will serve until it is convenient to place the intermediate pegs.

So many inquiries as to the details of this tent have been made, and so many requests for measurements and directions for making copies of it have occurred, that diagrams and measurements are here given.

Any tent-maker can reproduce it, for amateurs have, and it lends itself easily to those who enjoy making their own equipment.

The original is made of Lonsdale cambric and lightly waterproofed, and weighs only four pounds. It has had hard usage and has proved altogether satisfactory. Any thin material closely woven will serve, and that, too, without waterproofing, with roofs so steep.

Sheeting is practical, but would give a weight in excess of that quoted here.

DIRECTIONS FOR CUTTING AND SEWING

Material: Light, closely-woven cambric or other close material, 36 inches wide.

TYPES OF LIGHT TENTS 89

Dimensions: Seven feet 6 inches square on ground and 7 feet 9 inches high to peak.

Form: Half pyramid. Front "A," perpendicular; roof sloping three ways from pointed peak. Front flaps or wings are made to overlap considerably, and are longer than are necessary to reach the ground when closed perpendicularly.

LAYOUT FOR SIDE WALLS (FIG. 50)

Join two breadths 10' 4" long by edges, overlaid and double-stitched. Pin these out on floor smooth, and from point 1' 9" from end on one side to point same distance from other end of other side pin down a cord tight; close at either side of cord pin or baste a narrow tape, leaving

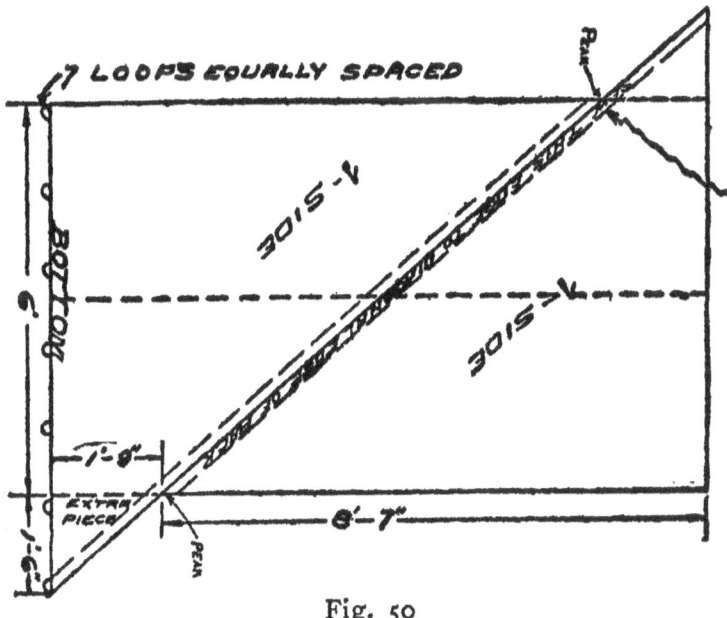

Fig. 50

tapes which cross the edges about two feet longer. Stitch these tapes down and divide goods in line between tapes. Sew to 1' 9" edge the selvage edge of a triangle 1' 9" by 1' 6" and sew tape to bias edge. These two triangles are the two side roofs.

LAYOUT OF MATERIAL FOR BACK (FIG. 51)

Pin out smooth one breadth 13' long, and between points 2' 2½" from each end on opposite side edges draw line or pin tight cord and sew tapes either side of line, leaving tapes which cross the edges two feet longer. Against

90 CAMPING AND WOODCRAFT

these edges and to the tapes sew triangles 2' 2" by 9". Divide the goods between the tapes. These two triangles to be turned with selvage edges together and when joined form the back roof.

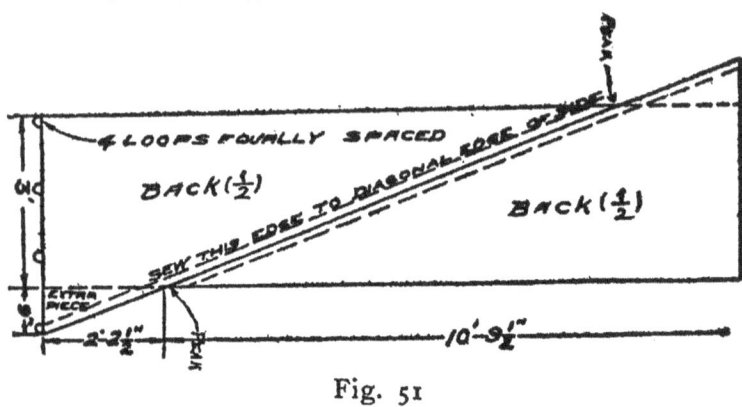

Fig. 51

This is to permit extending the front 2½ feet triangularly and still closing it tight; also allowing the wings to be extended 5 feet 6 inches in plane with the side roofs, producing a pyramid 13 feet by 7½ feet open at one end to the peak.

LAYOUT OF MATERIAL FOR WINGS (FIG. 52)

Pin out one breadth 8' 7½" long. From one corner to point on opposite side, and 3' 10½" from the opposite end,

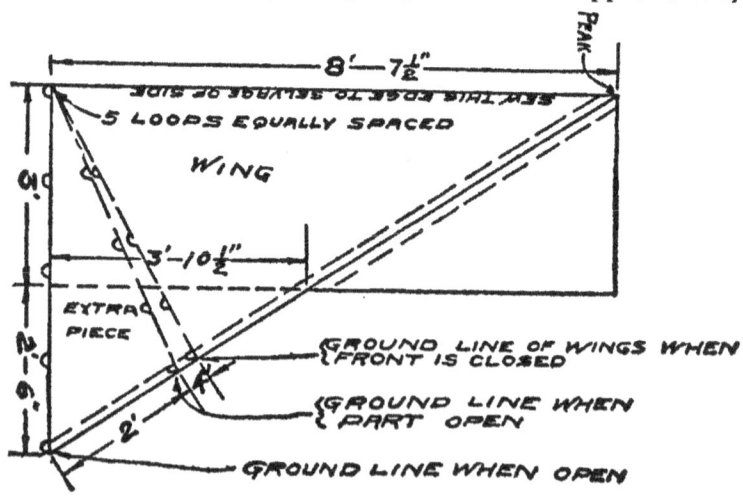

Fig. 52

draw line and sew tape on side of line toward larger piece, leaving tape about 4' 9" longer than reaching to the sel-

TYPES OF LIGHT TENTS 91

vage edge.. Against this 3′ 10½″ selvage edge sew triangle cut from other side of line, using right angled triangle 3′ 10½″ by 2′ 6″, binding bias edge with overhanging tape. This makes only one flap or wing. Duplicate.

HOW TO SET IT UP

Join to each diagonal edge of the back one of the diagonal edges of each sidepiece; and to the selvage edge of each side-piece a selvage edge of one of the wings.

Close the peak around a ¾-inch metal ring. Leave front wings open clear to peak. Turn in ground edge a little all around and attach strong tape loops for pegs at corners and five between on each side and back and four on bottom of each wing; also on a line from lower attached corner of each wing to a point 2 feet up from bottom of free edge of each wing put four loops on outside and again on a line from corner to a point 4 inches still higher four more loops. These loops are for pegging down wings in the three positions of extension in plane with sides, in partial extension, and when closed with perpendicular front.

If sod-cloth is desired, a breadth of cloth 7½ feet long split in three strips will make about a 10-inch sod cloth if attached to lower edge of sides and back before putting on a heavy tape which will finish the lower edge. No sod-cloth is needed at front as wings will turn in sufficient in all positions except when fully extended.

For light tent, flap-ties are best of tape and should be spaced along the free edges of each wing and also at line where edges fall when overlapped so as to make front bottom line of tent measure 7½ feet. Wings need hem or tape for free edges. A ⅛-inch braided cord 15 feet long is needed from peak where it can be attached to a metal ring just too large to pull through the peak ring. From this inside ring it is well to lead like cords down to the back corners of the tent and out through eyelet-holes through the sod-cloth just under the corner peg-loops. These two add to the trimness of tent, especially if of very light material, and can be run to front corners as well, if desired.

MATERIAL

36-inch wide stuff ....20½ yards.
½-inch tape ....75 feet.
¾-inch tape for bottom edge ....23 feet.
⅛ cord, peak 15 feet   }..................40 feet.
⅛ cord 2 back seams 25

92 CAMPING AND WOODCRAFT

WEDGE OR "A" TENTS.— The wedge tent is an "old stand-by" for those who go where portages must be made or camp shifted every day or two. It is light, cheap, easy to pitch with or without poles, and is well adapted to uneven ground.

In wooded country the camper often may find two trees or saplings from which to stretch a rope, above the level of his head, where it is out of the way. The tent is then pegged out and suspended by its ridge from the rope. This is a quick and satisfac-

Fig. 53.— Wedge Tent, Outside Ridge Rope

tory "set" in level forest. On rough ground it may be hard to find a place for the tent with trees growing just where you want them.

Common wedge tents are made with rope running through, under the ridge. The ridge then sags in what engineers call a catenary curve. This makes the sides sag inward, reducing the roominess all around, and the wind makes matters worse. A better plan is to have tapes on the outside of the ridge (Fig. 53), run the rope high and taut, then tie the middle tapes closer to the rope than the outer ones.

The bottom of a wedge tent with rope ridge should be pegged in such way that the sides will be in arcs of a circle, instead of straight along the ground (Fig. 54): this takes up slack. The ground-cloth, if there

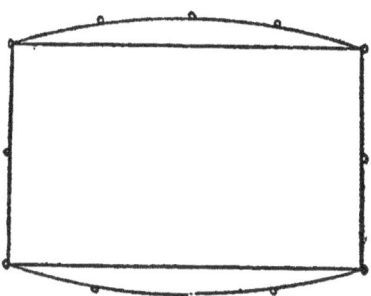

Fig. 54.—Pegging Bottom of Tent

is one, should be cut accordingly. The thinner the material, the more a tent will sag when erected without a ridge pole. Partially to obviate this, and to stiffen the tent in a gale, it is a good scheme to attach parrels (Figs. 55, 58) to ropes or strong seams in the sides. These pull outward and turn the

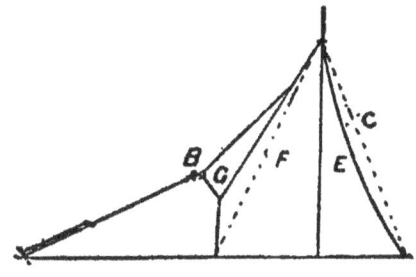

Fig. 55.—Side Parrels

wedge into a semi-wall tent. Referring to Fig 55, C shows the theoretically straight side of a wedge tent and E the actual inward sag from ridge droop and wind pressure. The dotted line F indicates the opposite side without parrels, and A is the same wall held out and made taut by the parrels BG. The illustration is adapted from one by T. H. Holding, of London.

Where no trees stand conveniently, a forked stake can be placed at each end of the tent, the rope run over the crotches and staked out as a guy fore and aft; but the front guy is much in the way. It is better to set up shears and a ridge pole, as in Fig. 11. Often a natural support can be found for one end of the pole.

When traveling where there are few or no trees, it will be necessary to carry jointed poles of wood, steel, or bamboo. There may as well be three of these, so that two can be straddled to leave the doorway free. A jointed ridge pole makes the tent stand trimmer; but, if all that weight can be carried, the party had better take a wall tent and be comfortable.

Wedge tents are not recommended in sizes larger than about 7 x 7 x 7 ft. Weights of a few examples are as follows:

TANALITE, EMERALITE	EXTRA LIGHT GREEN
$4\frac{1}{3}$ x 7 x 5. 6 lbs.	$4\frac{3}{4}$ x $6\frac{1}{2}$ x 5. 5 lbs.
7 x 7 x 7. 8 lbs.	$6\frac{1}{2}$ x $6\frac{1}{2}$ x 7. $6\frac{1}{2}$ lbs.
Balloon silk a bit heavier.	

TANO, NILO	GREEN EGYPTIAN.
$4\frac{1}{2}$ x $7\frac{1}{2}$ x 5. $4\frac{1}{2}$ lbs.	5 x $7\frac{1}{3}$ x 5. $6\frac{1}{2}$ lbs.
$7\frac{1}{2}$ x $7\frac{1}{2}$ x 7. $7\frac{1}{4}$ lbs.	$7\frac{1}{3}$ x $7\frac{1}{3}$ x 7. $9\frac{1}{2}$ lbs.

The alpine tent shown in Fig. 58 was designed by Edward Whymper, and has been used by many other famous mountaineers, such as Sir Martin Conway, Douglas Freshfield, Dr. Hunter Workman, and the Duke of the Abruzzi, for exploration among the highest mountains of the globe. It is made of Willesden canvas or drill, with a sewed-in groundsheet, and a " sill " at the door, to cut out draughts and ground chill. Few pegs are required. When the floor is stretched taut, every peg finds its proper place. The poles form shears at each end, over

TYPES OF LIGHT TENTS 95

which the ridge rope is guyed out fore and aft. This is a very stanch "set." The standard size is 7 x 7 x 6½ ft.

Fig. 56.— Whymper Alpine Tent

MODIFIED WEDGE TENTS.— An angular lap or extension may be added to the lower edge of each door flap to serve as a wind shield for a cooking fire in bad weather. If the rear end of a wedge tent is made rounded instead of square, extra room for duffle is provided, with little additional weight.

The Hudson Bay tent (Fig 57) saves weight by

Fig. 57.— Hudson Bay Tent

having both ends rounded and the ridge short. It does not sag so much as a regular wedge tent, and is more stable in a wind, but affords less head-room.

To get more head-room in a tent without walls, the Ross alpine tent (Fig. 58) is fitted over a sectional bent frame. It has side parrels, and a door at each end. The dimensions are 7 x 7 x 6½ ft.

Fig. 58.— Ross Alpine Tent

SEPARABLE SHELTER TENTS.— When men travel in pairs, going light, it is a good plan for each to carry a "shelter-half," adequate to protect him if he should become separated from his companion, and so fitted with ridge flap and tapes that it can quickly be attached to its mate to form a low, broad wedge tent.

Fig. 59.— Separable Shelter Tent

The old-fashioned army shelter half was merely a rectangle of 7½- or 8-oz. duck, two of which, buttoned together, made an A-shaped roof open at both

TYPES OF LIGHT TENTS

ends. It was little protection against shifting winds. In the present military shelter tent, the halves, when joined, close at the rear end, which is lower than the front. A rifle stood up at the front is all the support needed, and it can instantly be recovered for emergency use by kicking the butt free.

For hikers, etc., a good separable tent consists of two lean-tos that close at both ends when joined (Fig. 59). Sometimes these halves are made with a 12 to 18-inch wall (Fig 60). Each half should be

Fig. 60.— Shelter Half with Wall

about 7 ft. long, 3½ or 3¾ ft. wide, and 4¼ ft. high, weighing about 3½ lbs.

SHELTER CLOTHS.— For side trips from camp, a simple rectangle of thin, closely woven waterproof cloth, with grommets and tapes, is all one needs in moderate weather. Set it up at an angle, facing the fire, and, if need be, thatch one or both sides with evergreen boughs or other windbreak. The cloth is useful as a "tarp" about camp and as a wrap for packs on the trail. One that I use, of Tanalite, 7 x 9 ft., weighs 2½ lbs. Set up with a 9-ft. slant,

98   CAMPING AND WOODCRAFT

it stands 6 ft. high in front and shelters 7 x 5 ft. of ground. A small pyramidal mosquito bar should be taken along in summer.

TARPAULIN TENT.— A larger shelter cloth cut as in Fig. 61, the seams reinforced with tapes, beckets for tent pins added along three sides, and door tapes along the other, as indicated, has many uses. It serves, as one wishes, either for a simple lean-to shelter, a wedge tent open at both ends, a semi-pyramidal enclosed tent, a dining fly, a tarpaulin, a ground-sheet, a pack-cloth, or an emergency sail on a

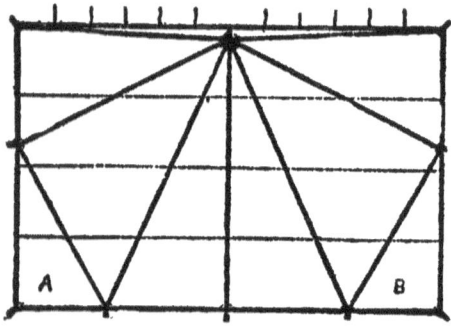

Fig. 61.— Tarpaulin Tent

boat. Referring to the diagram, it will be seen that when the triangular corners A and B are tucked under we have practically the George tent, and the cloth is erected in the same way.

These "tarp" tents are furnished by outfitters ready-made, in various materials, and in sizes from 7½ x 12 to 10 x 13 ft., making semi-pyramidal shelters from 4¾ x 9 x 6 to 7 x 7 x 6½ ft., waterproofed, weighing from 3½ to 6¾ lbs. Full directions for making one at home are given in *The Boy Scout's Hike Book* by Edward Cave.

BAKER TENT.— For a light tent in the hunting season, East or South, I prefer one with a shed-roof, rear wall, and a front that can be closed when one is away for the day, or when a contrary wind springs up with driving rain. Usually the front is left open, and in cold weather a good fire with back-logs of

TYPES OF LIGHT TENTS 99

green wood is kept going all night, about five feet in front of the tent. Of course, this takes a lot of wood, a good-sized hardwood tree being consumed in a single night, and the labor of chopping is rather severe to any one but a good axeman; but the work is well repaid by the exquisite comfort of lying before the blazing backlogs on a cold night, warm as toast, and breathing deeply the fresh air of the forest. Such a tent is never damp and cheerless, as closed tents are apt to be. The heat rays are reflected downward by the sloping roof, drying the ground and warming one's bed in a comparatively short time.

Fig. 62.—Baker Tent

A baker tent may be set up on shears (Fig. 62), or on stakes (Fig. 63), or on a pole nailed from one tree to another, or in various other ways suggested by the location. At the rear a stake is driven for each corner guy and a pole laid outside it, on the ground, to which the other guys are made fast; or a frame is made.

If the door is stretched straight forward as shown in these illustrations, it will prevent having a fire close in front where it should be. Ordinarily the

100 CAMPING AND WOODCRAFT

flap is thrown backward over the roof when a camp-fire is going. A long pole on each side of the tent, run diagonally upward from rear to front, will lift the awning high enough to be out of the way. However, I prefer to have the door-flap separate, and so fitted with grommets or eyelets that it can be attached either to the top or to one side of the tent, as preferred. In warm weather, when no all-night fire is needed, it may be hung from the top as an awning, and the tent may be closed up by it when the occupants are away; but on nights when a fire is kept going the flap should be stretched forward vertically from the windward side of the tent front, so as to

Fig. 63.— Camp-fire Tent

check the draught from that direction, and the fire should be built close to the tent, the front of which is left wide open.

A fall of snow on the roof of an ordinary baker tent may cause trouble, unless an outside framework has been built and thatched with browse. The camp-fire tent (Fig. 63) has a steeper roof, which sheds rain and snow much better, and it affords more head-room without increased weight. This is the best pattern of baker tent. Sizes and weights of some examples are as follows, the dimensions being width, depth, height of front, center, and back, in turn:

TYPES OF LIGHT TENTS

Extra Light Green
6½ x 6½ x 6 – 7 – 2.   8 lbs.
8   x 6½ x 6 – 7½ – 2½.   10 lbs.

Green Egyptian
7⅓ x 7⅓ x 6 – 7½ – 2½.   11 lbs.
9¾ x 7⅓ x 6 – 7½ – 2½.   13 lbs.

Green Wpf. Standard
7⅙ x 7⅙ x 6 – 7½ – 2½.   14   lbs.
9½ x 7⅙ x 6 – 7½ – 2½.   16½ lbs.

Weight in other materials may be judged from tables previously given of other patterns of tents.

One advantage of the baker or camp-fire type is that, in rainy weather, one has a dry, open space to move around in, and he can cook under shelter by building a *small* fire under the awning and feeding it a little at a time.

Such a tent is good for commissary quarters in fixed camp, as it is open and handy to work under. It is not recommended for parties that move frequently, nor for " bad fly-country."

But in a cool climate, where wood is plentiful and mosquitoes scarce, then for me the open lean-to or baker tent, before a hardwood fire, with the free breath of the forest filling my lungs! Let the sleet drive; let the mercury go where it listeth; my axe is my weapon against old Jack Frost. For me, a hunter's camp without a good log fire, burning all the night, is just no camp at all.

But understand: all my camping has been where I was free as an Indian to do with the forest whatever I pleased. I could cut down and burn any tree, any number of them — sweet birch, hickory, white ash, sugar maple, anything — heedless of what such timber might be worth if ever it got to market. I could burn choice wood when I did not need fire; burn just for the incense and comradry of it all.

Not so the average camper of to-day. He must cull old dead no-account stuff that he finds on the

102 CAMPING AND WOODCRAFT

ground — peradventure he even be permitted to light a fire in the woods at all. Alas! the lean-to, and the hissing red logs that cheered us and kept us cosy through the long frosty nights under the hunter's moon.

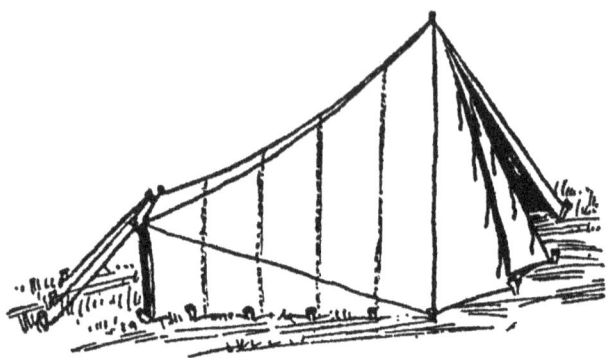

Fig. 64.— Canoe Tent with Pole

CANOE TENTS.— The old pattern canoe tent (Fig. 64) is erected with a single pole. The front is semi-circular, and the strain from it, pulling forward, does away with the need of a guy rope, unless

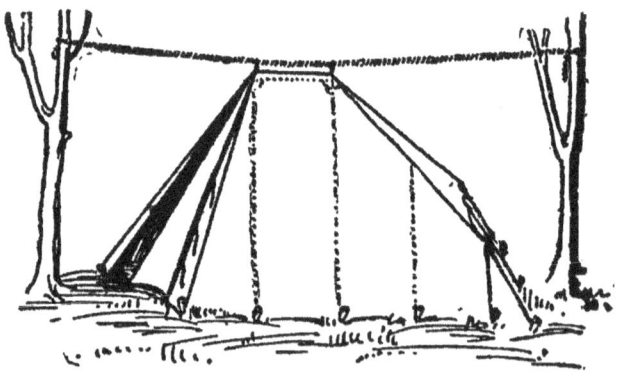

Fig. 65.— Canoe Tent with Ridge

the whole front is left open to the camp-fire, in which case two guys are run forward on either side of the fire.

A canoe tent with short ridge is shown in Fig. 65, suspended by a rope. When this pattern is used in

TYPES OF LIGHT TENTS 103

the open it is erected on a pair of shears, as in Fig. 68.

These models are advertised as "quick and easy to erect," but a glance at the cuts will show that they take too many pegs and stakes to really belong in that category. Still they are very popular, especially the one with ridge. Dimensions (not including the rounded front), and weights in various materials, are tabulated below. Other sizes and cloths are supplied by outfitters. The two patterns do not vary noticeably in weight.

TANALITE, EMERALITE
7 x 4½ x 6 − 1½. 7¼ lbs.
7⅓ x 7⅓ x 7 − 2. 10¼ lbs.
8¾ x 7⅓ x 7½ − 3. 12½ lbs.

TANO, NILO
7½ x 4½ x 6 − 1½. 5½ lbs.
7½ x 7½ x 7 − 2. 8½ lbs.
9 x 9 x 7½ − 2½. 11 lbs.

KIRO, DRIKI
7 x 4¾ x 7 − 2. 9¼ lbs.
7 x 7 x 7 − 2. 11¾ lbs.
9½ x 9½ x 8½ − 3. 17 lbs.

EXTRA LIGHT GREEN
6½ x 4¾ x 7 − 2. 6½ lbs.
6½ x 6½ x 7 − 2. 7¾ lbs.
8 x 6½ x 7½ − 3. 10 lbs.

GREEN EGYPTIAN
7⅓ x 4¾ x 7 − 2. 7½ lbs.
7⅓ x 7⅓ x 7 − 2. 10¼ lbs.
9¾ x 7⅓ x 7½ − 3. 13 lbs.

GREEN WPF. STANDARD
7⅙ x 4¾ x 7 − 2. 9½ lbs.
7⅙ x 7⅙ x 7 − 2. 13 lbs.
9½ x 7⅙ x 7½ − 3. 15¾ lbs.

"COMPAC" TENT.— This is a very light tent for pedestrians, canoeists, or others who want to get along with the least practicable outfit. For its size and weight, I have found it a good thing. It has a floor sewed to its walls; so, when the door flaps are snapped shut, nothing can get in. You can defy not only rain and wind, but bugs, flies, spiders, scorpions, snakes, skunks, wood rats, and all other vermin. Ventilation is provided by four little windows covered with bobbinet, with storm flaps that raise or lower from the inside. The cloth is very closely woven, and waterproofed. It may be had in tan, green, or the natural yellowish-white of unbleached cotton.

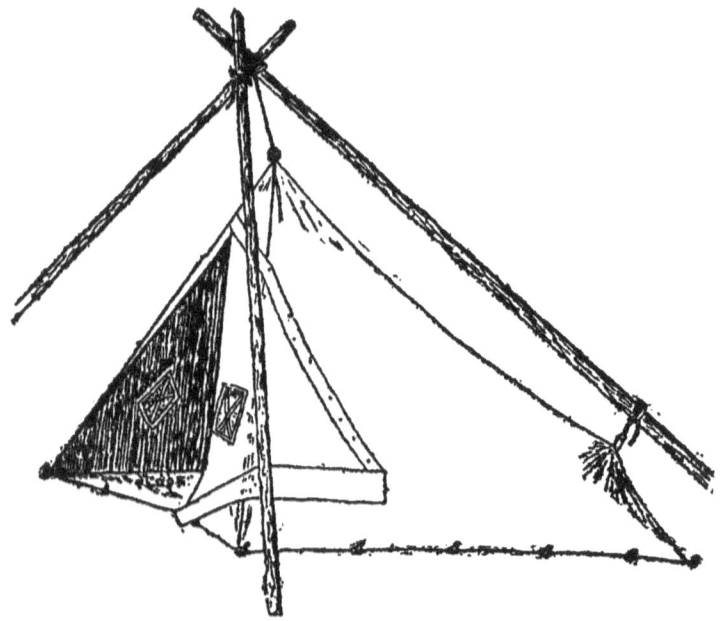

Fig. 66.— Compact Tent

This tent is easy to set up on any kind of ground. If a sapling happens to stand in the right place, peg out the corners of the floor and suspend the peak by its cord from a convenient limb. Otherwise, pitch with shears in front and a pole slanting backward from them, as shown in Fig. 66. Only a few pegs are required.

Being so low and so well braced, this pocket house will stand up against a gale that might overthrow wall tents and send their flies a-kiting. In cold

TYPES OF LIGHT TENTS 105

weather it can be warmed by radiation from a camp fire in front. It will accommodate two men and their duffle. Of course it is only high enough to sit up in, but that is all the room one needs on such trips, and it is best for a cloth floored tent anyhow, for it balks muddy feet. However, I do not like a sewed-in floor, for general camping. The reasons are given at the end of this chapter.

I have called this clever contrivance a "pocket-house." It deserves the name, being waterproof, wind-proof, bug-proof, ventilated, sheltering a space

Fig. 67.— Snow Tent

8 x 6 x 4–2 feet, and yet it rolls up into a 16 x 4-inch parcel, and weighs, with its rope, only 3¾ pounds.

SNOW TENT.— This pattern (Fig. 67) gets its name from the steepness of its slopes which makes it shed snow instead of holding it. With front flaps spread as shown, it can be warmed by a fire in front. The back has a low wall, and there is a short ridge; otherwise its qualities are those of a semi-pyramidal tent. It is made in sizes from 6½ x 6½ x 7½–2½ ft. to 9¾ x 9¾ x 7½–2½ ft., and the weights, in different materials, run from 7½ to 17 lbs.

The same model, with sewed-in floor, closed front, an oval door of bobbinet, and a ventilator, is known as the "explorer's" tent (Fig. 68). It is perfectly insect-proof. For the tropics a fly is added. A

Fig. 68.— Explorer's Tent

large number of these tents have been used by the Alaska Boundary Survey and by other scientific expeditions. The weights complete are only from 1½ to 2 lbs. greater than for same size of the snow tent.

INSECT-PROOF TENTS.— I have spoken several times of the desirability of good ventilation in a tent (the smaller the tent, the stuffier it will be if tightly enclosed) and of the necessity of protection from insects in their season. The reader who has followed me thus far can readily understand the construction of an ideal tent, in these respects, for countries like Alaska, central Canada, the tropics, and other places where poisonous or germ-bearing insects abound. I quote from Emerson Hough:

"The most perfect mosquito tent I ever saw I ran across this summer for the first time. It was made in a western city after a design said to have been invented by a member of the Geological Survey in Alaska. If it will work in Alaska it will anywhere. The material was not of heavy duck, but a light Egyptian cotton sometimes called 'balloon silk.' In size 7 x 7, very high in the ridge and on the walls, the tent in its bag weighs only about 12 pounds. A light waterproof floor is sewn into it. Both ends are sewn into it. On each side there are two large netted windows, affording abundant ventilation. There are flaps arranged for these windows which can be buttoned down in case of rain.

In each end of this tent there is yet another large window for ventilation. The roof projects three or four inches all around over the walls, making eaves which keep the water out of the open windows in case of rain. The front door is not a door at all, but a hole, round, and not triangular. This hole is fitted with a sleeve, like the trap of a fyke-net, the sleeve, or funnel, itself being made of light material. You crawl through this hole and, so to speak, pull it in after you and tie a knot in it. At least there is a puckering string by which you can close the bag which makes the entrance of the tent. Once inside it, you have a large, roomy house in which you can stand up with comfort, lay down your beds in comfort, and do light housekeeping. No mosquito can get at you unless you brought it in on your clothes. In case you have done that you can put a wet sock into operation. At first you will think the tent a little close, but soon will see that the ventilation is perfect." (*Out of Doors*).

SEWED-IN FLOORS.— On the other hand, there are objections to a sewed-in floor. Muddy boots make it odious, and hob-nailed ones are its ruin. Every bit of snow that you track in will help make a puddle. A lantern is dangerous in such structures as the last two we have been considering, and one must be very careful about matches. In the case of the explorer's tent, which lacks the windows of the other, you can't cook inside, even on a vapor stove, without risk of disaster, and certainty of steam condensing where it cannot escape. Even the moisture of one's breath amounts to a good deal in the course of a night, and in cold weather it will keep the interior of such a tent constantly damp or coated with rime. As for the sewed-in floor serving as a mattress cover, to keep your bed of browse or leaves in place, if that bed is thick enough for comfort, the tent will not set well, and there will be too much strain on the pegs and seams.

So, anywhere but in extremely bad mosquito country, or on bleak and windy mountains, it is better to have a wide sod-cloth around the bottom of the tent, and a separate ground-sheet, overlapping, that you can roll aside when you want a bare spot, and can take out and wash when it needs it.

CHAPTER VII

LIGHT CAMP EQUIPMENT

The problem of what to take on a trip resolves itself chiefly into a question of transportation. If the party can travel by wagon, and intends to go into fixed camp, then almost anything can be carried along — trunks, chests, big wall tents and poles, cots, mattresses, pots and pans galore, camp stove, kerosene, mackintoshes and rubber boots, plentiful changes of clothing, books, folding bath-tubs — what you will. Such things are right and proper if you do not intend to move often from place to place. But in any case beware of impedimenta that will be forever in the way and seldom or never used.

It is quite another matter to fit out a man or a party for wilderness travel. First, and above all, be plain in the woods. In a far way you are emulating those grim heroes of the past who made the white man's trails across this continent. We seek the woods to escape civilization for a time, and all that suggests it. Let us sometimes broil our venison on a sharpened stick and serve it on a sheet of bark. It tastes better. It gets us closer to Nature, and closer to those good old times when every American was considered " a man for a' that " if he proved it in a manful way. And there is a pleasure in achieving creditable results by the simplest means. When you win your own way through the wilds with axe and rifle you win at the same time the imperturbability of a mind at ease with itself in any emergency by flood or field. Then you feel that you have red blood in your veins, and that it is good to be free and out of doors. It is one of the blessings of wilderness life that it shows us how few things we need in order to be perfectly happy.

Let me not be misunderstood as counseling anybody to "rough it" by sleeping on the bare ground and eating nothing but hardtack and bacon. Only a tenderfoot will parade a scorn of comfort and a taste for useless hardships. As "Nessmuk" says: "We do not go to the woods to rough it; we go to smooth it — we get it rough enough in town. But let us live the simple, natural life in the woods, and leave all frills behind."

An old campaigner is known by the simplicity and fitness of his equipment. He carries few "fixings," but every article has been well tested and it is the best that his purse can afford. He has learned by hard experience how steep are the mountain trails and how tangled the undergrowth and downwood in the primitive forest. He has learned, too, how to fashion on the spot many substitutes for "boughten" things that we consider necessary at home.

The art of going "light but right" is hard to learn. I never knew a camper who did not burden himself, at first, with a lot of kickshaws that he did not need in the woods; nor one who, if he learned anything, did not soon begin to weed them out; nor even a veteran who ever quite attained his own ideal of lightness and serviceability. Probably "Nessmuk" came as near to it as any one, after he got that famous ten-pound canoe. He said that his load, including canoe, knapsack, blanket-bag, extra clothing, hatchet, rod, and two days' rations, "never exceeded twenty-six pounds; and I went prepared to camp out any and every night." This, of course, was in summer.

In the days when game was plentiful and there were no closed seasons our frontiersmen thought nothing of making long expeditions into the unknown wilderness with no equipment but what they carried on their own persons, to wit: a blanket, rifle, ammu-

LIGHT CAMP EQUIPMENT

nition, flint and steel, tomahawk, knife, an awl, a spare pair of moccasins, perhaps, a small bag of jerked venison, and another of parched corn, ground to a coarse meal, which they called "rockahominy" or "coal flour." Their tutors in woodcraft often traveled lighter than this. An Indian runner would strip to his G-string and moccasins, roll up in his small blanket a pouch of rockahominy, and, armed only with a bow and arrows, he would perform journeys that no mammal but a wolf could equal. General Clark said that when he and Lewis, with their men, started afoot from the mouth of the Columbia River on their return trip across the continent, their total store of articles for barter with the Indians for horses and food could have been tied up in two handkerchiefs. But they were woodsmen, every inch of them.

Now it is not needful nor advisable for a camper in our time to suffer hardships from stinting his supplies. It is foolish to take insufficient bedding, or to rely upon a diet of pork, beans, and hardtack, in a country where game may be scarce. The knack is in striking a happy medium between too much luggage and too little. *Ideal outfitting is to have what we want, when we want it, and not to be bothered with anything else.* A pair of scales are good things to have at hand when one is making up his packs. Scales of another kind will then fall from his eyes. He will note how the little, unconsidered trifles mount up; how every bag or tin adds weight. Now let him imagine himself toiling uphill under an August sun, or forging through thickety woods, over rocks and roots and fallen trees, with all this stuff on his back. Again, let him think of a chill, wet night ahead, and of what he will really need to keep himself warm, dry, and well ballasted amidships. Balancing these two prospects one against the other, he cannot go far wrong in selecting his outfit.

In his charming book, *The Forest,* Stewart Edward White has spoken of that amusing foible, common to us all, which compels even an experienced woodsman to lug along some pet trifle that he does not need, but which he would be miserable without. The more absurd this trinket is, the more he loves it. One of my camp-mates for five seasons carried in his "packer" a big chunk of rosin. When asked what it was for, he confessed: "Oh, I'm going to get a fellow to make me a turkey-call, some day, and this is to make it 'turk.'" Jew's-harps, camp-stools, shaving-mugs, alarm-clocks, derringers that nobody could hit anything with, and other such trifles have been known to accompany very practical men who were otherwise in light marching order. If you have some such thing that you know you can't sleep well without, stow it religiously in your kit. It is your "medicine," your amulet against the spooks and bogies of the woods. It will dispel the koosy-oonek. (If you don't know what that means, ask an Eskimo. He may tell you that it means sorcery, witchcraft — and so, no doubt, it does to the children of nature; but to us children of guile it is the spell of that imp who hides our pipes, steals our last match, and brings rain on the just when they want to go fishing.)

No two men have the same "medicine." Mine is a porcelain teacup, minus the handle. It cost me much trouble to find one that would fit snugly inside the metal cup in which I brew my tea. Many's the time it has all but slipped from my fingers and dropped upon a rock; many's the gibe I have suffered for its dear sake. But I do love it. Hot indeed must be the sun, tangled the trail and weary the miles, before I forsake thee, O my frail, cool-lipped, but ardent teacup!

There is something to be said in favor of individual outfits, every man going completely equipped and quite independent of the others. It is one of the delights of single-handed canoeing, whether you go alone or cruise in squadron, that every man is fixed to suit himself. Then if any one carries too much or too little, or cooks badly, or is too lazy to be neat, or lacks forethought in any way, he alone suffers the penalty; and this is but just. On the other hand, if one of the cruisers' outfits comes to grief, the others can help him out, since all the eggs are not in one basket. I like to have a complete camping outfit of my own, just big enough for two men, so that I can dispense a modest hospitality to a chance acquaintance, or take with me a comrade who, through no fault of his own, turns up at the last moment; but I want this outfit to be so light and compact that I can easily handle it myself when I am alone. Then I am always "fixed," and always independent, come good or ill, blow high or low.

Still, it is the general rule among campers to have "company stores." In so far as this means only those things that all use in common, such as tent, utensils, tools, and provisions, it is well enough; but it should be a point of honor with each and every man to carry for himself a complete kit of personal necessities, down to the least detail. As for company stores, everybody should bear a hand in collecting and packing them. To saddle this hard and thankless job on one man, merely because he is experienced and a willing worker, is selfish. Depend upon it, the fellow who "hasn't time" to do his share of the work before starting will be the very one to shirk in camp.

AXE.— A full-sized axe should be carried, in cold weather, if means of transportation permit. Its head need not weigh over 3 or 3½ pounds, but let the handle be of standard 36-inch length for a full-arm sweep. A single-bitt is best for campers, as the poll is useful for driving stakes, knocking off pine knots, to rive timber (striking with a mallet), and as an anvil (bitt stuck in a log or stump).

With this one tool a good axeman can build anything that is required in the wilderness, and he can quickly fell and log-up a tree large enough to keep a hot fire before his lean-to throughout the night.

If an axe is bought ready handled, see that the helve is of young growth hickory, straight grained, and free from knots. Sight along the back of the helve to see if it is straight in line with the eye of the axe, then turn it over and see if the edge of the axe ranges exactly in line with the center of the hilt (rear end of handle), as it should, and that the hilt is at right angles to the center of the eye. A good chopper is as critical about the heft and hang of his axe as a shooter is about the balance of his gun. If the handle is straight, score a 2½-foot rule on it, in inches. Get the axe ground by a careful workman. The store edge is not thin enough or keen enough. One cannot be too careful in selecting this indispensable tool: some grades are of the best steel and hand-forged, but many others are just "bum."

Have a leather sheath for the axe-head, to prevent accidents when traveling. Some are made with strap attached for carrying on one's back, but this is needless: in the few cases that you carry an axe that way, tie it to outside of pack with a string.

An axe lying around camp has a fatal attraction for men who do not know how to use it. Not that they will do much chopping with it; but somebody will pick it up, make a few bungling whacks at a projecting root, or at a stick lying flat on the ground, drive the blade through into the earth and pebbles, and leave the edge nicked so that it will take an hour's hard work to put it in decent order again. And the fellow who does this is the one who could not sharpen an axe to save his life. It never seems to occur to him that an axe is of no use unless its edge is kept keen, or that the best way to ruin it is to strike it into the ground, or that a chopping block will prevent that. You may loan your last dollar to a friend; but never loan him your axe, unless you are certain that he knows how to use it.

LIGHT CAMP EQUIPMENT 115

If a full-grown axe cannot be carried, then take a hatchet with handle as long as practicable (see Chapter X).

OTHER TOOLS.— A small spade, or an army entrenching tool, is a handy implement about camp. One outfitter has produced a good thing in this line which he calls a trekking spade. The handle is detachable. In shoveling hot coals at the fire-place, work quickly, so as not to draw the temper of the steel.

A useful tool, when it can be carried, is one I found recently in the catalogue of a certain mail-order house: a nail-cutting compass saw (just like any compass saw except that it is tempered for nails, sheet metal, etc., as well as wood), with 12-inch blade and weighing only 5 ounces. It can be used, too, in butchering big game, saving your axe edge. A folding saw, sold by sporting-goods dealers, will do well enough in most outfits.

If you want to weigh the game you kill, carry what is called a Little Giant scale (Fig. 69). Although of pocket size and 12-oz. weight, it weighs by the small hook up to 40 lbs. by 2 lbs., and by the larger one up to 350 lbs. by 5 lbs. For fish, of course, a small spring balance is the thing.

A pair of side-cutting pliers, of the very best steel, is almost a necessity. I always carry a small one when fishing, to snip off the barb of an imbedded hook, which otherwise is a mighty mean thing to get rid of. The pliers are in daily use for other purposes.

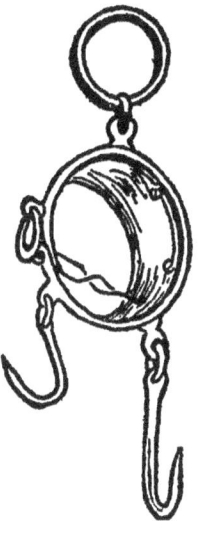

Fig. 69.— Little Giant Scale

A 6 to 8-inch mill file, and a carborundum stone, will keep the axe and other cutlery in order. (A mill file is cut diagonally and parallel, instead of criss-cross like a common flat file.)

CAMPING AND WOODCRAFT

Select from the following list such articles as you *know* you will need, and make a light wooden box in which they will stow properly.

Folding Saw.
Mill File.
Triangular File.
Side-cutting Pliers.
Carborundum Stone.
Scales.
Gun Screw-driver.
Reel Screw-driver.
Small Hand Drill.
Tape Line.
Copper Wire (two sizes).
Nails, Brads, Tacks, Screws.
½ gill Le Page's Glue.
Marine Glue.
Solderene.
Winding Silk (or Dental Floss).
Rod Varnish.
Ferrule Cement.
Spare Tips and Guides.
Rubber Mending Tissue.

Gun or Rifle Cleaning Rod and Brush.
Gun Oil.
Gun Wipers.
Sandpaper.
Emery Cloth.
Shears.
Needles.
Thread.
Wax.
Spare Buttons.
Safety Pins.
Horse-blanket Pins.
Rubber Bands (large).
Spare Shoe Laces.
Lock-stitch Awl.
Shoe Nails.
Hob-nails.
Sail Needles.
Twine (in tobacco bag).
Split Rivets.
10 yds. 2-inch Adhesive Plaster.

Adhesive plaster (zinc oxide plaster) can be bought at any drug store. Besides its regular use to hold a dressing in place where bandaging is difficult (never apply it directly to a wound), and for protecting sore spots, such as a cut finger or a blistered foot, it is a lightning repairer for all sorts of things. When warmed it will stick to any dry surface, wood, metal, glass, cloth, leather, or skin. It can be peeled off and reapplied several times. As an instantaneous mender of rents and stopper of holes or cracks it has no equal. It is waterproof and airtight. With a broad strip you can seal a box or chest watertight, stop a leak in a canoe ("iron" it on with a hot spoon or stone) or mend a paddle, a gunstock, or even an axe-handle (first nailing it). A chest or cupboard can be extemporized from any

LIGHT CAMP EQUIPMENT 117

packing box, in a jiffy, by cleating the top and using surgeon's plaster for hinges.

One of the most bothersome things in shifting camp is to secure opened cans and bottles from spilling. Surgeon's plaster does the trick in a twinkling. Put a little square of it over each hole in the milk can that you opened for breakfast, and there will be no leakage. To hold a cork in a bottle, stick a narrow strip of the plaster over the cork and down opposite sides of the bottle's neck. To protect the bottle from breaking, run a strip around it at top and one at bottom. The caps of baking powder cans or similar tins can be secured to the bodies in the same way.

If your fishing rod sticks at the ferrules, wrap a bit of the plaster around each joint to give you a grip, then pull without twisting.

Rubber mending tissue (any dry-goods store) is good to patch a tent, a canoe, or rubber articles (waders, etc.). Cut canvas patch and tissue of same size, place the latter over rent and the patch on top, then press with a hot iron or rub with a hot, smooth stone.

Dental floss is fine for quick rod repairing, or to use as an emergency leader. It is very strong, ready waxed, waterproof, and durable.

The list of tools and supplies given above is, of course, only suggestive, and for trips where the going is fairly easy. To each according to his needs.

When traveling with horses, take along a hammer, a few spare horseshoes and their nails, leather mending kit, and the necessary ropes.

LANTERN.— Kerosene is a nuisance in carriage; if so much as a drop escapes anywhere near your provisions, it will taint them. Carbide is easy to carry, and, aside from its regular use in an acetylene lantern, makes it easy to start a fire when everything is wet. A folding pocket lantern of Stonebridge or Alpina type, for candles, is best for men in light marching order; but let it be of tin or brass; those made of aluminum are much too frail.

HORN.— When camping in a canebrake country have a huntsman's horn in the outfit. Leave it with the camp-keeper, who will blow it every evening about an hour before supper. The sound of a horn carries far, and its message is unmistakable. It is a dulcet note to one who is bewildered in a thick wood or brake.

SUNDRIES.— A length of small rope, such as braided sash cord, and a ball of strong twine, spare cloth and leather for mending, a few rawhide thongs, and some broad rubber bands, are likely to be needed.

A few yards of mosquito netting should be taken along to protect meat from blow-flies, and for various other purposes.

COOKING KIT.— In rough country, especially if camp is to be shifted frequently, a stove is out of the reckoning. If pack animals are taken, or the trip is by canoe, without long and difficult portages, it pays to take along either a folding grate or a pair of fire irons (see Chapter IV).

On light marching trips no support for the utensils will be carried. Rocks or logs will take their place. There may be a little more spilling and swearing, but less tired backs.

It is commonly agreed that four is the ideal number for a camping party, at least among hunters and fishermen. Certainly no larger number should attempt their own cooking. Utensils and table ware for such a party, going light, should include: a large frying-pan (more serviceable than two small ones); a pan to mix dough in and wash dishes (common milk pan); a stout, seamless, covered pot for boiling or stewing meat, baking beans, etc.; a medium pot or pail for hot water (always wanted, substitute for tea kettle); a smaller one for cereals, vegetables, fruit; and either a coffee pot low enough to nest in the latter, or a covered pail in its place.

LIGHT CAMP EQUIPMENT 119

There should be six plates (two for serving) and four each of cups, knives, forks, teaspoons, tablespoons. This is about as little as the party can well get along with.

It will be bothersome to bake bread for four in the frying-pan. Add a reflector or a sheet-steel oven, if practicable. A wire broiler, a tea percolator, and a corkscrew and can opener will nest with this set. If the cook wears no sheath knife a butcher knife is essential. Several dish towels (some to be divided into clouts) and a couple of yards of cheesecloth for straining and to hang meat in should be taken. Sapolio will be needed, or Bon Ami if the utensils are of aluminum.

The common utensils of the shops will not nest. They are all spouts and handles, bail ears and cover knobs. Still, a good deal can be done by substitution. Covered pails or pots (Fig. 70) do the work

Fig. 70.—
Cooking Pot

Fig. 71.—
Pot Chain

Fig. 72.—
Coffee Pot

Fig. 73.—
Miner's
Coffee Pot

of sauce pans and kettles, and are better all round, for they can either be set upon the coals or hung above the fire; besides, you can carry water in them, and their covers keep heat in and ashes out. All such vessels should be low and broad; then they will boil quickly and pack well. Good proportions are:

```
3 quarts....diameter  6¾ in. x 5¼ in. height.
4    "         "      7½  "  x 5¾  "    "
6    "         "      8½  "  x 6½  "    "
8    "         "      9¼  "  x 7½  "    "
```

Bail ears should project as little as possible. Lids should have fold-down rings instead of knobs, so they will nest well.

A set of pot-chains with hooks (Fig. 74) is worth taking. With one of these (weight 2 oz.) a kettle can be suspended at any desired height above the fire.

Ordinary coffee pots are not suitable for camping. A good pattern for the purpose is shown in Fig. 72. It has a bail, folding handles, and a solid spout that cannot melt off. A cheaper but very good article in tin (Fig. 73) is known as a "miner's coffee pot." When very compact nesting is sought, discard the coffee pot for a lidded pail: it has the merit that no aroma escapes through a spout. For tea, have an aluminum tea-ball; then you will not commit the cardinal sin of steeping the leaves too long.

Cups, to nest inside the coffee pot, have the lower part of the handle free (Fig. 74). In tin, the 1½-pint size is best (5 x 2⅛ in.). Small cups and small plates are impertinences to anybody with a woods appetite. Tin is not so bad for coffee, but aluminum blisters the unwary mouth. Enamel is best for cups and plates, no matter what the material of the rest of the kit may be. It is so much easier to clean than tin or aluminum. If the plates are deep and generous (9½-inch soup plates, nest-

Fig 74.— Cup   Fig. 75.— Miller Frying Pan

ing in the frying-pan) there will be no need of bowls for soup and porridge.

The frying-pan handle is a perennial problem. If detachable, it is likely to be lost. The best folding handled pan that I have used is the Miller pattern (Fig. 75). A common pan may be adapted by cutting off all but two inches of the handle and riveting a square socket to the top of the stub so that a stick may be fitted to it when you cook (if

LIGHT CAMP EQUIPMENT 121

the socket is round the stick will twist unless carefully fitted). I prefer the folding handle, because it saves time, and, on the very few occasions when one needs a long stick for handle, he can insert it in the rings of the Miller handle. Get a pan with hinge that won't work loose.

Some sort of baker is almost essential for comfortable life in the woods. The most portable form is the folding reflector sold by most outfitters. It is similar to those that our great-grandmothers used to bake biscuit in, before a hearth fire. The top slants like a shed roof, and the bottom like another shed roof turned upside down, the bread pan being in the middle. The slanting top and bottom reflect heat downward upon the top of the baking and upward against its bottom, so that bread, for instance, bakes evenly all around.

A prime advantage of this cunning utensil is that baking can proceed immediately when the fire is kindled, without waiting for the wood to burn down to coals, and without danger of burning the dough. Fish, flesh, and fowl can be roasted to a turn in this contrivance. It has several better points than an oven, chief of which is its portability, as it folds flat; but it is inferior for corn bread, army bread, etc., and impossible for pot-roasts or braising. How to use it is shown in Chapter XVI.

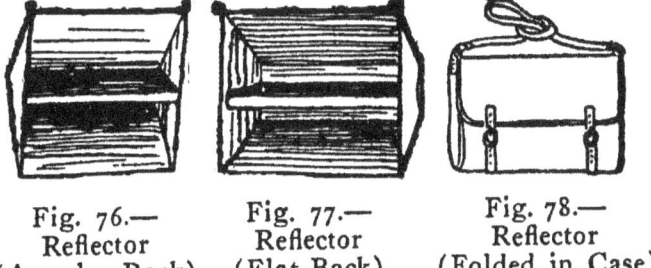

Fig. 76.—
Reflector
(Angular Back)

Fig. 77.—
Reflector
(Flat Back)

Fig. 78.—
Reflector
(Folded in Case)

There are two models of reflectors, one with a single joint at the rear (Fig. 76), the other with two (Fig. 77) and a flat back. The latter is more compact, but not so stiff as the other.

122 CAMPING AND WOODCRAFT

These ovens may be bought in tin or aluminum.

Tin	Aluminum	Aluminum
9 x 12 pan. 4 lbs.	8 x 12 pan. 2 lbs.	12 x 15 open. 2 lbs.
11 x 14 pan. 5½ lbs.	8 x 18 pan. 2¾ lbs.	15 x 18 open. 3 lbs.
	10 x 18 pan. 5 lbs.	15 x 24 open. 4 lbs.

An 8 x 12-in. pan holds just a dozen biscuits. A canvas carrying case (Fig. 78) which is needed, for the baker is frail, adds another pound. A wire broiler packs inside the reflector; it is not necessary for broiling meat, but it is handy for the purpose, and especially for broiling fish.

A reflector must be kept bright to do good baking. The sheet steel oven shown in Fig. 79 is much cheaper than a reflector. It consists of two halves that nest, each 4 x 12 inches, and a perforated shelf on which a roast or a bake-pan may be placed. It is managed like a Dutch oven (see Chapter XX), but requires more attention, as the material is thin. A reflector is better for the amateur, as he can see at all times how the baking or roasting progresses.

Fig. 79.—Sheet Steel Oven

Men who have neither time nor inclination to rummage the stores for "calamities" that will nest would do well to pay extra for outfits already kitted by camp outfitters. Using one outfitter's sets for illustration, we are offered:

Set for	Size, nested		In "Aluminol"	In "Amorsteel"
Two persons..	9½ x 8¾ in.	6¾ lbs.	$4.00 6⅜ lbs.	$9.85
Four persons..	10 x 11¼ in.	12 lbs.	6.25 10⅞ lbs.	16.60
Six persons...	11 x 12⅞ in.	17½ lbs.	8.50 17¼ lbs.	26.50
Eight persons.	11 x 12⅞ in.	19¼ lbs.	9.40 18¾ lbs.	30.00

In the four-men and eight-men sets the coffee pots will be found rather stingy. An 8 x 18 folding aluminum reflector, broiler, canvas case, butcher knife, cooking spoon, percolator, and canvas water bucket, would add exactly 4½ pounds weight and $6.90 to the price.

LIGHT CAMP EQUIPMENT

Such sets as these are very nice for what I may call confirmed campers; but if the party is likely to split up after the first trip, and no one cares to buy a first-class outfit for future use, go to the department store and get, in tin or enameled ware, the articles I have listed. The reflector you must order from an outfitter, or make for yourself.

CHAPTER VIII
CAMP BEDDING

One's health and comfort in camp depend very much upon what kind of bed he has. In nothing does a tenderfoot show off more discreditably than in his disregard of the essentials of a good night's rest. He comes into camp after a hard day's tramp, sweating and tired, eats heartily, and then throws himself down in his blanket on the bare ground. For a time he rests in supreme ease, drowsily satisfied that this is the proper way to show that he can "rough it," and that no hardships of the field can daunt his spirit. Presently, as his eyes grow heavy and he cuddles up for the night, he discovers that a sharp stone is boring into his flesh. He shifts about, and rolls upon a sharper stub or projecting root. Cursing a little, he arises and clears the ground of his tormentors. Lying down again, he drops off peacefully and is soon snoring. An hour passes, and he rolls over on the other side; a half hour, and he rolls back again into his former position; ten minutes, and he rolls again; then he tosses, fidgets, groans, wakes up, and finds that his hips and shoulders ache from serving as piers for the arches of his back and sides.

He gets up, muttering, scoops out hollows to receive the projecting portions of his frame, and again lies down. An hour later he reawakens, this time with shivering flesh and teeth a-chatter. How cold the ground is! The blanket over him is sufficient cover, but the same thickness beneath, compacted by his weight and in contact with the cold earth, is not

CAMP BEDDING 125

half enough to keep out the bone-searching chill that comes up from the damp ground. This will never do. Pneumonia or rheumatism may follow. He arises, this time for good, passes a wretched night before the fire, and dawn finds him a haggard, worn-out type of misery, disgusted with camp life and eager to hit the back trail for home.

The moral is plain. This sort of roughing it is bad enough when one is compelled to submit to it. It kills twice as many soldiers as bullets do. When it is endured merely to show off one's fancied toughness and hardihood it is rank folly. Even the dumb beasts know better, and they are particular about making their beds.

This matter of a good portable bed is the most serious problem in outfitting. A man can stand almost any hardship by day, and be none the worse for it, provided he gets a comfortable night's rest; but without sound sleep he will soon go to pieces, no matter how gritty he may be.

In selecting camp bedding we look for the most warmth with the least weight and bulk, for durability under hard usage, and for stuff that will not hold moisture long, but will dry out easily.

Warmth depends upon insulation. The best insulation is given by dry air confined in the interstices of the covering, this covering being thick enough to keep one's animal heat from escaping too readily.

Of course, materials vary in conductivity — cotton and other vegetable fibers being coldest, silk and wool warmer, fur and feathers warmest of all — but, irrespective of materials, the degree of insulation afforded by a covering depends upon its fluffiness, or looseness of texture, and its thickness of body. This means bulk; there is no way of getting around it; there must be room for confined air.

Innumerable expedients have been tried to keep down bulk by using impermeable insulators, such as paper, oiled cotton or silk, and rubber or rubberized fabric, but all such "skins to keep heat in" are total failures. The vapor from one's body must have an outlet or a man will chill, to say nothing of other unpleasant consequences.

The degree of insulation afforded by confined air may be judged roughly by a few comparisons. Here is a pack cloth of close-woven cotton duck; there is a cotton bed comforter of the same spread and weight, but thicker, of course. Size, weights, and materials are the same, yet what a difference in warmth! Well, it is just the enclosed air that makes the comforter "comfy," and lack of it that leaves the canvas cold as a covering. Similarly, a three-pound comforter filled with lamb's wool batting is as warm as a five-pound all-wool blanket, because it holds more dead air. Down filling is still warmer than wool, being fluffier, and its elasticity keeps it so — it does not mat from pressure.

After a cotton comforter has been used a long time, or kept tightly rolled up, its batting becomes matted down and then the cover is no warmer than a quilt of equal weight. Quilts — ugh! In the dank bedroom of a backwoods cabin, where the "kivvers" were heirlooms, but seldom had been aired, I have heaped those quilts on me till their very weight made my bones ache, and still shivered miserably through the long winter night.

Batting of any sort (but cotton the worst) will also mat from wet, and then its elasticity is gone. Water, moreover, is a good conductor of heat, and so a bed covering of any kind is cold when it is wet.

Note this, also, that the weight of one's body presses out a good deal of air from the bedding under him. Moreover, earth, being a good conductor, draws off one's animal heat faster than the air does. So, when sleeping on the ground, one needs more bedding underneath than over him — a cold, hard fact that some designers of sleeping bags have unaccountably overlooked. A bag with two thicknesses of blanket over the sleeper and only

CAMP BEDDING

one under him is built upside-down. The man will have at least part of his back only half protected; and one's vertebral region is the very part of him that is most vulnerable to cold.

BLANKETS.— The warmest blanket for its weight is not a close-woven one but one that is loose-woven and fluffy. An army blanket is made for hard service, and so must be of firm weave, but a third of its weight is added for that purpose only, not for warmth. For use in a sleeping bag, where they are protected from wear, blankets of more open texture are better. Two three-pound blankets are warmer than a six-pound one of the same grade, owing to the thin stratum of air between them. Hence the best bags are made up of several layers of light, fluffy blanketing, instead of a thick, felted bag.

Camp blankets should be all-wool. A cotton or part-cotton one is much more prone to absorb moisture from the damp woods air and to hold that which exudes from the body of the sleeper, hence it is clammier and colder than wool. The difference may not be so noticeable in the dry air of a heated bedroom, but it will quickly make itself felt in the woods. Another bad quality of cotton is that fire will spread through it from an ember cast out by the camp-fire, whereas the coal would merely burn a hole in wool.

The warmest blankets for their weight are those made of camel's hair. They are expensive, but one of them is as much protection as two common woolen blankets. They are favorites among experienced travelers all over the world.

Hudson Bay blankets have a well-justified reputation, being much like the well-nigh everlasting products of the old hand-loom. Their size is distinguished by "points" (four points, three-and-a-half points, three points) and they are marked accordingly by black bars in one corner.

Blankets should be of dark or neutral color, so

as not to show dirt or attract insects. If used without a canvas cover they may well be waterproofed with lanolin, by the process that I will describe in the next chapter.

To roll up in a blanket in such a way that you will stay snugly wrapped, lie down and draw the blanket over you like a coverlet, lift the legs without bending at the knee, and tuck first one edge smoothly under your legs then the other. Lift your hips and do the same there. Fold the far end under your feet. Then wrap the free edges similarly around your shoulders one under the other. You will learn to do this without bunching, and will find yourself in a sort of cocoon.

Often it is convenient to use a blanket as a garment while drying out your clothes, or as a cape in cold weather. Wear it as a Mexican does his sérape. As a bed blanket is larger than a sérape, one end must first be folded, say about two feet, depending upon size and your own height. This fold being turned under, stand with your back toward the blanket and draw its right-hand corner snugly up under the right armpit so that the triangle hangs down in front of you, and hold it firmly there. With left hand then draw the blanket up over left shoulder from behind, tight against nape of neck, and down in front. That leaves the left corner trailing on the ground before you. With a quick flirt throw this corner up over right shoulder and let it hang down your back, where it will stay of its own weight. You are now wrapped up but with right arm free. The blanket can be cast off in an instant.

COMFORTERS.— Sometimes these are miscalled quilts, but they are knotted together instead of quilted, and have thicker, fluffier filling than quilts. Cotton comforters are wholly unsuitable for outdoor use. They are warm only when perfectly dry, and it is impossible to keep them so in the damp air of a forest. But a comforter filled with wool bat-

CAMP BEDDING

ting is very warm for its weight and does not take up moisture so readily. It is cheaper than a blanket, and makes a softer bed, but is bulkier. Comforters are much used by Western campers, along with a canvas " tarp." Whenever extreme compactness of outfit is not necessary, I recommend that each member of a party take with him a wool comforter, even if for no other use than as a mattress.

Warmest of all coverings of this sort are the so-called eiderdown quilts (really goose down). They are expensive, and must carefully be protected from the wet.

SLEEPING BAGS.— There is a good deal of waste material in blankets and comforters, especially at the foot end. Suppose we cut them into a sort of coffin shape, to conform to the outlines of the body, sew up a side and an end and the lower third of the other side, then attach buttons or laces or clasps to close the bag after one has got into it. A good deal of weight and bulk are saved.

The objections are that such an arrangement is hard to air and dry out, it is not readily adjustable to varying temperatures, and the occupant has a feeling of constraint when cooped up in the thing. Still, in some kinds of camping, it is essential that the bed be very warm, waterproof, windproof, and yet as portable as possible. Hence the sleeping bag.

It may be laid down as an axiom at the start that no sleeping bag is worthy of serious notice unless its blankets or other lining can be removed quickly and spread out on a line to dry. A lining sewed inside a waterproof cover is an abomination. So is a nest of blanket bags that can only be aired by propping each one open with a stick. Such things get musty and dirty. They are so bothersome to air that they will be neglected.

Of course, if the bag is of but a single thickness it may be sunned first on the outside and then turned inside out. But no single bag is practical, except for a polar climate, when one adopts a fur bag.

Bedding, to be comfortable and healthful, must be adaptable to variations of temperature. Remember that the night gets colder and colder till daylight. This is much more noticeable out-of-doors than indoors, and yet, even at home, when one goes to bed he generally has a spare cover handy to pull over him towards morning.

Now a tent is far less insulated than a house. So if one muffles himself up when he goes to bed in enough covering to meet the last few hours before dawn, he soon will be roasted out, whereas if he has only enough bedding for comfort through the first watches of the night, he will find the last one *his watch* in literal truth, for he won't sleep. The only sleeping bag worth talking about is one that

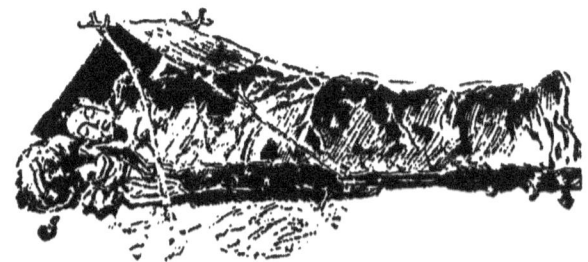

Fig. 80.— D. T. Abercrombie Sleeping Bag

has at least four layers of blanketing. Then one can turn in under one layer and the canvas; in the cold hours after midnight, he can emerge and crawl back under more cover (Fig. 80).

It is from lack of attention to these simple and obvious requirements that most designers of sleeping bags have failed. They have turned out contrivances that either were insufferably hot in the early part of the night or confoundedly cold before morning.

The explorer, Anthony Fiala, who has patented an extremely light and warm bag for use in high latitudes (Fig. 81), claims that not only the bag itself but its cover should be porous so as to throw off the bodily moisture which otherwise condenses

CAMP BEDDING

around the sleeper and chills him. So he uses plain khaki for a bag cover instead of waterproofed material. However, his type of sleeping bag is a snugger "fit" than the average, and so arranged with hood and closing flaps that it ventilates only through the cloth itself. The larger and heavier bags commonly used are roomy enough to provide considerable ventilation from the unconscious wriggling of the sleeper. Besides, the cover, though waterproof, is not impermeable to air, as rubber or oilskin would be.

If several layers of blanketing are used within a roomy cover of waterproofed canvas the outer layer will take up what little "sweating" occurs inside

Fig. 81.— Fiala Sleeping Bag

the canvas. Such a cover is desirable to protect the occupant from damp ground, from moist air, and from rain when he bivouacs away from camp. It also keeps the bedding dry while *en route,* as, for example, in a boat or canoe when water is shipped. If the bag is opened out and its lining sunned frequently, as should be done with any sort of bedding, no trouble from condensed moisture will be experienced in ordinary climates.

I have spoken of fur bags. They are much too hot for our climate, except in the high mountains where one must bivouac perhaps in wind and snow. The warmest of all coverings for its weight is a bag made of caribou or reindeer-skin. The hair of this animal is extraordinarily close and thick, and each hair is hollow, like a quill, and contains air (this is true of the whole deer family). Caribou pelts are in their prime when in the summer coat, in August and early September. After this the hair becomes too long and brittle. Skins of young animals should be used, being lighter than those of old ones, although almost as warm, and their hair is less liable to come out under conditions of dampness. They weigh about the same per square foot as raccoon or goat-skins ($4\frac{1}{2}$ to 5 ounces, as compared with $6\frac{1}{2}$ for wolf and 7 for black bear, on the average). A bag made from such skins will weigh about twelve pounds, from the adult caribou about sixteen pounds. Sleeping bags made in Norway from skins of domesticated reindeer could be purchased, before the war, through the Army and Navy stores in London for about £5. Alaska reindeer skins can be bought from trading firms in Seattle.

In the old *Book of Camping and Woodcraft* I discoursed as follows *re* sleeping bags:

> It is snug, for a while, to be laced up in a bag, but not so snug when you roll over and find that some aperture at the top is letting a stream of cold air run down your spine, and that your weight and cooped-upness prevent you from readjusting the bag to your comfort. Likewise a sleeping bag may be an unpleasant trap to be in when a squall springs up suddenly at night, or the tent catches fire.
>
> I think that one is more likely to catch cold when emerging from a stuffy sleeping bag into the cold air than if he had slept between loose blankets. A waterproof cover without any opening except where your nose sticks out is no more wholesome to sleep in than a rubber boot is wholesome for one's foot. Nor is such a cover of much practical advantage, except underneath. The notion that it is any substitute for a roof overhead, on a rainy night, is a delusion.
>
> Blankets can be wrapped around one more snugly, they do not condense moisture inside, and they can be thrown open instantly in case of alarm. In blankets you can sleep double in cold weather. Taking it all in all, I choose the separate bed tick, pillow bag, poncho, and blanket, rather than the same bulk and weight of any kind of sleeping

CAMP BEDDING 133

bag that I have so far experimented with. There may be better bags that I have not tried.

In his excellent book on *The Way of the Woods*, Dr. Edward Breck replied:

"I have always looked up to Mr. Kephart as a woodsman *sans reproche*, but I am forced to believe that he has never made fair trial of a good sleeping bag; for, if there is one thing a bag does *not* do, it is letting in streams of cold air down your spine, and, to me at least it almost goes without saying that a man is wrapped up much more tightly in blankets than in a bag, and hence far more helpless to rearrange his bed without pulling things to pieces. It is just precisely the ability to turn over in comfort that makes me love a sleeping bag, and this springs from its general 'stay-puttedness.' As for the stuffiness of a bag I confess I have yet to discover it. A proper bag opens down the side and ventilates easily. It is a little more difficult to air out in the morning, but not much. The comparison with a rubber boot is most unjust, and, though harder to get into, it takes no longer to do so than to wrap oneself up properly in blankets. As to getting caught inside if a fire breaks out, I will engage to get outside of mine [a 'Comfort sleeping pocket'] in less than three seconds if necessary. The sleeping bag has come to stay. My Indians have made themselves a couple out of blankets and waterproof canvas. Mr. Kephart asserts that the waterproof cover is no substitute for a roof overhead on a rainy night; and yet I can assure him that I have slept out in mine without a tent many times in hard rain without getting wet in the *slightest degree,* except when rising. Imagine, if you please, the state I should have been in with blankets only. A lean-to of some kind would have been imperative, and even then misery would have been the result. Of course, spending the night without some kind of shelter is not to be recommended, but my experience shows what the bag is capable of."

As for the roof overhead, what I meant was that gun and duffel need protection, and so do you when you crawl out on a rainy morning. The weight of a sleeping-bag cover put into a little waterproof tent that you can carry in your pocket, and a ground sheet to go with it, will give you better protection from the elements at night and a sheltered place to dress and cook breakfast in. This for side trips from camp, or for long hikes.

134 CAMPING AND WOODCRAFT

Otherwise it is a matter of finding a *proper* sleeping bag, and I have tried here to make the essentials plain. Beyond this, one's personal taste must be the decisive factor. Let us hear from another old-timer, Emerson Hough:

"As to your bed, let us have one more whack at the sleeping bag — that accursed invention of a misguided soul. Leave your sleeping bag at home, in the Adirondacks or in the Minnesota woods. Take a pair of good wool blankets which will weigh not less than ten pounds — more weight is better. Don't despise a good wool comforter or a 'Katy' which will fold double and make a nice mattress under you. And whatever you do, don't fail to have for your own use a good, big bed 'tarp' as it is known in the West. On the stock ranches we always used to have the tarpaulin of 20-oz. duck, about 7 x 14 ft., and sometimes it had harness hooks on it, sometimes not. It surely would turn rain. For the pack travel of today you will not need canvas of quite so much weight. But canvas and wool in abundance you surely should have for your bed. No hunting trip is a success when you don't sleep well and dry at night. Canvas and wool together are the correct dope for the mountains. Take an air mattress if you insist, or if your dealer does: don't blame me if you sleep cold."

When all is said, plain blankets are cheaper than sleeping bags, and they can be used at home: that settles the matter for most folks.

MATTRESSES AND PILLOWS.— It is folly to sleep on bare ground if one can help it. A bed of balsam browse is not excelled, if properly made and frequently renewed; but it takes fully an hour to make one right, and on many a camp ground there is no browse, not even spruce. As a substitute one may use pine needles, grass, ferns, the moss off old fallen trees, or even dead leaves. Such stuff, however, packs hard and spreads from under one unless confined in a bag. For years I carried a bag of common bed ticking for this purpose, $2\frac{1}{2}$ feet wide by $6\frac{1}{4}$ feet long, and weighing only $1\frac{1}{3}$ pounds. Such a bag made of tanalite is more practical than any kind of carryall or bed-sheet, for it serves just as well to

CAMP BEDDING

protect the bedding *en route,* and then is easy to turn into a mattress when you make camp. A pillow bag, similarly stuffed, with spare clothing atop, was not the least important item in my very light kit. When one has room, it pays to carry a small feather pillow or a down cushion about 12 x 18 inches.

AIR MATTRESSES.— An air bed is luxurious in moderate weather, but too cold to use late in the season unless well insulated with blankets or a felt pad. The thinner the bed the less objectionable it is in this respect, as it does not then steal so much of one's animal heat.

There are sleeping bags combined with air mattresses, full-length or only "body size," that are good for canoe cruising, horseback journeys, or other trips when camp is changed every day or so and good sites are not always to be found. They save much work, and sometimes a good deal of anxiety. There is then no night wood to cut, no browse to gather, no tent to trench, and little bother about smoothing the ground. Wherever one may be, in damp forest or on sandy dune, on rocky ground or mucky ground, down goes the bundle, it is unrolled, and one inflates his "blow bed" with the bellows that nature gave him. In ten minutes he is assured of a dry, warm, elastic bed for the night, in spite of Jupiter Pluvius, or Boreas, or both of them allied. If water runs in on the floor, let it run. If the tent blows down, let it alone until you feel like getting up. Come morning there is no bed making to do, if you are too hurried to air things, except to deflate the mattress and roll the bag up. It straps into a waterproof pack that stows conveniently anywhere.

But such a bed is quite expensive. For ordinary service, blankets and a bed tick will do just as well. In any case, study your health and your ease at night. There is a veteran's wisdom in what Chauncey Thomas says: "I go camping to have a good time, and a third of that time is spent in bed."

BED ROLLS.— If one carries loose blankets he will need a waterproof canvas cover to protect them *en route* and to serve as a ground sheet between them and the damp earth when he sleeps on the ground. A bed roll made with flaps at sides and

Fig. 82.— U. S. A. Regulation Bed Roll

end is best for this purpose. It is also a good thing when you sleep on a narrow cot, to keep cold air from coming up under the overhang of your blankets. The army regulation bed roll (Fig. 82) is

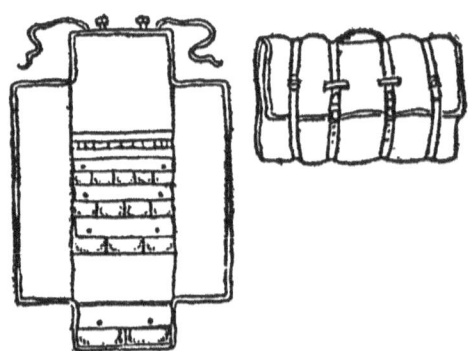

Fig. 83.— Shattuck Camp Roll

one type. There is a pocket for spare clothing that serves as pillow, and the blankets and a folding cot are rolled up in the main part of the sheet, covered by the flaps, and strapped up.

Another camp roll is shown in Fig. 83. It con-

CAMP BEDDING

tains a detachable wall pocket for small articles, which is to be hung up in the tent, and bellows pockets at the end.

There is a combination carryall and bed (Fig. 84) that I think a good deal of. In principle it is like the other bed rolls mentioned, but the bottom is double and open at both ends. A pair of stiff poles convert it into a stretcher bed (Fig. 86); cross poles

Fig. 84.—
Comfort Sleeping Pocket

Fig. 85.—
Combination Bed Roll, Stretcher Bed and Bed Tick

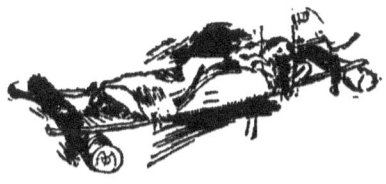
Fig. 86.—
Combination as Stretcher Bed

Fig. 87.—
Combination as Hammock

Fig. 88.—Combination as Bed Roll

added and lashed at the ends make a hammock frame (Fig. 87). The double bottom serves as a bed tick, to be filled with browse, grass, or whatever soft stuff the camp site affords. The ends can be closed with horse-blanket pins, after stuffing the bag. The roll is made of 12-oz. army duck, and weighs 7 or 8 pounds. It can be had with blanket lining, but this I do not recommend. Use separate blankets; then you can have as much thickness under as over you.

CHAPTER IX
CLOTHING

In a wild country one soon learns that the difference between comfort and misery, if not health and illness, may depend upon whether he is properly clad. Proper, in this case, does not mean modish, but suitable, serviceable, proven by the touchstone of experience to be best for the work or play that is in hand. When you seek a guide in the mountains he looks first in your eyes and then at your shoes. If both are right, you are right.

The chief uses of clothing are to help the body maintain its normal temperature, and to protect it from sun, frost, wind, rain and injuries. To *help,* mind you — the body must be allowed to do its share.

Perspiration is the heat-regulating mechanism of the body. Clothing should hinder its passage from the skin as little as possible. For this reason one's garments should be *permeable to air.* The body is cooled by rapid evaporation, on the familiar principle of a tropical water-bag that is porous enough to let some of the water exude. So the best summer clothing is that which permits free evaporation — and this means all over, from head to heel. In winter, just the same, there should be free passage for bodily moisture through the underclothes; but extra layers or thicknesses of outer clothing are needed to hold in the bodily heat and to protect one against wind; even so, all the garments should be permeable to air. If a man would freeze most horribly, let him, on a winter's night, crawl into a bag of India rubber and tie the opening tight about his neck.

CLOTHING

Cloth can be processed in such a way as to be rainproof and still self-ventilating (this will be considered later), but rubber garments and oilskins cannot safely be worn the day long, unless they are very roomy, and the wearer exercises but little. Rubber overshoes, boots, waders, are endurable only in cool weather or cold water, and then only if very thick oversocks are worn to hold air and absorb moisture.

All clothing worn by an outdoorman should be of such texture and fit as will allow free play to his muscles, so he may be active and agile, and should bind as little as possible, especially over vital organs. Garments that are too thick and stiff, or too loose at points of friction, will chafe the wearer.

These are general principles; now for particulars.

UNDERCLOTHING.— In discussing "togs" we usually begin on the wrong side — the outside. Now the outer garments will vary a great deal, according to climate, season, the terrain or waters, and according to the sport or work that one is to do; but the integument that comes next to one's skin should vary little for an outdoorman except in weight.

The material and quality of one's underwear are of more consequence than the shell he puts over it, for his comfort and health depend more on them. Whenever a man exercises heartily he is sure to perspire freely, no matter how cold the air may be. Arctic explorers all agree that their chief misery was from confined moisture freezing on them. How it is in the dog-days everybody knows — a glowing sun, humidity in the air, and sweat trickling from every pore because the atmosphere is not dry enough to take it up.

Permeability of cloth to air and moisture is largely a matter of *texture*. Consider the starched linen collar and the soft collar of an outing shirt; consider a leather sweat-band in the hat and a flannel one, or no sweat-band at all.

Underclothing, for any season, should be *loosely*

woven, so as to hold air and take up moisture from the body. The air confined in the interspaces is a non-conductor, and so helps to prevent sudden chilling on the one hand and over-heating on the other. A loose texture absorbs sweat but does not hold it — the moisture is free to pass on to and through the outer garments. In town we may endure close-woven underwear in summer, if thin enough, because we exercise little and can bathe and change frequently. In the woods we would have to change four times a day to keep near as dry.

WOOL VERSUS COTTON.— Permeability also depends upon material. Ordinary cotton and linen goods do not permit rapid evaporation. They absorb moisture from the skin, but hold it up to the limit of saturation. Then, when they can hold no more, they are clammy, and the sweat can only escape by running down one's skin.

After hard exertion in such garments, if you sit down to rest, or meet a sudden keen wind, as in topping a ridge, you are likely to get a chill — and the next thing is a " bad cold," or lumbago, rheumatism, or something worse.

Wool, on the contrary, is permeable. That is why (if of suitable weight and loose weave) it is both cooler in summer and warmer in winter than cloth made from vegetable fibre. " One wraps himself in a woolen blanket to keep warm — to keep the heat *in.* He wraps ice in a blanket to keep it from melting — to keep the heat *out.*" In other words, wool is the best material to maintain an equable, normal temperature.

However, the broad statement that one should wear nothing but wool at all seasons requires modification. It depends upon quality and weave. Some flannels are less absorptive and less permeable (especially after a few washings by the scrub-and-wring-out process) than open-texture cottons and linens.

And, speaking of washing, here comes another

CLOTHING

practical consideration. If woolen garments are washed like cotton ones — soap rubbed in, scrubbed on a washboard or the like, and wrung out — they will invariably shrink. The only way to prevent shrinkage is to soak them in lukewarm suds (preferably of fels-naphtha or a similar soap), then merely squeeze out the water by pulling through the hand, rinse, squeeze out again, stretch, and hang up to dry. This is easy, but it requires a large vessel, and such a vessel few campers have. The alternative is to buy your undershirts and overshirts a size too large, allowing for shrinkage. Drawers must not be oversize, or they will chafe. But one's legs perspire much less than his body, and need less protection; so, up to the time of frost, let the drawers be of ribbed cotton, which is permeable and dries out quickly. Cotton drawers have the further advantage that they do not shrink from the frequent wettings and constant rubbings that one's legs get in wilderness travel. Wool, however, is best for wading trout streams. For riding, the best drawers are of silk.

I conclude that for cold weather, for work in high altitudes where changes of temperature are sudden and severe, and for deep forests where the night air is chilly, woolen underclothes should be worn. In hot climates, and for summer wear in open country, a mixture of silk and wool is best, but open-texture linen or cotton does very well. Pajamas should be of flannel, at all seasons, if one sleeps in a tent or out-of-doors.

UNION SUITS are not practical in the wilds. If you wade a stream, or get your legs soaked from wet brush or snow, you can easily take off a pair of drawers to dry them, but if wearing a union suit you must strip from head to foot. Moreover, a union suit is hard to wash, and it is a perfect haven for fleas and ticks — you can't get rid of the brutes without stripping to the buff.

DRAWERS must fit snugly in the crotch, and be not too thick, or they will chafe the wearer. They should be loose in the leg, to permit free knee action. Full-length drawers are best because they protect the knees against dirt and bruises, and safety-pins can be used to hold up the socks (garters impede circulation).

SOCKS.— If trousers of full length are worn, then socks are preferable to stockings; they bulk less, weigh less, cost less, and are easier to wash. For forest travel, regardless of season, socks should be of soft wool, thick enough to cushion the feet and absorb moisture, and not closely knit but of rather open texture. But for open country, in hot sunny weather, cotton is better, because wool " draws " the feet at such times. On an all-day hike it pays to change to a fresh pair at noon.

The fit of socks is very important. If too loose, they wrinkle and chafe the feet; if too small, they are unendurable. To prevent woolen ones from shrinking is not difficult. Every night, or every time you come in with wet feet, remove your socks, put on fresh ones (having bathed the feet, of course), and put those you have worn to soak in a running stream; then draw them through the hand to squeeze out water, do not wring, but pull them gently into shape, and hang up to dry. On a long trip you will find means, now and then, to soak them in tepid suds, as they do not require a large vessel.

Take along enough socks so that when a pair gets "more holey than righteous" you can throw them away. Darned socks cause blisters, especially when a man does the darning.

OVERSHIRTS.— For summer wear the U. S. A. chambray shirt is as good as any. It is durable, does not fade, and shows dirt and perspiration stains less than khaki or common outing shirts. Army shirts have two roomy Stanley pockets with buttoned flaps. These are just right for pipe and tobacco, note-book and pencil, or whatever you want handy at all times without crowding the trousers pockets.

Later in the season, or for a cool climate, the

CLOTHING 143

standard infantry or officer's service shirt of olive-tan wool is excellent. It is always natty, and wears better than common flannel. The cloth is shrunk before making up, but will do some more shrinking from repeated wettings and washings, so get a size larger than what is worn at home. Gray is also a good color for overshirts.

NECKERCHIEFS.— A neckerchief worn with the peak in front is convenient to wipe perspiration from the face. Slewed around the other way, it shields the neck from sunburn. In a high wind, or in dense thickets, it can be used to hold the hat on by tying over the head; and it will protect one's ears when frost nips. It serves as a nightcap, or as a shield against insects, when folded and worn as shown in Figs. 89, 90.

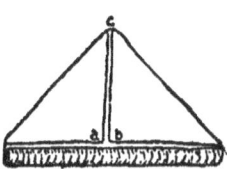
Fig. 89.—
Neckerchief
Folded for Hood

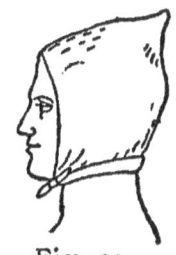
Fig. 90.—
Neckerchief
Hood Adjusted

Lay the kerchief out flat, fold over the upper corners a and b till they meet, roll the square lower edge toward the triangle thus formed, place kerchief over head with the slit ac in front, tie extremities of the roll under chin, and over ab, with a reef knot.

The neckerchief should be large (the army size, 27 x 27 in., or navy, 36 x 36 in.) and of silk. Silk neckerchiefs in any desired color can be bought of military outfitters. The army or navy size can be used as a doubled triangular bandage (or cut into two of them) in emergency. Tied around the abdomen it helps to keep a man warm when he is caught out at night, and it is a good thing in case of cramps.

TROUSERS.— Khaki, of standard army grade, is good for summer wear, as it is cool and can be washed. "Duxbak," or other closely woven cravanetted cotton, is better late in the season, since it sheds a good deal of wet and keeps out wind. Both of these materials dry readily. They are too noisy for still-hunting.

For cold weather the army trousers of olive-tan wool are good, unless one goes out for very rough travel. The woolen cloth called kersey is first choice in a cool, rainy climate, or wherever much wading is to be done. It is the favorite among those most practical of men, the log-drivers and lumberjacks generally.

Woolen trousers do not wear so well as firmly woven cotton ones. They "pick out" in brush, "snag," and collect burs. What has been said of cotton drawers applies also to trousers. Best of all trouser material, for rough service, is genuine English moleskin, which is a very strong, tough, twilled cotton cloth, with a fine pile or nap, the surface of which is "shaved" before dyeing. It wears like iron, is wind-proof, dries out quickly, and is comfortable in either warm or cold weather. Cheap moleskin is worthless.

Corduroy is easily torn, heavy, likely to chafe one, and it is notoriously hard to dry after a wetting. When wearing corduroy trousers there is a *swish-swash* at every stride that game can hear at a great distance.

Trousers should not be lined; it makes them stiff and hard to dry.

To wear with leggings the "foot breeches" of our infantry, which lace or button in front below the knee, fit better than trousers that must be lapped over; but for wilderness wear I prefer common trousers cut off about six inches below the knee: they are easier to put on and they dry out quicker.

Riding breeches are best for the saddle. They are cut too tight at the knee for foot travel, espe-

CLOTHING

cially for climbing. Knickerbockers are too baggy for the woods: they catch on snags and tear, or throw a man.

BELTS.— A belt drawn tight enough to hold up much weight is not only uncomfortable but dangerous. It checks circulation, interferes with digestion, and may cause rupture if one gets a fall. If common suspenders are objectionable, then wear the " invisible " kind that go under the overshirt. They prevent chafing, by holding the trousers snug up in the crotch. For ordinary service there is no need of a belt more than an inch wide. A cartridge belt should be worn sagging well down on the hips; or, if a heavy weight is to be carried on the belt (bad practice, anyway), by all means have shoulder-straps for it.

LEGGINGS.— Never buy leggings that strap under the instep. The strap collects mud, and it is soon cut to pieces on the rocks. Any legging that laces over hooks will catch in brush or high grass and soon the hooks bend outward or flatten. The present U. S. A. canvas legging (Fig. 91) has only one

Fig. 91.— U. S. Army Canvas Legging

Fig. 92.— Canvas Strap Puttee

Fig. 93.— Woolen Spiral Puttee

hook, in front; it is quickly adjusted. The strap puttee (Fig. 92) is better for a woodsman or mountaineer. Leather puttees are suitable only for horsemen; in walking and climbing they cut one in front and rear of the ankle joint. Genuine pigskin is the only leather that will stand hard service and frequent wettings.

For still-hunting I like spiral puttees (Fig. 93), not spat but plain, as here illustrated. They are strips of woolen cloth with selvage edges, specially woven and "formed," which wind round the leg like a surgeon's bandage and tie at the top. Do not wind too tightly. They are pliable, noiseless against brush, help to keep ticks and chiggers from crawling up one's legs, and, with the clothing underneath, are a sufficient defense against any snakes except the great diamond-back rattlers. "In experiments, only in rare instances has snake virus stained blotting-paper placed behind two thicknesses of heavy flannel."

German socks, instead of leggings, are good for still-hunting in severe cold weather.

Many dispense with leggings by wearing their trousers tucked inside boots or high-topped shoes. This will do when the woods are dry, but when all the bushes are wet from rain, or from heavy dew, the water runs down inside your shoes until they *slush-slush* as if you had been wading a creek.

COATS.— The conventional American hunting coat of tan-colored cotton is designed primarily for fishermen, bird-hunters, and others who can reach home or permanent camp every night. Being nearly "all pockets but the button-holes," its wearer needs no pouch or game-bag. A man can stuff all the pockets full (he generally does) and still cross fences and slip through thickets without anything catching or dangling in the way. A cravenetted coat of this sort turns rain and keeps out the wind. It is an excellent defence against burrs and briers. It is no heavier than a poncho, and more serviceable for everything but as a ground-sheet or shelter-cloth. These are good points.

On the other hand, the coat is too hot for summer (barring trout fishing), it impedes athletic movements, and, unless sleeveless, it is a poor thing to shoot in, as a gun butt is likely to slip from the shoulder. For summer hikes, canoeing, and big-

CLOTHING 147

game hunting (except when it is cold enough for Mackinaws) any coat is a downright nuisance.

Have the coat roomy enough to wear a sweater or thick vest under it. Never mind "fit"—the thing is hideous anyway. Of course, one can wear a modish and well-fitting shooting suit, or the like, in the fields near "civilization," but for wilderness travel it is as *outré* as a stag shirt and caulked boots would be on Fifth Avenue.

The coat should not be lined. Most linings are so tightly woven that they check ventilation of the skin, and they make a garment hard to dry out.

SWEATERS.— A sweater, or sweater jacket, is comfortable to wear around camp in the chill of the evening and early morning, and its elasticity makes it a good bed garment when there are not enough blankets. With nothing over it, a sweater is not serviceable in the woods, as it "picks out," "snags," and catches up burrs as a magnet does iron filings.

When you want such a garment at all, you need warmth a-plenty: so get a thick one of good quality, and don't kick at the price. It should have cuffs to draw down over the knuckles, and a wide collar to protect the neck and base of the head. The best colors are neutral gray and brown or tan. A sweater jacket that buttons up in front is more convenient than the kind that is drawn over one's head, but it is not so warm as the latter.

Personally, I usually discard the sweater in favor of a mackinaw shirt, worn hunting fashion with tail outside. It has all the good points of a sweater, except great elasticity, and has the advantages of shedding rain and snow, keeping out wind, wearing well under hard service, and not picking up so much trash.

LEATHER JACKETS.— In the cold dry air of the Far West a buckskin jacket or hunting shirt is often the best outer garment. It keeps out the keenest wind, is pliable as kid, noiseless, less bulky than a sweater or mackinaw, wears forever, and is proof against thorns and burrs. But when wet it is as cold and clammy as tripe.

Genuine buckskin shirts are still listed in the catalogues of certain dealers in the Northwest. Be sure the skins are "smoke-tanned," so that they will dry soft and not shrink so badly as those dressed by a commercial tanner. A fringed shirt dries better than a plain one, as the water tends to drip off the fringes.

Swedish dogskin jackets are rain-proof, but not so pliable as buckskin.

If one can get them (Hudson Bay posts) light caribou skins are better than buckskin. Caribou or reindeer hide has the singular property of not stretching when wet. When tanned with the hair on it is the warmest of all coverings.

VESTS.— A vest without coat may not be sightly, but it is mighty workmanlike. Suspenders can be worn under it without desecrating the landscape — and stout suspenders, say what you please, are a badge of good common sense on a woodsman.

But the vest worn in town is not fit for the wilderness. One's back is more vulnerable to cold than his chest; hence the thick cloth of a waistcoat should go all the way round. There should be four *roomy* pockets, the lower ones with buttoned flaps. Tabs fitted at the bottom will keep the vest from flapping when worn open.

WATERPROOFING WOOLENS.— Wet clothing is heavy and uncomfortable. It is much less permeable to air than dry clothing; consequently it interferes with evaporation of sweat; and it is chilly, because water, which is a good conductor of heat, has replaced the air, which is a non-conductor. Air passes through dry cloth more than twice as freely as through wet material.

The problem is to waterproof the outer garments and still leave them permeable to air. This is done with cotton goods by cravenetting the material, or,

CLOTHING 149

less effectively, by the alum and sugar-of-lead process which fixes acetate of alumina in the fibers.

It is easier to waterproof woolens than cotton clothing. Simply make a solution of anhydrous lanolin in benzine or gasoline, soak the garment in it about three minutes, wring out gently, stretch to shape, and hang up to dry, shifting position of garment frequently, until nearly dry, so that the lanolin will be evenly distributed. This process is very cheap, and old clothing can be treated by it as well as new, without injuring the buttons or anything else.

Cloth so treated permits the ready evaporation of sweat, and so may be worn without ill effects, no matter what the weather may be. In fact the perspiration escapes more freely than from plain woolen cloth, because moisture cannot penetrate the fibers and swell them — the interstices are left open for air to pass through. And yet woolens impregnated with lanolin shed rain better than cloth treated by any of the chemical processes. The goods are not changed in weight, color, or odor. Instead of being weakened, they are made stronger. The waterproofing is permanent.

Lanolin can be bought at any drug-store. It is simply purified wool fat. Wool, in its natural state, contains a grease known as suint. This suint is removed by alkalis before spinning the fiber into cloth. If it had been let alone, as in a Navajo blanket of the old type, the cloth would have shed water. But suint has an unpleasant odor, which is got rid of by purifying the fat into lanolin.

This lanolin, although it is a fat, has the singular property of taking up a great deal of water, and water is purposely added to it in preparing the common (hydrous) lanolin that is used as an ointment base and in cosmetics. In buying, specify that it be anhydrous (water-free). Cloth treated with lanolin absorbs little moisture because water cannot penetrate the fiber and is repelled from the interspaces.

The strength of solution to be used depends upon climate. For a hot, rainy climate, use four ounces of lanolin to a gallon of benzine; for average conditions in the temperate zone, three ounces to the gallon; for cold climate, or winter use exclusively, two ounces to the gallon, as cold has a tendency to stiffen cloth that has been steeped in a strong solution. The three-ounce formula is right for blankets.

If trouble is experienced in making a solution of lanolin, dissolve it first in a little chloroform, then pour into the benzine.

FOOTWEAR.— It is a truism that " a soldier is no better than his feet." Neither is anybody else who has much walking to do. Such shoes as we wear in town are wholly unfit for the field. They are too light, too short, and too narrow. We do little walking in town, and none that we do is over rough ground. We carry no burdens on our backs. So the " snug fit " is tolerated, and the thin socks.

On the trail it is different. One *must* have free play for his toes, or his feet will be cramped and blistered within a few hours — then misery! In marching with a pack, one's foot lengthens about half an inch every time his weight is thrown on it, and broadens nearly as much. And after hiking some distance the feet begin to swell.

The only way to insure a good fit is to put on thick socks, pick up a weight equal to the load you are to carry, slip a tape-measure under the sole, then throw your whole weight on that foot, and have someone do the measuring. Then the other foot similarly; for in many cases the two differ. Have the shoe made a half inch longer than the foot measurement, and wide enough to give a snug but easy fit over the ball when poised as above. Around the heel it should be snug enough to prevent slipping and chafing. These are the army rules, and they are right for anyone who marches and has equipment to carry.

When starting afield, lace the shoes rather tightly

CLOTHING

across the instep; then ease the lacing when your feet begin to swell. By the way, some people are always having their shoe laces come undone, because tied with a granny bow. A true bow knot (Fig. 94) is made like a reef knot (Figs. 95, 96) except that the ends are doubled back before tying.

Carry spare laces. They come handy for many purposes. Rawhide laces may be hardened at the ends by slightly roasting them.

SHOES.— It is not enough that the shoes be roomy. The lasts over which they are made should be anatomically correct. In 1911 a board of officers of our army was appointed to select a soldier's shoe. They tried many models, instituted thorough marching tests by thousands of men, and finally adopted a

Fig. 94.— True Bow Knot. Double the Ends Back and Tie as in a Reef Knot

Fig. 95.— Reef Knot Formed

Fig. 96.— Reef Knot Drawn Tight

shoe made over lasts designed by Surgeon-Major Munson, the well-known expert on military hygiene (Fig. 97). These lasts are straight on the inside, so that the big toe can point straight ahead, as Nature intended. The front is broad enough to give all the toes free play. There is no compression over the ball or arch of the foot. This is the perfect model, easy on one's feet from the word " go."

The army shoe has now been in use, by all arms of the service, long enough to have proved beyond question its merits. Lieutenant Whelan, so well known to us as a sportsman and military authority, says of it: " In the light of what the army now knows, sore feet are absolutely inexcusable. The presence of sore feet in an officer's command is a cause for investigation as to the efficiency of that officer."

To break in a new pair of shoes the soldier stands in about three inches of water for five minutes, then goes for a walk on level ground. When the shoes are not in use, care is taken that they shall not be packed away tightly or otherwise compressed out of the true shape that the breaking in gave them.

At night the shoes are dried by hanging them upside down on stakes before the fire — not too close, for wet leather "burns" easily. Or, fill a frying pan with clean pebbles, heat them (not too hot) over the fire, put them in the shoes, and shake them

Fig. 97.—
U. S. Army Shoe

Fig. 98.—
Sole of Army Shoe, Showing Proper Method of Placing Hobnails

around after a while. Before the shoes are quite dry, rub just a little neatsfoot oil into them. The remaining dampness prevents the oil from striking clear through, but helps it to penetrate on the outside, as the oil follows the retreating water.

The army shoe has a single sole; so it is flexible — a prime desideratum for good walking. The heel is low, broad, and longer than usual, giving firm footing and having less tendency to "run down" than the common pattern of heel. The tongue is loose,

CLOTHING 153

making the shoe cool and easy to dry out. There are no hooks to catch in grass and bend out of shape. A pair of these shoes weighs only 2 to 2½ pounds, according to size. This is a proper weight for marching on ordinary roads, but is too light, of course, for rough service, such as a sportsman's shoes often are put to. For the hardscrabble of mountaineering, or going anywhere over sharp rocks or among thorns and saw-briers, the leather is too thin; when it gets wet it goes to pieces.

When buying shoes go to a maker who has made, and kept, a reputation for using none but good leather. There is no severer test of leather than hard usage during frequent wettings and dryings; so, when you find a firm of shoemakers that lumberjacks swear by, trust it to turn you out a good article.

WATERPROOFED SHOES.— The army board decided positively against using any waterproofing compound on shoe leather, because waterproofed shoes steam the feet in perspiration, congest them, and make them tender, if worn for any considerable time, especially in warm weather.

However, it is one thing to march on ordinary roads and another thing to follow wilderness trails or go where there are none at all. And sportsmen often are out in cold slush or wet snow. It is true that no harm comes from wet feet so long as one keeps moving; but if a man has much standing around to do with his feet cold and wet he will suffer discomfort and quite likely catch a cold. Besides, no matter how good the quality of leather may be, when it gets soggy it wears badly. Consequently, although the army shoe is just right for warm weather and marching on roads, it is neither strong enough nor dry enough for continuous wilderness use.

My advice is to get shoes made over the Munson last, of weight suitable for the service in view, and have them viscolized or otherwise waterproofed if you are to be out a good deal in the wet. Have a pair of the regulation army shoes for hot weather and easy going.

No leather is absolutely waterproof. The skin from which it is tanned is porous, and a waterproofing preparation only partially fills those pores, making the leather shed water so long as the filling remains intact, but not preventing air and moisture from gradually seeping through. This is as it should be. If the pores were completely and permanently stopped up, the shoe would be as uncomfortable and unhealthful to wear as if made of rubber. All we can reasonably ask is that the shoe shall shed water under marching conditions; not that we may wade or stand in water indefinitely and still keep dry feet.

There are several good waterproofing preparations on the market, to be bought of almost any dealer in sporting goods. If you prefer to make your own, either of the following recipes will do very well. Do not use a mineral oil on shoes: it "burns" leather; but vaseline and paraffine are harmless.

TO WATERPROOF LEATHER.— A rather thick dubbing melted and rubbed into warmed leather is better than an oil, as it "stays put" and does not mix so much with water. Have the leather perfectly dry and apply the compound with a small brush, blowing it into the crack between the sole and upper, then rub well with the hand. Usually two coats, sometimes three, should be applied.

(1) Melt together one part paraffine and two parts yellow vaseline. Apply as above.

(2) Melt together equal parts paraffine or beeswax, tallow, and harness oil or neatsfoot oil.

(3) Boil together two parts pine tar and three parts cod-liver oil. Soak the leather in the hot mixture, rubbing in while hot. It will make boots waterproof, and will keep them soft for months, in spite of repeated wettings. This is a famous Norwegian recipe.

(4) Get a cake of cocoanut butter from a drug store and a small quantity of beeswax. Melt the cocoanut butter and add the beeswax in the proportion of about one

CLOTHING 155

part of beeswax to six of the cocoanut butter. Warm the shoe as thoroughly as possible to open the pores of the leather, and rub your melted waterproofing on while hot. Repeated warming of the shoe and application of the preparation will thoroughly fill the pores of the leather and also the stitching. The cocoanut butter when cold hardens somewhat like paraffine but not sufficiently to seal the stitching. The beeswax gets in its work there. A mixture of tallow or neatsfoot oil applied hot and with melted rubber mixed in, is also good. To melt the rubber, first chip it as small as possible. Rubber cuts easiest when wet. Apply to stitching with a stiff brush.— *Recreation,* April, 1911.

HOBNAILS.— If one is not traveling by canoe or on horseback, a few cone-headed Hungarian nails should be driven into the shoe soles in the pattern here shown (Fig. 98). The "natives" may stud their soles thickly, but that is only to save shoe leather. Too many nails hurt the feet, make the shoe stiff (whereas it can scarcely be too springy), cause the shoe to ball up in snow, and do not grip so well as a few nails well placed. I am not speaking here of mountaineering above snow-line, but of ordinary climbing, especially where leaves or pine needles may be thick, and of following the beds of trout streams. The nails under the instep are invaluable for crossing streams on fallen trees or poles.

The sharp points of cone-headed nails soon wear off, but edges are left that "bite" well. Broad hobnails with corrugated faces are good at first, but they quickly wear smooth, and then slip worse on the rocks than small ones. They also pull out sooner.

Many recommend short screw caulks. These, if sharp pointed, pick up trash at every step when you are in the woods; if blunt, they are treacherous on the "slick rocks," as they are made of hard steel.

Some prefer ⅜-inch round head blued screws instead of hobnails or caulks. They claim that these "bite" better, and that they are easy to insert or remove.

Rubber heels save much jarring on a long hike,

but they do not grip on slippery roots, on footlogs, or on leaf-strewn mountain sides.

BOOTS.— By boots I mean any soled footgear with tops more than eight inches high. Engineers who do more standing around than walking may be all right in high-topped boots that lace up the legs, and have buckles besides, but there are mighty few places where a sportsman should be seen in such rig. The importance of going lightly shod when one has to do much tramping is not appreciated by a novice.

Let me show what it means. Suppose that a man in fair training can carry on his back a weight of forty pounds, on good roads, without excessive fatigue. Now shift that load from his back and fasten half of it on each foot — how far will he go? You see the difference between carrying on your back and lifting with your feet. Very well; a pair of single-soled low shoes weighs about two and a half pounds. A pair of boots with double soles and sixteen or seventeen-inch tops weighs about four and a half pounds. In ten miles there are 21,120 average paces. At one extra pound to the pace the boots make you lift, in a ten-mile tramp, over ten tons more footgear than if you wore the shoes.

Nor is that all. The boots afford no outlet for hot air and perspiration. They are stiff, clumsy, and very likely to blister your feet and ankles. When they are brand new, you can wade shallows in them and keep your feet dry; but soon the seams are bound to open and no dubbing will ever close them again. Anyhow, if you fall in fording, or step half an inch too deep, it will take five minutes to remove those boots, pour out the water, and put them on again. Then if they dry out overnight you are uncommonly lucky.

And how are the boots in warm, dry weather? They keep the feet and legs wet all the time with stagnant perspiration. No — take six-inch shoes and light leggings, with a pair of waterproofed "pacs" in reserve for wet going. If you hunt in a

CLOTHING

marsh, wear rubber boots, which are waterproof in something more than name.

There are times and places where an eight or ten-inch hunting shoe that started out to be waterproof is all right.

High-topped "cruisers" have all the faults of the boots except that they are lighter. They scald the feet on a warm day, and chill or freeze them on a cold one, from lack of ventilation and confinement of moisture.

PACS.— A "shoe-pac" or "larrigan" is a beef-hide moccasin with eight to ten-inch top, and with or without a light, flexible sole. It is practically waterproof so long as the seams (which are on top where they get less strain than those of a shoe) remain sound, and they are kept well greased. They are lighter and more pliable than shoes, and are first-rate "extras" to take along for wet days, dewy mornings, and swampy ground, or as the regular footwear for still-hunting. Get them big enough to accommodate heavy lumbermen's socks over your soft thinner ones. Otherwise your feet will generally be either too hot or too cold.

Pacs without soles are fine in a canoe. In trout fishing they can be worn with a pair of hemp sandals to prevent slipping. In extremely cold weather the oil-tanned leather freezes as stiff as horn, and gets dangerously "slick."

MOCCASINS.— In dry weather, on ground that is not too steep or stony, give me the velvety and pliant, pussy-footed moccasin, of real moose-hide, "smoke-tanned" so it will dry soft if I do get wet. I will see more that is worth seeing in the woods than anybody who wears shoes.

If your feet are too tender, at first, for moccasins, add insoles of good thick felt, or birch bark or the dried inner bark of red cedar. After a few days the feet will toughen, the tendons will learn to do their proper work without crutches, and you will be able to travel farther, faster, more noiselessly, and with less exertion, than in any kind of boots or shoes. This, too, in rough country. I have often gone tenderfooted from a year's office work and have traveled in moccasins for weeks, over flinty Ozark hills, through canebrakes, through cypress swamps where the sharp little immature "knees" are hidden under the needles, over unballasted railroad tracks at night, and in other rough places, and enjoyed nothing more than the lightness and ease of my footwear. After one's feet have become accustomed to this most rational of all covering they become almost like hands, feeling their way, and avoiding obstacles as though gifted with a special sense. They can bend freely. One can climb in moccasins as in nothing else. So long as they are dry, he can cross narrow logs like a cat, and pass in safety along treacherous slopes where thick-soled shoes might bring him swiftly to grief. Moccasined feet feel the dry sticks underneath, and glide softly over the telltales without cracking them. They do not stick fast in mud. One can swim with them as if he were barefoot. It is rarely indeed that one hears of a man spraining his ankle when wearing the Indian footgear.

Moccasins should be of moose-hide, or, better still, of caribou. Elk-hide is the next choice. Deerskin is too thin, hard on the feet for that reason, and soon wears out. The hide should be Indian-tanned, and "honest Injun" at that — that is to say, not tanned with bark or chemicals, in which case (unless of caribou-hide) they would shrink and dry hard after a wetting, but made of the raw hide, its fibers thoroughly broken up by a plentiful expenditure of elbow-grease, the skin softened by rubbing into it the brains of the animal, and then smoked, so that it will dry without shrinking and can be made as pliable as before by a little rubbing in the hands. Moccasins to be used in a prickly-pear or cactus country must be soled with rawhide.

Ordinary moccasins, tanned by the above process (which properly is not tanning at all), are only

CLOTHING

pleasant to wear in dry weather. But they are always a great comfort in a canoe or around camp, and are almost indispensable for still-hunting or snowshoeing. They weigh so little, take up so little room in the pack, and are so delightfully easy on the feet, that a pair should be in every camper's outfit. At night they are the best foot-warmers that one could wish, and they will be appreciated when one must get up and move about outside the tent.

In a mountainous region that is heavily timbered, moccasins are too slippery for use after the leaves fall.

Moccasins should be made over a regular shoe last (Fig. 99). Those commonly sold are too narrow at the toe. Remember that they will shrink some after getting wet, and that you must wear thick socks in them, or perhaps two pairs, so get them big enough.

Heavy men, tenderfooted from town, enjoy moccasins best in a hammock. In fact, most city

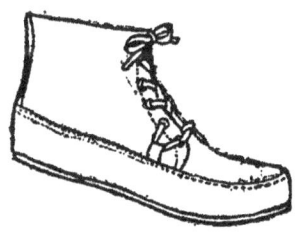

Fig. 99.— Soled Moccasin (Made Over Last)

men will get on better in soled moccasins, but these should be pliable and of not over 1½ pounds to the pair. Or canvas "sneakers" may be used. But beware the rubber soled variety. They are very hot, and will make your feet more tender than ever. Canvas with leather sole is cool and dries out quickly.

Either moccasins or sneakers are needed in camp to rest the feet, and to slip on at night if you stir out.

HEADWEAR.— For general use a soft felt hat, of good quality that will stand rain, is the best head covering. The rim should be just wide enough to shield the eyes from glare and the back of the neck from rain. I like a creased top, wearing it so until a hot sun beats down, then I push up the crown and have a good air space over my pate. The hat should have eyelets for ventilation. A strap or cord under one's "back hair," or chin if need be, holds the hat on in a wind.

A stiff rim is suitable only for mounted men; in the woods it is a plaything for brush and low branches.

A flannel sweat-band absorbs perspiration instead of holding it back like a leather one. (The Jaeger stores have them in stock.) It also helps to hold the hat on. In attaching, do not sew through the hat but through the narrow band under original sweat-band, otherwise the hat will leak.

A cap is of no account in the rain, and its crown is too low to protect one's head from the sun rays.

HEAD NETS.— A head net and gauntlets are the only adequate protection against insects when these are at their worst. The best net is of Brussels silk veiling of fine mesh, black, because that is the easiest color to see through. A net that tears easily is useless.

GLOVES.— Buckskin gloves are needed in mountain climbing and in a region where thorns and briers are common. Buy the regular army ones: they are real buck, and dry out soft. Cavalry gauntlets are better for horseback trips. By folding the hand of a gauntlet back against its cuff the latter serves as a drinking cup.

For "fly time" Dillon Wallace recommends "old loose kid gloves with the fingers cut off and farmer's satin elbow sleeves to fit under the wristbands of the outer shirt."

WATERPROOFS.— Rubber tears easily. Oilskins are superior, regular weight for the saddle and the duck blind, "feather-weight" for fishing and the like. A slicker should be quite roomy, to admit as much air as possible. Oilskin overalls are good things, at a fixed camp, to wear of a morning when dews are heavy and where the brush is thick.

On a hike there is no need of rubber or oilskins if you wear cravenetted or lanolined clothing; but one usually carries a light poncho as a ground-sheet

CLOTHING

at night, and on the march it will protect gun and pack, as well as the bearer, and let plenty of air circulate underneath it. A poncho makes a fair temporary shelter, a good wind-break, and is nice to sit on when the woods are damp. In a canoe it forms a waterproof cover for the pack. There are ponchos of " impervo " and similar oiled fabrics that outwear rubber ones two to one. A poncho is a nuisance on horseback; wear a pommel slicker.

Go over your oilskins each winter with an oil that the dealers sell for the purpose; then they will last for a long time.

RUBBER FOOTWEAR.— I never wear waders for summer trout fishing, but early spring fishing is a different matter. Wading stockings require special hobnailed shoes to go over them. I prefer a pair of light hip boots and separate wading sandals studded with nails. This combination costs less than the other, is more durable, and the boots by themselves are serviceable for general wet weather wear, marsh shooting, and the like. Light rubber boots of first-class quality will last as long as the common heavy ones, and have the advantage that the legs can be turned inside out clear to the ankle for drying. They need not weigh over 3 or 3½ pounds to the pair, and the sandals a pound more — together no more than the high-topped leather boots that I have been objurgating. Have them large enough for both socks and oversocks, then your feet are not likely to get " scalded." Carry a couple of " eezy-quick " menders, and have a rubber repair kit among your possibles in camp.

For hunting big game in wet snow and slush the best footwear is a pair of rubber shoes with ten-inch leather uppers, weighing a bit over two pounds. They should have heels, if you go into a hilly country, and rough corrugated soles. Dress the feet with soft woolen socks, and over these draw a pair of long, thick " German socks " that strap at the top. The latter are warmer than the loose felt boots worn by lumbermen, lighter, more flexible, fit better, and are easier to dry out. The rubbers should fit properly over the heavy socks, neither too tight nor too loose, but especially not too tight or you risk frostbite. Thus equipped, a still-hunter is "shod with silence." For cold weather the vital necessity is suppleness of the foot, and here you have it.

COLD WEATHER CLOTHING.— The main fault of most cold weather rigs is that, paradoxically, they are too hot. You go out into "twenty-some-odd" below zero, all muffled up in thick underwear, overshirt, heavy trousers, and a 32-ounce (to the yard) Mackinaw coat. Very nice, until you get your stride. In half an hour the sweat will be streaming from you enough to turn a mill. By and by you may have to stand still for quite a while. Then the moisture begins to freeze, and a buffalo robe wouldn't keep you warm.

Conditions vary; but for average winter work put on two suits of medium weight all-wool underwear, instead of one heavy one, moleskin trousers (heavy Mackinaws chafe), wool overshirt, Mackinaw shirt worn with tail outside, so it can easily be removed and worn behind you when not needed, the rubber "overs" and socks mentioned above, a Mackinaw cap with visor and ear laps, large, old kid gloves, and thick, woolen mittens held by a cord around the neck.

In buying Mackinaws get none but the best quality. Cheap Mackinaw is shoddy, or part cotton, and soaks up moisture like a sponge. A good grade sheds rain so long as the nap is not worn off; then it can be waterproofed by the lanolin process. It is noiseless, and stands rough usage. The natural gray color is best, except where the law requires you to wear red for protection against gun-bearing fools. (About this, saith our friend Crossman: "Yes, some fellow might take you for a deer if you wore an inconspicuous color in the woods, but what would you? He'd take you for a zebra if you wore

CLOTHING 163

green and yellow, or shoot you for a forest fire if you wore flaming crimson.")

CLOTHING FOR WOMEN.— So far as materials go, the same rules hold good for women in field and camp as for men.

The skirt, of course, should be short. For canoeing or forest travel it should come just below the knee. A Norfolk jacket, flannel waist or shirt, bloomers, cloth leggings, strong but light-weight and flexible shoes with broad, low heels, a soft felt hat, sweater jacket, and waterproofs — these suggest themselves. Ribbed cotton underwear may be worn on hot days, but fine woolen garments should be in reserve for the inevitable wet and chilly times.

Properly dressed for the woods, and not overburdened, the average woman can keep up anywhere with the average office man; but in a tight or draggy skirt she is simply hopeless. For real wilderness travel riding breeches, cut full at the knee, are far better than a skirt. A buttoned skirt that can be slipped on readily may be worn over them on occasion, as when approaching some village or camp where people are not yet civilized enough to approve common sense in a woman's costume. Alice MacGowan was fairly driven out of a mountain county in Kentucky because she wore riding breeches, and yet many's the time I have seen a mountain woman riding astride a man's saddle in an undivided long skirt. O Modesty, what crimes have been committed in thy name!

CHAPTER X
PERSONAL KITS

When one is going into fixed camp, the best carrier for his personal belongings is a common steamer trunk — a light one, but long enough to take in the fishing rods. For canoe, pack train, or automobile, the kit will be much smaller, of course, and may be carried in one of the bed rolls already described, or in a knapsack, or a dunnage bag, according to circumstances.

DUNNAGE BAG.— A common sailor's bag or "war bag" (simple canvas sack closed by a puckering cord) has the merit of simplicity, but it is not

Fig. 100.—
Dunnage Bag

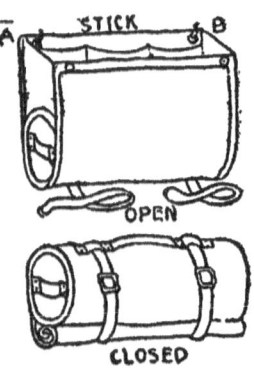
Fig. 101.—
Kit or Provision Pack

Fig. 102.—
Screw Hook Fastening for Box Lid

water-tight. If a bag is used for packing, get from a camp outfitter what he calls a duffel bag (Fig. 100), of waterproof canvas, made with an inside neck or throat-piece that is tied tightly before the

PERSONAL KITS

outside is closed. Then it will keep the contents dry even if your craft should fill or capsize. It should be about 3 feet long and 12 inches in diameter. Get a good quality, reasonably snag-proof, and with extra-strong seams and handles. If it is to be shipped as baggage, have it fasten with chain and padlock. I would not use a bag at all unless it was perfectly water-tight, for that is its only point of superiority; on the other hand, it is bothersome to pack, and when you want anything out of a bag you generally have to dump all the contents on the ground to find it.

The pack shown in Fig. 101 is almost as good protection against wet, and a deal handier. The top edge, AB, is stiffened by a stick, to hang it up by in camp, and there are pockets to keep things separated. To close it, fold in the sides, bringing front and back together, roll up, and strap.

DITTY BOXES, POUCHES.— Everyone will fit up these things to suit himself. When practicable to carry it, I prefer to put my small odds-and-ends in one or two low cigar boxes (the 50-size), with partitions, the lid being secured by a small screw-hook (Fig. 102). Otherwise little bags of cloth or soft leather answer the purpose.

As for pouches to carry on one's person, my reasons for not liking them will be given under the head of WALKING TRIPS, in Volume II.

HATCHET.— A woodsman should carry a hatchet, and he should be as critical in selecting it as in buying a gun. The notion that a heavy hunting knife can do the work of a hatchet is a delusion. When it comes to cleaving carcasses, chopping kindling, blazing thick-barked trees, driving tent pegs or trap stakes, and keeping up a bivouac fire, the knife never was made that will compare with a good tomahawk. The common hatchets of the hardware stores are unfit for a woodsman's use. They have broad blades with beveled edge, and they are generally made of poor, brittle stuff. A camper's hatchet should have the edge and temper of a good axe. It must be light enough to carry in or on one's knapsack, yet it should bite deep in timber. The best hatchet I have used (and it has been with me in the mountains for seven or eight years) is one shown in Fig. 103, except that the handle is a straight one, 17-inch, that I made myself. Its weight, with leather sheath, is 1 lb. 10 oz. With this keen little

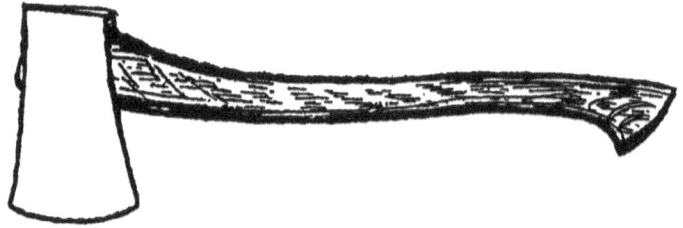

Fig. 103.— Hatchet

tool I have cut many a cord of the hardest woods — hickory, oak, dogwood, beech, etc.— up to young trees eight or more inches thick, often laying in a winter night's wood with it. (The way to learn chopping is to go slow, give all your attention to making every blow tell just where it is needed, and don't strike too hard.)

SHEATH KNIFE.— On the subject of hunting knives I am tempted to be diffuse. In my green and callow days I tried nearly everything in the knife line from a shoemaker's skiver to a machete, and I had knives made to order. The conventional hunting knife is, or was until recently, of the familiar dime-novel pattern invented by Colonel Bowie. It is too thick and clumsy to whittle with, much too thick for a good skinning knife, and too sharply pointed to cook and eat with. It is always tempered too hard. When put to the rough service for which it is supposed to be intended, as in cutting through the ossified false ribs of an old buck, it is an even bet that out will come a nick as big as a saw-tooth — and Sheridan forty miles from a grindstone! Such a knife is shaped expressly for stabbing, which

PERSONAL KITS 167

is about the very last thing that a woodsman ever has occasion to do, our lamented grandmothers to the contrary notwithstanding.

Many hunters do not carry sheath knives, saying (and it is quite true) that a common jackknife will skin anything from a squirrel to a bear. Still, I like a small, light sheath knife. It is always open and "get-at-able," ready not only for skinning game and cleaning fish, but for cutting sticks, slicing bread and bacon and peeling "spuds." It saves the pocket knife from wet and messy work, and preserves its edge for the fine jobs.

For years I used knives of my own design, because there was nothing on the market that met my notion of what a sensible, practical sheath knife should be; but we have it now in the knife here shown (Fig. 104). It is of the right size (4½-inch blade), the

Fig. 104.— Sheath Knife

right shape, and the proper thinness. I ground the front part of the back of mine to a blunt bevel edge for scaling fish and disarticulating joints. The sheath being flimsy, and the buttoned band a nuisance, I made one of good leather that binds well up on the handle and is fastened together with copper rivets besides the sewing.

Cutlery should be of the best steel obtainable. Knicks and dull edges are abominations, so use knives and hatchets for nothing but what they were made for, and whet them a little every day that they are in service.

POCKET KNIFE.— The jackknife has one stout blade equal to whittling seasoned hickory, and two small blades, of which one is ground thin for such surgery as you may have to perform (keep it clean). Beware of combination knives; they may be passable corkscrews and can openers, but that is about all.

COMPASS.— This instrument may not often be needed to guide one's course, but it is like the proverbial pistol in Texas. Besides, it is useful in reading a map, and indispensable for route sketching. If you get one of the common kind with both ends simply pointed and the north one blued or blackened scratch B = N (Blue equals North) on the case. This seems like an absurd precaution, does it not? Well, it will not seem so if you get lost. The first time that a man loses his bearings in the wilderness his wits refuse to work. He cannot, to save his life, remember whether the black end of the needle is north or south. The first time I ever got lost in the big woods I was not frightened, and yet I did a perfectly idiotic thing: to hold my compass level and steady I set it on the thick muzzle of my rifle barrel! That made the needle swing away out of true. It was ten minutes before I thought of this, and tried again, with all iron carefully put aside. That shows what a dunderhead a fellow can be, even when he is fairly cool.

If dust accumulates inside the case of a compass it may interfere a little with its true pointing, and moisture will do so. But, so long as the needle moves freely, *do not quarrel with it,* no matter how sure you may think you are that it has been bewitched.

A compass with revolving dial (card compass) is somewhat easier to use than one with a needle, because the *N* on the dial always points north, no matter which way you turn; but it must be rather bulky, to traverse freely, is not so sensitive as a needle, and wears the pivot faster.

There are compasses with dials illuminated by a radio-active substance that are handy to use at night. The old-fashioned "luminous" compasses that have to be exposed to sunlight every day are not worth the extra cost, for you will forget to attend to them.

PERSONAL KITS 169

Anyway, a woodsman should carry a pocket electric flasher, and, with that along, a common compass serves very well.

My favorite compass is of a pattern known as the "Explorer's," as here shown (Fig. 105), except that it has a hinged cover. Twice I have crushed the glasses of open faced compasses and ruined the pivots. The moveable arrow is to be set toward one's objective, when the needle points north; it then indicates the general direction of the course. The dial is of 1¾ inches diameter, and is divided into spaces of two degrees, reading from left to right, which is better for an amateur than the contrary reading of a surveyor's compass.

Fig. 105.— Compass with Course Arrow

The use of the compass will be explained in Vol. II, under the head of ROUTE SKETCHING.

I wear the instrument in a small pocket sewed on my shirt for that purpose, so it fits, and attach it to a button-hole by a short, strong cord. A long cord would catch in brush. If the compass is carried in a large pocket it will flop out when you stoop over or fall down. Sometimes, when mapping, I have worn one in a leather bracelet, like a wristwatch; but a better way is to attach it, at such time, to the little board that your cross-section paper is tacked on.

WATCH.— Ordinarily a cheap watch is good enough for the woods. If you do carry a good one, and it is open-faced, there is a good way to protect it from wet that I read some years ago in a sportsman's journal. This also helps to keep it from falling out of a pocket. "To keep one's watch dry, even though you go overboard, take a piece of pure rubber dental dam 8 inches square, put the watch in the center, and bring the rubber together at the stem, tying the puckered up rubber with a bit of string. When you wish to see the face, simply stretch the rubber over the front and you can see the hands clearly through it."

If it is desired to make a sketch-map of some region for which you cannot obtain a government topographical sheet, and the country is too rough for pacing, it will help if one member of the party carries a stop-watch, with which to estimate distances by the sound of pistol shots, as described in Vol. II.

WHISTLE.— A party traveling in thick woods with only an old line of blazes to guide them may have to deploy to find the marks. It will save time, and perhaps a good deal of searching for each other, if they have shrill whistles and a prearranged code of signals. The army officer's whistle is a good one.

MAPS.— Write to The Director, U. S. Geological Survey, Washington, D. C., for an index map showing what topographical sheets have been published for the State that you are to travel in. These sheets are sold at ten cents each (no stamps). Their character is described as follows:

The United States Geological Survey has been engaged since its organization in making a topographic survey and map of the United States. The unit of survey is a quadrangle 15', 30', or 1° in extent each way, covering an area of one-sixteenth, one-fourth, or one " square degree." The unit of publication is an atlas sheet 16½ by 20 inches, and each sheet is a topographic map of one of the above areas. As the atlas sheets are uniform in size, the greater the area covered the smaller the scale of the map. The scale of the full degree sheet is 1: 250,000, that of the 30' sheet is 1: 125,000, and that of the 15' sheet 1: 62,500. A sheet is designated by the name of some well-known place or feature appearing on it, and the names of adjoining published sheets are printed on the margins. The maps are engraved on copper and printed from stone. The cultural features, such as roads, railroads, cities, towns, etc., as well as all lettering, are in black; all water features are printed in blue; while the hill features are shown by brown contour lines. The contour interval varies with the scale of the map and the relief of the country.

These maps vary in merit. For some of the wilder and rougher regions they are only recon-

PERSONAL KITS 171

noissance maps and full of minor inaccuracies; but they are revised from time to time. A good part of the continental United States has already been surveyed.

Maps may be cut in sections and mounted on muslin in such way that they fold conveniently for the pocket, but there should be a cover to protect them from soiling and wet.

A better way is to use what the French call a *liseur de cartes*. There are many models and sizes, but all are alike in principle. The simplest form is a leather pocket to contain map sections, faced with

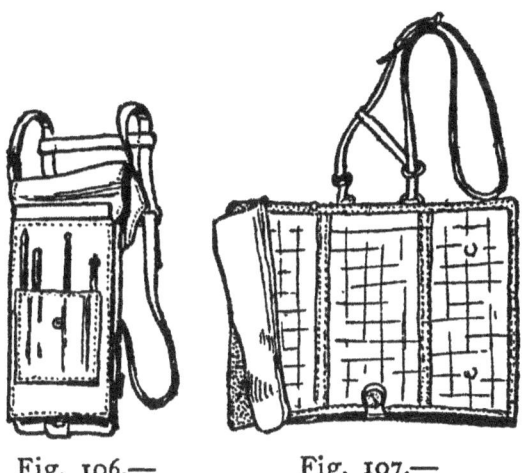

Fig. 106.—
Map Case

Fig. 107.—
U. S. A. Dispatch Case

transparent celluloid, ruled in squares, for the particular section in use at the time. Then there is no need of mounting the map on cloth (such a backing is likely to loosen in the humid air of the forest, and the edges will fray), nor is there risk of the map being soiled, torn, injured by rain, or blown away.

If one has much mapping, sketching, or writing to do, he may well carry a military dispatch case, of which one pattern is shown in Fig. 106, made of olive drab web, with celluloid windows divided into

1-inch squares, pockets for stationery, pencils, dividers, etc., and fitted with a military compass, or not, as one desires. The regulation U. S. Army dispatch case is of leather (Fig. 107).

For ordinary purposes a pocket case is more convenient. The London tackle makers, C. Farlow & Co., sell, at 5s. 6d. postpaid, a leather "fly and cast case," 5 x 4½ inches, with six transparent pockets of celluloid. A topographical sheet by the U. S. Geological Survey cuts into twelve sections that fit these pockets, two in each, back to back. Number the sections to show how they join. Small sheets of quadrille ruled paper for notes and route sketching go in the same case. The maps can readily be consulted without the bother of unfolding in a wind, and are protected.

STATIONERY.— Note-books and writing paper should be quadrille ruled, for convenience in mapping and drawing to scale. A loose-leaf memorandum book is best: then you can file your notes in a safe place every evening. Postal cards may suffice for correspondence. If envelopes are carried, let them be of linen, and take along a small stick of sealing-wax. Linen wears better than paper in the pocket of a native messenger. Gummed envelopes, in a moist climate, seal themselves before you want to use them. Sealing-wax thwarts the inquisitive rural postmaster and his family. On the route out from camp your mail may go through many hands: *à bon entendeur salut!* Carry stamps in books, not sheets.

A self-filling fountain pen, and a bottle of ink with screw top held tight by a spring, an indelible pencil for marking specimens or packages for shipment, and several large rubber bands, may be needed, according to circumstances.

Take along an almanac to regulate the watch, show the moon's changes (tides, if near the coast), and, by them, to determine the day of the month and week, which one is very apt to forget when he

PERSONAL KITS

is away from civilization. Have a time-table of the railroad that you expect to return by.

MATCHBOX.— Do not omit a *waterproof* matchbox, of such pattern as has a cover that cannot drop off. I prefer a flat one. It can be opened with one hand. The matches in this box are to be used only in emergency. Carry the daily supply loose where you can get at them. For this purpose I like a pigskin pocket with snap-button, worn on the belt. The matches I waterproof, before starting, by dipping them half-length in shellac varnish thinned with alcohol to the right consistency, which is found by experiment, and laying them out separately on a newspaper to dry. This is better than using paraffine or collodion, because shellac does not wear off, and it is itself inflammable, like sealing-wax. Matches so treated can be left a long time in water without spoiling.

A bit of candle is a handy thing to start fire with wet wood, besides its other obvious use in an emergency. Sick-room candles are less bulky than common ones, burn brighter, and last longer.

FLASHLIGHT.— To find things in the tent at night, or to find one's way if belated, a pocket electric flasher is so useful that a camper should always carry one. Get one with round edges that will not wear holes in the pocket. The kind shaped like a fountain pen is all right in some cases, but not on hunting or fishing trips: the less bright metal you expose, the better.

EYE GLASSES.— If you wear them, carry a spare pair; the woods are hard on such things.

The glare of the sun on water, or snow, or in deserts, is often very trying. The best sun glasses are what are called shooting glasses, of amber color, which excludes the ultra-violet rays. They are large enough to protect the eyes against wind, dust, and flying insects. They come handy when one is pursued for an hour by a swarm of " red pepper " gnats that are bent on suicide and on blinding somebody in doing it.

FIRST AID KITS.— There are many kinds of pocket medicine cases, and of first aid boxes fitted with both medical and surgical supplies. Most of them are too large and heavy to be carried constantly on the person when a man is afield: they will be left in camp — and camp is not the place where accidents are most likely to occur.

It is quite important that the little store of first aid appliances that one does keep always at hand should be contained in a case that is *air-tight and aseptic,* yet easy to open and close. I have not seen a ready fitted emergency case that is so, except the soldier's first aid packet, which is hermetically sealed in either tin or impermeable cloth. This package contains a triangular bandage, one or two compresses of sublimated gauze, two safety pins, and instructions.

A triangular bandage is made by dividing a piece of muslin a yard square into halves by a diagonal cut joining two opposite corners, and thoroughly sterilizing it. Cuts are printed on it showing how to bandage any major part of the body. Roller bandages are difficult for untrained people to handle, but anyone can see almost at a glance how to use the triangular one. A folded neckerchief, or any triangular piece of cloth, will do as a makeshift, if an aseptic dressing is first applied, in case of an open wound. How to fold the bandage before applying is shown in Fig. 108. A tourniquet to check bleeding is made by folding into a narrow cravat, as indicated, and then twisting into rope form.

The soldier's packet is intended for a first dressing of gunshot wounds, fractures (with the aid of improvised splints), and other serious injuries. One would not care to open it if he merely had cut his thumb, skinned his knuckle, or blistered his heel. Yet it is the lesser injuries that we are most apt to suffer, and they certainly should be treated anti-

PERSONAL KITS

septically on the spot, lest grave consequences follow.

So, get a small tin tobacco box, flat, with rounded corners; boil it in two waters, and dry thoroughly. Then pack it as follows: From the American National Red Cross, Washington, D. C., get a packet of dressings for small cuts, etc., and one of finger dressings. The former dressing is a gauze compress, 3 x 3 inches, sewed to a muslin bandage an inch wide and a yard long; the latter is similar but smaller. Get from them also a few ampules of 3½% tincture of iodine in wooden containers. All these are cheap, but very effective and easy to apply. Put one large dressing, a couple of smaller

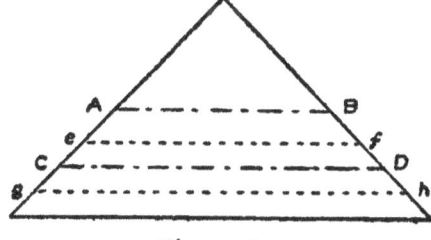

Fig. 108.—
To Fold Triangular Bandage. A B C D — Folds for Broad Cravat. AB, ef, gh — Folds for Narrow Cravat

ones, and an ampule, in your tin box, and the rest in the camp medical kit.

At the druggist's get some large capsules, and tablets of cascara, intestinal antiseptic, aspirin, potassium permanganate, and strychnine. Put a few tablets of each in capsule, label, and stow in box. Calomel and epsom salts may be added (one dose of the latter), or what you please. Fill whatever room is left with absorbent cotton. Then seal the box air-tight by running a narrow strip of the adhesive plaster around it. This is easy to open, and can be used over again many times.

In treating a wound, seize the end of the ampule that is encased in gauze and break off or crush the point of the glass, then hold the broken end down until the gauze is saturated with the iodine, clap directly to the surface of the wound, and apply either the larger or smaller dressing. A little emergency case of this sort is one of the most valuable pocket pieces that a man can carry on an outing.

Insect "dopes" are discussed in Chapter XIV.

POCKET REPAIR KIT.— Only a little of this and that, fitted into a quite small wallet. A pair of tiny, sharp-pointed scissors for trimming dressings, rigging tackle, and so on; pointed tweezers that can be used as dressing forceps, to remove splinters, and in manipulating gut for flies or leaders; some dental floss for emergency repairs on rods and the like; some 1-inch adhesive plaster; a needle or two, waxed linen thread on card, spare buttons, safety pins; one or two large rubber bands; a spare shoe lace; some strong twine; two feet of copper snare wire; a short rigged fishline, a few assorted hooks, minnow hooks with half the barb filed off, two or three split shot (tackle invaluable if you get lost); pipe cleaners (if you smoke): this exhausts the list of my own selection.

TOILET ARTICLES.— A small cake of soap in an oiled silk bag or a rubber tobacco pouch is convenient for light marching: compact, and does not rattle around. "Grandpa's" tar soap makes a good lather in any kind of water, hard or soft, warm or cold. Towels should be old (soft) and rather small (easy to wash and dry out). A pocket mirror is handy not only for toilet purposes but to examine mouth and throat or in removing a foreign substance from the eye. Other articles as required. On a hard trip cut out all but towel, soap, toothbrush, comb, and mirror.

CAMERA.— One cuts his coat according to his cloth, but if you can afford a camera with quick lens and high-speed shutter, it will pay well in good pictures. On wilderness trips it is the rule, not the exception, that you must "shoot" when the light is poor.

PERSONAL KITS

Again, you want a picture that *tells a story,* a true story, and, nine times out of ten, the only way to get it is by a snapshot taken unawares. When people pose for a camp scene or any other picture they are self-conscious, stiff, or showing off.

Your chance to get a story-picture always pops up unexpectedly. You must work quickly, or not at all. There is no chance to manœuvre for position, no time to wait on the sun. And if your camera is too large to carry in a pocket or on your belt, then, two to one, you haven't got it with you. So get a camera not over $3\frac{1}{4}$ x $4\frac{1}{4}$, with special lens and shutter, if you can. At best you will spoil a good many exposures, and you can well afford to have the really good ones enlarged.

A handy way to carry a camera is to remove the sling, cut two slits in back of leather case, and wear it on your belt over the hip. Then it is out of the way, does not dangle when you stoop nor flop when you run, and yet is instantly at your service.

FIELD GLASSES.— The only satisfactory ones are those small enough to go with you everywhere, yet with good definition and wide field of view. This means prism binoculars of moderate power, say 6 diameters, or perhaps 8 for sheep or goat hunting.

Opera glasses do very well for bird study.

Some other articles of personal equipment, such as knapsacks and their substitutes, canteens, and individual cooking kits, will be discussed in Vol. II under the head of WALKING TRIPS.

CHAPTER XI
PROVISIONS

When a party camps where fresh meat and farm products can be procured as they are wanted, its provisioning is chiefly a matter of taste, and calls for no special comment here. But to have good meals in the wilderness is a different matter. A man will eat five or six pounds a day of fresh food. That is a heavy load on the trail. And fresh meat, dairy products, fruit, and vegetables, are generally too bulky, too perishable. So it is up to the woodsman to learn how to get the most nourishment out of the least weight and bulk, in materials that " keep " well.

Light outfitting, as regards food, is mainly a question of *how much water* we are willing to carry in our rations. For instance, canned peaches are 88 per cent. water. Can one afford to carry so much water from home when there is plenty of it at camp? The following table is suggestive:

More than ¾ Water.
Fresh milk, fruit, vegetables (except potatoes).
Canned soups, tomatoes, peaches, pears, etc.

More than ½ Water.
Fresh beef, veal, mutton, poultry, eggs, potatoes.
Canned corn, baked beans, pineapple.
Evaported milk (unsweetened).

More than ⅛ Water.
Fresh bread, rolls, pork chops.
Potted chicken, etc.
Cheese.
Canned blackberries.

PROVISIONS

Less than ⅛ Water.

Dried apples, apricots, peaches, prunes.
Fruit jelly.

Less than ⅕ Water.

Salt pork. Bacon. Dried fish. Butter.
Desiccated eggs. Concentrated soups.
Powdered milk.
Wheat flour, corn meal, etc. Macaroni.
Rice, oatmeal, hominy, etc.
Dried beans, split peas.
Dehydrated vegetables.
Dried dates, figs, raisins.
Orange marmalade. Sugar. Chocolate.
Nuts. Nut butter.

Although this table is good in its way, it is not a fair measure of the relative value of foods. Even the solid part of some foodstuffs contains a good deal of refuse (fresh potatoes 20 per cent.), while others have none.

NUTRITIVE VALUES.— The nutritive elements of foodstuffs are protein, a little mineral matter, fats, and carbohydrates. Protein is the basis of muscle, bone, tendon, cartilage, skin, and the corpuscles of the blood. Fats and carbohydrates supply heat and muscular energy. In other words, the human body is an engine; protein keeps it in repair; fats and carbohydrates are the fuel to run it.

Familiar examples of proteids are lean meat and white of egg. The chief food fats are fat meat, butter, lard, oil, and cream. Carbohydrates are starchy foods (flour, cereals, etc.) and sugar (sweets of almost any kind).

Protein is the most important element of food, because nothing else can take its place in building up tissues and enriching the fluids of the body, whereas, in emergency, it can also supply power and heat, and thus run the human machine for a while without other fuel.

Men can live on foods deficient in protein, such as rice and potatoes, but they become anemic, weak, and subject to beriberi, pellagra, or other serious disease. Anyone can observe for himself the evil effects of a diet poor in protein but rich in heating power by traveling through our "hog and hominy belt." Fat pork contains hardly any protein; neither do the cabbage and potatoes that usually flank it on the negro's or poor-white's table. As for corn bread, when made as a plain hoecake or the like, it is in much the same class, and what protein it does contain is difficult to digest.

On the other hand, an undue proportion of lean meat, fish, dried beans, and other high-proteid foods, brings another train of ills. As Dr. Atwater says, "A dog can live on lean meat: he can convert its material into muscle and its energy into heat and muscular power. Man can do the same; but such a one-sided diet would not be best for the dog, and it would be still worse for the man."

The problem of a well-balanced ration consists in supplying daily the right proportion of nutritive elements in agreeable and digestible form. The problem of a campaign ration is the same, but cutting out most of the water and waste in which fresh foods abound. However, in getting rid of the water in fresh meats, fruits, and vegetables, we lose, unfortunately, much of the volatile essences that give these foods their good flavors. This loss — and it is a serious one — must be made up by the camp cook changing the menu as often as he can, by varying the ingredients and the processes of cooking.

VARIETY is quite as welcome at the camp board as anywhere else — in fact more so, for it is harder to get. Variety need not mean adding to the load. It means *substituting,* say, three 5-lb. parcels for one 15-lb. parcel, so as to have something "different" from day to day.

There is an old school of campers who affect to scorn such things. "We take nothing with us," they say, "but pork, flour, baking powder, salt, sugar, and coffee — our guns and rods furnish *us* variety." This sounds sturdy, but there is a deal

PROVISIONS

of humbug in it. A spell of bad weather may defeat the best of hunters and fishermen. Even granting that luck is good, the kill is likely to be of one kind at a time. With only the six articles named, nobody can serve the same game in a variety of ways. Now, consider a moment: How would you like to sit down to nothing but fried chicken and biscuit, three times a day? Chicken everlastingly fried in pork grease — and, if you tire of that, well, eat fried "sow-belly," and sop your bread in the grease! It is just the same with trout or bass as it is with chicken; the same with pheasant or duck, rabbit or squirrel or bear. The only kind of wild meat that civilized man can relish for three consecutive meals, served in the same fashion, is venison of the deer family. Go, then, prepared to lend variety to your menu. Food that palls is bad food — worse in camp than anywhere else, for you can't escape to a restaurant.

FOOD AS A SOURCE OF ENERGY.— The energy developed by food is measured in calories. A calorie is the amount of heat required to raise one pound of water through four degrees Fahrenheit. A man at moderately active muscular work requires about 3,400 calories of food-fuel a day; one at hard muscular work, about 4,150; one at very hard work, about 5,500 calories (Atwater's figures).

According to the latest data supplied me by the U. S. Department of Agriculture (February, 1916) the fuel value of protein is about 1,815 calories per pound, that of carbohydrates is the same, and that of fats is about 4,080 calories per pound.

"A pound of wheat flour, which consists largely of starch, has an average fuel value of about 1,625 calories, and a pound of butter, which is mostly fat, about 3,410 calories. These are only about one-eighth water. Whole milk, which is seven-eighths water, has an average fuel value of 310 calories per pound; cream, which has more fat and less water, 865 calories, and skim milk, which is whole milk after the cream has been removed, 165 calories.

182   CAMPING AND WOODCRAFT

This high fuel value of fat explains the economy of nature in storing fat in the body for use in case of need. Fat is the most concentrated form of body fuel."

I have compiled the following table of food values, with special reference to the camp commissariat, from various reports of the U. S. Department of Agriculture. Some of the figures for fuel value, I am informed, were computed by using the factors given above; others were derived from actual determinations of the heat of combustion and the digestibility of the food materials.—

AVERAGE NUTRIENTS OF FOODS
REMAINING PERCENTAGES CONSIST OF WATER AND REFUSE

Food materials (as purchased)	Protein	Fat	Carbohydrates	Ash	Fuel value per pound
	Per ct.	Per ct.	Per ct.	Per ct.	Calories
ANIMAL FOOD					
Beef, fresh:					
Loin	16.1	17.5	—	0.9	1,025
Ribs	13.9	21.2	—	0.7	1,135
Round	19.0	12.8	—	1.0	890
Beef, cured:					
Corned	14.3	23.8	—	4.6	1,245
Dried	26.4	6.9	—	8.9	790
Salted (mess beef)	11.2	39.9	—	5.9	1,890
Tongue, pickled	11.9	19.2	—	4.3	1,010
Beef, canned:					
Boiled	25.5	22.5	—	1.3	1,425
Corned	26.3	18.7	—	4.0	1,280
Roast	25.9	14.8	—	1.3	1,105
Tongue, ground	19.5	23.2	—	4.0	1,340
Pork, cured:					
Bacon, smoked	9.1	62.2	—	4.1	2,715
Ham, smoked	14.2	33.4	—	4.2	1,635
Salt pork	1.9	86.2	—	3.9	3,555
Lard	—	100.0	—	—	4,080
Pork, canned:					
Ham, deviled	19.0	34.1	—	3.3	1,790
Sausage:					
Bologna	18.2	19.7	—	3.8	1,155
Summer	24.5	42.1	—	7.0	2,230
Sausage, canned:					
Frankfort	14.9	9.9	—	2.8	695
Oxford	9.9	58.5	0.6	2.1	2,665
Pork	14.5	21.6	—	1.8	1,180
Soups, canned (not dried):					
Beef	4.4	0.4	1.1	1.2	120
Chicken	2.9	3.3	5.1	1.6	300
Cream of celery	2.1	2.8	5.0	1.5	235
Tomato	1.8	1.1	5.6	1.5	185
Poultry, fresh:					
Chicken	14.4	12.6	—	0.7	910

Table continued.

PROVISIONS

Food materials (as purchased)	Protein	Fat	Carbohydrates	Ash	Fuel value per pound
	Per ct.	Per ct.	Per ct.	Per ct.	Calories
Duck	15.4	16.0	—	1.1	1,085
Goose	14.8	25.5	—	1.0	1,475
Pheasant	21.5	4.2	—	1.0	730
Quail	22.3	6.1	—	1.4	835
Turkey	19.0	16.2	—	1.0	1,185
Poultry, canned:					
Chicken, boned	27.7	12.8	—	2.2	1,245
Chicken, potted	19.4	20.3	—	2.5	1,390
Terrine de foie gras	13.6	38.2	4.3	2.6	2,075
Turkey, potted	17.2	22.0	—	3.0	1,390
Frogs' legs:	10.5	0.1	—	0.7	195
Fish, fresh, dressed:					
Bass, small-mouthed	11.7	1.3	—	0.7	263
Perch, white	8.8	1.8	—	0.5	231
Pickerel	12.0	0.2	—	0.7	227
Salmon	15.0	9.5	—	0.9	658
Trout, brook	11.9	1.3	—	0.7	268
Trout, lake	11.0	6.2	—	0.7	449
Fish, cured:					
Cod, salt	16.0	0.4	—	18.5	325
Halibut, smoked	19.3	14.0	—	1.9	916
Herring, smoked	20.5	8.8	—	7.4	755
Fish, canned:					
Salmon	19.5	7.5	—	2.0	658
Sardines	23.7	12.1	—	5.3	916
Shellfish, fresh:					
Clams, round	10.6	1.1	5.2	2.3	331
Oysters, " solids ".	6.0	1.3	3.3	1.1	222
Eggs:					
Fresh hen's	13.1	9.3	—	0.9	635
Evaporated, whole	46.9	36.0	7.1	3.6	2,525
Evaporated, yolk	33.3	51.6	5.7	3.5	2,794
Milk:					
Fresh milk, whole	3.3	4.0	5.0	0.7	310
Cream	2.5	18.5	4.5	0.5	865
Condensed, sweetened	8.8	8.3	54.1	1.9	1,430
Evaporated, plain	7.4	8.5	11.1	1.7	683
Milk powder, from skimmed milk	34.0	3.1	51.9	8.0	1,785
Butter, Cheese:					
Butter	1.0	85.0	—	3.0	3,410
Cheese, full cream	25.9	33.7	2.4	3.8	1,885
VEGETABLE FOOD					
Flour, etc.:					
Corn meal	9.2	1.9	75.4	1.0	1,635
Corn, parched	11.5	8.4	72.3	2.6	1,915
Corn, popped	10.7	5.0	78.7	1.3	1,882
Hominy (grits)	8.6	0.6	79.6	0.3	1,671
Oats, rolled	16.1	7.4	66.5	1.8	1,759
Macaroni, etc.	13.4	0.9	74.1	1.3	1,645
Rice	6.9	0.3	80.0	0.5	1,546
Rye flour	6.8	0.9	78.7	0.7	1,620
Tapioca	0.4	0.1	88.0	0.1	1,650
Wheat breakfast food	12.1	1.8	75.2	1.3	1,680
Wheat flour, entire	13.8	1.9	71.9	1.0	1,650
Wheat flour, roller process	11.4	1.0	75.1	0.5	1,635

184 CAMPING AND WOODCRAFT

Food materials (as purchased)	Protein	Fat	Carbohydrates	Ash	Fuel value per pound
Bread, etc.:	Per ct.	Per ct.	Per ct.	Per ct.	Calories
Boston brown bread	6.3	2.1	45.8	1.9	1,110
Cake, sweet	6.3	9.0	63.3	1.5	1,630
Crackers, soda	9.8	9.1	73.1	2.1	1,875
Hoecake (plain corn bread)	4.0	0.6	40.2	2.4	885
Johnnycake	7.8	2.2	57.7	2.9	1,385
Rye bread	9.0	0.6	53.2	1.5	1,170
Wheat bread, white	9.2	1.3	53.1	1.1	1,200
Whole-wheat bread	9.7	0.9	49.7	1.3	1,130
Sweets:					
Candy, plain	—	—	96.0	—	1,680
Cane molasses	—	—	70.0	—	1,225
Cherry jelly	1.1	—	77.2	0.7	1,445
Honey	—	—	81.0	—	1,420
Maple sirup	—	—	71.4	—	1,250
Orange marmalade	0.6	—	84.5	0.3	1,585
Sugar, granulated	—	—	100.0	—	1,820
Vegetables, fresh:					
Onions	1.4	0.3	8.9	0.5	190
Potatoes	1.8	0.1	14.7	0.8	295
Vegetables, canned:					
Beans, baked	6.9	2.5	19.6	2.1	555
Corn, sweet	2.8	1.2	19.0	0.9	430
Peas	3.6	0.2	9.8	1.1	235
Tomatoes	1.2	0.2	4.0	0.6	95
Vegetables, dried:					
Beans, navy	22.5	1.8	59.6	3.5	1,520
Carrots, desiccated	7.7	0.6	80.3	4.9	1,790
Peas, split	24.6	1.0	62.0	2.9	1,565
Nuts:					
Almonds	21.4	54.4	16.8	2.5	2,895
Cocoanut, desiccated	6.3	57.4	31.5	1.3	3,125
Peanuts	29.8	43.5	17.1	2.2	2,610
Peanut butter	29.3	46.5	17.1	5.0	2,825
Pecans	12.1	70.7	12.2	1.6	3,300
Fruits, fresh:					
Apples	0.4	0.5	14.2	0.3	290
Bananas	1.3	0.6	22.0	0.8	460
Cranberries	0.4	0.6	9.9	0.2	215
Lemons	1.0	0.7	8.5	0.5	205
Oranges	0.8	0.2	11.6	0.5	240
Fruits, canned:					
Blackberries	0.8	2.1	56.4	0.7	1,150
Cherries	1.1	0.1	21.1	0.5	415
Olives, pickled	1.1	27.6	11.6	1.7	1,400
Peaches	0.7	0.1	10.8	0.3	220
Pineapples	0.4	0.7	36.4	0.7	715
Fruits, dried:					
Apples	1.6	2.2	68.1	2.0	1,350
Apricots	4.7	1.0	62.5	2.4	1,290
Dates, pitted	2.1	2.8	78.4	1.3	1,615
Figs	4.3	0.3	74.2	2.4	1,475
Prunes, pitted	2.1	—	73.3	2.3	1,400
Raisins	2.6	3.3	76.1	3.4	1,605
Miscellaneous:					
Chocolate	12.9	48.7	30.3	2.2	2,625
Cocoa	21.6	28.9	37.7	7.2	2,160
Olive Oil	—	100.0	—	—	4,080

PROVISIONS 185

Coffee, "cereal coffee," tea, condiments, and common beef extracts contain practically no nutriment, their function being to stimulate the nerves and digestive organs, to add agreeable flavor, or, in the case of salt, to furnish a necessary mineral ingredient.

DIGESTIBILITY.— In applying the above table we must bear in mind the adage that "we live not upon what we eat but upon what we digest." Some foods rich in protein, especially beans, peas, and oat meal, are not easily assimilated, unless cooked for a longer time than campers generally can spare. A considerable part of their protein is liable to putrefy in the alimentary canal, and so be worse than wasted. An excess of meat or fish will do the same thing. Other foods of very high theoretical value are constipating if used in large amounts, as cheese, nuts, chocolate.

The protein of animal food is more digestible than that of vegetable food by about 13 per cent. (average), and the protein of wheat is more easily assimilated than that of corn or oats. I quote the following from an article on army rations by Dr. Woods Hutchinson:

"Every imaginable grain, nut, root, pith or pulp that contains starch has been tried out as a substitute for it [wheat] because these are either cheaper in proportion to their starch content than wheat or can be grown in climates and latitudes where wheat will not flourish. Corn has been tried in the subtropics, rice in the tropics, oats, rye and barley in the north temperate zone, potatoes, sago from the palm, and tapioca from the manioc root.

"Only the net result can be given here, which is that no civilized nation that can raise the money or provide the transportation to get wheat will allow its army to live on any other yet discovered or invented grain or starch. Rice, corn meal, potatoes, sago and tapioca are, of course, ruled out at once, because they contain only starch and nothing to match in the slightest degree the twelve or fourteen per cent. of gluten, or vegetable meat, that gives wheat its supreme value.

"After our first food analyses a desperate attempt was made to substitute corn for wheat, because it contained from five to seven per cent. of protein — called zein — a perfectly good protein in the books and in the laboratories;

but it simply would not work in the field. Armies fed on it promptly showed signs of nitrogen starvation; and, about thirty years later, up came our physiologists with the belated explanation that, though zein was a right-enough protein in composition and chemical structure, only about a third of it could be utilized in the human body.

"Even the purely Oriental nations — the Japanese, Chinese and Hindus — born and brought up on rice, have formally abandoned it in their army ration and have endeavored to substitute wheat for it, though expense and the inborn prejudices of their soldiers have proved considerable obstacles. Troops or nations fed on rice are subject to beriberi and are cured by a diet rich in protein, either vegetable or animal, wheat or meat. Meat and wheat in the ration have wiped out four-fifths of the beriberi in the Japanese army and navy. Those fed on corn become subject to pellagra, which is ravaging our Southern States to-day.

"As for the northern grains, barley, rye and oats, which also contain some gluten, these are all inferior to wheat — rye and barley on account of their low protein content and considerable bulk of innutritious, gelatinous and gummy materials, which disturb the digestion; and oats on account of the irritating bitter extractives with which their high percentage of protein is combined. Nobody but a Scotchman can live on oatmeal as his sole breadstuff; and it has taken generations of training and gallons of whisky on the side to enable him to do it."

This is not saying that the grains here condemned are not good and proper food when used in the right combination with other nutrients; but it is saying that neither of them is fit for continuous use as the mainstay of one's rations.

FOOD COMPONENTS.— Let us now consider the material of field rations, item by item.—

Bacon.— Good old breakfast bacon worthily heads the list, for it is the campaigner's stand-by. It keeps well in any climate, and demands no special care in packing. It is easy to cook, combines well with almost anything, is handier than lard to fry things with, does just as well to shorten bread or biscuits, is very nutritious, and nearly everybody likes it. Take it with you from home, for you can seldom buy it away from railroad towns. Get the boneless, in 5 to 8-lb. flitches. Let canned bacon

PROVISIONS

alone: it lacks flavor, and costs more than it is worth. A little mould on the outside of a flitch does no harm, but reject bacon that is soft and watery, or with yellow fat, or with brownish or black spots in the lean.

Salt Pork (*alias* middlings, sides, bellies, Old Ned, *et al.*).— Commendable or accursed, according to how it is used. Nothing quite equals it in baking beans. Savory in some boiled dishes. When fried, as a *pièce de résistance,* it successfully resists most people's gastric juices, and is nauseous to many. Purchaseable at most frontier posts and at many backwoods farms.

Smoked Ham.— Small ones generally are tough and too salty. Hard to keep in warm or damp weather; moulds easily. Is attractive to blow-flies, which quickly fill it with "skippers," if they can get at it. If kept in a cheesecloth bag, and hung in a cool, airy place, a ham will last until eaten up, and will be relished. Ham will keep, even in warm weather, if packed in a stout paper bag so as to exclude flies. It will keep indefinitely if sliced, boiled, or fried, and put up in tins with melted lard poured over it to keep out air.

Dried Beef.— Cuts from large hams are best. Of limited use in pick-up meals. A notorious thirst-breeder. Not comparable to "jerked" beef, which, unfortunately, is not in the market. (For the process of jerking venison, see Chapter XV.)

Canned Meats and Poultry of all descriptions are quite unfit for steady diet. Devilled or potted ham, chicken, tongue, sausage, and the like, are endurable at picnics, and valuable in emergencies, as when a hard storm makes outdoor cooking impossible. Canned corned beef makes a passable hash.

There is a great difference in quality of canned meats. The cheaper brands found in every grocery store are, generally, abominations. Common canned "roast beef," for example (which has never been roasted at all, but boiled) is stringy, tasteless, and repugnant. Get catalogues from well-known grocers in the large cities who handle first-class goods.

Never eat meat that has been standing in an opened can: it soon undergoes putrefactive changes. A bulged can (unless frozen) indicates spoiled contents. If ever you have to treat a case of ptomaine poisoning you will not soon forget it.

Canned Soups.— These are wholesome enough, but the fluid kinds are very bulky for their meagre nutritive value. However, a few cans of consommé are fine for " stock " in camp soups or stews, and invaluable in case of sickness. Here, as with canned meat, avoid the country grocery kind.

Condensed Soups.— Soup powders are a great help in time of trouble — but don't rely on them for a full meal. There are some that are complete in themselves and require nothing but 15 to 20 minutes' cooking; others take longer, and demand (in small type on the label) the addition of ingredients that generally you haven't got. Try various brands at home, till you find what you like.

Cured Fish.— Shredded codfish, and smoked halibut, sprats, boneless herring, are portable and keep well. They will be relished for variety sake.

Canned Fish.— Not so objectionable as canned meat. Salmon and sardines are rich in protein. Canned codfish balls save a great deal of time in preparation, and are sometimes welcome when you have no potatoes for the real thing. But go light: these things are only for a change now and then, or for emergency use in bad weather.

Eggs.— To vary the camp bill of fare, eggs are simply invaluable, not only by themselves, but as ingredients in cooking. Look at the cook's timetable at the end of this volume and observe how many of the best dishes call for eggs in making them up.

When means of transportation permit, fresh eggs may be carried to advantage. A hand crate holding 12 dozen weighs about 24 pounds, filled.

Eggs can be packed along in winter without danger of breakage by carrying them frozen. Do not try to boil a frozen egg: peel it as you would a hard-boiled one, and then fry or poach.

To test an egg for freshness, drop it into cold water; if it sinks quickly it is fresh, if it stands on end it is doubtful, if it floats it is surely bad.

To preserve eggs, rub them all over with vaseline, being careful that no particle of shell is uncoated. They will keep good much longer than if treated with lime water, salt, paraffine, water-glass or any of the other common expedients.

On hard trips it is impracticable to carry eggs in the shell. Some campers break fresh eggs and pack them in friction-top cans. The yolks soon break, and they will keep but a short time. A *good* brand of desiccated eggs is the solution of this problem. It does away with all risk of breaking and spoiling, and reduces bulk and weight very much, as will be seen below.

Desiccated eggs vary a great deal in quality according to material and process employed. Condemned storage eggs have been used by unscrupulous manufacturers, and so, it is said, have the eggs of sea-fowl. I have tried some brands that were uneatable by themselves, nor did they improve any dish I combined them with. On the other hand, I have had five or six years' experience with evaporated eggs made by an Iowa firm which make excellent omelettes and scrambled eggs and are quite equal to fresh ones in bakestuffs and for various other culinary purposes. They are made from fresh hens' eggs (*whole,* but with sometimes more yolk added) by a strictly sanitary process. A 1-lb. can, equal to about 3 dozen fresh eggs, measures 6 x 3 x 3 inches and weighs 1 lb. 5 oz. gross. It costs little more than fresh eggs, and the powder will never spoil if kept dry. Of course, it cannot be used as fried, boiled, or poached eggs. For omelettes, etc., the powder must soak about an hour in cold or lukewarm water before using; it can be used dry in mixing dough. Thanks to this invention, the camp flapjack need no longer be a culinary horror.

Desiccated eggs made of the yolks only are merely useful as ingredients in cooking.

Milk.— Sweetened condensed milk (the "salve" of the lumberjacks) is distasteful to most people. Plain evaporated milk is the thing to carry — and don't leave it out if you can practicably tote it. The notion that this is a "baby food," to be scorned by real woodsmen, is nothing but a foolish conceit. Few things pay better for their transportation. It will be allowed that Admiral Peary knows something about food values. Here is what he says in *The North Pole*: "The essentials, and the only essentials, needed in a serious artic sledge journey, no matter what the season, the temperature, or the duration of the journey — whether one month or six — are four: pemmican, tea, ship's biscuit, condensed milk. . . . The standard daily ration for work on the final sledge journey toward the Pole on all expeditions has been as follows: 1 lb. pemmican, 1 lb. ship's biscuit, 4 oz. condensed milk, ½ oz. compressed tea."

Milk, either evaporated or powdered, is a very important ingredient in camp cookery. Look again at the cook's time-table previously mentioned.

Years ago I used to get an excellent powdered milk from a New York outfitter. It dissolved readily, was quite creamy rich, and had none of the scalded taste that one notices in most brands of evaporated milk. Then it went out of the market, and I have looked for it in vain. It was made of whole milk, retaining the butter fat. That was why it was rich, and that is why it was not a commercial success, for it would not keep well in storage — the fatty part would turn rancid, or at least grow stale.

I do not know of any but skim milk powders now on sale, excepting certain high-priced ones sold as food for infants or invalids, and none of these has the fresh milk flavor of the kind I got from the

PROVISIONS

outfitter. However, skim milk powder is useful in cooking, and I would carry it where evaporated milk would be too heavy.

Butter.— This is another " soft " thing that pays its freight. Look up its nutritive value in the table already given.

There is a western firm that puts up very good butter hermetically sealed in 2-lb. cans. It will keep indefinitely.

For ordinary trips it suffices to pack butter firmly into pry-up tin cans which have been sterilized by thorough scalding and then cooled in a perfectly clean place. Keep it in a spring or in cold running water (hung in a net, or weighted with a rock) whenever you can. When traveling, wrap the cold can in a towel or other insulating material.

If I had to cut out either lard or butter, I would keep the butter. It serves all the purposes of lard in cooking, is wholesomer, and, beyond that, it is the most concentrated source of energy that one can use with impunity.

Cheese.— Cheese has nearly twice the fuel value of a porterhouse steak of equal weight, and it contains a fourth more protein. It is popularly supposed to be hard to digest, but in reality is not so, if used in moderation. The best kind for campers is potted cheese, or cream or " snappy " cheese put up in tin foil. If not so protected from air it soon dries out and grows stale. A tin of imported Camembert will be a pleasant surprise on some occasion.

Bread, Biscuits.— It is well to carry enough yeast bread for two or three days, until the game country is reached and camp routine is established. To keep it fresh, each loaf must be sealed up in waxed paper or parchment paper (the latter is best, because it is tough, waterproof, grease-proof). Bread freezes easily; for cold-weather luncheons carry toasted bread.

Hardtack (pilot bread, ship biscuit) can be recommended only for such trips or cruises as do not permit baking. It is a cracker prepared of plain flour and water, not even salted, and kiln-dried to a chip, so as to keep indefinitely, its only enemies being weevils. Get the coarsest grade. To make hardtack palatable, toast it until crisp, or soak in hot coffee and butter it, or at least salt it.

Swedish hardtack, made of whole rye flour, is good for a change.

Plasmon biscuit, imported from England, is the most nutritious breadstuff I have ever used. It is a round cracker, firm but not hard, of good flavor, containing a large percentage of the protein of milk, six of the small biscuits holding as much proteid as a quarter of a pound of beef. Plasmon will be discussed in Volume II, under EMERGENCY RATIONS.

Flour.— Graham and entire-wheat flours contain more protein than patent flour, but this is offset by the fact that it is not so digestible as the protein of standard flour. Practically there is little or no difference between them in the amount of protein assimilated. The same seems to be true of their mineral ingredients.

Many campers depend a good deal on self-raising flour because it saves a little trouble in mixing. But such flour is easily spoiled by dampness, it does not make as good biscuit or flapjacks as one can turn out in camp by doing his own mixing, and it will not do for thickening, dredging, etc.

Flour and meal should be sifted before starting on an expedition: there will be no sieve in camp.

Baking Powder.— Get the best, made with pure cream of tartar. It costs more than the alum powders, and does not go so far, bulk for bulk; but it is much kinder to the stomach. Baking soda will not be needed on short trips, but is required for longer ones, in making sour-dough, as a steady diet of baking-powder bread or biscuit will ruin the stomach, if persisted in for a considerable time. Soda also is useful medicinally.

Corn Meal.— Some like yellow, some prefer white. The flavor of freshly ground meal is best, but the ordinary granulated meal of commerce keeps better, because it has been kiln-dried. Corn meal should not be used as the leading breadstuff, for reasons already given, but johnnycake, corn pancakes, and mush, are a welcome change from hot wheat bread or biscuit, and the average novice at cooking may succeed better with them. The meal is useful to roll fish in, before frying.

Breakfast Cereals.— These according to taste, and for variety sake. Plain cereals, particularly oat meal, require long cooking, either in a double boiler or with constant stirring, to make them digestible; and then there is a messy pot to clean up. They do more harm than good to campers who hurry their cooking. So it is best to buy the partially cooked cereals that take only a few minutes to prepare. Otherwise the "patent breakfast foods" have no more nutritive quality than plain grain; some of them not so much. The notion that bran has remarkable food value is a delusion: it actually makes the protein of the grain less digestible. As for mineral matter, to "build up bone and teeth and brawn," there is enough of it in almost any mixed diet, without swallowing a lot of crude fiber.

Rice, although not very appetising by itself, combines so well in stews or the like, and goes so well in pudding, that it deserves a place in the commissariat.

Macaroni, etc.— The various *paste* (pas-tay), as the Italians call them, take the place of bread, may be cooked in many ways to lend variety, and are especially good in soups, which otherwise would have little nourishing power. Spaghetti, vermicelli, and noodles, all are good in their way. Break macaroni into inch pieces, and pack so that insects cannot get into it. It is more wholesome than flapjacks, and it "sticks to the ribs."

Sweets.— Sugar is stored-up energy, and is assimilated more quickly than any other food. Men in the open soon get to craving sweets.

The "substitute" variously known as saccharin,

saxin, crystallose, is no substitute at all, save in mere sweetening power (in this respect one ounce of it equals about eighteen pounds of sugar). This drug, which is derived from coal tar, has medicinal qualities and injures one's health if persistently taken. It has none of the nutritive value of sugar, and supplies no energy whatever. Its use in food products is forbidden under the Federal pure-food law.

Maple sugar is always welcome. Get the soft kind that can be spread on bread for luncheons. Sirup is easily made from it in camp by simply bringing it to a boil with the necessary amount of water. Ready-made sirup is mean to pack around.

Sweet chocolate (not too sweet) has remarkable sustaining power. It will be mentioned further in Volume II, under EMERGENCY RATIONS.

When practicable, take along some jam and marmalade. The commissaries of the British army were wise when they gave jam an honorable place in Tommy Atkins' field ration. Yes: jam for soldiers in time of war. So many ounces of it, substituted, mind you, for so many ounces of the porky, porky, porky, that has ne'er a streak of lean. So, a little currant jelly with your duck or venison is worth breaking all rules for. Such conserves can be repacked by the buyer in pry-up cans that have been sterilized as recommended under the heading *Butter*.

Fresh Vegetables.— The only ones worth taking along are potatoes and onions. Choose potatoes with small eyes and of uniform medium size, even if you have to buy half a bushel to sort out a peck. They are very heavy and bulky in proportion to their food value; so you cannot afford to be burdened with any but the best. Cereals and beans take the place of potatoes when you go light.

Fresh onions are almost indispensable for seasoning soups, stews, etc. A few of them can be taken along almost anywhere. I generally carry at least one, even on a walking trip. Onions are good for the suddenly overtaxed system, relieve the inordinate

PROVISIONS

thirst that one experiences the first day or two, and assist excretion. Freezing does not spoil onions if they are kept frozen until used.

Beans.— A prime factor in cold weather camping. Take a long time to cook ("soak all day and cook all night" is the rule). Cannot be cooked done at altitudes of five thousand feet and upward. Large varieties cook quickest, but the small white navy beans are best for baking. Pick them over before packing, as there is much waste.

Split Peas.— Used chiefly in making a thick, nourishing soup.

Dehydrated Vegetables.— Much of the flavor of fresh vegetables is lost when the juice is expressed or evaporated, but all of their nutriment is retained and enough of the flavor for them to serve as fair substitutes when fresh vegetables cannot be carried. They help out a camp stew, and may even be served as side dishes if one has butter and milk to season them. Generally they require soaking (which can be done overnight); then they are to be boiled slowly until tender, taking about as much time as fresh vegetables. If cooking is hurried they will be woody and tasteless.

Dehydrated vegetables are very portable, keep in any climate, and it is well to carry some on trips far from civilization.

Canned Vegetables.— In our table of food values it will be noticed that the least nourishing article for its weight and bulk is a can of tomatoes. Yet these " airtights " are great favorites with outdoorsmen, especially in the West and South, where frequently they are eaten raw out of the can. It is not so much their flavor as their acid that is grateful to a stomach overtaxed with fat or canned meat and hot bread three times a day. If wanted only as an adjuvant to soups, stews, rice, macaroni, etc., the more concentrated tomato purée will serve very well.

Canned corn (better still, "kornlet," which is

the concentrated milk of sweet corn) is quite nourishing, and everybody likes it.

A few cans of baked beans (*without* tomato sauce) will be handy in wet weather. The B. & M. ¾-lb. cans are convenient for a lone camper or for two going light.

Nuts.— A handful each of shelled nuts and raisins, with a cake of sweet chocolate, will carry a man far on the trail, or when he has lost it. The kernels of butternuts and hickory nuts have the highest fuel value of our native species; peanuts and almonds are very rich in protein; Brazil nuts, filberts, and pecans, in fat. Peanut butter is a concentrated food that goes well in sandwiches. One can easily make nut butter of any kind (except almonds or Brazil nuts) for himself by using the nut grinder that comes with a kitchen food-chopper, and can add ground dates, ground popcorn, or whatever he likes; but such preparations will soon grow rancid if not sealed air-tight. Nut butter is more digestible than kernels unless the latter are thoroughly chewed.

Fruits.— All fruits are very deficient in protein and (except olives) in fat, but dried fruit is rich in carbohydrates. Fruit acid (that of prunes, dried apricots, and dehydrated cranberries, when fresh fruit cannot be carried) is a good corrective of a too fatty and starchy or sugary diet, and a preventive of scurvy. Most fruits are laxative, and for that reason, if none other, a good proportion of dried fruit should be included in the ration, no matter how light one travels; otherwise one is likely to suffer from constipation when he changes "from town grub to trail grub."

Among canned fruits, those that go farthest are pineapples and blackberries.

Excellent jelly can be made· in camp from dried apples (see recipe in Chapter XXII).

There is much nourishment in dates, figs (those dried round are better than layer figs) and raisins.

PROVISIONS

Pitted dates and seedless raisins are best for light outfits. And do not despise the humble prune; buy the best grade in the market (unknown to landladies) and soak overnight before stewing: it will be a revelation. Take a variety of dried fruits, and mix them in different combinations, sweet and tart, so as not to have the same sauce twice in succession; then you will learn that dried fruits are by no means a poor substitute for fresh or canned ones.

In hot weather I carry a few lemons whenever practicable. Limes are more compact and better medicinally, but they do not keep well. Lime juice in bottles is excellent, if you can carry it.

Citric acid crystals may be used in lieu of lemons when going light, but the flavor is not so good as that of lemonade powder that one can put up for himself. The process is described by A. W. Barnard: "Squeeze out the lemons and sift into the clear juice four to six spoonfuls of sugar to a lemon; let stand a few days if the weather is dry, or a week if wet, till it is dried up, then pulverize and put up into capsules." Gelatin capsules of any size, from 1-oz. down, can be procured at a drugstore. They are convenient to carry small quantities of spices, flavorings, medicines, etc., on a hike.

Vinegar and pickles are suitable only for fixed camps or easy cruises.

Fritures.— Lard is less wholesome than olive oil, or "Crisco," or the other preparations of vegetable fat. Crisco can be heated to a higher temperature than lard without burning, thus ensuring the "surprise" (see Chapter XVI), which prevents getting a fried article sodden with grease; it does as well as lard for shortening; and it can be used repeatedly without transmitting the flavor of one dish to the next one. Olive oil is superior as a friture, especially for fish, but expensive.

Beverages.—The best coffee can only be made from freshly roasted berries. Have it roasted and ground the day before you start, and put up in small air-tight canisters. It loses strength rapidly after a tin has been opened. If you are a connoisseur you will never be tempted more than once by any condensed coffee or substitute.

Tea is a better pick-me-up than coffee or liquor. Even if you don't use it at home, take along on your camping trip enough for midday meals. Tea tabloids are not bad, but I advise using the real thing. On a hike, with no tea-ball, I tie up enough for each pint in a bit of washed cheesecloth, loosely, leaving enough string attached whereby to whisk it out after exactly four minutes' steeping.

However it may be with you at home, leading a sedentary life, you probably will find that tea and coffee do you a world of good when working heartily out-of-doors.

There are exceptions, to be sure; but old campaigners generally will agree with Dr. Hutchinson when, having discussed the necessary solids for a soldier's ration, he says this:

"But is even this dietetic trinity of bread, beef and sugar, with greens and dessert on the side, sufficient? The results of a hundred campaigns have shown that it is not. Man is not merely a stomach and muscles — he is also a bundle of nerves; and they require their share of pabulum. In the early days the nerve-steadier in the soldier's diet used to be supplied in the form of grog, beer, wine, whisky; and up to about one hundred years ago alcohol in some form was considered to be an absolutely indispensable part of the army ration.

"Gradually, however, and by bitter experience, it was realized that alcohol's way of steadying and supporting the nerves was to narcotize them, which practically means poison them; that it gave no nourishment to the body and, instead of improving the digestion and utilization of food, really hindered and interfered with them. Man must have something to drink as well as to eat; but what can be found as a substitute?

"About two centuries ago two new planets swam into our human ken above the dietetic horizon — tea and coffee. They were looked on with great suspicion at first, partly because they were attractive and partly because they were new. They were denounced by the Puritan be-

PROVISIONS

cause they were pleasant, and by the doctor because they were not in the pharmacopœia; but, in spite of bitter opposition, they won their way.

"It is doubtful whether any addition to the comfort of civilized man within the last two hundred years in the realm of dietetics can be mentioned that equals them. Certainly, if we take into consideration the third new article of food, which came in and still goes down with them — sugar — it would be impossible to match them with anything of equal value."

Cocoa is not only a drink but a food. It is best for the evening meal, because it makes one sleepy, whereas tea and coffee have the opposite effect.

Get the soluble kind, if you want it quickly prepared.

Condiments.— Do not leave out a small assortment of condiments wherewith to vary the taste of common articles and serve a new sauce or gravy or pudding now and then.

Salt is best carried in a wooden box. The amount used in cooking and at table is small, but if pelts are to be preserved or game shipped out, considerably more will be needed.

White pepper is better than black. Some Cayenne or Chili should also be taken. Red pepper is not only a good stomachic, but also is fine for a chill (made into a tea with hot water and sugar).

Among condiments I class beef extract, bouillon cubes or capsules, and the like. They are of no use as food, except to stimulate a feeble stomach or furnish a spurt of energy, but invaluable for flavoring camp-made soups and stews when you are far away from beef. The powder called Oystero yields an oyster flavor.

When one is not going into a game country, it is worth while to carry Worcestershire sauce and pure tomato catchup, to relieve the monotony of cured and canned meats or of too much fish.

Mustard is useful not only at table but for medicinal purposes; cloves, not only for its more obvious purposes, but to stick in an onion for a stew, and perchance for a toothache.

Celery and parsley can now be had in dehydrated form. Some sage may be needed for stuffing.

If you aim at cake-making and puddings, ginger and cinnamon may be required. Curry powder is relished by many; its harshness may be tempered with sweet fruits or sugar.

Finally, a half-pint of brandy is worth its weight, for brandy-sauce — but keep it where it can't be filched, or somebody will invent a bellyache instanter.

On short trips, salt and pepper will meet all requirements.

RATION LISTS.— A ration list showing how much food of each kind is required, per man and per week, cannot be figured out satisfactorily unless one knows where the party is going, at what season of the year, how the stuff is to be carried, whether there is to be good chance of game or fish, and something about the men's personal tastes. Still, I may offer some suggestions.

Our army garrison ration often is used as a guide. Introducing the permissible substitutions in ratios given below, it works out as follows: —

U. S. ARMY GARRISON RATIONS
FOR ONE MAN ONE WEEK

Meats, Etc.:

	Lbs.	Oz.		
(½ time) Fresh meats, @ 20 oz. per day	4	6		
(½) Cured or canned, @ 12 oz.	2	10		
Lard, @ 0.64 oz.		4½		
Milk, evaporated, @ 0.5 oz.		3½		
Butter, @ 0.5 oz.		3½		
			7 lbs.	11½ oz.

Bread, Etc.:

	Lbs.	Oz.		
(¼) Hard bread, @ 16 oz.	1	12		
(¾) Flour, meal, @ 18 oz.	5	14½		
Baking powder, @ 1 oz. per lb. flour		6		
(½) Rice, hominy, @ 1.6 oz.		5½		
			8 lbs.	6 oz.

PROVISIONS

Vegetables:

	Lbs.	Oz.		
(½) Beans, @ 2.4 oz.		8½		
Potatoes, canned tomatoes, etc., @ 20 oz.	8	12		
	—	—	9 lbs.	4½ oz.

Fruits, Etc.:

	Lbs.	Oz.		
Prunes, dried apples or peaches, jam, @ 1.28 oz.		9		
Vinegar, @ 0.16 gill		4½		
	—	—		13½ oz.

Sugar, Etc.:

	Lbs.	Oz.		
Sugar, @ 3.2 oz.	1	6½		
Sirup, @ 0.32 gill		10		
	—	—	2 lbs.	½ oz.

Beverages:

	Lbs.	Oz.		
(⅔) Coffee, @ 1.12 oz.........		5¼		
(⅓) Tea, @ 0.32 oz.		¾		
	—	—		6 oz.

Condiments:

	Lbs.	Oz.		
Salt, @ 0.64 oz.		4½		
Pepper, @ 0.04 oz.		¼		
Spices, @ 0.014 oz............		1/10		
Flavoring extracts, @ 0.028 oz.		⅕		
	—	—		5 oz.

One man one week.................	28 lbs.	15 oz.
One man one day	4 lbs.	2 oz.

This is a very liberal ration, but would be so monotonous, if strictly adhered to, that much of it would be unused. Accordingly the soldier's mess is allowed to commute its surplus of staples for luxuries in which the ration is deficient.

For some years it was my practice to weigh personally, and note down at the time, the amount of provisions taken on my camping tours, and often I recorded the quantities left over at the end of the trip. I have also collected many ration lists compiled by practical woodsmen, and have spent considerable time in studying and comparing them. These varied remarkably, not so much in aggregate weights as in the proportions of this and that.

Still, a few general principles have been worked out:

1. When going as light as practicable, and taking the most concentrated (water-free) foods that will digest properly and sustain a man at hard work in the open air, the ration should not be cut down below 2¼ pounds (a ration being one man's food for one day). This is the minimum for mountaineering, arctic exploration, and wherever equipment must be "pared to the bone." This sort of provisioning will be considered in Volume II.

2. People leading an easy life in summer camp do not require so much actual nutriment as those engaged in hard travel, big game hunting, and the like; but they should have plenty of fruits and vegetables, and these things are heavy and bulky.

3. Men working hard in the open, and exposed to the vicissitudes of wilderness life, need a diet rich in protein, fats (especially in cold weather), and sweets. This may not agree with theories of dieticians, but it is the experience of millions of campaigners who know what their work demands. A low-proteid diet may be good for men leading soft lives, and for an occasional freak outdoorsman, but try it on an army in the field, or on a crew of lumberjacks, and you will face stark mutiny.

As a basis upon which the supplies for a party may be calculated, I offer, in the following table, two ration lists, called "light" and "heavy," for one man, one week. The first figures out about 4,900 calories, and the second about 5,300 calories, per man, per day. Either of these is sufficient for a man engaged in hard outdoor work; so the terms "light" and "heavy" do not refer to food values but to actual weights, the first being 3 pounds, aud the second a bit over 5 pounds, per man, per day. The difference is due chiefly to canned goods and fresh vegetables.

Observe that both of these lists include fresh

PROVISIONS

meat. It is assumed that the travelers will go either where they can supply this with game killed or where they can buy fresh meat as it is needed. Otherwise, substitute two-thirds its weight in cured meat.

For men not undergoing great strain, the "light" ration may be reduced, say to 2½ pounds a day.

CRUISER'S AND CAMPER'S RATIONS
FOR ONE MAN ONE WEEK

(Weights are *net*, not including tins, bags, wrappers.)

Meats, Etc.:	LIGHT. Lbs.	Oz.	HEAVY. Lbs.	Oz.	
Fresh meat	3	..	3	..	
Bacon	2	..	2	..	
Canned meat, poultry, fish	..	4	..	4	
Cured fish	..	4	..	4	
Canned soups	..	..	..	10	(1 can)
Dried soups	..	2	..	..	
Fresh eggs	..	..	1	8	(1 doz.)
Dried eggs	..	4	..	..	
Butter	..	8	..	8	
Cheese	..	4	..	4	
Crisco	..	4	..	4	
Evaporated milk	..	6	..	12	
	7	4	9	6	

Bread, Etc.:	Lbs.	Oz.	Lbs.	Oz.
Biscuits (crackers) or fresh bread	1	..	1	..
Wheat flour	4	..	4	..
Corn meal	1	..	1	..
Baking powder	..	4	..	4
Macaroni, etc.	..	4	..	4
Rice	..	6	..	6
Other cereal	..	8	..	8
	7	6	7	6

Vegetables:	Lbs.	Oz.	Lbs.	Oz.	
Fresh potatoes	..	..	5	..	
Fresh onions	..	8	..	8	
Canned tomatoes	..	..	2	..	(1 can)
Canned corn	..	..	..	10	(½ can)
Dried beans	..	8	..	8	
Dehydrated vegetables	..	8	..	..	
	1	8	8	10	

CAMPING AND WOODCRAFT

Fruits, Acids, Nuts:	LIGHT Lbs.	LIGHT Oz.	HEAVY Lbs.	HEAVY Oz.	
Fresh lemons	..	..	1	..	(½ doz.)
Lemonade capsules	..	6	..	..	
Canned fruits	..	..	4	..	(2 cans)
Dried apples, apricots, prunes, cranberries	..	12	..	..	
Raisins, dates, figs	..	8	..	8	
Pickles (sour)	..	..	..	6	
Shelled nuts, or nut butter	..	4	..	4	
	1	14	6	2	

Sweets:	Lbs.	Oz.	Lbs.	Oz.
Sugar (granulated)	..	14	..	14
Maple sugar (soft)	..	8	..	8
Chocolate (medium sweet)	..	12	..	8
Jam, jelly, marmalade	..	..	..	12
	2	2	2	10

Beverages:	Lbs.	Oz.	Lbs.	Oz.
Coffee	..	8	..	8
Tea	..	1	..	1
	..	9	..	9

Condiments:	Lbs.	Oz.	Lbs.	Oz.
*Salt	..	4	..	4
White pepper	..	¼	..	¼
Red pepper	..	⅛	..	⅛
Mustard (mixed)	..	....	..	1
Celery, parsley (dehydrated)	..	⅜	..	⅜
Bouillon cubes	..	1	..	1
Nutmeg, cloves, cinnamon, ginger, curry powder	..	¼	..	¼
Worcestershire sauce	..	..	..	2
Tomato catsup	..	..	..	2
	..	6	..	11
One man one week	21	1	35	6
One man one day	3	..	5	1

If butter is not carried, its weight in bacon should be added to the list; similarly other substitutions can be made to suit taste and circumstances.

The second list provides enough eggs and milk

* Not allowing for preparing skins and salting horses.

PROVISIONS

to allow their use liberally in cooking. Its ration is of about the same weight as that of the U. S. Navy.

PACKING FOOD.— Meat of any kind will quickly mould or spoil if packed in tins from which air is not exhausted. Wrap your bacon, pork, etc., in parchment paper, which is grease-proof (you can buy it from a mail-order house — for small quantities get parchment paper ice blankets and cut to suit), then enclose the meat in loose cheesecloth bags that can be hung up in camp, secure from insects.

Flour should not be carried in the original sacks: they wet through or absorb moisture from the air, snag easily, and burst under the strain of a lashrope. Pack your flower, cereals, vegetables, dried fruits, etc., in the round-bottomed paraffined bags sold by outfitters (various sizes, from 10 lbs. down), which are damp-proof and have the further merit of standing up on their bottoms instead of always falling over. Put a tag on each bag and label it in *ink*. These small bags may then be stowed in 9-inch waterproof canvas provision bags (see outfitter's catalogues), but in that case the thing you want is generally at the bottom. A much handier pack for horse or canoe is the side-opening one shown in Fig. 101.

Butter, lard, ground coffee, tea, sugar, jam, matches, go in pry-up tin cans, sold by outfitters (small quantities in mailing tubes), or in common capped tins with tops secured by surgeon's plaster. Get pepper and spices in shaker-top cans, or, if you carry common shakers, cover tops with cloth and snap stout rubber bands around them.

Salt, as it draws moisture, is best carried in a wooden box or in mailing tubes.

Often it is well to carry separately enough food to last the party between the jumping-off place and the main camp site, as it saves the bother of breaking bulk *en route*.

When transportation is easy it pays to pack the bread, bags of flour, etc., in a tin wash-boiler or two, which are wrapped in burlaps and crated. These make capital grub boxes in camp, securing their contents from wet, insects and rodents. Ants in summer and mice at all times are downright pests of the woods, to say nothing of the wily coon, the predatory mink, the inquisitive skunk, and the fretful porcupine. The boilers are useful, too, on many occasions, to catch rain-water, boil clothes, waterproof and dye tents, and so forth. After all these things have been done in them they are properly seasoned for cooking a burgoo.

Camp chests are very convenient when it is practicable to carry them. In fixed camp an old trunk will do; but if you are traveling from place to place, the boxes should be small, weighing not over fifty or sixty pounds each when packed, so that one man can easily handle them unassisted. If they are specially made, cottonwood is the best material (if thoroughly seasoned boards can be had—otherwise it warps abominably). It is the strongest and toughest wood for its weight that we have, and will not splinter. For the ends and lids of small chests, ⅝-inch stuff is thick enough, and ⅜-inch for the sides, bottoms and trays. The bottom should have a pair of ⅝-inch cleats for risers and the top a similar pair to keep it from warping, unless the chests are to go on pack animals. Straphinges and hasp, a brass padlock and broad leather end-straps (not drop-handles) should be provided, and the chest painted.

The best size is 24 x 18 x 9 inches, this being convenient for canoes and pack-saddles. A pine grocery box of this size, with ¾-inch ends and ⅜-inch sides, top, and bottom, weighs only 10 pounds, and will answer the purpose very well. Screw a wooden handle on each end, say 5 x 2 inches, with a hand-hold gouged out of the under side.

PROVISIONS

Chests intended to be used as hanging cupboards in camp should have shelf boards packed in them, and a bread board for rolling out biscuit dough and pastry. One box should be selected with a view to using it as a camp refrigerator or spring box (see Chapter XII). For a trip by wagon a regular "chuck box" may be built, with a drop front for serving table (held by light chains when open). This box is carried upright at the rear end of the wagon *à la* cow outfit.

When cruising where there are no portages it saves lots of time and bother if you build beforehand a light mess chest partitioned to hold utensils and all the food needed for, say, a week. This may be fitted with detachable legs, and the lid so fitted that it is supported level when opened, forming a table.

A LAST LOOK AROUND.— Check off every article in the outfit as it is stowed, and keep the inventory for future reference. Then note what is left over at the end of the trip. This will help in outfitting for the next season.

There are several things to be looked after in good season before starting on a camping trip. If your shoes are new, oil them and break them in. If your rifle is new, do not dream of carrying it into the wilderness until you have "sighted it up," testing the elevations at various ranges, and making sure that the sights are accurately aligned. If your fishing tackle is old, overhaul and test it thoroughly. If you have a hollow tooth, get it filled. Pare your nails closely, or they will soon be badly broken. Get your hair cropped short. See that you have a good supply of small change when you start. Don't carry off your bunch of keys. Be on hand early at the station and see to it personally that your humble but precious duffel all gets aboard.

And now, *bon voyage!*

CHAPTER XII
CAMP MAKING

As a rule, good camp sites are not found along the beaten road. Of course, water is the prime essential, and in a country where water is scarce, you will stop at an old camping ground; otherwise it is best to avoid such a place: for one thing, you don't want to be bothered with interlopers, and for another, the previous occupants will have stripped the neighborhood of good kindling and downwood, and may have left a legacy of rubbish and fleas.

A pleasant stopping-place is seldom far to seek in a hilly country that is well wooded. There are exceptions, as in the Ozarks, where the rock is a porous limestone, the drainage mostly is underground, and there are no brooks, nor are springs as common as one would expect, though when you do strike one it is a big one. Here a traveler must depend for water chiefly on the creeks and rivers, which may be miles apart.

In a level region, whether it be open plain or timbered bottom land, good water and a high and dry site may be hard to find.

In any case, when men are journeying through a wild country that is strange to them, they should begin at least two hours before sunset to keep a bright lookout for a good place on which to spend the night, and when such is found they had better accept it at once than run the risk of "murdering a night" farther on, wherever the powers of darkness may force them to stop.

CAMP SITES.— The essentials of a good camp site are these:

CAMP MAKING

1. Pure water.
2. Wood that burns well. In cold weather there should be either an abundance of sound downwood or some standing hardwood trees that are not too big for easy felling.
3. An open spot, level enough for the tent and campfire, but elevated above its surroundings so as to have good natural drainage. It must be well above any chance overflow from the sudden rise of a neighboring stream. Observe the previous flood marks.
4. Grass or browse for the horses (if there are any) and bedding for the men.
5. Straight poles for the tent, or trees convenient for attaching the ridge rope.
6. Security against the spread of fire.
7. Exposure to direct sunlight during a part of the day, especially during the early morning hours.
8. In summer, exposure to whatever breezes may blow; in cold weather, protection against the prevailing wind.
9. Privacy.

Water, wood, and good drainage may be all you need for a " one-night stand," but the other points, too, should be considered when selecting the site for a fixed camp.

WATER.— Be particularly careful about the purity of your water supply. You come, let us say, to a mountain brook, that issues from thick forest. It ripples over clean rocks, it bubbles with air, it is clear as crystal, and cool to your thirsty throat. " Surely that is good water." But do you know where it comes from? Every mountain cabin is built close to a spring-branch. Somewhere up that brook there may be a clearing; in that clearing, a house; in that house, a case of dysentery or typhoid fever. I have known several cases of infection from just such a source. It is not true that running water purifies itself.

When one must use well-water let him note the

surrounding drainage. If the well is near a stable or outhouse, or if dishwater is thrown near it, let it alone. A well in sandy soil is more or less filtered by nature, but rocky or clayey earth may conduct disease germs a considerable distance underground. Never drink from the well of an abandoned farm: there is no telling what may have fallen into it.

A spring issuing from the living rock is worthy of confidence. Even if it be but a trickle you can scoop out a basin to receive it that soon will clear itself.

Sometimes a subaqueous spring may be found near the margin of a lake or river by paddling close inshore and trailing your hand in the water. When a cold spot is noted, go ashore and dig a few feet back from the water's edge. I have found such spring exits in the Mississippi some distance from the bank, and, by weighting a canteen, tying a string to it and another to the stopper, have brought up cool water from the river bed.

Disease germs are of animal, not vegetable, origin. Still waters are not necessarily unwholesome, even though there be rotting vegetation in them: the water of cedar and cypress swamps is good to drink, wherever there is a deep pool of it, unless polluted from some outside source. Lake water is safe if no settlements are on its border; but even so large a body as Lake Champlain has been condemned by state boards of health because of the sewage that runs into it.

When a stream is in flood it is likely to be contaminated by decayed animal matter.

Alkaline Water.— When traveling in an alkali country, carry some vinegar or limes or lemons, or (better) a glass-stoppered bottle of hydrochloric acid. One teaspoonful of hydrochloric (muriatic) neutralizes about a gallon of water, and if there should be a little excess it will do no harm, but rather assist digestion. In default of acid, you may

CAMP MAKING

add a little Jamaica ginger and sugar to the water, making a weak ginger tea.

Muddy Water.—I used to clarify Mississippi water by stirring cornmeal in it and letting it settle, or by stirring a lump of alum in it until the mud began to precipitate, and then decanting the clear water. Lacking these, one can take a good handful of grass, tie it roughly in the form of a cone six or eight inches high, invert it, pour water slowly into the grass, and a runnel of comparatively clear water will trickle down through the small end.

The following simple method of purifying muddy water is recommended by H. G. Kegley:

"Dip up what is needed, place it in such vessels as are available, and treat it to condensed milk, in the proportion of two tablespoonfuls of milk to five gallons of water. The sediment settles in a very short time. Next morning, if you desire to carry some of the water with you through the day, pour it from the settlings, and then boil the water and skim it. In that way the cream and any possibility of sourness will be removed. Water thus clarified remains palatable so long as it lasts."

Stagnant Water.— A traveler may be reduced to the extremity of using stagnant or even putrid water; but this should never be done without first boiling it. Some charred wood from the camp fire should be boiled with the water; then skim off the scum, strain, and set the water aside to cool. Boiling sterilizes, and charcoal deodorizes.

I quote the following incident from Johnson's *Getting Gold.*—

"I once rode forty-five miles with nearly beaten horses to a native well, or rock hole, to find water, the next stage being nearly fifty miles further. The well was found, but the water in it was very bad; for in it was the body of a dead kangaroo, which had apparently been there for weeks. The wretched horses, half frantic with thirst, did manage to drink a few mouthfuls, but we could not. I filled our largest billycan, holding about a gallon, slung it over the fire and added, as the wood burnt down, charcoal, till the top was covered to a depth of two inches. With the charcoal there was, of course, a little ash containing bi-carbonate of potassium. The effect was marvellous. So soon as the horrible soup came to the boil, the impurities coagulated, and after keeping it at boiling temperature for about half an hour, it was removed from the fire, the cinders skimmed out, and the water allowed to settle, which it did very quickly. It was then decanted off into an ordinary prospector's pan, and some used to make tea (the flavor of which can be better imagined than described); the remainder was allowed to stand all night, a few pieces of charcoal being added. In the morning it was bright, clear, and absolutely sweet."

Filters are not to be depended upon to purify water. At best they only clarify; they do not sterilize it. A filter, to be of any use, must be cleaned out every day or two, and the sand forming the upper layer must be thoroughly washed or replaced; otherwise the filter itself becomes a breeding-place for germs.

To Cool Water.— Travelers in arid regions carry water bags of heavy canvas or linen duck. These, when filled, constantly " sweat " or exude enough moisture to cool the contents of the bag by evaporation. Wet canteens do the same. A covered pail or other vessel can be used: wrap cloths around it, keep them wet, and hang in a current of air.

FUEL.— In summer camping little firewood is used, but in cold weather an abundance is required. Some kinds of wood make fine fires, others are poor fuel or worthless: they are classified in the next chapter. In any case there should be plenty of sound dead wood to cook with.

When traveling with a team where fuel is scarce, make a practice of tossing into the wagon any good chunks that you may find along the road.

TENT GROUND.—Avoid low ground. Seek an open spot that is level enough for the purpose, but one that has good natural drainage. Wherever you may be, pitch your tent on a rise or slight slope instead of in a depression where water will gather if it rains. Don't trust a fair sky.

If you camp on the bank of a stream, be sure to

get well above the flood-marks left by previous freshets or overflows. Observe the more or less continuous line of dead grass, leaves, twigs, mud, and other flotsam or hurrah's-nests left in bushes along the water-front.

Precautions as to elevation and drainage are especially needful in those parts of our country that are subject to cloudbursts. I have seen a ravine that had been stone-dry for months fill fifteen feet deep, in a few minutes, with a torrent that swept trees and bowlders along with it; and it is quite common in many parts of the West for wide bottoms to be flooded in a night. When I was a boy in Iowa, a "mover" camped for the night on an island in Coon River, near our place. He had a bag of gold coin, but was out of rations. A sudden flood left him marooned the next morning on a knoll scarce big enough for his team and wagon. He subsisted for a week, like his horses, on the inner bark of cottonwood, and when a rescue party found him he was kicking his bag of gold over the few yards of dry ground that were left of his domain.

Bottom lands, and deep woods where the sun rarely penetrates, should be avoided, when practicable, for they are damp lairs at best, and in warm weather they are infested with mosquitoes. Keep away from thickets in summer: they are stifling and "buggy."

A ravine or narrow valley between steep hills is a trap for fog, and the cold, heavy air from the head of the hollow pours down it at night, while an undertow of warmer air drawing upward now and then makes the smoke from one's camp-fire shift most annoyingly. Besides a ravine gets too little sunlight.

New clearings in the forest are unhealthy, for the sun gets in on plants that are intolerant of strong light, they rot, and poisonous gases arise from their decay, as well as from the recently disturbed soil.

If one is obliged to camp in a malarial region he should not leave the camp-fire until the sun is up and the fog dispelled.

Sandy beaches, and low, gravelly points, are likely to swarm in summer with midges.

Sandy soil does not afford good holding-ground for the tent pegs; neither does a loamy or clayey soil after it gets soaked from rain. The best ground is gravelly earth: it holds well, and permits the rapid filtering through of surface water. A clay top-soil holds water and is soon trodden into sticky mud after a rain.

PRECAUTIONS AGAINST FIRE.— If the camp site is strewn with leaves, cut an evergreen branch, or, with some other makeshift broom or rake, clear all the ground of leaves, pile them in the bare spot, and burn them, lest a spark set the woods afire. In evergreen or cypress forests there is often a thick scurf on the ground (dead needles, etc.) that is very inflammable. Always scrape this away before building a fire. In a dry forest carpet, or in a punky log, fire may smoulder unnoticed for several days; then, when a breeze fans it into flame, it may start a conflagration. *One can't be too careful about fire in the woods.* Never leave a camp fire or a cooking fire to burn itself out. Drench it with water, or smother it absolutely by stamping earth upon it.

NEIGHBORHOOD OF TREES.— It is a common blunder to pitch the tent directly under the " natural shelter " of a big tree. This is pleasant enough at midday, but makes the tent catch drip from dew and keeps it from drying after a rain; besides, it may be positively dangerous. One of the first things to do in choosing the tent site is to see that it is not within reach of falling limbs. A tree branch falling forty or fifty feet, and striking a tent at night, is something to be remembered — if you survive. Shun the neighborhood of tall trees that are shallow-rooted, and of those with brittle limbs (the aspens,

CAMP MAKING 215

poplars, cottonwood, catalpa, butternut, yellow locust, silver maple), and any with unsound branches.

Dead trees are always unsafe. Every woodsman has often known them to come thundering down without the least warning when there was not so much as a zephyr astir. A tree that leans toward camp from a steep hillside hard by is a menace, and so is any near-by tree with a hollow butt.

TREES AND LIGHTNING.—I have never seen, nor heard of, a beech tree that had been struck by lightning, although beeches are plentiful on many battle-scarred mountains where stricken trees of other species can be noted by the score. Miss Keeler says on this point: " There was so firm a belief among the Indians that a beech tree was proof against lightning that on the approach of a thunder-storm they took refuge under its branches with full assurance of safety. . . . This popular belief has recently had scientific verification. . . . The general conclusion from a series of experiments is that trees ' poor in fat ' like the oak, willow, poplar, maple, elm and ash, oppose much less resistance to the electric current than trees ' rich in fat ' like the beech, chestnut, linden and birch."

In this connection I may note that there is no truth in the old adage that " lightning does not strike twice in the same place." At Takoma Park, a suburb of Washington, on July 19, 1915, a bolt of lightning struck an oak tree standing in the garden before the administration building of the Seventh-Day Adventists. After the storm had passed, several people went out from the building to view the damage done to the tree. Three of them lingered. A second bolt, from a clear sky, struck the same tree, killed two of the people under it, and knocked the other unconscious.

Electricity follows not only the trunk of a tree but also the drip that falls from it in a rain.

SHADE.— In summer it is well to camp where one's tent will be shaded from the afternoon sun, as otherwise it will get very hot, but morning sun should strike the tent fairly, to dry it, lest the canvas mildew and the interior get damp and musty. The wetter the climate, and the thicker the surrounding forest, the greater need of such exposure. Mildew attacks leather first, then woolens, and cottons last of all.

EXPOSURE.— As a general rule, an easterly or southeasterly frontage is best, not only to admit early sunlight and rouse you betimes, but also because, in most regions, it is the quarter least given to high winds and driving rains. Sudden and violent storms usually come up out of the southwest. This is true nearly everywhere: hence the sailor calls his tarp hat a " sou-wester."

Other considerations may govern the case. In hot weather we want exposure to whatever cool breezes may blow, and they are governed by local features. Late in the season we will take advantage of whatever natural windbreak we can find, such as the edge of a forest, the lee of a cliff, of a large rock, or of an evergreen thicket. This may make a difference of 10° or 15° in temperature. A rock absorbs the sun's heat slowly all day and parts with it slowly at night.

A grassy glade or meadow is colder than bare earth, sand, or rock. The air on a knoll is considerably warmer than that of flat land only a few feet below it.

PRIVACY.— A camp should not be exposed to view from a public road nor be in the track of picnickers, idle countrymen, vagabonds, or other unwelcome guests. One can save much annoyance by a little forethought in this matter.

GOOD CAMP SITES.— Often in traveling a party must put up for the night on unfavorable ground; but granting that there is much choice in the matter, then select, in summer, an open knoll, a low ridge, or, better, still, a bold, rocky point jutting out into a river or lake. A low promontory catches the

CAMP MAKING

breezes from both sides, which disperse fog and insects, and it is soon dried whenever the sun shines.

In cold weather seek an open, park-like spot in the forest, where surrounding trees will break the wind; or a " bench " (natural terrace backed by a cliff) on the leeward side of a hill. In the latter case, build your fire against the cliff, and shield the tent with a wind-break. The rock will reflect heat upon the tent, and will serve as a smoke-conductor as well.

On a hillside that is mostly bare, if there be a thicket or a cluster of evergreen trees, get on the downhill side of it. The stream of cold air from above will jump this obstacle and will leave an eddy of comparatively warm, still air immediately below it.

The best site for a fixed camp is near a river or lake, or on a bold, wooded islet, with a bathing beach, boating and fishing waters. A picturesque outlook is desirable, of course, but not if it makes the camp too prominent a landmark and so robs it of the privacy that refined people appreciate in camp as anywhere else.

SYSTEM IN CAMPING.— The celerity with which a camp is made depends upon the training and willingness of the men, and the system by which their duties are parceled. Let us suppose that there are four in the party, besides the teamster or packer. Then let No. 1, who is cook, get out the provisions and utensils, rig up the fireplace, build a fire, and prepare the food for cooking, while No. 2 is rustling wood and water. Meantime Nos. 3 and 4 clear the ground and smooth it off, cut tent pegs and poles, unpack the tent, and summon all hands for a minute, if they are needed, to assist in raising the tent and pegging it " square." Then the cook goes on with his proper duties, the axeman cuts and beds a chopping-block and gets in night-wood, and the canvasmen turn bed-makers. Thus, by the time supper is ready, which will be within an hour, or less, the camp will be properly made, and every one's work is done save the unfortunate scullion's.

When camping with a pack-train, pile the packs neatly together and cover them with canvas, and similarly pile and protect the saddles, making especially sure that the lash ropes cannot get wet, and that nothing will be buried out of sight, off somewhere by itself, if snow falls during the night. Soldierly system in all such matters pays a big dividend in time and good temper.

Even when stopping overnight, have a place for everything and let everything be in its place. Novices or shiftless folk strew things about and can't find them when needed. That is one reason why it takes them twice as long as it should to make or break camp, and it is why they are forever losing this and that, or leaving them behind and forgetting them till they reach the next stopping place.

If obliged to pitch the tent where there is not good natural drainage, trench it, if the weather be at all dubious. It is miserable business to crawl out into a driving storm at night and dig a ditch by lantern-light — worse still to awake to a realization that trenching is too late to save your soaking possessions. "Make yourself ready in your cabin for the mischance of the hour, if so it hap."

DINING PLACE.— It is wearisome to eat from the ground; and as Thoreau says, "None is so poor that he need sit on a pumpkin — that is shiftlessness." If stopping more than a day in one place, set up a rustic table and benches, away from the tent and near the cooking fire. Drive four stakes into the ground for legs, nail cleats across the ends, and cover the top with boards or straight sticks. If you have no nails, use forked stakes.

By the way, nearly every made-up picture of a camp shows crotches cut like Fig. 109. Why, good artists — why? You may hunt half a day in the woods to find such a natural crotch, and, if you should find it, the thing would be good-for-nothing

CAMP MAKING

as a stake, because you couldn't drive it without splitting it. A fork like Fig. 110 can be found anywhere; cut it as shown by the dotted lines, and

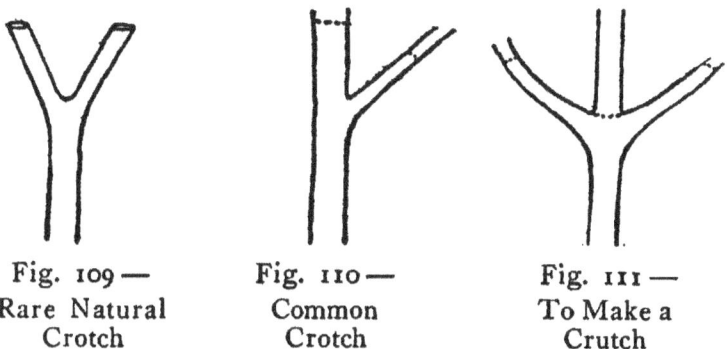

Fig. 109 —
Rare Natural
Crotch

Fig. 110 —
Common
Crotch

Fig. 111 —
To Make a
Crutch

it will drive all right. If somebody is injured and needs a crutch, pick out a sapling with limbs growing opposite, as in Fig. 111, cut out the central stem, trim, and shave down.

A comfortable height for the table is 30 inches, for the benches 18 inches. The latter are made in the same way as the table. Three widths of 10-inch boards make a good table top, and one suffices for each bench.

If you have a spare tent fly or tarpaulin, rig it over the dining table as a canopy. If no trees stand convenient for stretching it, set up two forked posts, lay a ridge pole on them, and guy out the sides to similar frames or to whatever may grow handy. To set a long stake, sharpen the butt end, hold the pole vertically, and make a hole in the ground by working the stick up and down as a quarryman does a long drill.

A table, bench, or shelf, can easily be set up wherever two trees grow close enough together. Nail a cross-piece from one to the other, and a similar one at same level on the other side, then cover with straight sticks or pieces of board.

COMMISSARIAT.— If food is carried in side-opening bags, suspend them from a horizontal pole run from tree to tree or from forked stakes. A cupboard made from packing boxes can be hung up in the same way, to keep vermin out. If ants are troublesome, the edibles can be hung up by wires, in a place where they will be sheltered from sun and rain.

In a stationary camp there should be a separate commissary tent, preferably of the baker style, as its door makes a good awning to work under in wet weather. Do not set boxes or bags of provisions on the ground, but on sticks, to keep dampness away from them.

RACKS or hangers for utensils, dish towels, etc., are improvised in many ways: a bush trimmed with stubs left on, and driven in the ground where it is wanted, inverted crotches nailed to a tree, and so on. Pegs of hard wood whittled to a blunt point can be driven into the trunk of a softwood tree by first making a vertical axe gash at the spot where the peg is to go.

COLD STORAGE.—Butter and milk should not be stored near anything that has a pronounced odor, for they would be tainted. As soon as the camp ground is reached the butter tin or jar should be placed in a net or bag and sunk in the spring or cold brook, the string being tied to the bank so that a freshet may not carry the food away or bury it out of sight. Later, if you stay in that place, a little rock-lined well can be dug near the spring, and covered securely so that 'coons and porcupines cannot plunder it.

Meat and fish may be kept fresh until consumed by digging a hole and putting a packing box in it, surrounding the sides and bottom of the box with six inches or more of gravel, and covering top of box with burlap or something similar. Keep the gravel and the burlap wet, and cover all with wet evergreen boughs.

If you have ice, a refrigerator can be made like the fireless cooker described in Chapter IV; or bore a few holes for drainage in the bottom of a box

CAMP MAKING

or barrel, sink it in the ground to its top, and cover with burlap or a blanket.

At a cabin in the Smokies, where I lived alone for three years, I had a spring box like the one shown in Fig. 112, which kept things cool and safe in the warmest weather, yet was easy for me to get

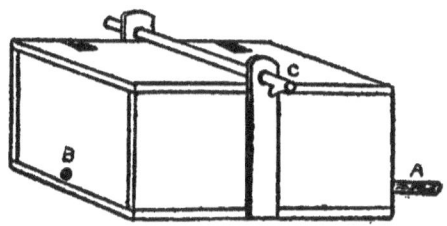

Fig. 112 — Spring Box

into. A short iron pipe at *A* entered the spring; the box inclined slightly toward the outlet *B;* pails and jars sat on flat rocks inside; the top was fastened by the round stick *C* passing through auger holes in the upright cleats.

Caches for provisions and other articles will be described in Volume II.

TENT FURNISHINGS.— If staying more than a night in one place, fit up the tent with hangers from which spare clothing, knapsacks and pouches, wall pockets, lantern, guns, and other loose articles may be suspended where they are kept dry, out of the way, and handy to get at. In a wall tent, plant a forked stake at each corner and lay a pole on them along each side, with nails in it. Guns are laid on shorter stakes underneath these. At the rear end you may set up a set of shelves for odds and ends.

If you have candles and no lantern, cut a stick long enough to hold the light as high as you want it, sharpen one end to shove in the ground, split the other end a little, put a loop of bark horizontally in the cleft, the candle in the loop, and draw tight against the stick. Half a potato, with a hole scooped in it, or a small can filled with earth, makes a portable candlestick.

FENCE.— Wild hogs are literally the *bêtes noires* of southern campers. Your thin-flanked, long-legged, sharp-nosed razorback, with tusks gleaming from his jaws — he or she of the third or further removed generation of feral lawlessness — is the most perverse, fearless, and maliciously destructive brute in America, wolverines or " Indian devils " not excepted. Shooting his tail off does not discourage him, rocks and clubs are his amusement, and no hint to leave that is weaker than a handful of red pepper baked inside a pone o' bread will drive him away. A hog-proof fence around camp, unsightly though it be, is one's only safeguard in southern wildwoods.

WASH-STAND.— A shelf between two trees, made as previously described, is best for this purpose. It should be so situated that wash-water will be thrown directly into a stream, or at least where it will quickly drain away from the camp, so as not to attract flies.

If one's ablutions are performed in the stream itself, drive a stick in the ground and nail the lid of a tin box to the top of it for a soap-dish.

CAMP SANITATION.— Nothing is cleaner, sweeter, wholesomer, than a wildwood unspoiled by man; and few spots are more disgusting than a " piggy " camp, with slops thrown everywhere, empty cans and broken bottles littering the ground, and organic refuse left festering in the sun, breeding disease germs, to be spread abroad by the swarms of flies. I have seen one of Nature's gardens, an ideal health resort, changed in a few months by a logging crew into an abomination and a pest-hole where typhoid and dysentery wrought deadly vengeance.

Destroy at once all refuse that would attract flies, or bury it where they cannot get at it.

Fire is the absolute disinfectant. Burn all solid kitchen refuse as fast as it accumulates. When a can of food is emptied toss it on the fire and burn it out, then drop it in a sink-hole, that you have

CAMP MAKING 223

dug for slops and unburnable trash, and cover it with earth or ashes so no mosquitoes can breed in it after a rainfall.

The sink should be on the downhill side of camp, and where it cannot pollute the water supply. Sprinkle kerosene on it, or burn it out frequently with a brush fire.

A latrine, as substitute for a closet, is one of the first things to be provided. A rude but sanitary

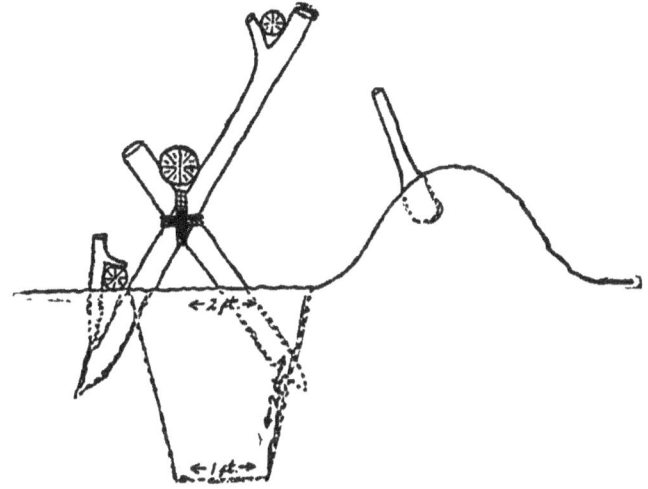

Fig. 113 — Latrine

one that can be made in a short time is shown in Fig. 113. The excavated earth is piled at the rear, and a paddle is left in it to cover excreta every time the place is used. (Whoever wrote Deuteronomy was a good camper.) The log used as seat, and the back-rest, are removable, so that a fire can be built in the trench every now and then from dead brush. Ashes and charcoal are good disinfectants in themselves. Dry earth does very well; but the trench should be burnt out after a rain.

A muslin or brush screen six feet high may be set around the latrine on stakes. A bathing screen can be similarly arranged at the water's edge.

CAMP CONVENIENCES.— A chopping-block is the first thing needed about a camp. The axe, when not in use, should always be stuck in that particular block, where any one can find it when wanted, and where it will not injure men or dogs.

Do not let the axe lie outdoors on a very cold night; the frost would make it brittle, so that the steel might shiver on the first knot you struck the next morning.

Stretch a stout line between two trees where the sunlight will strike, and air your blankets on it every day or two when the weather is pleasant. Against a straight tree near the tent make a rack, somewhat like a billiard-cue rack, in which fishing rods can be stood, full rigged, without danger of being blown down.

Of course, it takes time and brisk work to make everything snug and trim around camp; but it pays, just the same, to spend a couple of days at the start in rigging up such conveniences as I have described, and getting in a good supply of wood and kindling. To rush right off hunting or fishing, and leave the camp in disorder, is to eat your dough before it is baked.

CHAPTER XIII
THE CAMP-FIRE

"I am a woodland fellow, sir, that always loved a great fire."— *All's Well that Ends Well.*

Cold night weighs down the forest bough,
  Strange shapes go flitting through the gloom.
But see — a spark, a flame, and now
  The wilderness is home!
—*Edwin L. Sabin.*

The forest floor is always littered with old leaves, dead sticks, and fallen trees. During a drought this rubbish is so tinder-dry that a spark falling in it may start a conflagration; but through a great part of the year the leaves and sticks that lie flat on the ground are too moist, at least on their under side, to ignite readily. If we rake together a pile of leaves, cover it higgledy-piggledy with dead twigs and branches picked up at random, and set a match to it, the odds are that it will result in nothing but a quick blaze that soon dies down to a smudge. Yet that is the way most of us tried to make our first outdoor fires.

One glance at a camper's fire tells what kind of a woodsman he is. It is quite impossible to prepare a good meal over a heap of smoking chunks, a fierce blaze, or a great bed of coals that will warp iron and melt everything else.

If one would have good meals cooked out of doors, and would save much time and vexation — in other words, if he wants to be comfortable in the woods, he must learn how to produce at will either (1) a quick, hot little fire that will boil water in a jiffy, and will soon burn down to embers that are not too ardent for frying; or (2) a solid bed of long-lived coals that will keep up a steady, glowing, smokeless heat for baking, roasting, or slow boiling; or (3) a big log fire that will throw its heat forward on the ground, and into a tent or lean-to, and will last several hours without replenishing.

LUNCHEON FIRE.— For a noonday lunch, or any other quick meal, when you have only to boil coffee and fry something, a large fire is not wanted. Drive a forked stake in the ground, lay a green stick across it, slanting upward from the ground, and weight the lower end with a rock, so you can easily regulate the height of the pot. The slanting stick should be notched, or have the stub of a twig left at its upper end, to hold the pot bail in place, and should be set at such an angle that the pot swings about a foot clear of the ground.

Then gather a small armful of sound, dry twigs from the size of a lead pencil to that of your finger. Take no twig that lies flat on the ground, for such are generally damp or rotten. Choose hardwood, if there is any, for it lasts well.

Select three of your best sticks for kindling. Shave each of them almost through, for half its length, leaving lower end of shavings attached to the stick, one under the other. Stand these in a tripod, under the hanging pot, with their curls down. Around them build a *small* conical wigwam of the other sticks, standing each on end and slanting to a common center. The whole affair is no bigger than your hat. Leave free air spaces between the sticks. Fire requires air, and plenty of it, and it burns best when it has something to climb up on; hence the wigwam construction. Now touch off the shaved sticks, and in a moment you will have a small blast furnace under the pot. This will get up steam in a hurry. Feed it with small sticks as needed.

Meantime get two bed-sticks, four or five inches

THE CAMP-FIRE

thick, or a pair of flat rocks, to support the frying pan. The firewood will all drop to embers soon after the pot boils. Toss out the smoking butts, leaving only clear, glowing coals. Put your bedsticks on either side, parallel and level. Set the pan on them, and fry away. So, in twenty minutes from the time you drove your stake, the meal will be cooked.

A man acting without system or forethought, in even so simple a matter as this, can waste an hour in pottering over smoky mulch, or blistering himself before a bonfire, and it will be an ill mess of half-burned stuff that he serves in the end.

DINNER FIRE.— First get in plenty of wood and kindling. If you can find two large flat rocks, or several small ones of even height, use them as andirons; otherwise lay down two short cuts off a five- or six-inch log, facing you and about three feet apart. On these rocks or billets lay two four-foot logs parallel, and several inches apart, as rests for your utensils. Arrange the kindling between and under them, with small sticks laid across the top of the logs, a couple of long ones lengthwise, then more short ones across, another pair lengthwise, and thicker short ones across. Then light it. Many prefer to light the kindling at once and feed the fire gradually; but I do as above, so as to have an even glow under several pots at once, and then the sticks will all burn down to coals together.

This is the usual way to build a cooking fire when there is no time to do better. The objection is that the supporting logs must be close enough together to hold up the pots and pans, and, being round, this leaves too little space between them for the fire to heat their bottoms evenly; besides, a pot is liable to slip and topple over. A better way, if one has time, is to hew both the inside surfaces and the tops of the logs flat. Space these supports close enough together at one end for the narrowest pot and wide enough apart at the other for the frying-pan.

If you carry fire-irons, as recommended in a previous chapter, much bother is saved. Simply lay down two flat rocks or a pair of billets far enough apart for the purpose, place the flat irons on them, and space them to suit the utensils.

If a camp grate is used, build a crisscross fire of short sticks under it.

Split wood is better than round sticks for cooking; it catches easier and burns more evenly.

CAMP CRANE.— Pots for hot water, stews, coffee, and so on, are more manageable when hung above the fire. The heat can easily be regulated, the pots hanging low at first to boil quickly, and then being elevated or shifted aside to simmer.

Set up two forked stakes about five feet apart and four feet to the crotches. Across them lay a green stick (lug-pole) somewhat thicker than a broomstick. Now cut three or four green crotches from branches, drive a nail in the small end of each, or cut a notch in it, invert the crotches, and hang them on the lug-pole to suspend kettles from. These pot-hooks are to be of different lengths so that the kettle can be adjusted to different heights above the fire, first for hard boiling, and then for simmering. If kettles were hung from the lug-pole itself, this adjustment could not be made, and you would have to dismount the whole business in order to get one kettle off. *

---

* It is curious how many different names have been bestowed upon the hooks by which kettles are suspended over a fire. Our forefathers called them pot-hooks, trammels, hakes, hangers, pot-hangers, pot-claws, pot-crooks, gallows-crooks, pot-chips, pot-brakes, gibs or gib-crokes, rackan-crooks (a chain or pierced bar on which to hang hooks was called a rackan or reckon), and I know not what else besides. Among Maine lumbermen, such an implement is called a lug-stick, a hook for lifting kettles is a hook-stick, and a stick sharpened and driven into the ground at an angle so as to bend over the fire, to suspend a kettle from, is a wambeck or a spygelia — the Red Gods alone know why! The frame built over a cooking-fire is called by the Penobscots *kitchi-plak-wagn*, and the Micmacs call the lug-stick a *chiplok-waugan*, which the white guides have partially anglicized into waugan-stick. It is well to know, and heresy to disbelieve, that, after boiling the kettle, it brings bad luck to leave the waugan or spygelia standing.

If this catalogue does not suffice the amateur cook to express his ideas about such things, he may exercise his jaws with the Romany (gipsy) term for pot-hook, which is *kekauviscoe saster*.

THE CAMP-FIRE

If forked stakes are not readily found in the neighborhood, drive straight ones, then split the tops, flatten the ends of the cross-poles and insert them in the clefts of the stakes.

You do not want a big fire to cook over. Many and many a time I have watched old and experienced woodsmen spoil their grub, and their tempers, too, by trying to cook in front of a roaring winter campfire, and have marveled at their lack of commonsense. Off to one side of such a fire, lay your bedlogs, as above; then shovel from the camp-fire enough hard coals to fill the space between the logs within three inches of the top. You now have a steady, even heat from end to end; it can easily be regulated; there is level support for every vessel; and you can wield a short-handled frying-pan over such an outdoor range without scorching either the meat or yourself.

FIRE FOR BAKING.— For baking in a reflector, or roasting a joint, a high fire is best, with a backing to throw the heat forward. Sticks three feet long can be leaned against a big log or a sheer-faced rock, and the kindling started under them.

Often a good bed of coals is wanted. The campfire generally supplies these, but sometimes they are needed in a hurry, soon after camp is pitched. To get them, take *sound hardwood*, either green or dead, and split it into sticks of uniform thickness (say $1\frac{1}{4}$-inch face). Lay down two bed-sticks, cross these near the ends with two others, and so on up until you have a pen a foot high. Start a fire in this pen. Then cover it with a layer of parallel sticks laid an inch apart. Cross this with a similar layer at right angles, and so upward for another foot. The free draft will make a roaring fire, and all will burn down to coals together.

The thick bark of hemlock, and of hardwoods generally, will soon yield coals for ordinary cooking.

To keep coals a long time, cover them with ashes,

or with bark which will soon burn to ashes. In wet weather a bed of coals can be shielded by slanting broad strips of green bark over it and overlapping them at the edges.

FIRE IN A TRENCH.— In time of drought when everything is tinder-dry, or in windy weather, especially if the ground be strewn with dead leaves or pine needles, build your fire in a trench. This is the best way, too, if fuel is scarce and you must depend on brushwood, as a trench conserves heat.

Dig the trench in line with the prevailing wind. The point is to get a good draught. Make the windward end somewhat wider than the rest, and deeper, sloping the trench upward to the far end. Line the sides with flat rocks, if they are to be found, as they hold heat a long time and keep the sides from crumbling in. Lay other rocks, or a pair of green poles, along the edges to support vessels. A little chimney of flat stones or sod, at the leeward end, will make the fire draw well. If there is some sheet-iron to cover the trench a quite practical stove is made, but an open trench will do very well if properly managed.

THE HUNTER'S FIRE.— Good for a shifting camp in the fall of the year, because it affords first a quick cooking fire with supports for the utensils, and afterwards a fair camp-fire for the night when the weather is not severe. Cut two hardwood logs not less than a foot thick and about six feet long. Lay these side by side, about fifteen inches apart at one end and six or eight inches at the other. Across them lay short green sticks as supports, and on these build a crisscross pile of dry wood and set fire to it. The upper courses of wood will soon burn to coals which will drop between the logs and set them blazing on the inner sides. (If the bed logs were elevated to let draught under them they would blaze all around, and would not last long.)

After supper, lay two green billets, about eight inches thick, across the bed logs, and put night-wood

THE CAMP-FIRE 231

on it, to be renewed as required. In the morning there will be fine coals with which to cook breakfast.

WINTER CAMP-FIRE.— Let " Nessmuk " describe how he and a companion kept an open camp comfortably warm through a week in winter, with no other cutting tools than their hunting hatchets:

"We first felled a thrifty butternut tree ten inches in diameter, cut off three lengths of five feet each, and carried them to camp. These were the back-logs. Two stout stakes were driven at the back of the fire, and the logs, on top of each other, were laid firmly against the stakes. The latter were slanted a little back, and the largest log placed at bottom, the smallest on top, to prevent tipping forward. A couple of short, thick sticks were laid with the ends against the bottom log by way of fire-dogs; a fore-stick five feet long and five inches in diameter; a well built pyramid of bark, knots and small logs completed the camp-fire, which sent a pleasant glow of warmth and heat to the furthest corner of the shanty. For night-wood we cut a dozen birch and ash poles from four to six inches across, trimmed them to the tips, and dragged them to camp. Then we denuded a dry hemlock of its bark by aid of tenfoot poles flattened at one end, and packed the bark to camp. We had a bright, cheery fire from the early evening until morning, and four tired hunters never slept more soundly.

"We stayed in that camp a week; and, though the weather was rough and cold, the little pocket-axes kept us well in firewood. We selected butternut for back-logs, because, when green, it burns very slowly and lasts a long time. And we dragged our smaller wood to camp in lengths of twenty to thirty feet, because it was easier to lay them on the fire and 'nigger' them in two than to cut them shorter with light hatchets. With a heavy axe we should have cut them to lengths of five or six feet."

The first camp I ever made was built exactly after the " Nessmuk " pattern, shanty-tent, camp-fire with butternut back-logs, and all (see chapters III. and IV. of his *Woodcraft*). My only implement, besides knives, was a double-bitted hatchet just like his, of surgical instrument steel, weighing, with its twelve-inch handle, only eighteen ounces. I was alone. I stayed in that camp five weeks, in October and November; and I was snug and happy all the time. But then I was camping just for the fun of it. It is quite a different matter to come in at nightfall, dog-tired, and have to get in night-wood with a mere hatchet. Don't try that sort of camping without a full-size axe.

If there is a big, flat-faced rock or ledge on the camp site, take advantage of it by building your fire against it, with the tent in front. Or build a wall of rocks for a fire-back, with stone "andirons." Wooden ones must be renewed every day or so. But if logs must be used, and you have an axe, cut the back-logs from a green tree at least a foot thick, choosing wood that is slow to burn. Plaster mud in the crevices between the logs, around the bottom of stakes, and around the rear end of "handjunks" or billets used as andirons; otherwise the fire will soon attack these places. The fire-back reflects the heat forward into the tent, conducts the smoke upward, and serves as a windbreak in front of camp; so the higher it is, within reason, the better.

Novices generally erect the fire-back too far from the tent. Conditions vary, but ordinarily the face of the back-logs should not be more than five feet from the tent front; with a small fire, well tended, it need not be over four feet.

THE INDIAN'S FIRE.— Best where fuel is scarce, or when one has only a small hatchet with which to cut night-wood. Fell and trim a lot of hardwood saplings. Lay three or four of them on the ground, butts on top of each other, tips radiating from this center like the spokes of a wheel. On and around this center build a small, hot fire. Place butts of other saplings on this, radiating like the others. As the wood burns away, shove the sticks in toward the center, butts on top of each other, as before. This saves much chopping, and economizes fuel. Build a little windbreak behind you, and lie close to the fire. Doubtless you have heard the Indian's dictum (southern Indians express it just as the northern

THE CAMP-FIRE

and western ones do): "White man heap fool; make um big fire — can't git near: Injun make um little fire — git close. Uh, good!"

KINDLING.—The best kindling is fat pine, or the bark of the paper birch. Fat pine is found in the stumps and butt cuts of pine trees, particularly those that died on the stump. The resin has collected there and dried. This wood is usually easy to split. Pine knots are the tough, heavy, resinous stubs of limbs that are found on dead pine trees. They, as well as fat pine, are almost imperishable, and those sticking out of old rotten logs are as good as any. In collecting pine knots go to fallen trees that have almost rotted away. Hit the knot a lick with the poll of the axe and generally it will yield; if you must chop, cut deep to get it all and to save the axe edge. The knots of old dead balsams are similarly used. Usually a dead stump of pine, spruce, or balsam, all punky on the outside, has a core very rich in resin that makes excellent kindling.

Hemlock knots are worthless and hard as glass — keep your axe out of them.

The thick bark of hemlock is good to make glowing coals in a hurry; so is that of hardwoods generally. Good kindling, sure to be dry underneath the bark in all weathers, is procured by snapping off the small dead branches, or stubs of branches, that are left on the trunks of small or medium-sized trees, near the ground. Do not pick up twigs from the ground, but choose those, among the downwood, that are held up free from the ground. Where a tree is found that has been shivered by lightning, or one that has broken off without uprooting, good splinters of dry wood will be found. In every laurel thicket there is plenty of dead laurel, and, since it is of sprangling growth, most of the branches will be free from the ground and snap-dry. They ignite readily and give out intense heat.

The bark of all species of birch, but of paper birch especially, is excellent for kindling and for torches. It is full of resinous oil, blazes up at once, will burn in any wind, and wet sticks can be ignited with it.

Tinder, and methods of getting fire without matches, will be considered in Volume II.

MAKING FIRE IN THE WET.— It is a good test of one's resourcefulness to make a fire out-of-doors in rainy weather. The best way to go about it depends upon local conditions. If fat pine can be found the trick is easy: just split it up, and start your fire under a big fallen log. Dry fuel and a place to build the fire can often be found under big uptilted logs, shelving rocks, and similar natural shelters, or in the core of an old stump. In default of these, look for a dead softwood tree that leans to the south. The wood and bark on the under side will be dry — chop some off, split it fine, and build your fire under the shelter of the trunk.

LIGHTING A MATCH.— When there is nothing dry to strike it on, jerk the tip of the match forward against your teeth.

To light a match in the wind, *face* the wind. Cup your hands, with their backs toward the wind, and hold the match with its head pointing toward the rear of the cup — *i. e.*, toward the wind. Remove the right hand just long enough to strike the match on something very close by; then instantly resume the former position. The flame will run up the match stick, instead of being blown away from it, and so will have something to feed on.

FIRE REGULATIONS.— On state lands and on National forest reserves it is forbidden to use any but fallen timber for firewood. Different States have various other restrictions, some, I believe, not permitting campers to light a fire in the woods at all unless accompanied by a registered guide.

In New York the regulations prescribe that " Fires will be permitted for the purpose of cooking, warmth, and insect smudges; but before such fires are kindled sufficient space around the spot where

THE CAMP-FIRE

the fire is to be lighted must be cleared from all combustible material; and before the place is abandoned, fires so lighted must be thoroughly quenched."

In Pennsylvania forest reserves no fire may be made except in a hole or pit one foot deep, the pit being encircled by the excavated earth. In those of California, no fire at all may be lighted without first procuring a permit from the authorities.

Fire regulations are posted on all public lands, and if campers disregard them they are subject to arrest.

These are wise and good laws. Every camper who loves the forest, and who has any regard for public interests, will do his part by obeying them to the letter. However, if he occupies private property where he may use his own judgment, or if he travels in a wilderness far from civilization, where there are no regulations, it will be useful for him to know something about the fuel value of all kinds of wood, green as well as dead, and for such people the following information is given:

The arts of fire-building are not so simple as they look. To practice them successfully in all sorts of wild regions we must know the different species of trees one from another, and their relative fuel values, which, as we shall see, vary a great deal. We must know how well, or ill, each of them burns in a green state, as well as when seasoned. It is important to discriminate between wood that makes lasting coals, and such as soon dies down to ashes. Some kinds of wood pop violently when burning and cast out embers that may burn holes in tents and bedding or set the neighborhood afire; others burn quietly, with clear, steady flame. Some are stubborn to split, others almost fall apart under the axe. In wet weather it takes a practiced woodsman to find tinder and dry wood, and to select a natural shelter where fire can be kept going during a storm of rain or snow, when a fire is most needed.

There are several handy little manuals by which

one who has no botanical knowledge can soon learn how to identify the different species of trees by merely examining their leaves; or, late in the season, by their bark, buds, and habit of growth.

But no book gives the other information that I have referred to; so I shall offer, in the present chapter, a little rudimentary instruction in this important branch of woodcraft.

It is convenient for our purpose to divide the trees into two great groups, hardwoods and softwoods, using these terms not so loosely as lumbermen do, but drawing the line between sycamore, yellow birch, yellow pine, and slippery elm, on the one side, and red cedar, sassafras, pitch pine and white birch, on the other.

As a general rule, hardwoods make good, slow-burning fuel that yields lasting coals, and softwoods make a quick, hot fire that is soon spent. But each species has peculiarities that deserve close attention. The knack of finding what we want in the woods lies a good deal in knowing what we *don't* want, and passing it by at a glance.

UNINFLAMMABLE WOODS.— The following woods will scarcely burn at all when they are green: basswood, black ash, balsam, box elder, buckeye, cucumber, black or pitch pine and white pine, poplar or aspen, yellow poplar or tulip, sassafras, service berry, sourwood, sycamore, tamarack, tupelo (sour gum), water oak. Butternut, chestnut, red oak, red maple, and persimmon burn very slowly in a green state. Such woods, or those of them that do not spit fire, are good for backlogs, hand-junks or andirons, and for side-logs in a cooking fire that is to be used continuously. Yellow birch and white ash, on the contrary, are better for a campfire when green than when seasoned. A dead pine log seldom burns well unless split. The outside catches fire readily, but it soon chars and goes out unless a blazing fire of sticks is kept up against it.

THE CAMP-FIRE

GREEN WOOD burns best in autumn and winter, when the sap is down. Trees that grow on high, dry ground, burn better than those of the same species that stand in moist soil. Chestnut cut on the summits of the Appalachians burns freely, even when green, and the mountain beech burns as ardently as birch. Green wood growing along a river bank is very hard to burn.

SPITFIRE WOODS.— Arbor-vitæ (northern " white cedar ") and chestnut burn to dead coals that do not communicate flame. They, as well as box elder, red cedar, hemlock, sassafras, tulip, balsam, tamarack, and spruce, make a great crackling and snapping in the fire. All of the soft pines, too, are prone to pop. Certain hardwoods, such as sugar maple, beech, white oak, and sometimes hickory, must be watched for a time after the fire is started, because the embers that they shoot out are long-lived, and hence more dangerous than those of softwoods; but they are splendid fuel, for all that.

STUBBORN WOODS.— The following woods are very hard to split: Blue ash, box elder, buckeye, cherry, white elm, winged elm, sour gum, hemlock (generally), liquidambar (sweet gum), honey locust, sugar maple, sycamore, tupelo. Some woods, however, that are stubborn when seasoned are readily split when green, such as hickory, beech, dogwood, sugar maple, birch, and slippery elm.

THE BEST FUEL.—Best of all northern firewoods is hickory, green or dry. It makes a hot fire, but lasts a long time, burning down to a bed of hard coals that keep up an even, generous heat for hours. Hickory, by the way, is distinctly an American tree; no other region on earth produces it. The live oak of the South is most excellent fuel, so is holly. Following the hickory, in fuel value, are chestnut oak, overcup, white, blackjack, post and basket oaks, pecan, the hornbeams (ironwoods), and dogwood. The latter burns finally to a beautiful white ash that is characteristic; apple wood does the same. Black birch also ranks here; it has the advantage of "doing its own blowing," as a Carolina mountaineer said to me, meaning that the oil in the birch assists its combustion so that the wood needs no coaxing. All of the birches are good fuel, ranking in about this order: black, yellow, red, paper, and white. Sugar maple was the favorite fuel of our old-time hunters and surveyors, because it ignites easily, burns with a clear, steady flame, and leaves good coals.

Locust is a good, lasting fuel; it is easy to cut, and, when green, splits fairly well; the thick bark takes fire readily, and the wood then burns slowly, with little flame, leaving pretty good coals; hence it is good for night-wood. Mulberry has similar qualities. The scarlet and willow oaks are among the poorest of the hardwoods for fuel. Cherry makes only fair fuel. White elm is poor stuff, but slippery elm is better. Yellow pine burns well, as its sap is resinous instead of watery like that of the soft pines.

In some respects white ash is the best of green woods for campers' fuel. It is easily cut and split, is lighter to tote than most other hardwoods, and is of so dry a nature that even the green wood catches fire readily. It burns with clear flame, and lasts longer than any other free-burning wood of its weight. On a wager, I have built a bully fire from a green tree of white ash, one match, and no dry kindling whatever. I split some of the wood very fine and "frilled" a few of the little sticks with my knife.

SOFTWOODS.— Most of the softwoods are good only for kindling, or for quick cooking fires, and then only when seasoned. For these purposes, however, some of them are superior, as they split and shave readily and catch fire easily.

Liquidambar, magnolia, tulip, catalpa, and willow are poor fuel. Seasoned chestnut and yellow poplar make a hot fire, but crackle and leave no

THE CAMP-FIRE

coals. Balsam fir, basswood, and the white and loblolly pines make quick fires but are soon spent. The gray (Labrador) pine or jack pine is considered good fuel in the far North, where hardwoods are scarce. Seasoned tamarack is good. Spruce is poor fuel, although, being resinous, it kindles easily and makes a good blaze for "branding up" a fire. Pitch pine, which is the most inflammable of all woods when dry and "fat," will scarcely burn at all in a green state. Sycamore and buckeye, when thoroughly seasoned, are good fuel, but will not split. Alder burns readily and gives out considerable heat, but is not lasting.

The dry wood of the northern poplar (large-toothed aspen) is a favorite for cooking fires, because it gives an intense heat, with little or no smoke, lasts well, and does not blacken the utensils. Red cedar has similar qualities, but is rather hard to ignite and must be fed fine at the start.

The best green softwoods for fuel are white birch, paper birch, soft maple, cottonwood, and quaking aspen.

As a rule, the timber growing along the margins of large streams is softwood. Hence driftwood is generally a poor mainstay, unless there is plenty of it on the spot; but driftwood on the seacoast is good fuel.

PRECAUTIONS.— I have already mentioned the necessity of clearing the camp ground of inflammable stuff before starting a fire on it, raking it toward a common center and burning all the dead leaves, pine needles, and trash; otherwise it may catch and spread beyond your control as soon as your back is turned. Don't build your fire against a big old punky log: it may smoulder a day or two after you have left, and then burst out into flame when a breeze fans it.

Never leave a spark of fire when breaking camp, or when leaving it for the day. Make absolutely sure of this, by drenching the camp-fire thoroughly, or by smothering it completely with earth or sand. Never drop a lighted match, a burning cigar stub, or the hot residue of your pipe, on the ground without stamping it out. Have you ever seen a forest fire? It is terrible. Thousands of acres are destroyed, and many a time men and women and children have been cut off by a tornado of flame and burned alive. The person whose carelessness starts such a holocaust is worse than a fool — he is a criminal, and a disgrace to the good earth he treads.

CHAPTER XIV
PESTS OF THE WOODS

Summer twilight brings the mosquito. In fact, when we go far north or far south, we have him with us both by day and night. Rather I should say that we have *her;* for the male mosquito is a gentleman, who sips daintily of nectar and minds his own business, while madame his spouse is a whining, peevish, venomous virago, that goes about seeking whose nerves she may unstring and whose blood she may devour. Strange to say, not among mosquitoes only, but among ticks, fleas, chiggers, and the whole legion of bloodthirsty, stinging flies and midges, it is only the female that attacks man and beast. Stranger still, the mosquito is not only a bloodsucker but an incorrigible wine-bibber as well — it will get helplessly fuddled on any sweet wine, such as port, or on sugared spirits, while of gin it is inordinately fond.

Such disreputable habits — the querulous sing-song, the poisoned sting, the thirst for blood, and the practice of getting dead drunk at every opportunity, are enough of themselves to make the mosquito a thing accursed; but these are by no means the worst counts in our indictment against it. We have learned, within the past few years, that all the suffering and mortality from malaria, yellow fever, and filariasis (including the hideous and fatal elephantiasis of the tropics) is due to germs that are carried in no other way than by mosquitoes. Flies spread the germs of typhoid fever and malignant eye diseases; fleas carry the bubonic plague;

the sleeping-sickness of Africa is transmitted by insects. There is no longer any guesswork about this: it is demonstrated fact. Professor Kellogg, summing up what is now known of the life history of malaria-bearing mosquitoes (*Anopheles*) says: "When in malarial regions, avoid the bite of a mosquito as you would that of a rattlesnake — one can be quite as serious in its results as the other."

The worst of it, from a sportsman's view-point, is that the farther we push toward the arctics or the tropics, the worse becomes the pest of dangerous insects. It is into just such countries that, nowadays and in future, we must go in order to get really first-class hunting and fishing. Consequently the problem of how best to fight our insect enemies becomes of ever increasing importance to all who love to hunt over and explore the wild places that are still left upon the earth.

Mosquitoes are bad enough in the tropics, but they are at their worst in the coldest regions of the earth.

MOSQUITOES.— Harry de Windt reports that at Verkhoyansk, in Siberia, which is the arctic pole of cold (where the winter temperature often sinks to $-75°$ Fahr., and has been known to reach $-81°$) the mosquitoes make their appearance before the snow is off the ground, and throughout the three summer months, make life almost unbearable to the wretched natives and exiles. The swamps and shoaly lakes in the surrounding country breed mosquitoes in such incredible hosts that reindeer, sledge-dogs, and sometimes even the natives themselves, are actually tormented to death by them.

Throughout a great part of central and western Canada, and Alaska, there are vast tundras of bog moss, called by the Indians muskegs, which in summer are the breeding-grounds of unending clouds of mosquitoes whose biting powers exceed those of any insects known in the United States. Even if the muskeg land were not a morass, this plague of

PESTS OF THE WOODS 243

mosquitoes would forever render it uninhabitable in summer. The insects come out of their pupæ at the first sprouting of spring vegetation, in May, and remain until destroyed by severe frosts in September. In Alaska, all animals leave for the snow-line as soon as the mosquito pest appears, but the enemy follows them even to the mountain tops above timber-line. Deer and moose are killed by mosquitoes, which settle upon them in such amazing swarms that the unfortunate beasts succumb from literally having the blood sucked out of their bodies. Bears are driven frantic, are totally blinded, mire in the mud, and starve to death. Animals that survive have their flesh discolored all through, and even their marrow is reduced to the consistency of blood and water. The men who penetrate such regions are not the kind that would allow toil or privation to break their spirit, but they become so unstrung from days and nights of continuous torment inflicted by enemies insignificant in size but infinite in number, that they become savage, desperate, and sometimes even weep in sheer helpless anger.

In regions so exceptionally cursed with mosquitoes no mere sportsman has any business until winter sets in. But even in the more accessible woodlands north and south of us the insect pest is by far the most serious hardship that fishermen and other summer outers are obliged to meet. Head-nets and gauntlets are all very well in their way, but one can neither hunt, fish, paddle, push through the brush, nor even smoke, when so accoutered. Consequently everybody tries some kind or other of "fly-dope," by which elegant name we mean any preparation which, being rubbed over the exposed parts of one's skin, is supposed to discourage insects from repeating their attacks.

The number of such dopes is legion. They may be classified in three groups:

(1) Thick ointments that dry to a tenacious glaze on the skin, if the wearer abstain from washing;

(2) Liquids or semi-fluid unguents that are supposed to protect by their odor alone, and must be renewed several times a day;

(3) Insecticides, which poison the little beasts.

Glazes.— Among the glazes, Nessmuk's recipe, published in his *Woodcraft,* is perhaps as well known and as widely used as any. He says this about it:

"I have never known it to fail: 3 oz. pine tar, 2 oz. castor oil, 1 oz. pennyroyal oil. Simmer all together over a slow fire, and bottle for use. You will hardy need more than a 2-oz. vial full in a season. One ounce has lasted me six weeks in the woods. Rub it in thoroughly and liberally at first, and after you have established a good glaze, a little replenishing from day to day will be sufficient. And don't fool with soap and towels where insects are plenty. A good safe coat of this varnish grows better the longer it is kept on — and it is cleanly and wholesome. If you get your face or hands crocky or smutty about the camp-fire, wet the corner of your handkerchief and rub it off, not forgetting to apply the varnish at once wherever you have cleaned it off. Last summer I carried a cake of soap and a towel in my knapsack through the North Woods for a seven weeks' tour, and never used either a single time. When I had established a good glaze on the skin, it was too valuable to be sacrificed for any weak whim connected with soap and water. . . . It is a soothing and healing application for poisonous bites already received."

Aside from my personal tests of many dopes, I have had some interesting correspondence on this topic with sportsmen in various parts of the world. I quote from one letter received from Norman Fletcher, of Louisville:

"Upon the swampy trout streams of Michigan on a warm May day . . . when the insects are abundant and vicious . . . pure pine tar is by far the best repellent when properly used. I give two recipes:

(1) Pure pine tar.......... 1 ounce,
Oil pennyroyal .... 1 ounce,
Vaseline .... 3 ounces.

Mix cold in a mortar. If you wish, you can add 3 per cent. carbolic acid to above. Sometimes I make it 1½ oz. tar.

(2) Pure pine tar.......... 2 ounces,
Castor oil .... 3 ounces,

PESTS OF THE WOODS 245

Simmer for half an hour, and when cool add

Oil pennyroyal   1 ounce.

There are many others of similar nature, but the above are as good as any. Now as to use of above: apply freely and frequently to all exposed parts of person, and *do not wash off until leaving* the place where the pests abound. You can wash your eyes in the morning, and wash the palms of your hands as often as may be necessary, but if you wish to be immune, don't wash any other exposed parts. When you get accustomed to it you will find some compensating comfort.... I have had to contend with mosquitoes, deer-flies, black-flies, and midges   and have found "dope" with tar in it the best. I know that where mosquitoes are not very bad, oil of citronella, oil of verbena or of lemon-grass or of pennyroyal mixed with vaselin will keep them off, if the mixture is applied frequently. These essential oils are quickly evaporated, however, by the heat of the body. Camphorated oil is also used by some; this is simply sweet oil with gum camphor dissolved in it: the camphor is volatile and soon evaporates.

. Now I don't much like tar dope because I can not wash my face and hands as often as I could wish; but when it is necessary to get some trout, without being worried too much by the insects, I can stand the tar for a few days."

Doctor L. O. Howard, Chief of the Bureau of Entomology, U. S. Department of Agriculture, recommends the following tar dope:

"Fishermen and hunters in the North Woods will find that a good mixture against mosquitoes and black-flies can be made as follows: Take 2½ pounds of mutton tallow, melt and strain it. While still hot add ½ pound black tar (Canadian tar), stir thoroughly, and pour into the receptacle in which it is to be contained. When nearly cool stir in 3 ounces of oil of citronella and 1½ ounces of pennyroyal."

It is my own experience that tar glazes do the work when the weather is comparatively cool, but when it is so hot that one perspires freely both by night and day there is no chance for a glaze to be established. The stuff melts and runs in your eyes. A hard rain will wash it off. Thick dopes, more or less sticky, are unpleasant at all times, and especially at night. For these reasons, and for appearance sake, most people will prefer to use a fluid or unguent that is less disagreeable, even though it must be renewed every hour or two.

Essential Oils.— As for protective liquids, it is safe to say that everything in the pharmacopœia that seemed the least promising has been tried. The oils of pennyroyal, cloves, lavender, citronella, eucalyptus, cedar and sassafras are used singly or in combination. Spirits of camphor is offensive to insects but soon evaporates.

Citronella is the favorite. All insect pests dislike it; but some people, too, find the odor intolerable. The oil of lavender flowers (genuine) has a pleasant odor, and is equally effective, but it is quite expensive. Both of these oils are bland, whereas most of the others are irritant and will make the eyes smart if the least bit comes in contact with them. Artificial oil of lavender is worthless.

The protection afforded by a given oil depends somewhat upon locality (number, species, persistence of insects), and, apparently, the personal equation cuts some figure, for what works satisfactorily with one man affords no immunity to another. Hence the more popular dopes are "shot-gun prescriptions," compounded on the principle that if one ingredient misses another may hit.

The trouble with all the essential oils is that their protective principles are volatile. To retard evaporation, add double or treble the amount of castor oil, which has a good body and is itself repugnant to the whole created kingdom. After mixing, put up some of this thick liquid in a small capped oil can (bicycle oiler), to carry in the field.

Thicker dopes, which can be put up in collapsible tubes like artists' colors, are made by mixing the oil with carbolated vaseline, or with borated lanolin. The latter is a particularly good base because it is not only antiseptic but it is also the best preventive of sunburn, excellent for blistered feet, and a particularly good application for slight wounds and abrasions. Add enough oil of lavender flowers

PESTS OF THE WOODS 247

to give it a strong odor, and put it up in tubes to keep out moisture. I know nothing better in the line of "elegant preparations" to keep off mosquitoes.

Insecticides.— One of these is creosote. Another is the tincture of *ledum palustre* (wild rosemary, a European relative of our Labrador tea). Oil of cassia (i.e., oil of cinnamon) is said to be an irritant poison to all kinds of insects, and "its power remains a long time after it has dried."

Another thing that flies of all sorts find bad for their systems is quassia. It is used as an ingredient of fly poisons, as a parasiticide, and in some fly dopes. Either the fluid extract or the solid may be employed, according to the base.

Carbolic acid in sweet oil (1 to 16) is often used where insects are very insistent. It has the obvious advantage of being a good antiseptic as well. On a trip to Hudson Bay, Dr. Robert T. Morris employed a very strong solution, of which he reported:

"We depended upon the mixture of one part of carbolic acid and nine parts of sweet oil to keep off various things that sought our acquaintance. A very little of this mixture on the face and hands was effective. It is a preparation that I learned to use in Labrador, where none of the common applications would suffice."

Doctor Durham, of the English Yellow Fever Commission, Rio de Janeiro, told Dr. L. O. Howard that

"He and the late Dr. Myers found that a 5 per cent. solution of sulphate of potash prevented mosquitoes from biting, and that they were obliged to use this mixture while at work in their laboratory in Brazil to prevent themselves from being badly bitten."

I judge this would also be a good preventive of attacks from ticks and chiggers, as they cannot stand sulphur.

Plain kerosene is certain death to all sorts of insect pests, so long as they have not burrowed beneath the skin, and one of the best preventives of their attacks. It is used everywhere by men whose constant exposure renders them less fastidious about personal greasiness and aroma than they are solicitous for comfort and health. Dr. W. H. Dade, an army surgeon in the Philippines, found that the addition of one part oil of bergamot to sixteen of kerosene made the odor less disagreeable and added enough body to prevent evaporation in less than six to eight hours. I have used Japanese oil of camphor for the same purpose.

Some Dopes.—The following mixtures may be particularly recommended:

Mr. C. A. Nash's.
Oil of citronella	1 oz.
Spirits of camphor	1 oz.
Oil of cedar	½ oz.

Doctor Howard says this is the most effective mixture he has tried. "Ordinarily a few drops on a bath towel hung over the head of the bed will keep *Culex pipiens* away for a whole night. Where mosquitoes are very persistent, however, a few drops rubbed on the face and hands will suffice."

Dr. Edward Beck's.
Pine tar	3 oz.
Olive (or castor) oil	2 oz.
Oil pennyroyal	1 oz.
Oil citronella	1 oz.
Creosote	1 oz.
Camphor (pulverized)	1 oz.
Carbolated vaseline	large tube.

Heat the tar and oil and add the other ingredients; simmer over slow fire until well mixed. The tar may be omitted if disliked, or for ladies' use. Above will rather more than fill a pint screw-top tin flask. This mixture not only discourages insect attacks but is also a good counter-irritant after being bitten. One may substitute for the olive oil its weight in carbolated vaseline and thus make an unguent that can be carried in collapsible tubes, and the Doctor now recommends this.

Col. Crofton Fox's.
Oil pennyroyal	1 dram.
Oil peppermint	1 dram.
Oil bergamot	1 dram.

PESTS OF THE WOODS 249

Oil cedar 1 dram.
Quassia .... 1 dram.
Gum camphor 4 drams.
Vaseline, yellow 2 drams.

Dissolve camphor in vaseline by heat; when cold add remainder.

I doubt if peppermint adds anything to the efficacy of this formula, and would substitute citronella or lavender.

The principles to be observed in compounding a dope of one's own are (1) choose your repellents or insecticides, or both; (2) add enough lanolin, vaseline, castor oil, or other base to give the desired "body." It is well to incorporate some good antiseptic with the stuff, to relieve irritation and poisoning from bites already received, and to serve as a healing ointment for abrasions, bruises, and other injuries, as already mentioned. Any ingredient that irritates the skin or makes the eyes smart should be avoided, except where insects are so bad that such addition may be necessary.

BITES AND STINGS.— To relieve the itching of insect bites the common remedies are ammonia or a solution of baking soda. A better one is to cover each bite with flexible collodion (" New Skin "); but be sure the bottle is always securely stoppered, for the ether of the solvent evaporates very quickly and then the stuff is useless.

A bee leaves its sting in the wound, and this of course should be removed; a wasp, hornet, or yellowjacket can sting repeatedly. For the pain, apply ammonia or baking powder solution, or a weak solution of carbolic acid, or wet salt, moistened clay, a mud poultice, a slice of raw onion, or a moist quid of tobacco.

FLEAS.— In the high mountains of North Carolina and adjoining States there are no mosquitoes, at least none that sing or bite; but if a man sits down on a log, it may be five miles from any house, the chance is good that he will arise covered with fleas. I have been so tormented by these nimble allies of Auld Reekie, when spending a night in a herder's cabin on the summit of the Smokies, that I have arisen in desperation and rubbed myself from head to foot with kerosene. That settled the fleas. Citronella will do as well.

If you catch a flea, don't try to crush it, for you can't, but roll it between the fingers; that breaks its legs; than you can open your fingers and kill it. A good way, if water is handy, is to keep a tight grip until you get your thumb and finger into some water — a flea can't swim — then, if it is not already filled with blood, it will sink, and drown, and go to meet its reward, which, let us hope, is a hot one.

When you have to occupy a cabin infested with fleas, scrub it out with hot soapsuds, and see that the site is well wet beneath the floor. Fleas will not stay in a wet place.

BLOOD-SUCKING FLIES.—In northern forests we have several species of flies that attack man. The deer-fly or "bull-dog" is a small gad-fly that drives her dagger-like mandibles into one's skin so viciously that she takes out a bit of flesh and makes the blood flow freely. The black-fly (*Similium molestum*) is a stout, hump-backed, black termagant with transparent wings, from one-sixth to one-quarter inch long. This creature is a common nuisance of the forests and along the streams of northern New England, the Adirondacks, the Lake region, and Canada. She keeps busy until late in the afternoon, poisoning everything that she attacks, and raising a painful lump as big as a dime at every bite. Closely related species are the buffalo-gnat and turkey-gnat of the South, which sometimes appear in incredible numbers, driving animals frantic and setting up an inflammatory fever that may prove fatal. Black-flies and their ilk are easily driven away by smudges. Mosquito dopes will protect one from them.

BLOW-FLIES.— Worst of all flies, though fortunately rare in the North (it has been known to reach Canada), is the screw-worm fly (*Compsomyia macellaria*), a bright metallic-green insect with golden re-

PESTS OF THE WOODS 251

flections and four black stripes on the upper part of the body. This is a blow-fly which has the sickening habit of laying its eggs in wounds, and even in the nostrils of sleeping men. Several fatalities from this cause have been reported in our country; they have been much more numerous in South America. The *gusanéro* of tropical America is described by a traveler as "a beast of a fly that attacks you, you know not when, till after three or four months you know that he has done so by the swelling up of the bitten part into a fair-sized boil, from which issues a maggot of perhaps an inch and a half in length." Another Amazonian fly of similar habits is the *birni*, whose larva generates a grub in one's skin that requires careful extraction, lest it be crushed in the operation, "and then," said a native, "gentlemen often go to *o outro mundo*" (the other world). The *motûca* of Brazil has ways similar to those of our black-fly, and, like it, can easily be killed with one's fingers.

PESTS OF THE TROPICS.—While I am on this topic, it may add a little to the contentment of those outers who are unable to seek adventure in faraway lands, but must needs camp within a hundred miles or so of home, if I transcribe from the pages of a well-known naturalist the following notes on some of the impediments to travel in the tropics:

"But the most numerous and most dreaded of all animals in the middle Amazons are the insects. Nearly all kinds of articulate life here have either sting or bite. The strong trade wind keeps the lower Amazons clear of the winged pests; but soon after leaving Manãos, and especially on the Marañon in the rainy season, the traveler becomes intimately acquainted with half a dozen insects of torture:

(1) The sanguinary mosquito. . . . There are several species, most of them working at night; but one black fellow with white feet is diurnal. Doctor Spruce experimented upon himself, and found that he lost, by letting the blood-letters have their own way, three ounces of blood per day. . . . The ceaseless irritation of these ubiquitous creatures makes life almost intolerable. The great Cortez, after all his victories, could not forget his struggles with

these despicable enemies he could not conquer. Scorpions with cocked tails, spiders six inches in diameter, and centipedes running on all dozens, are not half so bad as a cloud of mosquitoes. . . .

(2) The *pium,* or sand-fly, a species of *trombidium* called mosquito in Peru. It is a minute, dark-colored dipter with two triangular, horny lancets, which leave a small, circular red spot on the skin. It works by day, relieving the mosquito at sunrise. It is the great scourge of the Amazons. Many a paradisiac spot is converted into an inferno by its presence. There are several species, which follow one another in succession through the day, all of them being diurnal. Their favorite region is said to be on the Cassiquiare and upper Orinoco.

(3) The *maruim,* which resembles the *pium.* They are infinitely numerous on the Juruá. Humboldt estimated there were a million to a cubic foot of air where he was.

(4) The *motúca,* called *tábono* on the Marañon (*Hadrus lepidotus*), resembling a small horse-fly, of a bronze-black color, with the tips of the wings transparent, and a formidable proboscis. . . .

(5) The *moquím* . . . a microscopic scarlet *acarus,* resembling a minute crab under the glass. It swarms on weeds and bushes, and on the skin causes an intolerable itching. An hour's walk through the grassy streets of Teffé was sufficient to cover my entire body with myriads of *moquíms,* which it took a week, and repeated bathing with rum, to exterminate.

(6) *Carapátos,* or ticks (*ixodes*), which mount to the tips of blades of grass, attach themselves to the clothes of passersby, and bury their jaws and heads so deeply in the flesh that it is difficult to remove them without leaving the proboscis behind to fret and fester. In sucking one's blood they cause no pain; but serious sores, even ulcers, often result. . . .

These few forms of insect life must forever hinder the settlement of the valley. . . . Besides there are ants . . . innumerable in species and individuals, and of all sizes, from the little red ant of the houses to the mammoth *tokandéra,* an inch and a half long. . . . The latter . . . bites fiercely, but rarely causes death. Doctor Spruce likens the pain to a hundred thousand nettles. . . . On the Tapajós lives the terrible fire-ant . . . whose sting is likened to the puncture of a red-hot needle. The *saübas* are not carnivorous, but they make agriculture almost impossible. . . . There are black and yellow wasps. . . . The large, hairy caterpillars should be handled with care, as the irritation caused by the nettling hairs is sometimes a serious matter. Cockroaches are great pests in the villages. Lice find a congenial home on the unwashed Indians of every tribe, but particularly the Andean. Jiggers and fleas prefer

PESTS OF THE WOODS 253

dry, sandy localities; they are accordingly most abounding on the mountains. The Pacific slope is worthy of being called flea-dom."— ORTON, *The Andes and the Amazons,* pp. 484-487.

NORTHERN CHIGGERS.— The *moquim* mentioned above answers the description of our own chigger, jigger, red-bug, as she is variously called, which is an entirely different beast from the real chigger or chigoe of the tropics. I do not know what may be the northern limit of these diabolic creatures, but have made their acquaintance on Swatara Creek in Pennsylvania. They are quite at home on the prairies of southern Illinois, exist in myriads on the Ozarks, and throughout the lowlands of the South, and are perhaps worst of all in some parts of Texas. The chigger, as I shall call it, is invisible on one's skin, unless you know just what to look for. Get it on a piece of black cloth, and you can distinguish what looks like a fine grain of red pepper. Put it under a microscope, and it resembles, as Orton says, a minute crab. It lives in the grass, and on the under side of leaves, dropping off on the first man or beast that comes its way. Then it prospects for a good place, where the skin is thin and tender, and straightway proceeds to burrow, not contenting itself, like a tick, with merely thrusting its head in and getting a good grip, but going in body and soul, to return no more. The victim is not aware of what is in store for him until he goes to bed that night. Then begins a violent itching, which continues for a week or two. I have had two hundred of these tormenting things in my skin at one time.

If one takes a bath in salt water every night before retiring, he can keep fairly rid of these unwelcome guests. A surer preventive is to rub kerosene on the wrists, neck, ankles, and abdominal region. Powdered sulphur dusted into one's drawers and stocking legs will do if one keeps out of the bushes. Naphthaline may be used successfully in the same manner.

The country people sometimes rub themselves

with salty bacon-rind before going outdoors, and claim that this is a preventive; also that kerosene will do as well. If one keeps an old suit of clothes expressly for chigger-time, puts the suit in a closet, and fumigates it thoroughly with the smoke of burning tobacco stems, no chigger will touch him. Alas! that the preventives should all be so disagreeable.

When chiggers have burrowed underneath the skin, neither salt, nor oil, nor turpentine, nor carbolized ointment, nor anything else that I have tried will kill them, save mercurial ointment or the tincture of stavesacre seed, both of which are dangerous if incautiously used. After much experiment, I found that chloroform, dropped or rubbed on each separate welt, will stop the itching for several hours. It is quite harmless, and pleasant enough to apply.

Moderately strong ammonia, or a saturated solution of baking soda, will suffice if applied as soon as the itching is felt, but they are useless if treatment is delayed. In the latter case, I would use tincture of iodine. It is said that collodion brushed over each welt will act as a specific, but I have had no chance to try it.

The chigger seems particularly fond of the butterfly-weed or pleurisy-root. It is seldom much of a nuisance until the middle of June, and generally disappears in the latter part of September.

TROPICAL CHIGOES.—The chigoe or sand-flea of Mexico, Central America, and South America, is a larger and more formidable pest than our little redbug. It attacks, preferably, the feet, especially under the nail of the great toe, and between the toes. The insect burrows there, becomes encysted, swells enormously from the development of her young, and thus sets up an intolerable itching in the victim's skin. If the female is crushed or ruptured in the tumor she has formed, the result is likely to be amputation of the toe, if nothing worse. She should be removed entire by careful manipulation with a needle. This chigoe is a native of tropical America, but seems to be gradually spreading northward.

PESTS OF THE WOODS 255

About 1872 it was introduced into Africa, and spread with amazing rapidity over almost the entire continent. It will probably soon invade southern Europe and Asia.

TICKS.—The wood-ticks that fasten on man are, like the chiggers, not true insects, but arachnids, related to the scorpions and spiders. They are leathery-skinned creatures of about the same size and shape as a bedbug, but of quite different color and habits. They "use" on the under side of leaves of low shrubs, and thence are detached to the person of a passer-by just as chiggers are. They also abound in old mulchy wood, and are likely to infest any log that a tired man sits on. They hang on like grim death, and if you try to pull one off your skin, its head will break off and remain in the epidermis, to create a nasty sore. The ticks that infest birds, bats, sheep, and horses, are true insects, in no wise related to the wood-ticks, dog-ticks, and cattle-ticks. The cattle-tick is responsible for the fatal disease among cattle that is known as Texas fever.

Preventive measures are the same as for chiggers.

To remove a tick without breaking off its head, drop oil on it, or clap a quid of moistened tobacco on it, or touch it with nicotine from a pipe, or stand naked in the dense smoke of a green-wood fire, or use whiskey externally, or hot water, or flame; in either case the tick will back its way out. The meanest ticks to get rid of are the young, which are known as "seed-ticks." They are hard to discover until they have inflamed the skin, and then are hard to remove because they are so small and fragile. A man may find himself covered with hundreds of them. In such case let him strip and rub himself with kerosene, or, lacking that, steep some tobacco or a strong cigar in warm water and do the same with it. They will drop off.

PUNKIES.—The punkie or "no-see-um" of our northern wildwoods, and its cousins the biting gnats and stinging midges of southern and western forests, are minute bloodsuckers that, according to my learned friend Professor Comstock, live, "under the bark of decaying branches, under fallen leaves, and in sap flowing from wounded trees." With all due deference to this distinguished entomologist, I must aver that they don't live there when I am around; they seem particularly fond of sap flowing from wounded fishermen. Dope will keep them from biting you, but it won't keep them out of your eyes. Punkies are particularly annoying about sunset. They seem to know just when and where you will be cleaning the day's catch of trout, and that you will then be completely at their mercy. At such times you will agree that they beat all creation for pure, downright cussedness. Oil of citronella will protect your face and neck, but you can't have it on your hands when cleaning the fish. Punkies can't stand a smudge.

INSECTS IN CAMP.— The common house-fly, which, as Dr. Howard suggests, should be called the typhoid-fly, is often a great nuisance in camps. Screening of tents and of food supplies is the only sure remedy. Burning insect powder (pyrethrum) will drive them out of a tent or cottage, and that is also a good way to get rid of the wood cockroaches that sometimes are attracted by the lights of the camp and proceed to make themselves offensively at home.

Sometime you may elect to occupy an abandoned lumber camp while on an outing. My advice is, pass it by: not all its inhabitants have moved away. Any shack in the woods may harbor bedbugs. If you must use such a place, don't forget the kerosene can.

If ants are troublesome about camp, try to find the nest by following the workers; then pour kerosene or boiling water into it. Red pepper or oil of sassafras sprinkled about may discourage them, but repellent substances are not to be depended upon. Kerosene is the sovereign remedy.

SMUDGES.— A good smudge is raised by using cedar "cigars," made as follows: Take long

PESTS OF THE WOODS 257

strips of cedar bark and bunch them together into a fagot six or eight inches in diameter, about one strip in three being dry and the others water-soaked; bind them with strips of the inner bark of green cedar. Ignite one end at the camp-fire, and set up two or more such cigars on different sides of the camp, according as the wind may shift. Punky wood piled on a bed of coals is also good. The ammoniacal vapors from a smudge of dried cow-dung is particularly effective. I have elsewhere referred to smudges made of dried toadstools; these are peculiarly repellent to punkies. A toadstool as large as one's two fists will hold fire for six or eight hours. A piece of one can be carried suspended by a string around one's neck, the burning end out. If the fungus is too damp at first, it can soon be dried out by placing it before the fire.

SCORPIONS.— Scorpions are not uncommon as far north as Missouri. I often used to find them in the neighborhood of St. Louis — little red fellows about 4 inches long. In the southwest, where they abound, they grow to a length of 6 or 7 inches. They hide by day under flat rocks, in dead trees, and in moist, dark places generally, and do their foraging at night. They are very belligerent, always fighting to the death. They carry their tails curled upward and forward, and can only strike upward and backward. They are sometimes unpleasantly familiar around camp, especially in rainy weather, having a penchant for crawling into bedding, boots, coat sleeves, trousers legs, etc.

The sting of a small scorpion is about as severe as that of a hornet; that of a large one is more serious, but never fatal, so far as I know, except to small children. After a person is stung a few times he is inoculated, and proof against the poison thereafter. If you get stung, take a hollow key or small tube, press the hollow with force over the puncture, causing the poison and a little blood to exude, hold firmly in place for several minutes, and, if the scorpion was a large one, you have a good excuse for drinking all the whiskey you want. Ordinarily a quid of moist tobacco locally applied eases the pain and reduces the swelling. Tobacco juice, by the way, is fatal to scorpions, tarantulas, and centipedes, and will set a snake crazy.

An uncommonly severe bite should be treated like snake-bite (see Volume II).

TARANTULAS.— I first witnessed the leaping powers of a tarantula one night when I was alone in a deserted log cabin in southern Missouri. The cabin had not been occupied for fifteen years, and there was no furniture in it. I had scarcely made my bed on the board floor when a tornado struck the forest. It was a grand sight, but scared me stiff. Well, the electric plant was working finely, just then, the lightning being almost a continuous glare. A tarantula that spread as broad as my hand jumped out of the straw that I was lying on and — it was hard to tell which was quicker, he or the lightning. He seemed disturbed about something. Not being able to fight the tornado, I took after the big spider with an old stumpy broom that happened to be in the cabin. When the broom would land at one side of the room, the tarantula would be on the other side. I was afraid he would spring for my face, but presently he popped into a hole somewhere, and vanished. The cabin somehow stuck to terra firma, and I returned to my pallet.

The tarantula's habits are similar to the scorpion's. The fangs are in its mouth. The bite is very severe, but not fatal to an adult. Cases of men being injured by either of these venomous arachnids are extremely rare, considering the abundance of the pests in some countries, and their habit of secreting themselves in clothes and bedding. If you want to see a battle royal, drop a scorpion and a tarantula into the same box. They

PESTS OF THE WOODS 259

will spring for each other in a flash, and both are absolutely game to the last.

CENTIPEDES.— I have had no personal experience with centipedes. Paul Fountain says:

"The centipedes were an intolerable nuisance for they had a nasty habit of hiding among the bed-clothes and under the pillows, attracted there to prey on the bugs, as I suppose; one evil as a set-off to another. But the centipedes were something more than a mere nuisance. It is all very well to be blandly told by gentlemen who think they know all about it that the bites of centipedes and scorpions are not dangerous. It may not be particularly dangerous to have a red-hot wire applied to your flesh, but it is confoundedly painful. Yet that is to be preferred to a centipede bite, which will not only make you dance at the time of infliction, but leave a painful swelling for many days after, accompanied by great disturbance of the system."

The cowpunchers' remedy for centipede bites, according to Mr. Hough, was "a chaw of tobacco on the outside and a horn of whiskey on the inside, both repeated frequently."

PORCUPINES.—In northern woods the porcupine is a common nuisance. It is a stupid beast, devoid of fear, and an inveterate camp marauder. You may kick it or club it unmercifully, yet it will return again and again to forage and destroy. The "porky" has an insistent craving for salt, and will gnaw anything that has the least saline flavor, anything that perspiring hands have touched, such as an axe-handle, a gunstock, a canoe paddle, and will ruin the article. He is also fond of leather, and will chew up your saddle, bridle, shoes, gloves, belts, the sweat-band of your hat, or any sweaty cloth or rope. Foodstuffs that are salty or greasy are never safe from him unless hung up on wires.

Porcupine quills, being barbed, are hard to extract. When they break off they work deep into the flesh. They are poisonous, in a way, and cause severe pain.

The porcupine is not found south of the Canadian faunal zone, which extends well down into our northern States.

SKUNKS.— Another notoriously fearless pest is the skunk. It will turn tail quickly enough, but nothing on earth will make it run. If a skunk takes it into his head to raid your camp he will step right in without any precautions whatever. Then he will nose through all of your possessions, walk over you if you be in his way, and forty men cannot intimidate him.

Once when I was spending the summer in a herders' hut, on a summit of the Smoky Mountains, a skunk burrowed under the cabin wall and came up through the earthen floor. It was about midnight. My two companions slept in a pole bunk against the wall, and I had an army cot in the middle of the room. It 'vas cold enough for an all-night fire on the hearth.

I awoke with the uneasy feeling that some intruder was moving about in the darkness. There was no noise, and my first thought was of rattlesnakes, which were numerous in that region. I sat up and lit the lantern, which hung over my head. One glance was enough. " Boys," I warned in a stage whisper, " for the love of God, don't breathe: there's a skunk at the foot of my bed!"

The animal was not in the least disconcerted by the light, but proceeded leisurely to inspect the premises. It went under my cot and nosed around there for five mortal minutes, while I lay rigid as a corpse.

Then Doc sneezed. I heard Andy groan from under his blanket: "You damn fool: now we'll get it!"

But we didn't. Madame Polecat waddled to their bunk, and I had a vision of two fellows sweating blood.

Then she moved over to the grub chest, found some excelsior lying beside it, and deliberately went to work making a nest.

An hour passed. I simply had to take a smoke. My tobacco was on a shelf right over the skunk. I risked all, arose very quietly, reached over the

PESTS OF THE WOODS

beast, got my tobacco, and retired like a ghost to the other end of the cabin to warm myself at the fire. We were prisoners; for the only door was a clapboard affair on wooden hinges that skreeked like a dry axle.

The visitor, having made its bed, did not yet feel like turning in, but decided to find out what for a bare-legged, white-faced critter I was, anyhow. It came straight over to the fireplace and sniffed my toes. The other boys offered all sorts of advice, and I talked brimstone back at them — we had found that pussy didn't care a hang for human speech so long as it was gently modulated.

That was a most amiable female of her species. True, she investigated all our property that was within reach, but she respected it, and finally she cuddled up in the excelsior, quite satisfied with her new home.

To cut an awfully long story short, the polecat held us spellbound until daybreak. Then she crawled out through her burrow, and we instantly fled through our skreeky door. Doc had a shotgun in his hand and murder in his heart. Not being well posted on skunk reflexes, he stepped up within ten feet and blew the animal's head clean off by a simultaneous discharge of both barrels. Did that headless skunk retaliate? It did, brethren, it did!

Many methods have been reported effective in deodorizing clothing that has been struck by the skunk's effluvium. Burying the clothes in earth is of no use unless they are left there long enough to rot them (they will smell again every time they get wet). Chloride of lime is objectionable for the same reason. Ammonia is said to neutralize the odor, and benzine or wood alcohol to extract it. An old trappers' remedy is to wrap the clothes in fresh hemlock boughs and leave them out-of-doors for twenty-four hours. A writer in one of the sportsmen's magazines states that, having met disaster in the shape of a skunk, he took an old farmer's advice, put some cornmeal on top of a hot stove, and, when it began to char and smoke, he held the clothes in the smoke for somewhat less than five minutes, by which time the scent was gone, nor did it ever reappear, even when the clothes were damp. Personally I never have had occasion to try any of these remedies.

The belief that skunk-bite is likely to cause hydrophobia is common in the Southwest, and to some extent it is borne out by the reports of army surgeons. A considerable number of soldiers and plainsmen bitten by the spotted or rock skunk of that region, which is a particularly aggressive creature, have undoubtedly died of hydrophobia. Yet the facts seem to be, as explained by W. Wade in the *American Naturalist,* that although men and other animals have been stricken mad by skunk-bite and have died therefrom, still this has only happened during an epidemic of rabies, in which skunks, being slow-moving and utterly fearless creatures, fell easy prey to rabid dogs or wolves. Becoming mad, in their turn, they would bite men sleeping in the open, and their bites would usually be inflicted upon the men's faces, hands and other exposed parts of their persons. In such cases, since none of the poisonous saliva was wiped off by clothing, the result was almost certain death. But rabies is very exceptional among skunks, and the bite of a healthy animal is not a serious matter.

The best insurance against skunks and predatory beasts in general is a good camp dog.

WOLVERINES.— The wolverine, also called glutton, carcajou, skunk bear, and Indian devil, is the champion thief of the wilderness. Lacking the speed of most of his family, the weasel and marten tribe, and devoid of special means of defence such as have been given the skunk and the porcupine, he has developed a diabolic cunning, which, coupled with his great strength and dogged persistence, makes him detested beyond all other creatures in the wild Northland that he inhabits. He systematically robs hunters of their game, trappers of

PESTS OF THE WOODS 263

their bait, and breaks into caches that defy almost any other animal. If he finds more food than his capacious paunch will hold, he defiles the rest so that no beast, however hungry, will touch it. So far as I know, the wolverine is practically extinct in our country except in the northwestern States bordering on Canada.

OTHER CAMP THIEVES.—The bushy-tailed pack rat of the West is noted for carrying off any and everything that he can get away with, but the eastern wood rats and wood mice seldom do much damage about a camp beyond chewing up canvas or other cotton goods to build nests with — a trick that flying-squirrels also are prone to play.

I have never been bothered by 'coons, although living where they are abundant. But "Nessmuk" had a different experience. Many years ago he told in *Forest and Stream* of his troubles with them in northern Pennsylvania.—

"A strong cache . . . is indispensable in this region, for there is not a night during the open season in which you can lay by meat, fish, or butter, where hedgehogs and 'coons will not find it. Their strength and persistence in digging out your larder is something surprising. I have a butter cup with a tight-fitting cover, and a square tin case for keeping pork, also with a tight cover. Time and again I have had these tins raided by raccoons, nosed around, wallowed in the mud, and moved yards away from the cache; but the covers stuck like burs, and it must drive a 'coon frantic to work half the night in unearthing a butter cup, and then, with only one thickness of tin between his nose and the longed-for butter, be unable to get a taste of it. Unless the 'coon dialect has plenty of cuss-words I don't see how he could ever get over it."

CHAPTER XV
DRESSING AND KEEPING GAME AND FISH

Butchering is the most distasteful part of a hunter's work—a job to be sublet when you can; but sometimes you can't.

When an animal is shot, the first thing to do is to bleed it, unless the bullet itself has gone clean through and left a large hole of exit through which much blood has drained.

Even birds and fish should be bled as soon as secured. The meat keeps better, and, in the case of a bird, the feathers are more easily plucked. Speaking, now, of large game, do not drop your gun and rush in on a dying beast to stick it, for it might prove an ugly customer in its death struggle. First put a bullet through its heart or spine.

To cut a deer's throat would ruin the head for mounting. Twist its head to one side, with the throat downhill, if possible, so that blood will not flow over the hide; then stick your knife in at the point of the breast, just in front of the sternum or breastbone, and work the point of the knife two or three inches back and forth, close up to the backbone, so as to sever the great blood-vessels. Then if you must hurry on, perhaps after another animal, toss some brush over the carcass, or hang a handkerchief over it, to suggest a trap, and *make a brush blaze* here and there as you go along, to guide you back to the spot.

If practicable, remove the entrails at once. To do this, it is not necessary to hang the animal up.

DRESSING GAME AND FISH

If you are in a hurry, or if the camp is not far away, it will do merely to take out the paunch and intestines; but if this is neglected gas will accumulate and putrefaction will soon set in. A bear, especially, will soon spoil, because the fur keeps in the vital heat, so that the body will smoke when opened, even after it has lain a long time in hard-freezing weather.

If the animal is not to be butchered on the spot, slit the skin only from vent to stomach, using the point of the knife, and taking care not to rupture the paunch. Sever the intestine at the rectum, cut the genitals free, then cut off the gullet as high as you can above the stomach, and pull all out. The carcass should lie so that this is done toward the downhill side.

DRAGGING A DEER.— If the ground is not too rough, nor the distance too great, a deer may be dragged to camp over the snow or leaves; but drag it head-foremost; if pulled the other way every hair will act as a barb against the ground. Before starting, tie the front legs to the lower jaw. The carcass will slide easier, and the hide will not be so disfigured, if you first drop a bush or small tree by cutting through the roots, leaving a stub of a root projecting for a handle, then tie the animal on the upper side of the bush, and drag away.

PACKING DEER ON A SADDLE.— To pack a deer on horseback: first, if your horse is green in the business, let him smell the deer, pet him, and, if necessary, blindfold him until you get the carcass lashed in place. Even then you may have trouble. I have seen a mule get such a conniption fit at the smell of blood that he bucked himself, deer, and saddle, off a cut-bank into a swift river; the girth broke, and that saddle is going yet.

It may be necessary to smear some of the deer's blood on your horse's nose to kill the scent.

If the animal is antlered, remove the head and make a separate parcel of it.

Re-cinch your saddle, and, if the deer is too

heavy to lift upon the horse's back, fasten your picket-rope to the deer's hind legs, throw the line over the saddle, get on the other side, and haul away until the deer's hocks are up even with the saddle; then quickly snub the rope around the saddle-horn, go around, swing the burden over the saddle, balancing it evenly, and lash it fast. Or, if you wish to ride, move the deer behind the saddle and lash it there, bringing the legs forward on either side and tying them to the rings of the cinch. For thongs, if the saddle has none, cut strips from the skin of the deer's fore legs. Be sure to fasten the load securely, so that it cannot slip, or you will have a badly frightened horse. By skinning the legs from hoofs to ankles, partly disarticulating the latter, and then tying the legs snugly, they will not dangle and scare the horse, nor catch in underbrush.

Another way is to place the deer in the saddle seat, back to horn, legs to rear. Tie one end of a short rope to latigo ring, pass rope around deer back of shoulders and once more through the ring. Bring rope out in front of deer's breast, take a half turn with it in rope back of shoulders, and pull all tight. Take two half hitches on saddle horn. Repeat on opposite side, but bring rope up between hind legs of deer, take the half turn, and fasten to saddle horn as before. Now tie deer's head on top of load. This method of packing is recommended by W. G. Corker, who says "no horse alive can buck it off."

A simpler but secure way is to cut slits for thongs above the hocks and knees and another slit along the brisket. Place the deer on the saddle in such manner that the saddle horn sticks through the slit brisket. Tie down the legs at their middle joints to the cinch-ring on each side. (Emerson Hough.)

CARRYING ON A LITTER.— Two men can carry a deer on a pole by tying its legs together in pairs, slipping the pole through, and tying the head to the pole. Unless the carcass is tied snugly to the pole,

DRESSING GAME AND FISH 267

such a burden will swing like a pendulum as you trudge along, especially if the pole is at all springy.

A more comfortable way is to make a litter of two poles by laying them parallel, about two and one-half feet apart, and nailing or tying cross-pieces athwart the poles. Whittle the ends of the poles to a size convenient for your hands, and fasten to each end of the litter a broad strap, in such a way that it may pass over the shoulders of the carrier and thus take up much of the weight. Then lash the animal securely to the top of the litter.

CARRYING SINGLE-HANDED.—One man can carry a small deer entire by dragging it to a fallen tree, boosting it up on the log, lengthwise and back down, then grasping one or both hind legs with one hand and the fore legs with the other, and carrying the load so that its weight is on the back of his neck and shoulders.

Or you may prop the deer on the log breast down, squat with back of your neck against the body, put one arm under near front leg, the other under near hind leg, get the carcass on your shoulders, and arise.

A better scheme is to cut a slit through the lower jaw and up through the mouth, and another slit through each of the legs between the tendons, just above the hoof; tie the head and legs together, but not too close, and then, by the loop thus formed, swing the burden over your shoulder.

To carry a larger animal pickaback: gut it, cut off the head and hang it up to be called for later, skin the legs down to the knees and hocks, cut off the shinbones, tie the skin of each fore leg to the hind leg on the same side, put the arms through the loops thus formed, and "git ep!" Or, remove the bones from the fore legs from knee to foot, leaving the feet on, tie the hind legs together and the fore legs to them, thrust your head and one arm through, and carry the burden as a soldier does a blanket-roll.

THE INDIAN PACK.— When one has a long way

to go, and can only carry the hide and the choicer parts of the meat, the best way is to make up an Indian pack, as shown in Fig. 114. Skin the deer, place a stick athwart the inside of the skin, pack

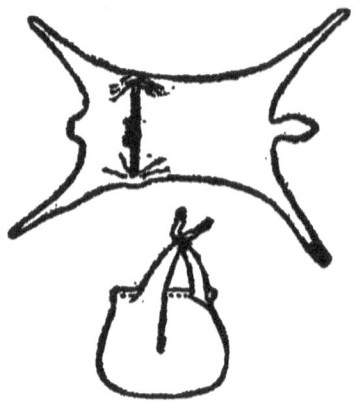

Fig. 114 — Indian Deer Pack

the saddles, hams, and tid-bits in the latter, and roll up and tie in a convenient bundle.

HANGING TO BUTCHER.— It is not necessary to hang a deer up to skin and butcher it; but that is the more cleanly way. One man, unassisted, can hang a pretty heavy animal in the following way: Drag it headforemost to a sapling that is just limber enough to bend near the ground when you climb it. Cut three poles, ten or twelve feet long, with crotches near the ends. Climb the sapling and trim off the top, leaving the stub of one stout branch near the top. Tie your belt, or a stout withe or flexible root, into a loop around the deer's antlers or throat. Bend the sapling down until you can slip the loop over the end of the sapling. The latter, acting as a spring-pole, will lift part of the deer's weight. Then place the crotches of the poles under the fork of the sapling, butts of poles radiating outward, thus forming a tripod. First push on one pole, then on another, and so raise the carcass free from the ground. If you do not intend to butcher it immediately, raise it up out of reach of roving dogs and "varmints."

DRESSING GAME AND FISH

It is common practice to hang deer by gambrels with the head down; but, when hung head up, the animal is easier to skin and to butcher, drains better, and does not drop blood and juices over the head and neck, which you may want to have mounted for a trophy. Dried blood is very hard to remove from hair or fur. If the skin is stripped off from rear to head it will be hard to grain. And if the animal is not to be skinned for some time it is best hung by the head, because the slope of the hair then sheds rain and snow instead of, holding them, and the lung cavity does not collect blood, rain, or snow.

The more common way of skinning a deer, when the head is not wanted for mounting, is to hang it up by one hind leg and begin skinning at the hock, peeling the legs, then the body, and finally the neck, then removing the head with skin on (for baking in a hole), after which the carcass is swung by both legs and is eviscerated.

If there is no time to hang the deer, open it, throw the entrails well off to one side, then cover the carcass with boughs as if it were a trap, or hang a handkerchief, or the blown-up bladder of the animal, over it, to scare away marauders. Place the deer so it will drain downhill. And don't neglect to blaze your way out, so you can find it again.

BUTCHERING DEER.— Now let us suppose that you have killed a deer far away from camp, and that you wish to skin and butcher it on the spot, saving all parts of it that are good for anything. You are alone. You wish to make a workmanlike job of it. You carry only the choicer parts with you that evening, and must fix the rest so it will not be molested overnight.

Of course, you have a jack-knife, and either a pocket hatchet or a big bowie-knife — probably the latter, if this is your first trip. First hang the deer, as described above. By the time you are through cutting those poles with the knife your hand will ache between thumb and forefinger; a tomahawk would have been better.

SKINNING.— This is your first buck, and you wish to save the head for mounting. For this the skin of the whole neck must be preserved, clear back to the shoulders. Cleanse away any blood that may have issued from the nose and mouth, and stuff some dry moss, or other absorbent, in the beast's mouth. Stick your big knife into a log alongside; it is only to look at, for the present.

Open your jack-knife, insert the point, edge up, where the neck joins the back, and cut the skin in a circle around the base of the neck, running from the withers down over the front of the shoulder-blade to the brisket or point of the breast on each side. Do not skin the head at present—you may not have time for that. Insert the point of the knife through the skin over the paunch, and, following the middle line of the chest, slit upward to meet the cut around the neck. Then reverse, and continue the slit backward to the end of the tail, being careful not to perforate the walls of the belly. Then slit along the inside of each leg from the hoof to the belly-slit. If you wish to save the feet for mounting, be particular to rip the skin in a straight line up the *under* side of the leg, starting by inserting the point of the knife between the heel-pads.

Now comes a nice trick, that of severing the shanks. Nearly every inexperienced person starts too high. Study the accompanying illustrations

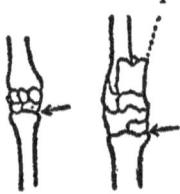

Fig. 115 — The Place to Use Your Knife. From *Forest and Stream*

of these joints, noting where the arrow points, which is the place to use your knife. In a

DRESSING GAME AND FISH

deer the joint is about an inch and a half below the hock on the hind leg, and an inch below the knee on the fore leg. Cut square across through skin and muscles, in front, and similarly behind; then, with a quick pull backward against your knee, snap the shank off. The joint of the fore leg is broken in a similar manner, excepting that it is snapped forward.

Having stripped the vertebræ from the tail, now peel the skin off the whole animal, from the shoulders downward, assisting with your closed fist, and, where necessary, with the knife; but wherever the knife is used be careful to scrape the skin as clean as you can, without cutting it, for every adhering bit of fat, flesh, or membrane must be thoroughly removed before the skin is ready for tanning, and that is easier to do now than after it dries. The whole operation of skinning is much easier while the animal is still warm than after the body has become cold. To skin a frozen animal is a desperately mean job. I have known four old hunters to work nearly a whole afternoon in skinning a frozen bear.

The skin of the body and limbs having been removed, stretch it out flat, hair side down, alongside of you to receive portions of the meat as it is butchered.

GRALLOCHING.— Now take up your big knife, insert its point alongside the breastbone, and cut through the false ribs to the point of the sternum. In a young animal this is easy; but in an old one the ribs have ossified, and you must search for the soft points of union between the ribs and the sternum, which are rather hard to find. Here your knife's temper, and perhaps your own, will be put to the test. The most trifling-looking pocket hatchet would do the trick in a jiffy.

Open the abdominal cavity, taking care not to rupture anything, and prop the chest open a few inches with a stick, or by merely pulling the ribs away from each other. Cut the diaphragm free at both sides and at the back. (It is the membrane that separates the organs of the chest from those of the abdomen.) Everything now is free from the body except at the throat and anus. Reach in and take in your grasp all the vessels that run up into the neck. With knife in the other hand, cut them across from above downward, taking care that you do not cut yourself. Now pull away gradually, helping a little here and there with the knife until all the contents of the visceral cavity lie at your feet, save the lower end of the rectum, which is still attached. With a hatchet, if you had one, you would now split the pelvis. The thing can be done with a large knife, if the animal is not too old, by finding the soft suture at the highest part of the bone and rocking the knife-edge on it. But you may not be able to accomplish this just now. So reach in with the jack-knife, cut carefully around the rectum and urinary organs, keeping as close to the bone as possible, and free everything from the cavity. If water is near, wash out the cavity and let it drain, or wipe with a dry cloth if you have one. Be particular to leave no clotted blood.

To remove the head; flay back the skin for several inches at base of neck, cut through flesh, etc., to the backbone. Search along this till you find the flat joint between the faces of two vertebræ, separate these as far as you can; then twist the attached part of the body round and round, until it breaks off.

Directions how to skin a head for mounting are given in Volume II.

In butchering, save the liver, heart, brain, milt (spleen), kidneys, and the caul fat. The caul is the fold of membrane loaded with fat that covers most of the intestines. In removing the liver you need not bother about a gall-bladder, for a deer has none. Many a tenderfoot has been tricked into looking for it. In the final cutting up, save the marrow-bones (especially of elk) for eating;

DRESSING GAME AND FISH

the ligaments that lie on either side of the backbone, from the head backward, for sinew thread; the hoofs for glue (if you are far from supply-stores and expect to remain a good while); and perhaps the bladder, paunch, large intestine, and pericardium (outer skin) of the heart, for pouches and receptacles of various kinds, and to make catgut. The scrotum of a buck, tanned with the hair on, makes a good tobacco-pouch.

BUTCHERING ON THE GROUND.— If one is in a hurry, and is not particular about the hide, he can do his butchering on the ground. In that case, lay the animal on sloping ground, with its head uphill; or bend its back over a log or rock; or turn it on its back with its head twisted around and wedged under one side. The old-time way of butchering a buffalo was to turn the carcass on its belly, stretching out the legs on either side to support it. A transverse cut was made at the nape of the neck; then the workman, gathering the long hair of the hump in one hand, separated the skin from the shoulder, laid it open to the tail, along the spine, freed it from the sides, and pulled it down to the brisket. While the skin was thus still attached to the belly it was stretched upon the ground to receive the dissected meat. Then the shoulder was severed, and the fleece, which is the mixed fat and lean that lies along the loin and ribs, was removed from along the backbone, and the hump ribs were cut off with a tomahawk. These portions were placed on the skin, together with the *boudins* from the stomach, and the tongue. The rest of the meat was left to feed the wolves.

ELK AND MOOSE.— Such large animals are generally butchered on the ground. If the beast has antlers, first remove the head. Then turn the body on its back and prop it in position with a couple of three-foot stakes sharpened at both ends, a hole being dug for a moose's withers. Sometimes only the haunches, sirloins and tongue are saved, these being cut away without skinning or gutting the carcass.

If there is a horse, or several men with a rope, to elevate the body, the animal's lower legs are skinned, the shanks removed, the hide split from throat to tail, the sides skinned free, the windpipe and gullet raised, the pleura and diaphragm cut loose, and the carcass then raised high enough so that the hide can be removed from the rump and back. The rectum, small intestines, and paunch are then loosened and allowed to roll out on the ground. The gullet is cut, the liver taken out, and the diaphragm, lungs and heart removed. Then the skinning is finished over the shoulders and fore legs.

It is best not to cut up the meat until it is quite cold and firm. Then split the carcass in halves along the backbone, and quarter it, leaving one rib on each hind quarter. The meat may then be put on a scaffold, and covered with the skin to protect it from moose-birds.

Two men can raise a very heavy animal clear of the ground with three stiff poles, say twelve feet long, which are sharpened at the butts and notched at the tips. Lay these on the ground with notched ends together over the animal's hind quarters and the sharpened ends radiating outward and equidistant from each other. Tie the notched ends rather loosely together with a short piece of rope, the other end of which is tied to a gambrel thrust through the hind legs under the hamstrings (or attach to antlers, nose, or through lower jaw). Lift the tripod until the rope is taut, shove one pole forward a few inches, then another, sticking the butts in the ground as you progress, until the hindquarters are raised, and so on until the beast swings free.

BEARS.— These beasts, too, are generally butchered on the ground. In skinning, begin the incisions at the feet, and leave at least the scalp, if not the skin of the whole head, attached. It is

DRESSING GAME AND FISH 275

quite a task to skin a bear, as the beast usually is covered with fat, which adheres to the hide and must be scraped free. All of the caul fat should be saved for rendering into bear's oil, which is better and wholesomer than lard. The brain, liver, and milt (spleen) are good eating.

Owing to its greasiness, the skin of a bear is very likely to spoil unless carefully scraped, especially at the ears. Slit the ears open on the inside, skin them back almost to the edge, and fill with salt; also salt the base of the ears. The feet likewise must be skinned out and well salted.

PRESERVING SKINS.— If a hide is to be preserved for some time in a green state, use nothing on it but salt. Spread it out flat, hair side down, stretch the legs, flanks, etc., and rub all parts thoroughly with salt, particular pains being taken to leave no little fold untreated. A moose-hide will take ten or even fifteen pounds of salt. As soon as the salting is done, fold in the legs and roll the hide up.

Methods of tanning, and of making buckskin and rawhide, will be discussed in Volume II.

CARE OF MEAT.— When a deer has merely been eviscerated and is hung up to be skinned, and cut up at a more convenient season, prop open the abdominal cavity with a stick, so that it may dry out quickly. If the weather is warm enough at any hour of the day for flies to come out, keep a smudge going under the carcass.* It takes flies but a few minutes to raise Ned with venison. If blows are discovered on the meat, remove them, looking especially at all folds and nicks in the meat, and around the bones, for the blows work into such places very quickly. So long as they have not bored into the flesh they do it no harm.

A surer way is described by Doctor Breck:

---

* This means in camp, where there is someone to look after it. Do not leave a smudge to take care of itself out in the woods: a wind springing up in your absence may cause it to set the forest afire.

"It is my practice to carry with me three or four yards of cheesecloth (which has been dipped in alum-water at home), and this I wrap closely round whatever parts of the animal I especially wish to preserve. If a round of venison is thus done up, preferably with a needle and thread, it is safe from fly-blows, which are the bane of hunters. If unskinned, a head may also be kept clean in like manner. The cheesecloth takes up little more room than a napkin, and amply repays the small bulge in the coat-pocket."—*The Way of the Woods.*

I always carry cheesecloth on fishing trips, too.

It may be said here that even smoked bacon is not immune from blows, and it should not be hung up without a cheesecloth cover. The fly that blows meats is the common "blue-bottle." Its eggs hatch into "skippers" within twelve hours.

CURING VENISON.— Venison keeps a long time without curing, if the climate is cool and dry. To cure a deer's ham, hang it up by the shank, divide the muscles just above the hock, and insert a handful of dry salt. The meat of the deer tribe gets more tender and better flavored the longer it is hung up. In warm weather dust flour all over a haunch or saddle of venison, sew it up in a loose bag of cheesecloth, and hang it in a shady place where there is a current of air. It will keep sweet for several weeks, if there is no crevice in the bag through which insects can penetrate. Ordinarily it is best not to salt meat, for salt draws the juices. Bear meat, however, requires much salt to cure it — more than any other game animal.

Hornaday recommends the following recipe for curing venison:—

The proportions of the mixture I use are:
Salt .... 3 lbs.
Allspice .... 4 table-spoonfuls,
Black Pepper .... 5 table-spoonfuls,
    all thoroughly mixed.

Take a ham of deer, elk, or mountain sheep, or fall-killed mountain goat, and as soon as possible after killing, dissect the thigh, muscle by muscle. Any one can learn to do this by following up with the knife the natural

DRESSING GAME AND FISH 277

divisions between the muscles. With big game like elk, some of the muscles of the thigh are so thick they require to be split in two. A piece of meat should not exceed five inches in thickness. Skin off all enveloping membranes, so that the curative powder will come in direct contact with the raw, moist flesh. The flesh must be sufficiently fresh and moist that the preservative will readily adhere to it. The best size for pieces of meat to be cured by this process is not over a foot long, by six or eight inches wide and four inches thick.

When each piece has been neatly and skilfully prepared rub the powder upon every part of the surface, and let the mixture adhere as much as it will. Then hang up each piece of meat, by a string through a hole in the smaller end, and let it dry in the wind. If the sun is hot, keep the meat in the shade; but in the North the sun helps the process. Never let the meat get wet. If the weather is rainy for a long period, hang your meat rack where it will get heat from the campfire, but no more smoke than is unavoidable, and cover it at night with a piece of canvas.

Meat thus prepared is not at its best for eating until it is about a month old; then slice it thin. After that no sportsman, or hunter, or trapper can get enough of it. . . .

No; this is *not* "jerked" meat. It is many times better. It is always eaten uncooked, and as a concentrated, stimulating food for men in the wilds it is valuable.

(*Camp-fires in the Canadian Rockies,* 201–203.)

It is a curious fact that blow-flies work close to the ground, and will seldom meddle with meat that is hung more than ten feet above the ground. Game or fish suspended at a height of twenty feet will be immune from "blows," if hung on a trimmed sapling well away from any foliage.

JERKED VENISON.— "Jerky" or jerked meat has nothing to do with our common word "jerk." It is an anglicized form of the Spanish *charqui,* which is itself derived from the Quichua (Peruvian) *ccharqui,* meaning flesh cut in flakes and dried without salt. It is the same as the African *biltong.* Those who have not investigated the matter may be surprised to learn that the round of beef is 61 per cent. water, and that even the common dried and smoked meat of the butcher shops contains 54 per cent. water. To condense the nutritive properties of these substances, the water, of course, must be exhausted. In ordinary dried beef this is only partially done, because the pieces are too thick.

In the dry air of uninhabited plains, meat does not putrefy, even when unsalted, and it may be dried in the sun, without fire. Elk flesh dried in the sun does not keep as well as that of deer.

As I have said, real jerky has been dried without salt; but it is common practice nowadays to use some salt in the process, proceeding as follows:—

If you can afford to be particular, select only the tender parts of the meat; otherwise use all of the lean. Cut it in strips about half an inch thick. If you have time, you may soak them a day in strong brine. If not, place the flakes of meat on the inside of the hide, and mix with them about a pint and a half of salt for a whole deer, or two or three quarts for an elk or moose; also some pepper. These condiments are not necessary, but are added merely for seasoning. Cover the meat with the hide, to keep flies out, and let it stand thus for about two hours to let the salt work in. Then drive four forked stakes in the ground so as to form a square, the forks being about four feet from the ground. Lay two poles across from fork to fork, parallel, and across these lay thin poles about two inches apart. Lay the strips of meat across the poles, and under them build a small fire to dry and smoke the meat. Do not let the fire get hot enough to cook the meat, but only to dehydrate it, so that the flesh becomes dry as a chip. The best fuel is birch, especially black birch, because it imparts a pleasant flavor. Only a thin smoke is wanted. To confine it, if a breeze is stirring, put up some sort of wind-break. This will reduce the weight of the meat about one-half, and will cure it so that it will keep indefinitely. You may have to keep up the fire for twenty-four hours. The meat of an old bull will, of course,

DRESSING GAME AND FISH 279

be as tough as sole leather; but, in any case, it will retain its flavor and sustenance. When pounded pretty fine, jerky makes excellent soup; but it is good enough as it is, and a man can live on it exclusively without suffering an inordinate craving for bread.

The breasts (only) of grouse and other game birds can be cured in the same way, and are good.

Some do not like their meat smoked. A way of jerking without smoking was described by " an old-timer " for the *New York Sun:*

"Cut the choicest of the meat into strips ten inches long and two inches square. Sprinkle them quite liberally with salt, but not enough to make them bitter. Let the salt work on them for a couple of hours. While it is doing it you go and put down two logs a foot or so in diameter side by side and about the same distance apart. Between the logs make a fire of dry hemlock bark.

"Hemlock, or a relative of hemlock, is always apt to be found in deer hunting regions, and I never go into camp without taking pains to gather up a lot of hemlock bark for use. It is the best material for the purpose because it will make a fire of hot coals without running to blaze or smoke. Birch bark would be ideal for the purpose, but it is all blaze with birch bark. Hickory wood couldn't be beat for jerking venison, but hickory wood would smoke the meat, and jerked venison isn't smoked venison, as a good many folks suppose it is, not by a long shot.

"Having got your bed of hemlock bark coals in fine shape, and having driven at the inside edge of the ends of each log a crotched stick long enough after it is securely driven to have the crotch perhaps a foot above the logs, and having extended from crotch to crotch in these sticks two poles that are thus suspended above the fire, cut as many half inch hardwood sticks as you need, long enough to reach across from one pole to another and rest securely on them. On these sticks string your strips of deer meat by thrusting them through the meat near one end of the strips, the sticks being sharpened at one end to facilitate that operation.

"This will leave the strips hanging from their sticks much as the candles used to hang from theirs in the old fashioned moulds, if any hunter of this generation is happy enough to have recollections of the days when we made our own candles. Place the sticks with their pendent meat over the coals. Turn the concave sides of lengths of hemlock bark over the top of the sticks. This will keep in the steam that will presently begin to rise from the meat, as the coals get their gradual but effective work in on it. Keep the fire down there between the logs so it won't make too rapid a heat, for if it does the juice will ooze out of the meat and be lost, and that would detract from the excellence of the finished product.

"If during the process of jerking your venison the meat is taken off the coals before it is done it will be soft and flabby. If it is hard when taken off it will be overdone. In either case your jerked venison might much better have remained unjerked, for it will be a failure. To prevent either of these catastrophes the meat should be tested frequently by pushing a sharp knife blade or other convenient probe into and through the strips. The moment it requires more than ordinary force to push the probe through, your venison is thoroughly and properly jerked. Then shove the coals from under the strips and let them cool with the dying embers."

COMPUTING WEIGHT.— Hornaday gives the following rule, in his *Natural History,* for computing the live weight of deer from the dressed weight: Add five ciphers to the dressed weight in pounds, and divide by 78,612; the quotient will be the live weight in pounds.

SMALL MAMMALS.— Now for what Shakespeare calls "small deer." The easiest way for a novice to skin a squirrel is the one described by "Nessmuk."—

"Chop off head, tail, and feet with the hatchet; cut the skin on the back crosswise, and, inserting the two middle fingers, pull the skin off in two parts (head and tail). Clean and cut the squirrel in halves, leaving two ribs on the hind quarters." The objection is that, in this case, you throw away the best part of the squirrel, the cheek meat and brain being its special tid-bits.

A better way is this: Sever the tail from below, holding your left forefinger close in behind it, and cutting through the vertebræ close up to the body, leaving only the hide on the top side. Then turn the squirrel over and cut a slit down along each ham. Put your foot on the tail, hold the rear end of the squirrel in your hand, and pull, stripping the skin off to the fore legs. Peel the

DRESSING GAME AND FISH

skin from the hind legs, and cut off the feet. Then cut off the fore feet. Skin to the neck; assist here a little with the knife; then skin to the ears; cut off the butts of the ears; then skin till the blue of the eyeballs shows, and cut; then to the nose till the teeth show, and cut it off. Thus you get no hair on the meat, and the whole thing is done in less than a minute, when you have gained deftness.

In dressing mammals larger than squirrels be particular to remove the scent glands. Even rabbits have them. Cut directly between the fore leg and body and you will find a small waxy " kernel " which is a gland. The degree to which this taints the flesh depends a good deal on the season; but in most of the fur-bearers it is always objectionable.

Dan Beard gives the following directions for dressing small animals:

" To prepare a musquash or any other small fur-bearing animal for the table, first make *a skinning stick* of a forked stick about as thick as your finger. Let the forks be about one inch to each branch, and the stick below long enough to reach up between your knees when the sharpened lower end is forced into the ground. If you squat on the ground the stick should be about a foot and one-half long, but longer if you sit on a camp stool, stump or stone. Hang the muskrat on the forks of the stick by thrusting the sharpened ends of the fork through the thin spot at the gambrel joints of the hind legs, that is, the parts which correspond with your own heels. Hung in this manner (with the one and one-half foot stick), the nose of the animal will just clear the ground. First skin the game, then remove all the internal organs, and, if it be a muskrat, not only remove all the musk glands, but cut into the inside of the forearms and the fleshy part of the thighs, and take out a little white substance you will find there which resembles a nerve. This done and the meat well washed, it may be cooked with little fear of the food retaining a musky flavor."
— (*Field and Forest Handy Book.*)

To skin a 'coon: begin with the point of the knife in the center of one hind foot and slit up the inside of the leg to the vent and down the other leg in a like manner. Cut carefully around the vent, then rip from it up to the chin. Strip the skin from the bone of the tail with a split stick gripped firmly in the hand. Then flay the animal, scrape the pelt clean, and put it on a stretcher to dry.

DRESSING BIRDS.— Turkeys, geese, ducks, and grouse are usually dry picked. If this could be done while the bodies were still warm, it would be no job at all; but after they are cold it generally results in a good deal of laceration of the skin — so much so that sometimes the disgusted operator gives up and skins the whole bird. It would be better to scald them first, like chickens. In dry picking, hang the bird up by one leg, pluck first the pinions and tail feathers; then the small feathers from shanks and inside of thighs; then the others. Grasp only a few feathers at a time between finger and thumb, as close to the skin as possible, and pull quickly toward the head. Then pick out all pin-feathers and quills. Singe the down off quickly, so as not to give an oily appearance to the skin. Ordinarily the down can be removed from a duck's breast by grasping the bird by the neck and giving one sweep of the open hand down one side of the body and then one down the other. In plucking geese or ducks some use finely powdered resin to remove the pin-feathers. The bird is plucked dry, then rubbed all over with the resin, dipped in and out of boiling water seven or eight times, and then the pin-feathers and down are easily rubbed off.

To draw a bird: cut off the head, and the legs at the first joint. Make a lengthwise slit on back at base of neck and sever neck bone close to body, also the membrane which holds the windpipe. Make a lengthwise incision from breastbone to (and around) the vent, so you can easily draw the insides, which must be done carefully, so as not to rupture the gall-bladder (pheasants have none).

The idea that ducks and other game birds should hang until they smell badly is monstrous. If you

DRESSING GAME AND FISH 283

want to know where such tastes originated, read the annals of medieval sieges.

Small game birds, such as snipe and plover, can be cleaned very quickly by pressing a thumb on each side of their breasts, and, with a swift push, break the skin back, carrying feathers, backbone and entrails with it, and leaving only the breast. Grouse can be treated in the same way if the skin of the breast is first slit. The legs and rump, if wanted, can be removed separately.

KEEPING SMALL GAME.— To ship rabbits, squirrels, etc.: do not skin them, but remove the entrails, wipe the insides perfectly dry, wrap in paper, and pack them back down.

Never pack birds in straw or grass without ice, for in damp or warm weather this will heat or sweat them. If they freeze they must be kept so, as they will quickly spoil after thawing. Food in a bird's crop soon sours; the crop should be removed.

To preserve birds in warm weather for shipment: draw them, wash the inside perfectly clean, dry thoroughly, and then take pieces of charcoal from the fireplace, wrap them in a thin rag, and fill the abdominal cavity with this. Also fill the bill, ears, eyes, and anal opening with powdered charcoal, to keep off flies and prevent putrefaction. Reject all pieces of charcoal that are only half-burnt or have the odor of creosote. Birds stuffed in this way will keep sweet for a week in hot weather.

CLEANING TROUT.— Brook trout have no noticeable scales, but they should be scraped free of slime. Rainbow trout need scaling.

Remove the vent, cut the gills free from the lower jaw and back of head, and slit open from head to anal fin. Draw the inside out by the gills, and scrape the clotted blood away from the backbone. If the fish are only for the pan, not to be exhibited, cut the heads off; then they are easier to clean. Large ones, anyway, should have heads and tails cut off before frying.

A small trout may be cleaned without splitting, by cutting out the vent, tearing out the gills with the fingers, and drawing the entrails with them.

CLEANING SCALY FISH.— To scale a fish: grasp it by the head (or lay it on a board and drive a fork through its tail), and, using a knife that is not over-keen, scale first one side and then the other, with swift, steady sweeps. The scales below the gills, and those near the fins, are removed by moving the point of the knife crosswise to the fish's length. Next place the knife just below the belly fin and with a slant stroke cut off this, the side fins, and the head, all in one piece. Then remove the back fin, and the spines beneath it, by making a deep incision on each side of the fin and pulling the latter out. The ventral part is removed in the same way. Open the fish, wash it in cold water, scrape off the slime, and then wipe it *dry* with a clean cloth or towel. Large fish, for broiling, should be split open along the back and the spine removed.

A special fish knife, with saw-tooth back for scaling, can be bought at a sporting-goods store. A good scaler is extemporized by nailing a common bottle cap on the flattened end of a stick.

A slippery, flabby fish is more easily handled for scaling if you sharpen one end of a stick as thick as your little finger and run it down through the fish's mouth about two-thirds the length of the body.

Fish taken from muddy or mossy water, or from cedar swamps, taste strong if cleaned in the ordinary way, unless special precautions are taken in cooking (see Chapter XVIII). The taint is not removed by scaling, for its cause is hidden deep in the roots of the scales. Such fish should be skinned. That is also the best way to prepare yellow perch.

SKINNING FISH.— Grasp the fish firmly, belly down. Cut across the nape of the neck, run the point of the knife along the back to the tail, and

DRESSING GAME AND FISH 285

on each side of the back fin. Remove the fin by catching lower end between thumb and knife blade and pulling smartly upward toward the head. Skin each side by seizing between thumb and knife the flap of skin at nape and jerking outward and downward; then the rest, by grasping skin as near the vent as possible and tearing quickly down to the tail, bring away the anal fin. Remove the head and the entrails will come with it. Trout and pickerel should be scraped free of slime.

Large fish for frying are best steaked. Robert Pinkerton gives the following directions:

" Cut off the head, run the knife down either side of the bones of the back the entire length. Cut down to the backbone and continue along the ribs. This gives you two slabs of boneless meat and leaves the entrails in the skeleton. Lay the pieces, skin side down, on a paddle blade and run a sharp knife between the flesh and skin. You now have boneless, scaleless, skinless fish, which may be rolled in flour or cornmeal, fried in bacon grease, and eaten with as little difficulty as though it were moose steak."

To skin a catfish or bullhead, do not scald it, for that makes the meat flabby and robs it of its fresh flavor. Cut off the ends of the spines, slit the skin behind and around the head, and then from this point along the back to the tail, cutting around the back fin. Then peel the two corners of the skin well down, sever the backbone, and, holding to the corners of the skin with one hand, pull the fish's body free from the skin with the other. A pair of pliers will be appreciated here.

Or, cut through the skin clear around the neck near the gills. Stick a large table fork into the gills and pin the fish to a board by its backbone. Then catch the skin at neck between thumb and knife-blade, and strip it off by a steady pull.

To skin an eel: drive a fork through the back of his neck (if you have no fork, roll him in ashes or dust and use a swab in the left hand), slit the skin around his neck with a sharp knife, make a longitudinal slit half the length of the body, peel the skin back at the neck until you get a good hold, and then strip it off.

Another way is to rub the tail under your foot until the skin splits, or nail the eel up by the tail, cut through the skin around the body just forward of the tail and work its edges loose, then draw the skin off over the head; this takes out all of the fin bones, and strips off the skin entire.

To KEEP FISH.— It is very bad practice to string fish together through the gills and keep them in water till you start for home. It makes them lose blood and torments them till they die of suffocation. Why sicken your fish before you eat them? If you must use a stringer, push its point through the fish's lower jaw. Then it can breathe freely. A single fish on a good length of line, strung in this way, can fight off turtles till you notice the commotion.

If you are not fishing from a boat, with live box or net, then by all means kill your fish as fast as you catch them. Some do this by giving the thing's head a quick jerk backward, breaking its neck; others hit it a smart rap on the back of the head with the handle of a sheath-knife (many English fishermen carry a "priest," which is a miniature bludgeon, for this very purpose). It is better to break the fish's throat-latch (the cord that joins head to body on the under side), because that not only kills the fish but bleeds it, and one's finger does the trick in a second.

The reason for killing fish at once is two-fold; first, it is humane; second, it keeps the meat firm, as it should be for the pan, and it will not spoil so soon as if the fish smothered to death.

Fish spoil from exposure to sun and moisture, especially the latter. They keep much better if wiped dry before carrying away. Never use fish that have been lying in the sun or that have begun to soften. Ptomaines work in a mysterious but effectual way.

DRESSING GAME AND FISH 287

To keep fish in camp: scale, behead, and clean them; then string them by a cord through their tails and hang them, head down, in a shady, breezy place. They drain well when hung in this way, and that is important.

If you stay long in one place, it will pay to sink a covered box in the sloping bank of a stream, to keep your fish in. Such a bank is always cool. Hang the fish up separately in the box with rods or cords. If you lack a box, make a rock-lined cache, covered with flat stones to keep out mink and other robbers.

Trout may be kept bright, with their spots showing lively, for many hours, if each is wiped and wrapped separately in some absorbent paper, such as toilet paper, as soon as caught.

To keep fish that must be carried some distance, in hot weather: clean them as soon as you can after they are caught, and *wipe them dry*. Then rub a little salt along their backbones, but nowhere else, for salt draws the juices. Do not pile them touching each other, but between layers of paper, cheesecloth, basswood leaves, or ferns.

If you are to pack fish in ice, the best way is to have with you some parchment paper (any mail-order house) to keep them from direct contact with the ice. This paper is strong and waterproof. Everybody ought to know that when fish get wet from ice the best of their flavor is stolen. For the same reason it is bad practice to carry fish in damp moss or grass. Keep them dry, whether you have ice or not.

There is a very good thing called a refrigerator grip, to be bought of dealers in sporting goods. Outside it looks like a common handbag. Within are two metal compartments. The upper section is filled with cracked ice and the cover is screwed on. The lower one contains food and drink for an outing, and holds your fish on the trip home. It is surrounded by a metal shell into which the water drips as the ice melts. No ice or water comes in contact with what you carry.

If you have no ice, and yet wish to transport your catch a considerable distance, try the following method recommended a good many years ago by Colonel Park (he says it is also a good way to pack venison). Some of my correspondents have enthusiastically given me credit for inventing it, but I got it out of a little *Sportsmen's Handbook* by the above-named gentleman, printed, as I remember, in Cincinnati, of which I have seen but one copy. For brevity's sake, I paraphrase the description.—

Kill the fish as soon as caught; wipe them clean and dry; remove the entrails; scrape the blood off from around the backbone; remove the gills and eyes; wipe dry again; split the fish through the backbone to the skin, from the inside; fill this split with salt; spread the fish overnight on a board or log to cool. In the morning, before sunrise, fold the fish in dry towels, so that there is a fold of towel between each fish and its neighbor; carefully wrap the whole package in a piece of muslin, and sew it up into a tight bag, and then in woolen blanketing, sewing up the ends and sides. Now put the roll in a stout paper bag, such as a flour sack. "Fish prepared in this way can be sent from Maine to New Orleans in August, and will remain fresh and nice."

Sugar, as it has antiseptic qualities, is a good preservative. Doctor O. M. Clay gives the following process for keeping trout a week or two:

"Clean well; remove heads; wash thoroughly; dry with cloth. Cook a syrup of sugar and water until it begins to candy. In this dip the fish, one at a time, and lay them on a board to glaze. Pack in a box. Before using, soak overnight in cold water."

To dry fish for future use: split them along the back, remove the backbones and entrails, and soak them in a weak brine overnight. Make a conical teepee of cloth or bark, suspend the fish in it, and dry and smoke them over a small fire for a couple of days. This is tedious, as the fire requires close

DRESSING GAME AND FISH 289

attention; but it pays when many fish are to be dried.

To salt fish: dress them as above, wash clean, and roll in salt. " Place them in a wooden vessel in a cool place for several days; then turn them out and let the brine drain off. Clean the vessel and put the fish back. Cover them with brine made strong enough to carry an egg or potato. Trout preserved in this way are excellent." (E. Kreps, *Camp and Trail Methods*.)

The following method of preserving fish is quoted from *Outdoor Life*:

"Put two handfuls of salt in two or three quarts of water. Let it come to a boil. Then put fish on a piece of cheesecloth or other white cloth so as to be able to handle them, and dip them in this water, allowing them to remain in it five to seven minutes, according to size of fish. Water should not boil after the fish are put in. Then put them in vinegar, allspice, cloves and bay leaves — using enough vinegar to submerge the fish. Leave them in this solution until used. We believe you will find fish preserved in this way the sweetest-tasting that you ever ate."

CHAPTER XVI
CAMP COOKERY

Meats

The main secrets of good meals in camp are to have a proper fire, good materials, and then to imprison in each dish, at the outset, its natural juice and characteristic flavor. To season fresh camp dishes as a French chef would is a blunder of the first magnitude. The raw materials used in city cuisine are often of inferior quality, from keeping in cold storage or with chemical preservatives; so their insipidity must be corrected by spices, herbs, and sauces to make them eatable. In cheap restaurants and boarding houses, where the chef's skill is lacking, "all things taste alike" from having been penned up together in a refrigerator and cooked in a fetid atmosphere.

In my chapter on Provisions I advised that a few condiments be taken along, but these are mostly for seasoning left-overs or for desserts — not for fresh meat, unless we have but one kind, to the surfeiting point. In the woods our fish is freshly caught, our game has hung out of doors, and the water and air used in cooking (most important factors) are sweet and pure. Such viands need no masking. The only seasoning required is with pepper and salt, to be used sparingly, and not added (except in soups and stews) until the dish is nearly or quite done. Remember this: salt draws the juices.

The juices of meats and fish are their most palatable and nutritious ingredients. We extract them purposely in making soups, stews, and gravies,

MEATS

but in so doing we ruin the meat itself. Any fish, flesh, or fowl that is fit to be eaten for the good meat's sake should be cooked succulent, by first coagulating the outside (searing in a bright flame or in a very hot pan, or plunging into smoking hot grease or furiously boiling water) and then removing farther from the fire to cook gradually till done. The first process, which is quickly performed, is "the surprise." It sets the juices, and, in the case of frying, seals the fish or meat in a grease-proof envelope so that it will not become sodden but will dry crisp when drained. The horrors of the frying-pan that has been unskillfully wielded are too well known. Let us campers, to whom the frying-pan is an almost indispensable utensil, set a good example to our grease-afflicted country by using it according to the code of health and epicurean taste.

Meat, game, and fish may be fried, broiled, roasted, baked, boiled, stewed, or steamed. Frying and broiling are the quickest processes; roasting, baking, and boiling take an hour or two; a stew of meat and vegetables, to be good, takes half a day, and so does soup prepared from the raw materials. Tough meat should be boiled or braised in a pot.

Do not eat freshly killed meat if you can help it. Game should hang at least two days; otherwise it will be tough and tasteless. Venison eaten before it has completely cooled through will cause diarrhœa and perhaps nausea.

FRYING.— Do not try to fry over a flaming fire or a deep bed of coals; the grease would likely burn and catch aflame. Rake a thin layer of coals out in front of the fire; or, for a quick meal, make your fire of small dry sticks, no thicker than your finger, boil water for your coffee over the flame, and then fry over the quickly formed coals.

If you have a deep pan and plenty of frying fat, it is much the best to immerse the material completely in boiling grease, as doughnuts are fried.

Let the fat boil until little jets of smoke arise (being careful not to burn the grease). When fat begins to smoke continuously it is decomposing and will impart an acrid taste. When a bread crumb dropped in will be crisp when taken out, the fat is of the right temperature. Then quickly drop in small pieces of the material, one at a time so as not to check the heat. Turn them once while cooking. Remove when done, and drop them a moment on coarse paper to absorb surplus grease, or hang them over a row of small sticks so they can drain. Then season. The fry will be crisp, and dry enough to handle without soiling the fingers. This is *the* way for small fish.

Travelers must generally get along with shallow pans and little grease. To fry (or, properly, to sauté) in this manner, without getting the article sodden and unfit for the stomach, heat the dry pan very hot, and then grease it only enough to keep the meat from sticking (fat meat needs none). The material must be dry when put in the pan (wipe fish with a towel) or it will absorb grease. Cook quickly and turn frequently, not jabbing with a fork for that would let juice escape. Season when done, and serve piping hot.

Lard used for frying fish must not be used again for anything but fish. Crisco does not transmit the flavor of one food to another. Surplus fat can be kept in a baking powder can, sealed, for transit, with surgeon's plaster.

Chops, fat meats, squirrels, rabbits, and the smaller game birds are best sautéd or fricasseed and served with gravy. A fricassee is made of meat or birds cut into small pieces, fried or stewed, and served with gravy. Sausage should be fried over a very gentle fire.

Bear meat is best braised (see under that heading); if to be fried, it should first be soaked for an hour in a solution of one tablespoon baking soda to a quart of water, then parboiled until tender.

BROILING.— Fresh meat that is tender enough to

MEATS 293

escape the boiling pot or the braising oven should either be broiled or roasted before a bed of clear, hard coals. Both of these processes preserve the characteristic flavor of the meat and add that piquant, aromatic-bitter " taste of the fire " which no pan nor oven can impart. Broil when you are in a hurry, but when you have leisure for a good job, roast your meat, basting it frequently with drippings from the pan below, so as to keep the surface moist and flexible and insure that precise degree of browning which delights a gourmet.

For broiling, cut the meat at least an inch thick. Only tender pieces are fit for broiling. Venison usually requires some pounding, but don't gash it in doing so. Have a bed of bright coals free from smoke, with clear flaming fire to one side. Sear outside of meat by thrusting for a moment in the flame and turning; then broil before the fire, rather than over it, so as to catch drippings in a pan underneath. Do not season until done, or, if you do salt it, observe the rule for chops, given below. A steak 1 inch thick should be broiled five minutes, 1½ inches ten minutes, 2 inches twenty minutes. Serve on hot dish with drippings poured over, or buttered.

To broil on a forked, green stick, tie the split-open bird, or whatever it be, to the fork with hemlock rootlets or others that do not burn easily.

To broil enough for a party, when you have no broiler, clean the frying-pan thoroughly and get it almost red hot, so as to seal pores of meat instantly. Cover pan. Turn meat often, without stabbing. A large venison steak will be done in ten minutes. Put on hot dish, season with pepper and salt, and pour juices over it. Equal to meat broiled on a gridiron, and saves the juices. To broil by completely covering the slice of meat with hot ashes and embers is a very good way.

To grill on a rock, take two large flat stones of a kind that do not burst from heat (not moist or seamy ones), wipe them clean of grit, place them one above the other, with a few pebbles between to keep them apart, and build a fire around them. When they are well heated, sweep away the ashes, and place your slices of meat between the stones.

Before broiling fish on an iron they should be buttered and floured to prevent sticking; or, grease the broiler.

There is no chop like an English mutton chop. It should be cut *thick*. How to cook it is told by an English camper, Mr. T. H. Holding, in his *Camper's Handbook:*

"First let the pan get warm, then rub with a piece of the fat from the meat. As this fat warms and melts on the bottom, put in the chop and slightly increase your flame [he is assuming that you cook on a Primus stove], and let it cook rapidly. Put a very free sprinkling of salt on the *top* of the chop. I will explain this. The salt that is so distributed melts, and runs into the pores of the meat and gets through it. As the heat forces up the blood, so the salt in melting trickles down till it fills the chop, so to say. Directly the latter begins to look red on the top, turn it over smartly and cleanly. Now the heat will drive back the blood to meet the fresh supply of salt that is put on the 'new' side. Cook it gently, moving it at intervals. Presently this salt will disappear, and in its place blood will begin to make its appearance and show the chop is cooked.

"Now, the hungry one who knows how to enjoy a chop, will be delighted with one thus cooked. It will be tender, tasty, and soft, if the meat is good. A chop should not be cooked till it is pale inside; if it loses its redness it loses its character and its flavor.

"The fat of a chop should not be cut off, unless there is too much of it. It will pay to cook it and so help to make gravy, into which a piece of bread or slices of potato may be put and fried. . . .

"If a couple of potatoes be peeled and washed, cut in slices not more than an eighth-of-an-inch in thickness, put in the pan around the chop, and the whole covered over with a plate, they will be cooked by the time the chop is done. I am free to say from experience that never do potatoes taste so sweet as when cooked under these conditions. . . . But to cut these potatoes thick is to foil the object, because they have not time then to cook through."

Chops of mountain sheep and other game may be cooked in the same way.

ROASTING.— To roast is to cook by the direct

MEATS

heat of the fire, as on a spit or before a high bed of coals. Baking is performed in an oven, pit, or closed vessel. No kitchen range can compete with an open fire for roasting.

Build a rather large fire of split hardwood (softwoods are useless) against a high backlog or wall of rocks which will reflect the heat forward. Sear the outside of the roast (not a bird or fish) in clear flames until outer layer of albumen is coagulated. Then skewer thin slices of pork to upper end; hang roast before fire and close to it by a stout wet cord; turn frequently; catch drippings in pan or green-bark trough, and baste with them. This is better than roasting on a spit over the fire, because the heat can be better regulated, the meat turned and held in position more easily, the roast is not smoked, and the drippings are utilized.

Just before the meat is done, baste it and sprinkle with flour, then brown it near the fire, and make gravy as directed on page 303.

A whole side of venison can be roasted by planting two stout forked stakes before the fire, a stub of each stake being thrust through a slit cut between the ribs and under the backbone. The forward part of the saddle is the best roasting piece. Trim off flanky parts and ends of ribs, and split backbone lengthwise so that the whole will hang flat. To roast a shoulder, peel it from the side, cut off leg at knee, gash thickest part of flesh, press bits of pork into them, and skewer some slices to upper part.

When roasting a large joint, a turkey, or anything else that will require more than an hour of steady heat, do not depend upon adding wood from time to time, unless you have a good supply of sound, dry hardwood sticks of stove-wood size. If green wood or large sticks must be used, build a bonfire of them at one side of your cooking-fire, and shovel coals from it as required. It will not do to check the cooking-fire.

Kabobs.— When in a hurry, cut a 1½ or 2 inch portion from the saddle or other tender part, break up the fiber by pounding, unless the animal was young, and divide the meat into several small fragments. Impale one of these on a sharpened stick, salt and pepper it, plunge it for a moment into a clear bright flame, then toast it slowly over the embers. Salt, in this case, is glazed on the surface and cannot draw the juice. While eating one bit, toast another.

Roasting in the Reflector.— Pin thin slices of pork or bacon over the roast. Put a little water in the bake-pan, lay the meat in, and set the baker before the fire. Baste occasionally. When the front is done, reverse the pan. Make gravy from the drippings.

Barbecueing.— To barbecue is to roast an animal whole, and baste it frequently with a special dressing, for which the following recipe is borrowed from Frank Bates:

"One pint of vinegar, half a can of tomatoes, two teaspoonfuls of red pepper (chopped pepper-pods are better), a teaspoonful of black pepper, same of salt, two tablespoonfuls of butter. Simmer together till it is completely amalgamated. Have a bit of clean cloth or sponge tied on the end of a stick, and keep the meat well basted with the dressing as long as it is on the fire."

Dig a pit somewhat longer and wider than the spread-out carcass of the animal. Build a log fire in it of hardwood. When this has burned to coals, place a green log at each end of the pit and one on each side of it, near the edges. Over the side logs lay green poles to support the meat, thick enough not to burn through (when it can be procured, a sheet of wire netting is laid over this frame). Tough meat is previously parboiled in large pots.

BRAISING.— Tough meat is improved by braising in a Dutch oven, or a covered pot or saucepan. This process lies between baking and frying. It is pre-eminently the way to cook bear meat, venison shoulders and rounds. Put the meat in the oven or

MEATS

pot with about two inches of hot water in the bottom, and a bit of bacon or pork (but not for bear). Add some chopped onion, if desired, for seasoning. Cover and cook about fifteen minutes to the pound. A half hour before the meat is done, season it with salt and pepper.

The gravy is made by pouring the grease from the pot, adding a little water and salt, and rubbing flour into it gradually with a spoon.

BAKING MEAT.—*Baking in a Hole.*—This is a modification of braising. Dig a hole in the ground, say 18 x 18 x 12 inches. Place kindling in it, and over the hole build a cob house by laying split hardwood sticks across, not touching each other, then another course over these and at right angles to them, and so on till you have a stack two feet high. Set fire to it. The air will circulate freely, and the sticks, if of uniform size, will all burn down to coals together.

Cut the fowl, or whatever it is, in pieces, season, add a chunk of fat pork the size of your fist, put in the kettle, pour in enough water to cover, put lid on kettle, rake coals out of hole, put kettle in, shovel coals around and over it, cover all with a few inches of earth, and let it alone over night. It beats a bake-oven. In case of rain, cover with bark.

Experiment with this two or three times before you risk much on it; for the right heat and the time required can only be learned by experience.

Grouse and the like can be cooked nicely by putting one in the bean-pot when baking beans.

Baking an Animal in Its Hide.— If the beast is too large to bake entire, cut off what you want and sew it up in a piece of the hide. In this case it is best to have the hole lined with flat stones. Rake out embers, put meat in, cover first with green grass or leaves, then with the hot coals and ashes, and build a fire on top. When done, remove the skin.

A deer's head is placed in the pit, neck down,

and baked in the same way: time about six hours.

Baking in Clay.— This hermetically seals the meat while cooking, and is better than baking in a kettle, but requires experience. Draw the animal, but leave the skin and hair on. If it be a large bird, as a duck or goose, cut off head and most of neck, also feet and pinions, pull out tail feathers and cut tail off (to get rid of oil sac), but leave smaller feathers on. If a fish, do not scale. Moisten and work some clay till it is like softened putty. Roll it out in a sheet an inch thick and large enough to completely encase the animal. Cover the latter so that no feather or hair projects. Place in fire and cover with good bed of coals and let it remain with fire burning on top from ¾ of an hour, for a small bird or medium trout, to two hours for a pheasant or duck. Larger animals require more time, and had best be placed in bake-hole over night.

When done, break open the hard casing of baked clay. The skin peels off with it, leaving the meat perfectly clean and baked to perfection in its own juices. This method has been practiced for ages by the gipsies and other primitive peoples.

Frank Bates recommends another way: " Have a pail of water in which stir clay until it is of the consistency of thick porridge or whitewash. Take the bird by the feet and dip into the water. The clay will gather on and between the feathers. Repeat till the bird is a mass of clay. Lay this in the ashes, being careful to dry the outside. Bake till the clay is almost burned to a brick."

Baking in the Embers.— To bake a fish, clean it — if it is large enough to be emptied through a hole in the neck, do not slit the belly — season with salt and pepper, and, if liked, stuff with Indian meal. Have ready a good bed of glowing hardwood coals; cover it with a thin layer of ashes, that the fish may not be burnt. Lay the fish on this, and cover it with more ashes and coals. Half an hour, more or less, is required, according to size.

MEATS

On removing the fish, pull off the skin, and the flesh will be found clean and palatable.

A bird, for example a duck, is baked in much the same way. Draw it, through a small slit at the vent, but do not remove the feathers. If you like stuffed duck, stuff with bread crumbs or broken biscuit, well seasoned with salt and pepper. Wet the feathers by dipping the bird in water; then bury it in the ashes and coals. A teal will require about half an hour; other birds in proportion.

BOILING.— The broader the pot, and the blacker it is, the quicker it boils. Fresh meats should be started in boiling water; salt or corned meats, and those intended for stews or soups, in cold water. The meat (except hams) should be cut into chunks of not over five pounds each, and soup bones well cracked. Watch during first half hour, and skim off all scum as fast as it rises, or it will settle and adhere to meat. Fresh meat should be boiled until bones are free, or until a fork will pierce easily (ten pounds take about two and a half hours). Save the broth for soup-stock, or make gravy of it by seasoning with pepper and thickening with flour. (See page 303.)

Meat that is to be eaten cold should be allowed to cool in the liquor in which it was boiled. A tablespoonful or two of vinegar added to the boiling water makes meat more tender and fish firmer. Turn the meat several times while boiling. If the water needs replenishing, do it with boiling, not cold, water. Season a short time before meat is done. If vegetables are to be cooked with the meat, add them at such time that they will just finish cooking when the meat is done (potatoes twenty to thirty minutes before the end; carrots and turnips, sliced, one to one and a half hours).

Remember this: put fresh meat in hard boiling water for only five minutes, to set the juices; then remove to greater height over the fire and boil very slowly — to let it boil hard all the time would make it tough and indigestible. Salt or corned meats go in cold water at the start and are gradually brought to a boil; thereafter they should be allowed barely to simmer.

Fish go in boiling salted water. Boiling meat must be kept covered.

In heating milk beware that you do not burn it. Bring it gradually to the simmering point, but do not let it actually boil.

At high altitudes it is impossible to cook satisfactorily by boiling, because water boils at a lower and lower temperature the higher we climb. The decrease is at the rate of about one degree for every 550 feet up to one mile, and one degree for 560 feet above that, when the temperature is 70°. With the air at 32° F., and the barometer at 30 inches, water boils at 212° at sea-level, 202.5° at 5,000 feet, 193.3° at 10,000 feet, and 184.5° at 15,000 feet. These figures vary somewhat according to the purity of the water, the material of the vessel, etc.

To parboil is to boil only until tender, before cooking in some other way.

STEWING.— This process is slow, and should be reserved for tough meats. Use lean meat only. First brown it with some hot fat in a frying-pan; or put a couple of ounces of chopped pork in a kettle and get it thoroughly hot; cut your meat into small pieces; drop them into the fat and "jiggle" the kettle until the surface of the meat is coagulated by the hot fat, being careful, the while, not to burn it. Add a thickening of a couple of ounces of flour and mix it thoroughly with the fat; then a pint of water or soup-stock. Heat the contents of the kettle to boiling and season with salt, pepper, and chopped onion. Curry powder, if you like it, is proper in a stew. Now cover the kettle closely and hang it where it will only simmer for four or five hours. Stews may be thickened with rice, potatoes, or oatmeal, as well as with flour. Add condiments to suit the taste. A ragout is nothing but a highly seasoned stew. The greater the variety

MEATS

of meats and vegetables, the better. Rice and tomatoes are especially suitable. Macaroni, spaghetti, vermicelli, and noodles, are fine in stews; you will need little or no bread if you have such pastes or some dumplings in the stew. To vary the flavor of game stews, add beef extract, such as Steero or other beef cubes, or Oysters. Desiccated vegetables may be used instead of fresh ones.

The method given above is the one I usually follow; but I take the liberty of adding another by Captain Kenealy:

"Stewing is an admirable way of making palatable coarse and tough pieces of meat, but it requires the knack, like all other culinary processes. Have a hot fry-pan ready, cut the meat up into small squares and put it (without any dripping or fat) into the pan. Let it brown well, adding a small quantity of granulated sugar and sliced onions to taste. Cook until the onions are tender and well colored. Then empty the fry-pan into a stew-pan and add boiling water to cover the meat, and let it simmer gently for two or three hours. Flavor with salt, pepper, sweet herbs, curry powder or what you will. The result will be a savory dish of tender meat, called by the French a ragout. It is easy to prepare it this way. Do not boil it furiously as is sometimes done, or it will become tough. This dish may be thickened with browned flour, and vegetables may be added — turnips, carrots, celery, etc., cut into small pieces and browned with the meat. The sugar improves the flavor vastly. The only condiments actually necessary are pepper and salt. Other flavorings are luxuries."

STEAMING.— To steam meat or vegetables: build a large fire and throw on it a number of smooth stones, not of the bomb-shell kind. Dig a hole in the ground near the fire. When the stones are red hot, fork them into the hole, level them, cover with green or wet leaves, grass, or branches, place the meat or potatoes on this layer, cover with more leaves, and then cover all with a good layer of earth. Now bore a small hole down to the food, pour in some water, and immediately stop up the hole, letting the food steam until tender. This is the Chinook method of cooking camass. Shellfish can be steamed in the same way.

MEAT GRAVIES AND SAUCES.— A gravy is seasoned with nothing but salt and pepper, the object being to preserve the flavor of the meat. A sauce is highly seasoned to disguise poor meat, or made-over dishes, or whatever has been served so often that it begins to pall on the appetite.

An abundance of rich gravy is relished by campers who do not carry butter. They have nothing else to make their bread "slip down." Good gravy cannot be made from meat that has been fried properly or broiled, because the juice is left in the meat. Our pioneer families seldom had butter, yet they had to eat a much larger component of bread than we do, from lack of side dishes. Hence the "fried-to-a-chip" school of cookery.

In such case, the right way is obvious, granting that you have plenty of meat. Fry properly enough meat for the party and leave enough more in the pan to make gravy. Gash or mince this remainder, cook all the juice out of it without scorching, throw out the refuse meat, rub in a thickening prepared in advance as directed below, salt and pepper, then thin to the desired consistency with boiling water. The thickening is made by rubbing cold milk, or water, or broth, a little at a time, into a spoonful of flour, until a smooth paste is formed that will just drop from a spoon; or thicken with roux. Chopped liver improves a gravy.

Roux (pronounced "roo") is a thickening for gravy or soups that can be prepared at any time and kept ready for emergencies. It will keep good for months in a covered jar. A teaspoonful thickens half a pint of gravy, or a pint of soup.

Brown roux is made thus: Melt slowly ½ lb. of butter, skim it well, let it stand for a minute to settle, and pour it off from the curd. Put the clear oily butter into a pan over a slow fire, shake into it enough sifted flour (7 or 8 oz.) to make a thick paste. Stir constantly and heat slowly and evenly until it is very thick and of a bright brown color. Put it into a jar. White roux is made in

MEATS

the same way except that it is stirred over a very gentle fire until it is thoroughly baked but not browned. It is used for white gravy on fish, etc.

Gravy for Boiled Meat.— Some of the liquor in which the meat was cooked can be thickened by melting a piece of butter the size of a small egg, mixing with it very smoothly a tablespoonful of flour, heating until lightly browned, adding the meat liquor and letting it boil up. Flavor to taste and serve separately from the meat.

Gravy for Roast Meat.— Use the drippings as above, and thin with boiling water in which half a teaspoonful of salt has been dissolved.

Dripping is the fat that drops from meat when roasting.

Gravy from Extract of Beef.— When there is no venison in camp, it will not be long before the men crave the taste of beef. Liebig's extract, or Bovril, or Steero, dissolved in boiling water and liberally salted will make a good beef gravy by letting it boil up, then simmer, and thicken in one of the ways described above.

Onion Gravy.— Rub up flour in water to a batter; salt it. Chop some onion very fine and fry it a little in the meat juice. Pour the batter on this, and stir till the flour is done.

Cream Gravy for Meat or Fish.—

> ½ pint milk.
> 1 tablespoonful butter.
> ½ tablespoonful flour.
> ½ tablespoonful salt.
> ⅛ tablespoonful pepper.

Heat butter in frying-pan. Add flour, stirring until smooth and frothy. Draw pan back and gradually stir in the milk. Then return the pan to the fire. Add salt and pepper. Stir until sauce boils. This must be used at once, and everybody's plate should be hot, of course.

Sauces.— A camp cook nearly always lacks the sweet herbs, fresh parsley, mushrooms, capers, anchovies, shrimps, tarragon, wine, and many other condiments to which standard sauces owe their characteristic flavors. He must make shift with spices and perhaps lemon, Worcestershire, vinegar, mustard, curry powder, or celery seed. How to use these to the best advantage cannot be taught in a book. Personal tastes and the materials at hand must govern. I give here the recipes for three simple sauces for meat. Others will be found in the chapters on GAME, FISH, and DESSERTS.

Mustard Sauce.— Brown two teaspoonfuls of flour in a pan with a little butter. Put two tablespoonfuls of butter on a plate and blend with it the browned flour, a teaspoonful of mustard, and a little salt. When these are smoothly mixed stir them into ¼ pint boiling water. Simmer five minutes. Add enough vinegar or lemon juice to flavor.

Venison Sauce.— Stir together one tablespoonful of butter with a teaspoonful of mustard and three tablespoonfuls of jelly (preferably currant). When these are well blended, add three tablespoonfuls of vinegar, some grated nutmeg, and a dash of Cayenne pepper. Heat together. When the sauce boils add three tablespoonfuls chopped pickles. Serve at once. Currant jelly alone goes well with venison.

Sauce for Broiled Venison.— Make the steak-dish very hot. Put on it for each pound of venison ½ tablespoonful of butter, a tablespoonful of currant jelly, one of boiling water, and a little pepper and salt. Turn the broiled steaks in the sauce once or twice and serve very hot.

Parsley Butter.— I confess to a weakness for the flavor of parsley. The fresh herb, of course, we cannot have in camp, but the dehydrated kind, or C. & B. dried parsley, will do very well. Make a thin mixture of flour and water, salt it, and add a pat of butter (not really necessary). Boil this until the rawness is gone from the flour, and use it with fish, flesh, or fowl, particularly the latter.

CHAPTER XVII
CAMP COOKERY

Game

The following additional details are supplementary to what has gone before, and presuppose a careful reading of the preceding pages.

Game and all other kinds of fresh meat should be hung up till they have bled thoroughly and have cooled through and through — they are tenderer and better after they have hung several days. Venison especially is tough until it has hung a week. In no case cook meat until the animal heat has left it: if you do, it is likely to sicken you. This does not apply to fish. Frozen meat or fish should be thawed in very cold water and then cooked immediately — warm water would soften it and steal its flavor.

All mammals from the 'coon size down, as well as duck and grouse, unless young and tender, or unless they have hung several days, should be parboiled (gently simmered) from ten to thirty minutes, according to size, before frying, broiling, or roasting. The scent glands of mammals and the oil sacs of birds should be removed before cooking. In small mammals look for pea-shaped, waxy or reddish kernels under the front legs and on either side of the small of the back.

As game has little natural fat, it requires frequent basting and the free use of butter or bacon grease in cooking.

VENISON.— *(Deer of all species, elk, moose, caribou.)*

Fried Venison.— See page 291.
Boiled Venison.— See page 292.
Roast Venison.— See page 294.
Braised Venison.— See page 296.
Baked Venison.— See page 297.
Boiled Venison.— See page 299.
Stewed Venison.— See page 300.
Steamed Venison.— See page 301.
Baked Deer's Head.— See page 297.
Braised Bear.— See page 296.
Fried Bear.— See page 292.

Brains.— Clean and wash them well. Fry; or boil slowly half an hour.

Brains and Eggs.— Desiccated eggs will do as well as fresh ones. Soak them as directed on can.

Chop fine some bacon and enough onion to season. Dice the brains into about ½-inch cubes. Fry bacon and onion together until brown. Add the brains, and cook until nearly done; then add the eggs, beaten slightly, and fry until they are scrambled. Season with salt and pepper.

Heart.— Remove valves and tough, fibrous tissue; then braise, or cut into small pieces and use in soups or stews.

Kidneys, Fried.— Halve them, slit twice the long way on the inside, but do not cut clear through; leave the fat on the kidneys. Fry until all blueness has disappeared.

Kidneys, Stewed.— Soak in cold water one hour. Cut into small pieces, and drop each piece into cold water, as cut. Wash well; then stew, seasoning with onion, celery (dehydrated), cloves, salt and pepper.

Liver.— Carefully remove the gall-bladder if the animal has one — deer have not. Parboil the liver and skim off the bitter scum that rises. Slice rather thin; put one slice of bacon in the pan and fry from it enough grease to keep liver from sticking. Salt the liver and fry until half done; then add more bacon and fry all until done. Liver should be thoroughly cooked; if you put all the

GAME

bacon in with it at the start the latter would be ruined before the liver was done.

Another way: cut liver into slices ¼-inch thick, soak it one hour in cold salt water, rinse well in warm water, wipe dry, dip each slice in flour seasoned with salt and pepper, and fry as above.

If in a hurry, put the liver on a green hardwood stick for a spit, skewer some of the caul fat around it, and roast before the fire.

Marrow Bones.— Cover ends with small pieces of plain dough made with flour and water, over which tie a floured cloth; place bones upright in kettle, and cover with boiling water. Boil two hours. Remove cloth and paste, push out marrow, and serve with dry toast.

Milt (Spleen).— Skewer a piece of bacon to it, and broil.

Moose Muffle (nose and upper lip).— Boil like pig's head. Add an onion.

Tongue.— Soak for one hour; rinse in fresh water; put in a kettle of cold water, bring to a boil, skim and simmer two hours, or until tender. A blade of mace and a clove or two improve the gravy; so also Worcestershire sauce.

Croquettes.— Two cups minced meat or game of any kind, ½ cup bread or cracker crumbs, 1½ egg, melted butter. Roll meat, seasoning, and enough of the butter to moisten, into pear-shaped balls. Dip in beaten eggs and crumbs. Fry, with enough butter, to a nice brown.

Venison Sausages.— Utilize the tougher parts of the deer, or other game, by mincing the raw meat with half as much salt pork, season with pepper and sage, make into little pats, and fry like sausages. Very good.

Game Pot Pie.— Take ½ teaspoonful baking powder to ½ pint of flour, sift together, and add a teaspoonful lard or butter by rubbing it in, also a pinch of salt. Make a soft biscuit dough of this, handling as little as possible and being careful not to mix too thin. Roll into a sheet and cut into strips about 1½ inches wide and 3 inches long, cutting two or three little holes through each to let steam escape. Meantime you have been boiling meat or game and have sliced some potatoes.

When the meat is within one-half hour of being done, pour off the broth into another vessel and lift out most of the meat. Place a layer of meat and potatoes in bottom of kettle, and partially cover with strips of the dough; then another layer of meat and vegetables, another of dough, and so on until the pot is nearly full, topping off with dough. Pour the hot broth over this, cover tightly, and boil one-half hour, without lifting the pot cover, which, by admitting cold air, would make the dough "sad." Parsley helps the pot, when you can get it.

Dumplings.— These add zest to a stew or to boiled meat of any kind. Plain dumplings are made of biscuit dough or the batter of dropped biscuit (recipes in chapter on BREAD). Drop them into the pot a short time before meat is done. See also page 358.

Bear, Braised.— See page 296.

SMALL GAME.—

Jambolaya.— This is a delicious Creole dish, easily prepared. Cut up any kind of small game into joints, and stew them. When half done, add some minced ham or bacon, ¼ pint rice, and season with pepper and salt. If rabbit is used, add onions. Serve with tomatoes as a sauce.

Curry of Game.— Cut some birds or other small game into rather small joints. Fry until lightly browned. Score each joint slightly, place a little curry powder in each opening, and squeeze lemon juice over it. Cover the joints with brown gravy and simmer gently for twenty minutes. Serve with rice around the dish. (See also *Curry Sauce,* page 320.)

Game Pie.— Make a plain pie crust as directed in the chapter on DESSERTS. Cut the game into joints. Season rather highly. Moisten the joints

GAME

with melted butter and lemon juice, or put a few thin strips of bacon in with them. Cover with top crust like a fruit pie and bake not too long; time according to size.

Squirrels, Fried.— Unless they are young, parboil them gently for ½ hour in salted water. Then fry in butter or pork grease until brown. A dash of curry powder when frying is begun improves them, unless you dislike curry. Make gravy as directed on page 303.

Squirrels, Broiled.— Use only young ones. Soak in cold salted water for an hour, wipe dry, and broil over the coals with a slice of bacon laid over each squirrel to baste it.

Squirrels, Stewed.— They are best this way, or fricasseed. For directions see pages 300 and 292.

Squirrels, Barbecued.— Build a hardwood fire between two large logs lying about two feet apart. At each end of the fire drive two forked stakes about fifteen inches apart, so that the four stakes will form a rectangle, like the legs of a table. The forks should all be about eighteen inches above the ground. Choose young, tender squirrels (if old ones must be used, parboil them until tender but not soft). Prepare spits by cutting stout switches of some wood that does not burn easily (sassafras is best — beware of poison sumach), peel them, sharpen the points, and harden them by thrusting for a few moments under the hot ashes. Impale each squirrel by thrusting a spit through flank, belly, and shoulder, on one side, and another spit similarly on the other side, spreading out the sides, and, if necessary, cutting through the ribs, so that the squirrel will lie open and flat.

Lay two poles across the fire from crotch to crotch of the posts, and across these lay your spitted squirrels. As soon as these are heated through, begin basting with a piece of pork on the end of a switch. Turn the squirrels as required. Cook slowly, tempering the heat, if needful, by scattering ashes thinly over the coals; but remove the ashes for a final browning. When the squirrels are done, butter them and gash a little that the juices may flow.

Rabbit, or Hare.— Remove the head; skin and draw, cut out the waxy glands under the front legs where they join the body; soak in cold salted water for one hour; rinse in fresh cold water and wipe dry. It is better, however, unless the animals are quite young, to parboil them for about fifteen minutes with salt, pepper, and an onion. Rabbits are not really good to eat until several days after killing.

To fry: parboil first, cut off legs at body joint, and cut the back into three pieces. Sprinkle with flour and fry brown on both sides. Remove rabbit to a dish kept hot over a few coals. Make a gravy as follows: Put into the pan a small onion previously parboiled and minced and add one cup boiling water. Stir in gradually one or two tablespoonfuls of browned flour; stir well, and let it boil one minute. Season with pepper, salt, and nutmeg. Pour it over the rabbit.

To roast in reflector: cut as above, lay a slice of pork on each piece, and baste frequently. The rabbit may be roasted whole before the fire.

To bake in an oven: stuff with a dressing made of bread crumbs, the heart and liver (previously parboiled in a small amount of water), some fat salt pork, and a small onion, all minced and mixed together, seasoned with pepper, salt, and nutmeg, and slightly moistened with the water in which heart and liver were parboiled. Sew up the opening closely; rub butter or dripping over rabbit, dredge with flour, lay thin slices of fat pork on back, and place it in pan or Dutch oven, back uppermost. Pour into pan a pint or more of boiling water (or stock, if you have it), and bake with very moderate heat, one hour, basting every few minutes if in pan, but not if in Dutch oven. Prepare a gravy with the pot juice, as directed above.

Rabbit is good stewed with onion, nutmeg, pep-

GAME

per, and salt for seasoning. Also curried, after the manner already described.

"The rabbity taste can be eliminated by putting a tablespoonful of vinegar in the water in which the rabbit is boiled. Hard boiling will toughen the meat; allow it to simmer gently for one or two hours. When tender add a minced onion and some bacon grease to the liquor and place in the baker to brown.

"The Germans prepare rabbit in a more ambitious manner, but one that well repays. The disjointed rabbit is simmered until tender. Pour the meat and liquor into a dressing made as follows: Fry until brown three or four pieces of bacon which have been diced. Add to this a tablespoonful of flour, a teaspoonful each of sugar and salt, a tablespoonful of vinegar, and a few cloves if possible. Stir well to keep from burning.

"In both cases time can be saved by simmering the rabbit in the evening, and, on the following day, browning in a baker or serving with the German dressing." (*Kathrene Pinkerton.*)

Rabbits are unfit to eat in late summer, as their backs are then infested with warbles, which are the larvæ of the rabbit bot-fly.

Possum.— To call our possum an opossum, outside of a scientific treatise, is an affectation. Possum is his name wherever he is known and hunted, this country over. He is not good until you have freezing weather; nor is he to be served without sweet potatoes, except in desperate extremity. This is how to serve " possum hot." —

Stick him, and hang him up to bleed until morning. A tub is half filled with hot water (not quite scalding) into which drop the possum and hold him by the tail until the hair will strip. Take him out, lay him on a plank, and pull the hair out with your fingers. Draw, clean, and hang him up to freeze for two or three nights. Then place him in a 5-gallon kettle of cold water, into which throw two pods of red pepper. Parboil for one hour in this pepper-water, which is then thrown out and the kettle refilled with fresh water, wherein he is boiled one hour.

While this is going on, slice and steam some sweet potatoes. Take the possum out, place him in a large Dutch oven, sprinkle him with black pepper, salt, and a pinch or two of sage. A dash of lemon will do no harm. Pack sweet potatoes around him. Pour a pint of water into the oven, put the lid on, and see that it fits tightly. Bake slowly until brown and crisp. Serve hot, *without* gravy. Bourbon whiskey is the orthodox accompaniment. If you are a teetotaler, any plantation darky can show you how to make "ginger tea" out of ginger, molasses, and water. Corn bread, of course.

It is said that possum is not hard to digest even when eaten cold, but the general verdict seems to be that none is ever left over to get cold.

When you have no oven, roast the possum before a high bed of coals, having suspended him by a wet string, which is twisted and untwisted to give a rotary motion, and constantly baste it with a sauce made from red pepper, salt, and vinegar.

Possum may also be baked in clay, with his hide on. Stuff with stale bread and sage, plaster over him an inch of stiff clay, and bake as previously directed. He will be done in about an hour.

Coon.— It is likewise pedantic to call this animal a raccoon. Coon he always has been, is now, and shall ever be, to those who know him best.

Skin and dress him. Remove the "kernels" (scent glands) under each front leg and on either side of spine in small of back. Wash in cold water. Parboil in one or two waters, depending upon the animal's age. Stuff with dressing like a turkey. If you have a tart apple, quarter it and add to the dressing. Bake to a delicate brown. Serve with fried sweet potatoes.

Porcupine.— I quote from Nessmuk: "And do not despise the fretful porcupine; he is better than he looks. If you happen on a healthy young specimen when you are needing meat, give him a show before condemning him. Shoot him humanely in the head, and dress him. It is easily done; there are no quills on the belly, and the skin peels as freely as a rabbit's. Take him to camp, parboil him for thirty minutes, and roast or broil him to a rich brown over a bed of glowing coals. He will need no pork to make him juicy, and you will find him very like spring lamb, only better."

The porcupine may also be baked in clay, without skinning him; the quills and skin peel off with the hard clay covering. Or, fry *quickly*.

As I have never eaten porcupine, I will do some more quoting — this time from Dr. Breck: "It may be either roasted or made into a stew, in the manner of hares, but must be parboiled at least a half-hour to be tender. One part of the porcupine is always a delicacy — the *liver,* which is easily removed by making a cut just under the neck into which the hand is thrust, and the liver pulled out. It may be fried with bacon, or baked slowly and carefully in the baker-pan with slices of bacon."

Muskrat.— You may be driven to this, some day, and will then learn that muskrat, properly prepared is not half bad. The French-Canadians found that out long ago. Remove the musk glands and the white stringy substance found on the inside of the forearms and thighs. I do not remember where I picked up the following recipe:

"Skin and clean carefully four muskrats, being particular not to rupture musk or gall sac. Take the hind legs and saddles, place in pot with a little water, a little julienne (or fresh vegetables, if you have them), some pepper and salt, and a few slices of pork or bacon. Simmer slowly over fire until half done. Remove to baker, place water from pot in the baking pan, and cook until done, basting frequently. This will be found a most toothsome dish."

Muskrat may also be broiled over the hot coals, basting with a bit of pork held on a switch above the beastie.

Woodchuck.— I asked old Uncle Bob Flowers,

one of my neighbors in the Smokies: "Did you ever eat a woodchuck?"

"Reckon I don't know what them is."

"Ground-hog."

"O la! dozens of 'em. The red ones hain't good, but the gray ones! man, they'd jest make yer mouth water!"

"How do you cook them?"

"Cut the leetle red kernels out from under their forelegs; then bile 'em, fust — all the strong is left in the water — then pepper 'em and sage 'em, and put 'em in a pan, and bake 'em to a nice rich brown, and — then I don't want nobody there but me!"

According to J. Alden Loring, "The only way to cook a woodchuck properly is to roast him whole on a stick over a camp-fire, turning him from time to time until he is well done. The skin keeps the fat from broiling out, and enough sinks into the flesh to make it tender and juicy."

Beaver Tail.— This tid-bit of the old-time trappers will be tasted by few of our generation, more's the pity. Impale the tail on a sharp stick and broil over the coals for a few minutes. The rough, scaly hide will blister and come off in sheets, leaving the tail clean, white, and solid. Then roast, or boil until tender. It is of a gelatinous nature, tastes somewhat like pork, and is considered very strengthening food. A young beaver, stuffed and baked in its hide, is good; old ones have a peculiar flavor that is unpleasant to those not accustomed to such diet.

Beaver tail may also be soused in vinegar, after boiling, or baked with beans. It makes a good soup if part of the backbone is added.

The liver, broiled on a stick and seasoned with butter, salt, and pepper, is the best part of the animal.

BIRDS.— If game birds are not hung a few days after killing they are likely to be tough; but, as I have remarked elsewhere, this should not be overdone.

Game Birds, Fried.— Birds for frying should be cut in convenient pieces, parboiled until tender in a pot with enough water to cover, then removed, saving the liquor. Sprinkle with salt, pepper, and flour (this for the sake of the gravy), fry in melted pork fat, take out when done, then stir into the frying fat one-half cupful dry flour till a dark brown, add parboiling liquor, bring to a boil, put game in dish, and pour gravy over it, or serve with one of the sauces described below.

Game Birds, Broiled.— Split them up the back, broil over the coals, and baste with a piece of pork on tined stick held over them. Fillets of ducks or other large birds may be sliced off and impaled on sticks with thin slices of pork.

Game Birds, Fricasseed.— Any kind of bird may be fricasseed as follows: Cut it into convenient pieces, parboil them in enough water to cover; when tender, remove from the pot and drain. Fry two or three slices of pork until brown. Sprinkle the pieces of bird with salt, pepper, and flour, and fry to a dark brown in the pork fat. Take up the bird, and stir into the frying fat half a cup, more or less, of dry flour, stirring until it becomes a dark brown; then pour over it the liquor in which the bird was boiled (unless it was a fish-eater), and bring the mixture to a boil. Put the bird in a hot dish, and serve with the gravy poured over it.

Wild Turkey, Roasted.— Pluck, draw, and singe. Wipe the bird inside and out. Rub the inside with salt and red pepper. Stuff the crop cavity, then the body, with either of the dressings mentioned below, allowing room for the filling to swell. Tie a string around the neck, and sew up the body. Truss wings to body with wooden skewers. Pin thin slices of fat pork to breast in same way. Suspend the fowl before a high bed of hardwood coals, as previously described, and place a pan under it to catch drippings. Tie a clean rag on the end of a stick to baste with. Turn and baste frequently. Roast until well done (two to three hours). (See also page 294.)

Meantime cleanse the gizzard, liver, and heart of the turkey thoroughly in cold water; mince them; put them in a pot with enough cold water to cover, and stew gently until tender; then place where they will keep warm until wanted. When the turkey is done, add the giblets with the water in which they were stewed to the drippings in pan; thicken with one or two tablespoonfuls of flour that has been stirred up in milk or water and browned in a pan; season with pepper and salt, and serve with the turkey. If you have butter, the fowl may be basted with it (melted, of course), and when stewing the giblets add a tablespoonful of butter and half a teacupful of evaporated milk.

Stuffing for Turkey.— (1) If chestnuts are procurable, roast a quart of them, remove shells, and mash. Add a teaspoonful of salt, and some pepper. Mix well together, and stuff the bird with them.

(2) Chop some fat salt pork very fine; soak stale bread or crackers in hot water, mash smooth, and mix with the chopped pork. Season with salt, pepper, sage, and chopped onion. No game bird save the wild turkey should be stuffed, unless you deliberately wish to disguise the natural flavor.

Wild Turkey, Boiled.— Pluck, draw, singe, wash inside with warm water, and wipe dry. Cut off head and neck close to backbone, leaving enough skin to turn over the stuffing. Draw sinews from legs, and cut off feet just below joint of leg. Press legs into sides and skewer them firmly. Stuff as above. Put the bird into enough hot water to cover it. Remove scum as it rises. Boil gently one and one-half to two hours. Serve with giblet sauce as above.

Waterfowl have two large oil glands in the tail, with which they oil their feathers. The oil in these glands imparts a strong, disagreeable flavor to the bird soon after it is killed. Hence the tail should always be removed before cooking.

To cook a large bird in a hurry.— Slice off several fillets from the breast; impale them, with slices of pork, on a green switch; broil over the coals.

Wild Goose, Roasted.— A good way to suspend a large bird before the fire is described by Dillon Wallace in his *Lure of the Labrador Wild:*

"George built a big fire — much bigger than usual. At the back he placed the largest green log he could find. Just in front of the fire, and at each side, he fixed a forked stake, and on these rested a cross-pole. From the center of the pole he suspended a piece of stout twine, which reached nearly to the ground, and tied the lower end into a noose.

"Then it was that the goose, nicely prepared for the cooking, was brought forth. Through it at the wings George stuck a sharp wooden pin, leaving the ends to protrude on each side. Through the legs he stuck a similar pin in a similar fashion. This being done, he slipped the noose at the end of the twine over the ends of one of the pins. And lo and behold! the goose was suspended before the fire.

"It hung low — just high enough to permit the placing of a dish under it to catch the gravy. Now and then George gave it a twirl so that none of its sides might have reason to complain at not receiving its share of the heat. The lower end roasted first; seeing which, George took the goose off, reversed it, and set it twirling again."

Time-table for Roasting Birds.— A goose or a middling-sized turkey takes about two hours to roast, a large turkey three hours, a duck about forty-five minutes, a pheasant twenty to thirty minutes, a woodcock or snipe fifteen to twenty minutes.

Wild Duck, Baked.— The bird should be dry-picked, and the head left on. Put a little pepper and salt inside the bird, but *no other dressing.* Lay the duck on its back in the bake-pan. Put no water in the pan. The oven must be hot, but not hot enough to burn; test with the hand. Baste frequently with butter or bacon. A canvasback requires about thirty minutes; other birds according to size. When done, the duck should be plump, and the flesh red, not blue.

This is the way to bring out the distinctive flavor

of a canvasback. Seasoning and stuffing destroy all that. A canvasback should not be washed either inside or outside, but wiped clean with a dry cloth. Duck should be served with currant jelly, if you have it. (See also page 297.)

Wild Duck, Stewed.— Clean well and divide into convenient pieces (say, legs, wings, and four parts of body). Place in pot with enough cold water to cover. Add salt, pepper, a pinch of mixed herbs, and a dash of Worcestershire sauce. Cut up fine some onions and potatoes (carrots, too, if you can get them). Put a few of these in the pot so they may dissolve and add body to the dish (flour or corn starch may be substituted for thickening). Stew slowly, skim and stir frequently. In forty-five minutes add the rest of the carrots, and in fifteen minutes more add the rest of the onions and potatoes, also turnips, if you have any. Stew until meat is done.

A plainer camp dish is to stew for an hour in water that has previously been boiled for an hour with pieces of salt pork. (See also page 300.)

Fish-eating Fowls.— The rank taste of these can be neutralized, unless very strong, by using plenty of pepper, inside and out, and baking with an onion inside. Or, skin, draw, and immerse overnight in a solution of ½ small teacup of vinegar to a gallon of water; then fry or bake.

Coots, sheldrake or old-squaw are rid of their fishy taste, without sacrificing the game flavor, by a process described by Mary Walsh:

"Pluck and draw the birds immediately; don't allow them to hang with the entrails in. Wash thoroughly with cold water both outside and in. Cut off the tail for about one inch with the fatty tissue at the base. Sprinkle with pungent white pepper both inside and out, using two teaspoonfuls to each bird. Place in the ice-box but not touching the ice, and keep for at least one week, better ten days. Then wash with salt water (handful to the pint), dry and roast for twenty minutes with an apple placed in each bird. Then serve, removing the apple before placing on the table."

The breast of a coot or rail may be broiled over the embers. Cut slits in it, and in these stick slices of fat salt pork. The broiled breast of a young bittern is good.

Grouse, Broiled.— Pluck and singe. Split down the back through the bone, and remove the trail. Wipe out with damp towel. Remove head and feet. Rub inside with pepper and salt. Flatten the breast, brush over with melted butter, or skewer bacon on upper side, and grill over a hot bed of coals.

Grouse, Roasted.— Dress and draw, but do not split. Place a piece of bacon or pork inside, and skewer a piece to the breast. Roast before the fire as described for turkey, or in a reflector.

Deviled Birds.— If drumsticks and breasts of birds are left over, they are better deviled than served cold. Mix up with a knife half an ounce of butter, half a teaspoonful each of mustard and salt, some white or black pepper, and enough cayenne or chile to give it "snap." Slit the meat, and insert this mixture, or chop the meat fine and add the seasoning. Heat well in the frying-pan, and serve.

Small Birds (quail, woodcock, snipe, plover, etc.).— These are good roasted before a bed of coals, searing them first as in broiling meat. Impale each bird on a green stick, with a slice of bacon on the point of the stick over the bird. Thrust butt of stick into the ground, and incline stick toward the fire. Turn frequently.

When a number of birds are to be roasted, a better way is to set up two forked stakes and a cross-pole before the fire. Hang birds from the pole, heads downward, by wet strings. Baste as recommended for turkey, and turn frequently. Serve very hot, without any sauce, unless it be plain melted butter and a slice of lemon.

To grill in a pan: pin a bit of bacon to the breast of each bird with a sliver like a toothpick; hold the pan close over the coals at first for searing;

then cook more slowly, but not enough to dry out the meat.

Such birds can also be served in a ragout. (See page 300.)

Woodcock are not drawn. The trail shrivels up and is easily removed at table.

SAUCES FOR GAME. (See also page 303.)—

Giblet Sauce.— See under *Wild Turkey, Roasted.*

Celery Sauce.— Having none of the vegetable itself, use a teaspoonful of celery seed freshly powdered, or five drops of the essence of celery on a piece of sugar. Flavor some melted butter with this, add a little milk, and simmer ten minutes.

Cranberry Sauce.— Put a pound of ripe cranberries in a kettle with just enough water to prevent burning. Stew to a pulp, stirring all the time. Then add syrup previously prepared by boiling a pound of sugar in $\frac{2}{3}$ pint of water. Canned or dehydrated cranberries will answer.

Curry Sauce.— This is used with stewed small game or meat (especially left-overs) that is served in combination with rice. (See page 308.)

Put a large spoonful of butter in a pan over the fire; add one onion cut into slices; cook until the onion is lightly browned. Then stir in one teaspoonful of curry powder and add gradually a generous cup of brown gravy, or soup stock, or the broth in which meat has been stewed, or evaporated milk slightly thinned. Boil fifteen minutes, and strain. Curry may be varied indefinitely by further flavoring with lemon juice, red pepper, nutmeg, mace, or Worcestershire sauce.

CHAPTER XVIII
CAMP COOKERY

Fish and Shellfish

Fish of the same species vary a great deal in quality according to the water in which they are caught. A black bass taken from one of the overflow lakes of the Mississippi bears no comparison with its brother from a swift, clear, spring-fed Ozark river. But however pure its native waters may be, no fish is good to eat unless it has been properly cared for after catching (see Chapter XV); and the best of fish is ruined if fried soggy with grease (see Chapter XVI under FRYING).

Fish, Fried.— Small fish should be fried whole, with the backbone severed to prevent curling up; large fish may be steaked (see Chapter XV); medium ones should have heads and tails removed so they will lie flat in the pan, and have the backbone cut in two or three places.

It is customary to roll fish in cornmeal or bread crumbs, thinly and evenly, before frying. That browns them, and keeps them from sticking to the pan; but it is best only for coarse fish; trout is of better flavor if simply wiped dry.

Fry in plenty of very hot grease to a golden brown, sprinkling lightly with pepper and salt just as the color turns. If the fish is not naturally full-flavored, a few drops of lemon juice will improve it.

Olive oil is best to fry fish in, especially small ones that can be quite immersed in it; but Crisco, bacon, salt pork, butter, or lard will do very well.

When butter is used, less salt is required. If the fish has not been wiped dry it will absorb too much grease. If the frying fat is not very hot when fish are put in it they will get soggy with it: put the pieces in one at a time so as not to check the heat.

Fish, Broiled.— (See also Chapter XVI.) If a broiling iron is used, first rub it with fat bacon to prevent fish from sticking to it. When broiling large fish, remove the head, split down the back instead of the belly, and lay on the broiler with strips of bacon or pork laid across. Broil over a rather moderate bed of coals so that the inside will cook done, but beware of cooking dry and " chippy." Small fish are best broiled quickly over ardent coals. They need not have heads removed.

When done, sprinkle with salt and pepper, spread with butter (unless you have been basting with bacon), and hold again over fire until butter melts.

If you have no broiler, sharpen a small green stick, thrust this through the mouth and into the body, and keep turning over the coals while you baste with the drippings from a bit of bacon held on another stick above the fish.

Fish, Skewered.— Small fish may be skewered on a thin, straight, greenwood stick, sharpened at the end, with a thin slice of bacon or pork between every two fish, the stick being constantly turned over the coals like a spit, so that juices may not be lost.

Another way is to cut some green hardwood sticks, about three feet long, forked at one end, and sharpen the tines. Lay a thin slice of pork inside each fish lengthwise, drive tines through fish and pork, letting them through between ribs near backbone and on opposite sides of the latter — then the fish won't drop off as soon as it begins to soften and curl from the heat. Place a log lengthwise of edge of coals, lay broiling sticks on this support, slanting upward over the fire, and lay a small log over their butts. Large fish should be planked.

FISH AND SHELLFISH

Fish Roasted in a Reflector.— This process is simpler than baking, and superior in resulting flavor, since the fish is basted in its own juices, and is delicately browned by the direct action of the fire. The surface of the fish is lightly moistened with olive oil (first choice) or butter; lacking these, use drippings, or bacon grease, or lard. Then place the fish in the pan and add two or three morsels of grease around it. Roast in front of a good fire, just as you would bake biscuit. Be careful not to overroast and dry the fish by evaporating the gravy. There is no better way to cook a large fish, unless it be planked.

Fish, Planked.— More expeditious than baking, and better flavored. Split and smooth a slab of sweet hardwood two or three inches thick, two feet long, and somewhat wider than the opened fish. Prop it in front of a bed of coals till it is sizzling hot. Split the fish down the back its entire length, but do not cut through the belly skin. Clean and wipe it quite dry. When plank is hot, grease it, spread fish out like an opened book, tack it, skin side down, to the plank and prop before fire. Baste continuously with a bit of pork on a switch held above it, or with butter. Reverse ends of plank from time to time. If the flesh is flaky when pierced with a fork, it is done. Sprinkle salt and pepper over the fish, moisten with drippings, and serve on the hot plank. No better dish ever was set before an epicure. Plenty of butter improves it at table.

Fish, Stuffed and Baked.— Clean, remove fins, but leave on head and tail. Prepare a stuffing as follows: put a cupful of dry bread-crumbs in a frying-pan over the fire with two tablespoonfuls of drippings, or the equivalent of butter, and stir them until they begin to brown. Then add enough boiling water to moisten them. Season this stuffing rather highly with salt, pepper, and either celery seed, or sage, or a teaspoonful of finely chopped onion. Stuff the fish with this and sew up the opening, or wind string several times around the fish. Lay several strips of salt pork or bacon in the pan, and several over the top of the fish. Sprinkle over all a little water, pepper, salt, and bread crumbs (or dredge with flour). Bake in a hot oven, basting frequently. When flakes of fish begin to separate, it will be done. This is best for coarse fish.

Fish, Steamed.— Smear some tissue Manila paper with butter. Clean the fish, leaving head and fins on. Season with salt and cayenne pepper. Roll each fish separately in a piece of the buttered paper. Place the fish in a pile and envelop them in a large sheet of paper. Then wrap the bundle in a newspaper, and dip this in water for five minutes, or long enough to saturate the newspaper. Scrape a hole in the middle of a bed of coals, and bury the package in the embers. Leave it there ten to twenty minutes, depending upon size. The newspaper will scorch, but the inner wrappers will not. The result is a dish fit for Olympus. (*Up De Graff.*)

Doctor Breck says of this dish:

"I am so fond of steamed trout that I never fail to take with me a dozen sheets of parchment paper (the kind in which butter is sold) in which to wrap my fish. . . . 'Steam-baked' trout are the *ne plus ultra* of woods cookery."

Small fish can be steamed in wet basswood leaves, or other large leaves, without buttering. For another method of steaming, see page 301.

Fish, Boiled.— None but fish of good size should be boiled. If the fish is started in cold water and not allowed to boil hard, it will be less likely to fall apart, but the flavor will not be so good. It is better to wrap the fish in a clean cloth and drop it into boiling water well salted. A tablespoonful of vinegar, or the juice of a lemon, improves the dish. Leave the head on, but remove the fins. Boil very gently until the fish will easily part from the bones. Skim off the scum as it rises. Time

FISH AND SHELLFISH

depends on species; from eight to ten minutes per pound for thick fish, and five minutes for small ones.

Boiled fish require considerable seasoning and a rich sauce, or at least melted butter, to accompany them. Besides vinegar or lemon, onions, carrots, cloves, etc., may be used in the water. Recipes for sauces follow. (See also pages 303 and 304.)

Butter Sauce.—

>2 heaped tablespoonfuls butter.
>1 heaped tablespoonful flour.
>1 teaspoonful salt.
>⅛ teaspoonful pepper.

Put the butter in a cold pan, and rub into it the flour, salt, and pepper, beating well. Then pour on a scant half-pint boiling water. Cook two minutes. Use immediately.

White Sauce.—

>2 tablespoonfuls butter.
>2 heaped tablespoonfuls flour.
>1 pint milk.
>½ teaspoonful salt.
>⅛ teaspoonful pepper.

For two, use half this.

Cook butter until it bubbles. Add flour, and cook thoroughly, until smooth. Remove from direct heat of fire, but let it simmer, and add the milk in thirds, rubbing into a smooth paste each time as it thickens. Season last. Thick white sauce is made by doubling the flour.

Cold fish that has been left over is good when heated in this sauce. It can be served thus, or baked and some chopped pickles sprinkled over the top.

India Sauce.— Make a white sauce as above, add a teaspoonful of curry powder, and some pickles, chopped small, with a little of the vinegar.

Lemon Sauce.—

>1 lemon.
>3 tablespoonfuls sugar.
>½ pint milk.
>1 scant tablespoonful butter.

Put the milk, sugar, and thin rind of the lemon into a pan and simmer gently ten minutes. Then add the juice of the lemon and the butter rolled in flour. Stir until butter is dissolved and strain or pour off clear.

Mustard Sauce (best for coarse fish).— Melt butter size of large egg in pan and stir in 1 tablespoonful flour and ½ teaspoonful mustard. Boil up once, and season (*Breck*).

Fish Chowder.— Cut the fish into pieces the right size for serving, and remove all the bones possible. For 5 or 6 lbs. of fish take ¾ lb. clear fat salt pork, slice it, and fry moderately. Slice two good-sized onions and fry in the fat. Have ready ten potatoes pared and sliced. Into your largest pot place first a layer of fish, then one of potatoes, then some of the fried onion, with pepper, salt, and a little flour, then a slice or two of the pork. Repeat these alternate layers until all has been used. Then pour the fat from the frying-pan over all. Cover the whole with boiling water, and cook from twenty to thirty minutes, according to thickness of fish. Five or ten minutes before serving, split some hard crackers and dip them in cold water (or use stale bread or biscuits similarly), add them to the chowder, and pour in about a pint of hot milk.

The advantage of first frying the pork and onion is that the fish need not then be cooked overdone, which is the case in chowders started with raw pork in the bottom of the kettle and boiled.

Another Fish Chowder.—Clean the fish, parboil it, and reserve the water in which it was boiled. Place the dry pot on the fire; when it is hot, throw in a lump of butter and about six onions sliced finely. When the odor of onion arises, add the fish. Cover the pot closely for fish to absorb flavor. Add a very small quantity of potatoes, and some of the reserved broth. When cooked, let each man season his own dish. Ask a blessing and eat. (*Kenealy.*)

FISH AND SHELLFISH

Fish Cakes.— Take fish left over from a previous meal and either make some mashed potatoes (boil them, and mash with butter and milk) or use just the plain cold boiled potatoes. Remove bones from fish and mince it quite fine. Mix well, in proportion of one-third fish and two-thirds potato. Season with salt and pepper. Then mix in thoroughly a well-beaten egg or two (or equivalent of desiccated egg). If it seems too dry, add more egg. Form into flat cakes about 2½ x ¾ inches, and fry with salt pork, or (preferably) in deep fat, like doughnuts.

Fish, Creamed.— See page 337. A good way of utilizing fish left over.

Fish from Muddy Waters.— To clean them properly, see directions in Chapter XV. Another method is here copied from the *Outer's Book:*

" Remove the scales, head, fins and intestines, wash and clean well, then place the fish in a large dishpan and pour boiling water over them, let them remain in this water for one minute, two minutes if the fish are very large, take them out of the water and remove the skin. When the skin is removed the meat will be clean and free from moss, mud or tule taste. All fish caught from lakes or streams where fish frequent places where moss or tules grow, will taste of the moss unless they are scaled and the skin removed; the moss taste is under the scales and in the skin. Fish that live in swift running water will not have the moss taste, and will not have to be scalded."

When it is necessary to eat fish caught in muddy streams, rub a little salt down the backbone, lay them in strong brine for a couple of hours before cooking, and serve with one of the sauces described above. Carp should have the gills removed, as they are always muddy from burrowing.

Eel, Broiled.— Skin, clean well with salt to remove slime, slit down the back and remove bone, cut into good-sized pieces, rub inside with egg, if you have it, roll in cornmeal or dry breadcrumbs, season with pepper and salt, and broil to a nice brown. Some like a dash of nutmeg with the seasoning.

Eel, Stewed.— Skin the eel, remove backbone, and cut the eel into pieces about two inches long; put in the stew-pan with just enough water to cover, and add a teaspoonful of strong vinegar or a slice of lemon, cover stew-pan and boil moderately until flesh will leave the bones (20 minutes to half an hour). Then remove, pour off water, drain, add fresh water and vinegar as before, and stew until tender. Now drain, add cream enough for a stew, season with pepper and salt (no butter), boil again for a few minutes, and serve on hot, dry toast. (*Up De Graff.*)

Parsley butter (see page 304) is a good dressing. Stew the eel until done, add parsley butter, and continue stewing until it thickens and the parsley is cooked.

An eel is too oily for direct frying; but after stewing until quite done it may be put in a pan and fried to a nice brown.

A plain stew is made by adding only a little salt and a bit of butter, simmer gently till done, then put enough fine bread or cracker crumbs in the water to make a thick white sauce.

Fish Roe.— Parboil (merely simmer) fifteen minutes; let them cool and drain; then roll in flour, and fry.

MISCELLANEOUS.— *Frog Legs.*— First, after skinning, soak them an hour in cold water to which vinegar has been added, or put them for two minutes into scalding water that has vinegar in it. Drain, wipe dry, and cook as below:

To fry: roll in flour seasoned with salt and pepper and fry, not too rapidly, preferably in butter or oil. Water cress is a good relish with them.

To grill: Prepare three tablespoonfuls melted butter, one-half teaspoonful salt, and a pinch or two of pepper, into which dip the frog legs, then roll in fresh bread crumbs, and broil for three minutes on each side.

To cream: same process as for codfish (page 336) except stir cream until simmering, season with pep-

FISH AND SHELLFISH

per, salt, and nutmeg, cover and cook twenty minutes.

Turtles.— All turtles (aquatic) and most tortoises (land) are good to eat, the common snapper being far better than he looks. Kill by cutting or (readier) shooting the head off. This does not kill the brute immediately, of course, but it suffices. The common way of killing by dropping a turtle into boiling water I do not like. Let the animal bleed. Then drop into a pot of boiling water for a few seconds. After scalding, the outer scales of shell, as well as the skin, are easily removed. Turn turtle on its back, cut down middle of under shell from end to end, and then across. Throw away entrails, head, and claws. Salt and pepper it inside and out. Boil a short time in the shell. Remove when the meat has cooked free from the shell. Cut up the latter and boil slowly for three hours with some chopped onion. If a stew is preferred, add some salt pork cut into dice, and vegetables. (See page 300.)

Crayfish.— These are the " craw-feesh!" of our streets. Tear off extreme end of tail, bringing the entrail with it. Boil whole in salted water till the crayfish turns red. Peel and eat as a lobster, dipping each crayfish at a time into a saucer of vinegar, pepper, and salt.

SHELLFISH.— *Oysters, Stewed.*— Oysters should not be pierced with a fork, but removed from the liquor with a spoon. Thoroughly drain the juice from a quart of shelled oysters. Add to the juice enough water (if needed) to make one-half pint. Place juice over fire, and add butter the size of a walnut. Remove all scum that arises when the juice boils. Put in the oysters. Let them cook quickly until the beards wrinkle, but not until oysters shrivel— they should remain plump. Add two-thirds pint of milk, let all scald through, remove from fire, and season to taste. Never boil oysters in milk.

Oysters, Fried.— Drain the oysters, and dry

them on a soft cloth (then they will not absorb grease). Have some desiccated egg prepared, or beat light the yolks of two or three eggs. Have enough smoking hot grease in the pan to cover all the oysters. Dip an oyster into the egg, then into rolled cracker or dry crumbs, and repeat this. Lay oysters in the pan one at a time, so as not to check the heat. When one side is brown, turn, and brown the other side. Serve piping hot.

Oysters, Scalloped.— Cover bottom of greased bake-pan with a layer of drained oysters, dot thickly over with small bits of butter, then cover with finely crumbled stale bread, and sprinkle with pepper and salt. Repeat these layers until the pan is full, with bread and butter for top layer. The bread crumbs must be in very thin layers. Bake in reflector or oven until nicely browned.

Oysters, Sauté.— Drain the oysters. Melt a little butter in the frying-pan, and cook the oysters in it. Salt when removed from pan.

Oysters, Roasted.— Put oysters unopened on broiler, and hold over the coals. When they open, put a little melted butter and some white pepper on each oyster, and they are ready.

Clams, Baked.— Lay down a bed of stones in disk shape, and build a low wall almost around it, forming a rock oven open at the top. Build a big fire in it and keep it going until the wood has burned down to embers and the stones are very hot. Rake out all smoking chunks. Throw a layer of sea-weed over the embers, and lay the clams quickly on this. Roasting ears in the husks, or sweet potatoes, are a desirable addition. Cover all with another layer of sea-weed, and let steam about forty minutes, or until clams will slip in the shell. Uncover and serve with melted butter, pepper, salt, and perhaps lemon or vinegar.

Clam Chowder.— Wash the clams, put them in a kettle, and pour over them just enough boiling water to cover them. When the shells open, pour off the liquor, saving it, cool the clams, and shell

FISH AND SHELLFISH

them. Fry two or three slices of pork in bottom of kettle. When it is done, pour over it two quarts of boiling clam liquor. Add six large potatoes, sliced thin, and cook until nearly done. Turn in the clams, and a quart of hot milk. Season with salt and pepper. When this boils up, add crackers or stale bread, as in fish chowder. Remove from fire and let crackers steam in the covered pot until soft.

Fried sliced onion and a can of tomatoes will improve this chowder. Cloves, allspice, red pepper, Worcestershire sauce, and other condiments, may be added according to taste.

Shellfish, Steamed.— See page 301.

Crabs, Deviled.— Boil hard-shell crabs a few minutes until red. Remove the back shells, and shred out the white meat. Meantime make a paste of flour rubbed up in cold water, to which add a few drops of olive oil and some chopped green peppers. Mix swiftly with the crab meat, add a dash of cayenne, and stuff back into the shells. Bake until done. (*Fortiss.*)

CHAPTER XIX
CAMP COOKERY

CURED MEATS, ETC.— EGGS

Bacon, Fried.— Slice quite thin. Remove the rind, as it not only is unsightly but makes the slices curl up in the pan. Put pan half full of water on fire; when water is warm, drop the bacon in, and stir around until water begins to simmer. Then remove bacon, throw out water, fry- over very few coals, and turn often. Remove slices while still translucent, and season with pepper. They will turn crisp on cooling. Some prefer not to parboil.

Bacon, Broiled.— Slice as above. Turn broiler repeatedly until bacon is of a light brown color. Time, three to four minutes.

Bacon, Boiled.— Put in enough cold water to just cover. Bring to a boil very gradually. Remove all scum as it arises. Simmer gently until thoroughly done. Two pounds take 1½ hours; each additional pound, ½ hour.

Bacon, Toasted.— Cut cold boiled bacon into thin slices. Sprinkle each with fine bread crumbs peppered with cayenne. Toast quickly in wire broiler.

Bacon and Eggs.— Poach or fry the eggs and lay them on fried bacon.

Bacon Omelet.— See *Ham Omelet*, near end of chapter.

Bacon Gravy, Thin.— Pour off the fat and save it for future use. Pour in enough water to supply the quantity of gravy desired. Add the juice of a lemon. Boil and pour upon the bacon. If a

CURED MEATS

richer gravy is desired, follow recipe given below.

Pork Gravy, Thickened.— This can be made with ham or salt pork, as well as with bacon. To make gravy that is a good substitute for butter, rub into the hot grease that is left in the pan a tablespoonful of flour, keep on rubbing until smooth and brown; then add two cups boiling water and a dash of pepper. A tablespoonful of catchup may be added for variety. If you have milk, use it instead of water (a pint to the heaping tablespoonful of flour), and do not let the flour brown; this makes a delicious white gravy.

Salt Pork, Fried.— Same as fried bacon, above. Pork should be firm and dry. Clammy pork is stale.

Salt Pork, Broiled.— Same as bacon; but it is usually so salty that it should be parboiled first, or soaked at least an hour in cold water.

Salt Pork, Boiled.— Nearly always cooked with vegetables or greens; hence need not be soaked or parboiled. See page 299.

Pork Fritters.— Make a thick batter of cornmeal one-third and flour two-thirds, or of flour alone. Fry a few slices of salt pork or bacon until the fat is tried out. Then cut a few more slices, dip them in the batter, drop them in the bubbling fat, season with salt and pepper, fry to a light brown, and eat while hot. It takes the stomach of a lumberjack to digest this, but it is a favorite variant in frontier diet.

Pork and Hardtack.— Soak hardtack in water until it is partly softened. Drop it into hot pork fat, and cook. A soldier's resource.

Ham, Fried.— Same as bacon. Parboil, first, for eight or ten minutes, if hard and salty.

Ham and Eggs.— Same as bacon and eggs.

Ham, Broiled.— If salty, parboil first. Cut rather thick slices, pepper them, and broil five minutes. Ham that has been boiled is best for broiling. A little mustard may be spread on the slices when served.

Ham, Boiled.— Wash the ham, and let it soak over night in cold water. In the morning, cover it well with fresh water, bring to a boil, and hang the kettle high over the fire where it will boil gently until dinner time. When the bone on the under side leaves the meat readily, the ham is done. If you have eggs, the nicest way to serve a boiled ham is to remove the skin, brush over the top of ham with yolk of egg, sprinkle thickly with finely grated crumbs or cracker-dust, and brown in an oven.

Ham and Macaroni.— " Boil an inch-thick slice of ham half an hour, at the same time boiling the required amount of macaroni in salted water. When the macaroni is done, drain off the water and put in a baking dish and pour over it a can of tomatoes, which should be seasoned with salt and pepper. Place slice of ham on top, and bake half an hour. A little grated cheese is an improvement when mixed with the macaroni, before adding the tomatoes." (*Arthur Chapman.*)

Ham Chow.— Slice the required amount of potatoes in thin slices, season with salt and pepper, and place in baking dish. Add one can of tomatoes. Cover and cook for an hour. Then place slices of boiled ham, or some well seasoned chops, over the potato and tomato mixture, return to the oven without the cover, and bake half an hour. Thinly sliced bacon will take the place of ham or chops, but must only be left in the oven a few minutes. (*Same.*)

Pork Sausages.— Cut links apart, prick each with a fork so it will not burst in cooking, and broil on forked stick; or, lay in cold frying-pan, and fry fifteen to twenty minutes over a slow fire, moving them about so they will brown evenly all over. Serve with mashed potatoes, over which pour the fat from the pan. Apples fried to a light brown in the sausage grease are a pleasant accompaniment.

Corned Beef, Boiled.— Put the ham into enough

CURED MEATS 335

cold water to cover it. Let it come slowly to a boil, and then merely simmer until done. Time, about one-half hour to each pound. Vegetables may be added toward the end, as directed on page 299. If not to be used until the next day, leave the meat in its liquor, weighted down under the surface by a clean rock.

Corned Beef Hash.— Chop some canned corned beef fine with sliced onions. Hash up with freshly boiled potatoes, two parts potatoes to one of meat. Season highly with pepper (no salt), and some mustard if liked. Put a little pork fat in a frying-pan, melt, add hash, and cook until nearly dry and a brown crust has formed. Dehydrated potatoes and onions can be used according to directions on packages.

Stew with Canned Meat.— Peel and slice some onions. If the meat has much fat, melt it; if not, melt a little pork fat. Add onions, and fry until brown. Mix some flour into a smooth batter with cold water, season with pepper and salt, and pour into the camp kettle. Stir the whole well together. Cut meat into slices, put into the kettle, and heat through.

Lobscouse.— Boil corned beef as above (if very salty, parboil first, and then change the water). About thirty minutes before it is done add sliced potatoes and hardtack.

Slumgullion.— When the commissariat is reduced to bacon, corned beef, and hardtack, try this sailor's dish, described by Jack London: Fry half a dozen slices of bacon, add fragments of hardtack, then two cups of water, and stir briskly over the fire; in a few minutes mix in with it slices of canned corned beef; season well with pepper and salt.

Dried Beef, Creamed.— Slice 3 oz. of dried beef into thin shavings, or chop fine. Pour over it a pint of boiling water, and let it stand two minutes. Turn off water, and drain beef dry. Heat a heaped tablespoonful of butter in the frying-pan;

then add the beef. Cook three minutes, stirring all the time. Then pour on ¼ pint cold milk. Mix 4 tablespoonfuls milk with 1 teaspoonful flour, and stir into the beef in the pan. Add an egg, if you have it. Cook two minutes longer and serve at once.

Canned Meats.— Never eat any that has been left standing open in the can. It is dangerous. If any has been left over, remove it to a clean vessel and keep in a cool place.

Canned corned beef and the like should not be eaten cold out of the can if you can help it. Place the can in water and boil it about ten minutes: the meat is more wholesome this way.

Cured Venison.— "Cut off the worst of the blackened casing and slice into steaks an inch thick. Dredge these with flour, salt, and pepper, and lay in hot bacon grease in a frying-pan. Pour in a small cup of water, cover tightly, and allow to steam until the water is gone. Then remove the cover, and brown." (*Kathrene Pinkerton.*)

CURED FISH.— *Salt Fish* requires from twelve to thirty-six hours' soaking, flesh downward, in cold water before cooking, depending on the hardness and dryness of the fish. Change the water two or three times to remove surplus salt. Start in cold water, then, and boil until the flesh parts from the bones. When done, cover with bits of butter, or serve with one of the sauces given in the chapter on FISH.

Broiled Salt Fish.— Freshen the flakes of fish by soaking in cold water. Broil over the coals, and serve with potatoes.

Stewed Codfish.— Soak over night in plenty of cold water, or one hour in tepid water. Put in pot of fresh, cold water, and heat gradually until soft. Do not boil the fish or it will get hard. Serve with boiled potatoes, and with white sauce made as directed under FISH.

(2) Put two tablespoonfuls of butter in a pan; when melted add one tablespoonful of flour, stir-

CURED MEATS

ring constantly; then a cup of rich milk and some pepper; then half a pint of desiccated codfish. Stir until boiling. Serve on toast, if you have light bread.

Codfish Hash.— Prepare salt codfish as above. When soft, mash with potatoes and onions, season with pepper, and fry like corned beef hash.

Codfish Balls.— Shred the fish into small pieces. Peel some potatoes. Use one pint of fish to one quart of raw potatoes. Put them in a pot, cover with boiling water, cook till potatoes are soft, drain water off, mash fish and potatoes together, and beat light with a fork. Add a tablespoonful of butter and season with pepper. Shape into flattened balls, and fry in very hot fat deep enough to cover.

Smoked Herrings.— (1) Clean, and remove the skin. Toast on a stick over the coals.

(2) Scald in boiling water till the skin curls up, then remove head, tail, and skin. Clean well. Put into frying-pan with a little butter or lard. Fry gently a few minutes, dropping in a little vinegar.

Smoked Sprats.— Lay them on a slightly greased plate and set them in an oven until heated through.

Canned Salmon, Creamed.— Cut into dice. Heat about a pint of them in one-half pint milk. Season with salt and Cayenne pepper. Cold cooked fish of any kind can be served in this way.

Canned Salmon, Scalloped.— Rub two teaspoonfuls of butter and a tablespoonful of flour together. Stir this into boiling milk. Cut two pounds of canned salmon into dice. Put a layer of the sauce in bottom of a dish, then a layer of salmon. Sprinkle with salt, Cayenne pepper, and grated bread crumbs. Repeat alternate layers until dish is full, having the last layer sauce, which is sprinkled with crumbs and bits of butter. Bake in very hot oven until browned (about ten minutes).

Canned Salmon on Toast.— Dip slices of stale bread in smoking-hot lard. They will brown at once. Drain them. Heat a pint of salmon, picked into flakes, season with salt and Cayenne, and turn into a cupful of melted butter. Heat in pan. Stir in one egg, beaten light, with three tablespoonfuls evaporated milk not thinned. Pour the mixture on the fried bread.

Sardines on Toast.— Fry them and give them a dash of red pepper. They are better if wiped free of oil, dipped into whipped egg, sprinkled thickly with cracker crumbs, fried, and served on buttered toast.

(2) Drain and remove skins from one dozen sardines, put a tablespoonful of butter in the pan, with two teaspoonfuls anchovy paste, and a little tabasco. Lay the sardines carefully in the pan. When well heated through, serve each on a tiny strip of toast.

EGGS.—

Desiccated Egg.— The baker's egg mentioned in the chapter on PROVISIONS is in granules about the size of coarse sand. It is prepared for use by first soaking about two hours in cold or one hour in lukewarm water. Hot water must not be used. Solution can be quickened by occasional stirring. The proportion is one tablespoonful of egg to two of water, which is about the equivalent of one fresh egg. Use just like fresh eggs in baking, etc., and for scrambled eggs or omelets. Of course, the desiccated powder cannot be fried, boiled, or poached.

Fried Eggs.— Have the frying-pan scrupulously clean. Put in just enough butter, dripping, or other fat, to prevent the eggs sticking. Break an egg with a smart but gentle crack on the side of a cup, and drop it in the cup without breaking yolk. Otherwise you might drop a bad one in the pan and spoil the whole mess. Pour the egg slowly into the pan so that the albumen thickens over the yolk instead of spreading itself out like a pancake. The fire should be moderate. In two or three minutes they will be done. Eggs fried longer than this, or on both sides, are leathery and unwholesome.

CURED MEATS

Scrambled Eggs.— Put into a well-greased pan as many eggs as it will hold separately, each yolk being whole. When the whites have begun to set, stir from bottom of pan until done (buttery, not leathery). Add a piece of butter, pepper, and salt. Another way is to beat the eggs with a spoon. To five eggs add one-fourth teaspoonful salt. Heat one tablespoonful butter in the frying-pan. Stir in the eggs, and continue stirring until eggs set. Before they toughen, turn them out promptly into a warm dish.

Scrambled Eggs, Fancy.— After turning in five eggs as above, add a cupful of canned tomatoes, drained and chopped quite fine; or, chopped ham or bacon instead of tomatoes.

Plain Omelet.— It is better to make two or three small omelets than to attempt one large one. Scrape the pan and wipe it dry after each omelet is made. Use little salt: it keeps the eggs from rising. Heat the fat in the pan very gradually, but get it hot almost to the browning point.

Beat four eggs just enough to break them well; or, break into a bowl with four tablespoonfuls milk, and whip thoroughly. Add a little salt. Put two heaped teaspoonfuls of butter in the pan and heat as above. Pour egg into pan, and tilt the pan forward so that the egg flows to the far side. As soon as the egg begins to set, draw it up to the raised side of the pan with a knife. Beginning then at the left hand, turn the egg over in small folds until the lower part of the pan is reached, and the omelet has been rolled into a complete fold. Let the omelet rest a few seconds, and then turn out into a hot dish. Work rapidly throughout, so that the omelet is creamy instead of tough. It should be of a rich yellow color.

Ham Omelet.— Cut raw ham into dice. Fry. Turn the beaten eggs over it and cook as above. Bacon can be used instead of ham.

Fancy Omelets.— Take tender meat, game, fish, or vegetable, hash it fine, heat it in white sauce (see page 325), and spread this over the omelet before you begin to fold it; or they can be put in with the eggs. Jam, jelly, or preserved fruit may be used in a similar way (two tablespoonfuls, say, of marmalade to six eggs).

Rum Omelet.— Beat three eggs, add a very small pinch of salt, a teaspoonful of powdered sugar, a slice of butter, and a tablespoonful of rum. Fry as described above. Lay the omelet on a hot dish, pour around it one-half tumberful of rum that has been warmed in a pan, light it, and serve with its blue flame rising round it.

Poached Eggs.— Put a pint of water in the frying pan, with one-half teaspoonful of salt. If you have vinegar, add two teaspoonfuls to the water: it keeps the whites from running too much. Bring the water to a gentle boil. Break the eggs separately into a saucer and slide them into the water. Let the water simmer not longer than three minutes, meantime ladling spoonfuls of it over the yolks. Have toast already buttered on a very hot plate. Lay eggs carefully on it. Eat at once. This may be varied by moistening the toast with hot milk.

Eggs, Boiled.— Eggs are boiled soft in two and one-half to three minutes, depending upon size and freshness. If wanted hard boiled, put them in cold water, bring to a boil, and keep it up for twenty minutes. The yolk will then be mealy and wholesome. Eggs boiled between these extremes are either clammy or tough, and indigestible. To boil eggs, soft, if you have no watch: put them in *cold* water and set the pot over the fire. Watch the water; when it begins to sing slightly, or when the first little bubbles arise, the eggs are done to a turn.

Eggs, Roasted.— This can be done by covering the eggs with hot ashes and embers, but the shells must be cracked a little at one end to prevent them exploding.

Eggs, Stirred.— Make half a cup of rich gravy. Melt a tablespoon of butter in a pan and add the gravy. When hissing hot, stir in five beaten eggs

CURED MEATS

until they thicken. Season with half a teaspoonful of salt, a dash of pepper, sprinkle with parsley, and serve on toast.

CHAPTER XX
CAMP COOKERY

BREADSTUFFS AND CEREALS

When men must bake for themselves they generally make biscuit, biscuit-loaf, flap-jacks, or corn bread. Bread leavened with yeast is either beyond their skill or too troublesome to make out of doors; so baking powder is the mainstay of the camp. Generally the batch is a failure. To paraphrase Tom Hood,

> Who has not met with camp-made bread,
> Rolled out of putty and weighted with lead?

It need not be so. Just as good biscuit or johnny cake can be baked before a log fire in the woods as in a kitchen range. Bread making is a chemical process. Follow directions; pay close attention to details, as a chemist does, from building the fire to testing the loaf with a sliver. It does require experience or a special knack to *guess* quantities accurately, but none at all to *measure* them.

In general, biscuit or other small cakes should be baked quickly by ardent heat; large loaves require a slow, even heat, so that the outside will not harden until the inside is nearly done.

The way to bake in a reflector or in a "baker" has been shown in the chapter on MEATS. If you have neither of these utensils, there are other ways.

Baking in a Dutch Oven.— This is a cast-iron pot with flaring sides and short legs, fitted with a thick iron cover, the rim of which is turned up to

BREADSTUFFS

hold a layer of coals on top. If it were not for its weight it would be the best oven for outdoor use, since it not only bakes but cooks the meat or pone in its own steam.

Place the Dutch oven and its lid separately on the fire. Get the bottom moderately hot, and the lid very hot (but not red, lest it warp). Grease the bottom and sprinkle flour over it, put in the bread or biscuits, set cover on, rake a thin layer of coals out in front of the fire, stand oven on them, and cover lid thickly with more live coals. Replenish occasionally. Have a stout pot-hook to lift lid with, so you can inspect progress of baking once or twice.

The sheet-steel oven mentioned in Chapter VII can be used in a similar way, or one of the pots made for fireless cookers, or a pudding pan inverted over a slightly smaller one; but with such thin utensils you must use a more moderate heat, of course, and watch the baking carefully lest you burn it.

Baking in a Kettle.— Every fixed camp that has no stove should have a bake-hole, if for nothing else than baking beans. The hole can be dug anywhere, but it is best in the side of a bank or knoll, so that an opening can be left in front to rake out of, and for drainage in case of rain. Line it with stones, as they hold heat and keep the sides from crumbling. Have the completed hole a little larger than your baking kettle.

Build a hardwood fire in and above the hole and keep it going until the stones or earth are very hot (not less than half an hour). Rake out most of the coals and ashes, put in the bake-pot, which must have a tight-fitting lid, cover with ashes and then with live coals; and, if a long heating is required, keep a small fire going on top. Close the mouth of the oven with a flat rock. This is the way for beans or for braising meat.

Bread is not to be baked in the kettle alone, because the sides are vertical and you would have a sweet time getting the bread out; but if you have a pudding-pan that will go inside the kettle, well and good. Put three or four pebbles in the bottom of the kettle for the pan to rest on, so the dough will not burn.

A shifty camper can make bread in almost anything. I have even baked beans to perfection in a thin, soldered lard-pail, by first encasing it in clay.

Baking in the Ashes.— Build a good fire on a level bit of ground. When it has burned to coals and the ground has thoroughly heated, rake away the embers, lightly drop the loaf on the hot earth, pat it smooth, rake the embers back over the loaf (some hot ashes first), and let it bake until no dough will adhere to a sliver thrust to the center of the loaf. This is the Australian damper. Ash cakes are similarly baked (see page 352). Dirty? No it isn't; try it.

Baking in a Frying-pan.— Grease or flour a frying-pan and put a flat cake of biscuit-dough in it. Rake some embers out in front of the fire and put pan on them just long enough to form a little crust on bottom of loaf. Then remove from embers, and, with a short forked stick, the stub of which will enter hole in end of handle, prop pan up before fire at such angle that top of loaf will be exposed to heat. Turn loaf now and then, both sidewise and upside down. When firm enough to keep its shape, remove it, prop it by itself before the fire to finish baking, and go on with a fresh loaf. A tin plate may be used in place of the frying-pan.

If you have in your kit a shallow pudding-pan of the right size, invert it over the dough in the pan and heap embers on top; or a second frying-pan can be used in the same way. Another way, with one pan and no cover, is described by Kathrene Pinkerton:

"Make a rich, moist baking-powder biscuit dough, using double the amount of lard. The dough should be so thin it can be smoothed with a knife. Heat a little lard in a frying-pan and pour in the dough. A bannock should never be baked in less than twenty-five minutes.

BREADSTUFFS

With a good cooking fire, the pan should be held three feet above the blaze until the bannock has risen to twice its original height. Then lower the pan and brown. Shake the pan occasionally to see that the bannock is not burning. When one side is done, slide the bannock onto a plate, heat more lard in the pan, gently replace the bannock upside down and brown again. The result is a golden-brown loaf."

Baking on a Slab.— Heat a thick slab of non-resinous green wood until the sap simmers. Then proceed as with a frying-pan.

Baking on a Stick.— Work dough into a ribbon two inches wide. Get a club of sweet green wood (birch, sassafras, maple), about two feet long and three inches thick, peel large end, sharpen the other and stick it into ground, leaning toward fire. When sap simmers wind dough spirally around peeled end. Turn occasionally. Several sticks can be baking at once. Bread for one man's meal can be quickly baked on a peeled stick as thick as a broomstick, holding over fire and turning. This is " corkscrew bread."

Clay Oven.— In fixed camp, if you have no oven, a good substitute can soon be made in a clay bank or steep knoll near by. Dig down the bank to a vertical front. Back from this front, about 4 feet, drive a 4 or 5-inch stake down to what will be the bottom level of the oven. Draw the stake out, thus leaving a hole for flue. It is best to drive the stake before excavating, as otherwise it might cause the roof of your oven to cave in from the shock of driving. Now, from the bottom of the face, dig a horizontal hole back to the flue, keeping the entrance as small as you can, but enlarging the interior and arching its top. When the oven is finished, wet the whole interior, smooth it, and build a small fire in the oven to gradually dry and harden it.

To bake in such an oven: build a good fire in it of split hardwood sticks, and keep it burning hard for an hour or two; then rake out the embers, lay your dough on broad green leaves (basswood, from choice) or on the naked floor, and close both the door and the flue with flat stones or bark.

If no bank or knoll lies handy, build a form for your oven by first setting up a row of green-stick arches, like exaggerated croquet wickets, one behind the other, and cover with sticks laid on horizontally like a roof. At the rear, set up a round stake as core for the chimney. Now plaster wet clay thickly over all except the door. Let this dry naturally for a day in hot sunlight, or build a very small fire within and feed it only as needed to keep up a moderate heat. When the clay has hardened, give it another coating, to fill up the cracks that have appeared. Then give it a final firing.

To Mix Dough Without a Pan.— When bark will peel, use a broad sheet of it (paper birch, basswood, poplar, cottonwood, slippery elm, etc.). It is easy to mix unleavened dough in the sack of flour itself. Stand the latter horizontally where it can't fall over. Scoop a bowl-shaped depression in top of flour. Keep the right hand moving round while you pour in a little water at a time from a vessel held in the left. Sprinkle a little salt in. When a thick, adhesive dough has formed, lift this out and pat and work it into a round cake about $2\frac{1}{2}$ inches thick.

WHEAT BREAD AND BISCUITS.— When baking powder is used, the secret of good bread is to *handle the dough as little as possible.* After adding the water, mix as rapidly as you can, not with the warm hands, but with a big spoon or a wooden paddle. To knead such bread, or roll it much, or even to mould biscuits by hand instead of cutting them out, would surely make your baking " sad." As soon as water touches the flour, the baking powder begins to give off gas. It is this gas, imprisoned in the dough, that makes bread light. Squeezing or moulding presses this gas out. The heat of the hands turns such dough into Tom Hood's " putty."

Biscuit Loaf.— This is a standard camp bread, because it bakes quickly. It is good so long as it

BREADSTUFFS

is hot, but it dries out soon and will not keep. For four men:

3 pints flour,
3 heaping teaspoonfuls baking powder,
1 heaping teaspoonful salt,
2 heaping tablespoonfuls cold grease,
1 scant pint cold water.

Amount of water varies according to quality of flour. Baking powders vary in strength; follow directions on can.

Mix thoroughly, with big spoon or wooden paddle, first the baking powder with the flour, and then the salt. Rub into this the cold grease (which may be lard, cold pork fat, drippings, or bear's grease), until there are no lumps left and no grease adhering to bottom of pan. This is a little tedious, but don't shirk it. Then stir in the water and work it with spoon until you have a rather stiff dough. Have the pan greased. Turn the loaf into it, and bake. Test center of loaf with a sliver when you think it probably done. When no dough adheres, remove bread. All hot breads should be broken with the hands, never cut.

To freshen any that is left over and dried out, sprinkle a little water over it and heat through. This can be done but once.

Biscuit.— These are baked in a reflector (12-inch holds 1 dozen, 18-inch holds 1½ dozen), unless a camp stove is carried or an oven is dug. Build the fire high. Make dough as in the preceding recipe, which is enough for two dozen biscuits. Flop the mass of dough to one side of pan, dust flour on bottom of pan, flop dough back over it, dust flour on top of loaf. Now rub some flour over the bread board, flour your hands, and gently lift loaf on board. Flour the bottle or bit of peeled sapling that you use as rolling-pin, also the edges of can or can cover used as biscuit cutter. Gently roll loaf to three-quarter-inch thickness. Stamp out the biscuit and lay them in pan. Roll out the culls and make biscuit of them, too. Bake until edge of front row turns brown; reverse pan and continue until rear row is similarly done. Time, twenty to twenty-five minutes in a reflector, ten to fifteen minutes in a closed oven.

Dropped Biscuit.— These do away with breadboard, rolling-pin, and most of the work, yet are about as good as stamped biscuit. Use same proportions as above, except turn in enough water to make a *thick batter* — one that will drop lazily from a spoon. In mixing, do not stir the batter more than necessary to smooth out all lumps. Drop from a big spoon into the greased bake-pan.

Army Bread.— This is easier to make than biscuit dough, since there is no grease to rub in, but it takes longer to bake. It keeps fresh longer than yeast bread, does not dry up in a week, nor mould, and is more wholesome than biscuit. It is the only baking-powder bread I know of that is good to eat cold — in fact, it is best that way.

- 1 quart flour,
- 1 teaspoonful salt,
- 1 tablespoonful sugar,
- 2 heaped teaspoonfuls baking powder.

Mix the dry ingredients thoroughly. Then stir in enough cold water (about 1½ pints) to make a thick batter that will pour out level. Mix rapidly with spoon until smooth, and pour at once into bake-pan. Bake about forty-five minutes, or until no dough adheres to a sliver. Above quantity makes a 1½-pound loaf (say 9x5x3 inches).

For variety, substitute for the sugar two or three tablespoonfuls of molasses, and add one to two teaspoonfuls of ginger.

Breakfast Rolls.—

- 1 quart flour,
- 2 level tablespoonfuls butter,
- 1 egg,
- 1 teaspoonful baking powder,
- 1 pint cold milk (or enough to make a soft dough).

Rub butter and flour well together, add beaten

BREADSTUFFS

egg, a pinch of salt, and the milk, till a soft dough is mixed. Form into rolls and bake quickly.

Salt-rising Bread.— This smells to heaven while it is fermenting, but is a welcome change after a long diet of baking-powder breadstuffs. For a baking of two or three loaves take about a pint of moderately warm water (a pleasant heat to the hand) and stir into it as much flour as will make a good batter, not too thick. Add to this one-half teaspoonful salt, not more. Set the vessel in a pan of moderately warm water, within a little distance of a fire, or in sunlight. The water must not be allowed to cool much below the original heat, more warm water being added to pan as required.

In six to eight hours the whole will be in active fermentation, when the dough must be mixed with it, and as much warm water (milk, if you have it) as you require. Knead the mass till it is tough and does not stick to the board. Make up your loaves, and keep them warmly covered near the fire till they rise. They must be baked as soon as this second rising takes place; for, unless the rising is used immediately on reaching its height, it sinks to rise no more.

Sour-dough Bread.— Mix a pail of batter from plain flour and water, and hang it up in a warm place until the batter sours. Then add salt and soda (not baking powder) and a spoonful of sugar, thicken with flour to a stiff dough, knead thoroughly, work into small loaves, and place them before the fire to rise. Then bake.

The following is by Mrs. Pinkerton:

"The sour-dough can ranks high in the list of woods time-savers. It is easy to manipulate, will supply yeast for both cakes and bread, and requires only one start, for it improves with age. Our sour-dough pail has now been going continuously for nine months and is getting better all the time.

"To make the 'sourings,' stir two cups of flour, two tablespoons of sugar and one of salt in sufficient water to make a creamy batter. Stir in a tablespoonful of vinegar and set near a fire or in the sun to sour. One author has said 'it requires a running start of thirty-six hours.' Two days' souring is better. Do not be dismayed by the odor. The woods axiom is, 'the sourer the better,' and it will not be at its best the first few days. Its great advantage for campers lies in the fact that it will raise either bread or pancakes in any temperature above freezing.

"Pancakes should be set in the evening. Beat until smooth; water and flour in proper proportions for batter. Stir this into the 'sourings' in the sour dough can. This rises overnight. In the morning the amount of batter necessary for breakfast should be taken out, leaving enough yeast for the next day. Into enough batter for two we stir two tablespoons of molasses, one teaspoon of salt, and one half teaspoon of soda, the last two dissolved in hot water. Then, small cakes are better and more easily handled than those the size of the frying pan.

"A quick, hot fire is necessary for pancakes, although, when frying in a pan, care must be taken or they will burn. Once a cake has burned to the pan you may as well stop and clean the pan thoroughly or every succeeding cake will be spoiled.

"Uneaten pancakes should be broken up and dropped into the sourings. It improves the cakes. Some woodsmen are almost superstitious about the mixture, and, with them, the sour dough pail rivals the garbage can as a receptacle for uneaten foods. When the yeast loses its sourness from overwork a tablespoon of vinegar will revive it. The 'sourings' can be carried in a pail or in a push-top tin. If you use the latter be sure to allow plenty of room for expansion. We still carry on a blanket evidences of too active 'sourings.'"

To Raise Bread in a Pot.— Set the dough to rise over a very few embers, keeping the pot turned as the loaf rises. When equally risen all around, put hot ashes under the pot and upon the lid, taking care that the heat be not too fierce at first.

Lungwort Bread.— On the bark of maples, and sometimes of beeches and birches, in the northern woods, there grows a green, broad-leaved lichen variously known as lungwort, liverwort, lunglichen, and lung-moss, which is an excellent substitute for yeast. This is an altogether different growth from the plants commonly called lungwort and liverwort — I believe its scientific name is *Sticta pulmonacea*. This lichen is partly made up of fungus, which does the business of raising

BREADSTUFFS

dough. Gather a little of it and steep it over night in lukewarm water, set near the embers, but not near enough to get overheated. In the morning, pour off the infusion and mix it with enough flour to make a batter, beating it up with a spoon. Place this "sponge" in a warm can or pail, cover with a cloth, and set it near the fire to work. By evening it will have risen. Leaven your dough with this (saving some of the sponge for a future baking), let the bread rise before the fire that night, and by morning it will be ready to bake.

It takes but little of the original sponge to leaven a large mass of dough (but see that it never freezes), and it can be kept good for months.

Unleavened Bread.— Quickly made, wholesome, and good for a change. Keeps like hardtack.

>2½ pints flour,
>1 tablespoonful salt (scant),
>1 tablespoonful sugar.

Mix with water to stiff dough, and knead and pull until lively. Roll out thin as a soda cracker, score with knife, and bake. Unleavened bread that is to be carried for a long time must be mixed with as little water as possible (merely dampened enough to make it adhere), for if any moisture is left in it after baking, it will mould.

A teaspoonful of lard worked in with the flour improves the taste, but the bread will not keep forever, as it would without the lard. If lard is used, you may as well make a good imitation of Maryland biscuit while you are about it. Lay the dough out on a board and beat it lustily with a paddle until it becomes elastic, then bake.

Dough Gods.—"Take ⅔ cupful of flour, 1 small teaspoonful of baking powder, ¼ teaspoonful of salt, and a slice of fat bacon minced fine as possible. Mix thoroughly in your bread-pan and add water slowly, stirring and working till you have a fairly stiff dough. Flour the loaf, top and bottom, flour your hands and pat the dough out into a couple of big cakes about half an inch thick. Bake in the ashes, or in the frying-pan. . . . This is the old way of baking with bacon instead of rendered grease or lard, used by men who carried nothing they could do without, and whose only food staples were flour, bacon, baking-powder, and salt." (*Edward Cave.*)

CORN BREAD.— Plain corn bread, without flour, milk, or egg, is hard to make eatable without a Dutch oven to bake it in. Even so, it is generally spoiled by being baked too fast and not long enough to be done inside.

Corn Pone.—

1 quart meal,
1 teaspoonful salt,
1 pint *warm* (but not scalding) water (1½ pints for old meal).

Stir together until light. Bake to a nice brown all around (about forty-five minutes), and let it sweat fifteen minutes longer in the closed oven, removed from the fire. Yellow meal generally requires more water than white. Freshly ground meal is much better than old.

Corn Dodgers.— Same as above, but mix to a stiff dough, and form into cylindrical dodgers four or five inches long and 1½ inches diameter, by rolling between the hands. Have frying-pan very hot, grease it a little, and put dodgers on as you roll them out. As soon as they have browned, put them in oven and bake thoroughly.

Ash Cake.— Same kind of dough. Form it into balls as big as hen's eggs, roll in dry flour, lay in hot ashes, and cover completely with them.

Johnny-cake.—" Mix at home, before starting, 1 quart of yellow, granulated corn meal, 1 pint of white flour, ½ cup of sugar, 1 teaspoonful of salt, 4 teaspoonfuls of baking-powder. In camp it should be mixed in the pan to make a fairly heavy batter and allowed to stand for a few minutes before frying so that it becomes light and puffy. It should then be dropped by spoonfuls, without further stirring,

BREADSTUFFS

into the hot, greased pan, and not turned until the top has begun to set. The bacon grease takes the place of butter.

"If less water is used, the entire mixture may be put in the frying-pan at once, baked from the bottom up over coals until the top has set, and then turned. It makes delicious johnny-cake. Try rolling the trout in a little of the dry mixture." (*Warwick S. Carpenter.*)

Corn Bread (Superior).—

>1 pint corn meal,
>1 pint flour,
>3 tablespoonfuls sugar,
>2 heaped tablespoonfuls butter,
>3 teaspoonfuls baking powder,
>1 teaspoonful salt,
>2 eggs,
>1 pint (or more) milk.

Rub butter and sugar together. Add the beaten eggs; then the milk. Sift the salt and baking powder into the meal and flour. Pour the liquid over the dry ingredients, beating well. Pour batter into well-greased pan, and bake thirty to forty minutes in moderately hot oven. Can also be made into muffins.

Corn Batter Bread.—

>1 pint corn meal,
>2 pints milk (or water),
>2 eggs,
>1 teaspoonful salt.

Beat the eggs light; add the salt; then the meal and milk, gradually, until well blended. Bake about thirty minutes. This is the standard breakfast bread of the South, easily made, and (if the meal is freshly ground) delicious. A little boiled rice, or hominy grits, may be substituted for part of the meal.

Snow Bread.— After a fall of light, feathery snow, superior corn bread may be made by stirring together

1 quart corn meal,
½ teaspoonful soda,
1 teaspoonful salt,
1 tablespoonful lard.

Then, in a cool place where the snow will not melt, stir into above one quart light snow. Bake about forty minutes in rather hot oven. Snow, for some unknown reason, has the same effect on bread as eggs have, two tablespoonfuls of snow equaling one egg. It can also be used in making batter for pancakes, or puddings, the batter being made rather thick, and the snow mixed with each cake just before putting in the pan.

Substitute for Baking Soda.— Take the *white* of wood ashes, same quantity as you would use of soda, and mix dry with the flour. It makes bread rise the same as soda, and you can't tell the difference. The best ashes are those of hickory, dogwood, sugar maple, and corncobs; but the ashes of beech, ash, buckeye, balsam poplar, and yellow poplar are also good.

"*Gritted Bread.*"—When green corn has just passed from the tucket, or soft and milky stage, and has become too hard for boiling, but is still too soft for grinding into meal, make a " gritter," as follows: Take a piece of tin about 7 x 14 inches (unsolder a lard pail by heating, and flatten the sides); punch holes through it, close together, with a large nail; bend the sheet into a half cylinder, rough side out, like a horseradish grater; nail the edges to a board somewhat longer and wider than the tin. Then, holding the ear of corn pointing lengthwise from you, grate it into a vessel held between the knees.

The meal thus formed will need no water, but can be mixed in its own milk. Salt it, and bake quickly. The flavor of "gritted bread" is a blend of hot pone and roasting ears — delectable! Hard corn can be grated by first soaking the ears over night.

BREADSTUFFS

Pancakes.—

Plain Flapjacks.—
  1 quart flour,
  1 teaspoonful salt,
  2 teaspoonfuls sugar, or 4 of molasses,
  2 level tablespoonfuls baking powder.

Rub in, dry, two heaped tablespoonfuls grease. If you have no grease, do without. Make a smooth batter with cold milk (best) or water — thin enough to pour from a spoon, but not too thin, or it will take all day to bake enough for the party. Stir well, to smooth out lumps. Set frying-pan level over thin bed of coals, get it quite hot, and grease with a piece of pork in split end of stick. Pan must be hot enough to make batter sizzle as it touches, and it should be polished. Pour from end of a big spoon successively enough batter to fill pan within one-half inch of rim. When cake is full of bubbles and edges have stiffened, shuffle pan to make sure that cake is free below and stiff enough to flip. Then hold pan slanting in front of and away from you, go through preliminary motion of flapping once or twice to get the swing, then flip boldly so cake will turn a somersault in the air, and catch it upside down. Beginners generally lack the nerve to toss high enough. Grease pan anew and stir batter every time before pouring. This is the "universal pancake" that "Nessmuk" derided. Much better and wholesomer are:

Egg Pancakes.— Made same as above excepting that you add two eggs, or their equivalent in desiccated egg.

Snow Pancakes.— Instead of eggs, in the above recipe, use four tablespoonfuls of freshly fallen snow. Make the batter rather thick, and add some clean, dry snow to each pancake before putting it in the pan.

Mixed Cakes.— When cold boiled rice is left over, mix it half and half with flour, and proceed as with flapjacks. It makes them tender. The batter is best mixed with the water in which the rice was boiled. Oatmeal, grits, or cold boiled potatoes, may be used in the same way. Stewed dried fruit is also a good addition; mix the flour with their juice instead of water.

Corn Batter Cakes.—

> ½ pint corn meal,
> ¼ pint flour,
> 1 heaped teaspoonful baking powder,
> 1 heaped teaspoonful sugar or 2 molasses,
> 1 level teaspoonful salt.

After mixing the dry ingredients thoroughly, add cold water, a little at a time, stirring briskly, until a rather thick batter results. Bake like flapjacks. Wholesomer than plain flour flapjacks. These are better with an egg or two added, and if mixed with milk instead of water. Snow can be substituted for eggs, as described above.

Buckwheat Cakes.—

> 1 pint buckwheat flour,
> ½ pint wheat flour,
> 2 tablespoonfuls baking powder,
> ½ teaspoonful salt.

Mix to a thin batter, preferably with milk. A couple of eggs make them light, or make snow cakes.

Syrup.— Mix maple or brown sugar with just enough water to dissolve it, and heat until clear. If white sugar is used, caramel it by putting it dry in a pan and heating until browned; then add water to dissolve it.

TOAST, FRITTERS, DUMPLINGS, ETC.—

Stale Bread.— Biscuit or bread left over and dried out can be freshened for an hour or two by dipping quickly in and out of water and placing in the baker until heated through; or, the biscuit may be cut open, slightly moistened, and toasted in a broiler.

If you have eggs, make a French toast by dipping the slices in whipped eggs and frying them.

With milk, make milk toast: heat the milk, add a

BREADSTUFFS

chunk of butter and some salt, toast the bread, and pour milk over it. Heat the milk gradually to the simmering point, but do not let it boil, lest it burn.

Stale bread may also be dipped into smoking hot grease. It will brown immediately. Stand it edgewise to drain, then lay on hot plate. Cut into dice for soups.

Fried Quoits.— Make dough as for biscuit. Plant a stick slanting in the ground near the fire. Have another small, clean stick ready, and a frying-pan of lard or butter heated sissing hot. There must be enough grease in the pan to drown the quoits. Take dough the size of a small hen's egg, flatten it between the hands, make a hole in the center like that of a doughnut, and quickly work it (the dough, not the hole) into a flat ring of about two inches inside diameter. Drop it flat into the hot grease, turn almost immediately, and in a few seconds it will be cooked.

When of a light brown color, fish it out with your little stick and hang it on the slanting one before the fire to keep hot. If the grease is of the right temperature, the cooking of one quoit will occupy just the same time as the molding of another, and the product will be crisp and crumpety. If the grease is not hot enough, a visit from your oldest grandmother may be expected before midnight. (Adapted from *Lees and Clutterbuck.*)

Fritters.— A dainty variety is added to the camp bill-of-fare by fritters of fruit or vegetables, fish, flesh, or fowl. They are especially relished in cold weather, or when the butter supply is low. Being easily made and quickly cooked, they fit any time or place.

The one essential of good and wholesome fritters is plenty of fat to fry them in, and fat of the right temperature. (The best friture is equal parts of butter and lard.) Set the kettle where the fat will heat slowly until needed; then closer over the fire until a bluish smoke rises from the center of the kettle. Drop a cube of bread into it; if it turns golden-brown in one minute, the fat is right. Then keep the kettle at just this temperature. Make batter as follows:

Fritter Batter.—
  1 pint flour,
  4 eggs,
  1 tablespoonful salt,
  1 pint water or milk,
  3 tablespoonfuls butter or other grease.

Blend the salt and the yolks of the eggs (or desiccated egg). Rub the butter into this; then the flour, a little at a time; then the water. Beat well, and, if you have time, let it stand a while. If fresh eggs are used, now beat the whites to a stiff froth and stir them in. When using, drop even spoonfuls into the fat with a large spoon. When golden-brown, lift fritter out with a forked stick (not piercing), stand it up to drain, and serve very hot. The base may be almost anything: sliced fruit, minced game or meat, fish or shellfish, grated cheese, boiled rice, grated potato or green corn, etc. Anything cut to the size of an oyster is dipped in the batter and then fried; if minced or grated it is mixed with the batter. Jam is spread on bread, covered with another slice, the sandwich is cut into convenient pieces, and these are dipped in the batter. Plain fritters of batter alone are eaten with syrup. Those made of corn meal instead of flour (mixed with *warm* milk and egg) are particularly good. The variety that can be served, even in camp, is well-nigh endless.

Dumplings.— Those of biscuit dough have already been mentioned. When specially prepared they may be made as follows:

  ½ pint flour,
  1 teaspoonful baking powder,
  ¼ teaspoonful salt,
  ½ teaspoonful sugar,
  ⅙ pint milk.

The stew that they are to be cooked with should

BREADSTUFFS

be nearly done before the dumplings are started. Then mix the dry ingredients thoroughly. Wet with the milk and stir quickly into a smooth ball. Roll into a sheet three-quarters of an inch thick, and cut like biscuit. Meantime bring the stew to a sharp boil. Arrange dumplings on top of it, cover the vessel, and cook exactly ten minutes.

MACARONI.—

Boiled Macaroni.— For one-half pound macaroni have not less than three quarts of salted water boiling rapidly. Break the macaroni into short pieces, and boil thirty-five minutes for the small, forty-five minutes for the large. Then drain, and pour sauce over it, or bake it. It is better if boiled in good broth instead of water.

Tomato Sauce.—

> 1 quart can tomatoes,
> 1 tablespoonful butter,
> 2 tablespoonfuls flour,
> 1 teaspoonful salt,
> ⅛ teaspoonful pepper,
> 1 teaspoonful sugar.

Rub the flour into the butter until they blend. Brown this in a pan. Add the tomatoes and simmer thirty minutes. Stir frequently. Add the seasoning, along with spices, if you wish. This makes enough sauce for 1½ pounds macaroni, but it keeps well in cold weather, and can be used with other dishes. Good in combination with the following:

Macaroni with Cheese.— After the macaroni is boiled, put it in a pan with a little butter and some grated cheese. Stir gently, and as soon as the cheese is melted, serve; or, pour the above sauce over it.

Macaroni, Baked.— Boil first, as above. Drain. Place in a deep pan, add a cupful of cold milk, sprinkle in three tablespoonfuls grated cheese and one tablespoonful butter. Then bake until brown.

Spaghetti.— This has the advantage over macaroni of not being so bulky to carry; but some do not like it so well. Speaking of bulk, if you cannot carry canned tomatoes, a very good sauce is made of Franco-American tomato purée (usually listed under SOUPS in grocers' catalogues) which is put up in cans as small as ½ pint.

"Dice one large onion and ¼ lb. of bacon and cook in a frying-pan until the onion is a light brown. Mix with this one small can of tomato purée, and, if you have it, a half cup of grated cheese. Season well and combine this with the spaghetti, which has been boiled, and blanched in cold water. Place in the baker in moderate heat for an hour. We buy plain American cheese and grate after drying: it should be packed in a push-top tin well lined with oiled paper." (*Mrs. Pinkerton.*)

PORRIDGE.—

Corn Meal Mush.— Mix two level tablespoonfuls salt with one quart meal. Bring four quarts of water (for yellow meal, or half as much for fresh white meal) to a hard boil in a two-gallon kettle. Mix the salted meal with enough *cold* water to make a batter that will run from the spoon; this is to prevent it from getting lumpy. With a large spoon drop the batter into the boiling water, adding gradually, so that water will not fall below boiling point. Stir constantly for ten minutes. Then cover pot and hang it high enough above fire to insure against scorching. Cook thus for one hour, stirring occasionally, and thinning with *boiling* water if it gets too thick.

Fried Mush.— This, as Father Izaak said of another dish, is "too good for any but very honest men." The only drawback to this gastronomic joy is that it takes a whole panful for one man. As it is rather slow to fry, let each man perform over the fire for himself. The mush should have been poured into a greased pan the previous evening, and set in a cool place over night to harden. Cut into slices one-third of an inch thick, and fry in very hot grease until nicely browned. Eat with syrup, or *au naturel*.

BREADSTUFFS

Polenta.— An Italian dish made from our native corn and decidedly superior to plain boiled mush. Cook mush as above for one hour. Partly fill the bake-pan with it, and pour over it either a good brown gravy, or the tomato sauce described under macaroni. Then sprinkle with grated cheese. Set the pan in the oven three minutes, or in the reflector five minutes, to bake a little.

Oatmeal Porridge.— Rolled oats may be cooked much more quickly than the old-fashioned oatmeal; the latter is not fit for the human stomach until it has been boiled as long as corn mush. To two quarts boiling water add one teaspoonful of salt, stir in gradually a pint of rolled oats, and boil ten minutes, stirring constantly, unless you have a double boiler. The latter may be extemporized by setting a small kettle inside a larger one that contains some water, with a few pebbles at the bottom to keep them apart.

CEREALS.—

Rice, Boiled.— Good precedent to the contrary notwithstanding, I contend that there is but one way to boil rice, and that is this (which is described in the words of Captain Kenealy, whose *Yachting Wrinkles* is a book worth owning):

"To cook rice so that each grain will be plump, dry, and separate, first, wash the measure of rice thoroughly in cold, salted water. Then put it in a pot of *furiously boiling* fresh water (1 cupful to 2 quarts water), no salt being added. Keep the pot boiling hard for twenty minutes, but *do not stir*. Then strain off the water, place the rice over a very moderate fire (hang high over camp-fire), and let it swell and dry for half an hour, in an uncovered vessel. Remember that rice swells enormously in cooking."

Plain boiled rice is not an appetising dish, particularly when you have no cream to eat it with; but no other cereal lends itself so well to varied combinations, not only as a breakfast food but also in soups and stews, in puddings, cakes, etc. Boiled rice with raisins is a standard dish; other dried fruit may be used. As a left-over, rice can be fried, made into pancakes or muffins, or utilized in a score of other ways, each dish tasting different from the others.

Rice, Fried.— When boiled rice is left over, spread it in a dish. When cold, cut it into cakes and fry it, for a hasty meal. It is better, though, in muffins.

Rice Muffins.— Mash very smooth half a pint boiled rice. Add slowly, stirring to a thinner paste, half a pint of milk, three beaten eggs, salt. Then make into a stiff batter with flour. Bake like dropped biscuits.

Rice with Onions.— A very good dish, quickly made, is boiled rice mixed with onions which have been chopped up and fried.

Spanish Rice.—" Mix two cupfuls of boiled rice, a large diced onion, and a can of tomato purée. Season with plenty of cayenne pepper and bake in the reflector for an hour." (*Mrs. Pinkerton.*)

Risotto.— Fry a sliced onion brown in a tablespoonful of butter. Add to this a pint of hot water and half a pint of washed rice. Boil until soft, adding more hot water if needed. Heat half a pint canned tomatoes, and stir into it a teaspoonful of sugar. When the rice is soft, salt it; add the tomato; turn into a dish and sprinkle over it a heaped tablespoonful of grated cheese.

Rice, Curried.— Same as Risotto, but put a teaspoonful of curry powder in the tomatoes and omit cheese.

Grits, Boiled.— Put in plenty of boiling unsalted water. Boil about thirty minutes; then salt and drain.

Grits, Fried.— Same as fried rice.

" Breakfast Foods."— According to directions on packages.

Left-over Cereals.— See MIXED CAKES, page 355.

CHAPTER XXI
CAMP COOKERY

Vegetables.— Soups

Fresh Vegetables.— Do not wash them until just before they are to be cooked or eaten. They lose flavor quickly after being washed. This is true even of potatoes.

Fresh vegetables go into plenty of fast-boiling salted water. Salt prevents their absorbing too much water. The water should be boiling fast, and there should be plenty of it. They should be boiled rapidly, with the lid left off the pan. If the water is as hot as it should be, the effect is similar to that which we have noted in the case of meats: the surface is coagulated into a waterproof envelope which seals up the flavor instead of letting it be soaked out. In making soup, the rule is reversed.

Dried Vegetables.— Beans and peas are to be cooked in unsalted water. If salted too soon they become leathery and difficult to cook. Put them in cold, fresh water, gradually heat to the boiling point, and boil slowly.

Dehydrated Vegetables.— When time permits they should first be soaked in cold water, according to directions on package; this makes them more tender. The onions and soup vegetables, however, can be boiled without previous soaking. Heat gradually to the boiling point and cook slowly in a covered vessel until done. When served alone they require butter for seasoning.

Canned Vegetables.— The liquor of canned peas, string beans, etc., is unfit for use and should be thrown away; this does not apply to tomatoes.

Cleaning Vegetables.— To clear cabbage, etc., from insects, immerse them, stalk upward, in plenty of cold water salted in the proportion of a large tablespoonful to two quarts. Vinegar may be used instead of salt. Shake occasionally. The insects will sink to bottom of pan.

Storing Vegetables.— To keep vegetables, put them in a cool, dry place (conditions similar to those of a good cellar). Keep each kind away from the other, or they will absorb each other's flavor.

Potatoes, Boiled.— Pick them out as nearly as possible of one size, or some will boil to pieces before the others are done; if necessary, cut them to one size. Remove eyes and specks, and pare as thinly as possible, for the best of the potato lies just under the skin. As fast as pared, throw into cold water, and leave until wanted. Put in furiously boiling salted water, then hang kettle a little higher where it will boil moderately, but do not let it check. Test with a fork or sliver. When the tubers are done (about twenty minutes for new potatoes, thirty to forty minutes for old ones) drain off all the water, dust some salt over the potatoes (it absorbs the surface moisture, and keeps leftovers from souring early), and let the pot stand uncovered close to the fire, shaking it gently once or twice, till the surface of each potato is dry and powdery. Never leave potatoes in the water after they are done; they become watery.

Potatoes, Boiled in Their Jackets.— After washing thoroughly, and gouging out the eyes, snip off a bit from each end of the potato; this gives a vent to the steam and keeps potatoes from bursting open. I prefer to put them in cold water and bring it gradually to a boil, because the skin of the potato contains an acid poison which is thus extracted. The water in which potatoes have been boiled will poison a dog. Of course we don't " eat 'em skin and all," like the people in the nursery rhyme; but

VEGETABLES

there is no use in driving the bitterness into a potato. Boil gently, but continuously, throw in a little salt now and then, drain, and dry before the fire.

Potatoes, Steamed.— Old potatoes are better steamed. A rough-and-ready method is shown on page 30.

Potatoes, Mashed.— After boiling, mash the potatoes with a peeled stub of sapling, or a bottle, and work into them some butter, if you have it, and milk. "The more you beat 'em, the better they be." Salt and pepper.

Potato Cakes.— Mould some mashed potato into cakes, season, and fry in deep fat. Or add egg and bake them brown.

Potatoes, Baked.— Nessmuk's description cannot be improved: "Scoop out a basin-like depression under the fore-stick, three or four inches deep, and large enough to hold the tubers when laid side by side; fill it with bright hardwood coals and keep up a strong heat for half an hour or more. Next, clean out the hollow, place the potatoes in it, and cover them with hot sand or ashes, topped with a heap of glowing coals, and keep up all the heat you like. In about forty minutes commence to try them with a sharpened hardwood sliver; when this will pass through them they are done and should be raked out at once. Run the sliver through them from end to end, to let the steam escape, and use immediately, as a roast potato quickly becomes soggy and bitter."

Potatoes, Fried.— Boiled or steamed potatoes that have been left over may be sliced one-quarter inch thick, and fried.

Potatoes, Fried, Raw.— Peel, and slice into pieces half an inch thick. Drop into cold water until frying-pan is ready. Put enough grease in pan to completely immerse the potatoes, and get it very hot, as directed under FRYING. Pour water off potatoes, dry a slice in a clean cloth, drop it into the sizzling fat, and so on, one slice at a time.

Drying the slices avoids a splutter in the pan and helps to keep from absorbing grease. If many slices were dropped into the pan together, the heat would be checked and the potatoes would get soggy with grease. When the slices begin to turn a faint brown, salt the potatoes, pour off the grease at once, and brown a little in the dry pan. The outside of each slice will then be crisp and the insides white and deliciously mealy.

Potatoes, Lyonnaise.— Fry one or more sliced onions until they are turning yellowish, then add sliced or diced potatoes, previously boiled; keep tossing now and then until the potatoes are fried somewhat yellow; salt and pepper to taste; you may add chopped or dehydrated parsley. Drain and serve.

Potatoes, Creamed.— Cut 1 pint cold potatoes in cubes or thin slices; put in pan and cover with milk; cook gradually until milk is absorbed. Then add 1 tablespoon butter, ½ teaspoonful salt, some pepper, and parsley. Stir a few moments, and serve.

Potatoes au Gratin.—" Chop cold boiled potatoes rather fine. Rub a tablespoonful of butter with one of flour, add ½ pint of milk, and season with salt and pepper. When this mixture has boiled, mix it with potatoes and turn into a baking dish. Sprinkle grated cheese over the top, pressing it down into the cream sauce. Bake in a quick oven until a golden brown." (*Arthur Chapman.*)

Potatoes, Stewed.— Cut cold boiled potatoes into dice, season with salt, pepper, butter, and stew gently in enough milk to cover them. Stir occasionally to prevent scorching. Or, peel and slice some raw potatoes. Cover with boiling water and boil until tender. Pour off the water. Roll a large piece of butter in flour, heat some milk, beat these together until smooth, season with salt and pepper, and bring to a boil. Then stew together five minutes. Serve very hot.

Sweet Potatoes, Boiled.— Use a kettle with lid.

VEGETABLES 367

Select tubers of uniform size; wash; do not cut or break the skins. Put them in boiling water, and continue boiling until, when you pierce one with a fork, you find it just a little hard in the center. Drain by raising the cover only a trifle when kettle is tilted, so as to keep in as much steam as possible. Hang the kettle high over the fire, cover closely, and let steam ten minutes.

Sweet Potatoes, Fried.— Skin the boiled potatoes and cut them lengthwise. Dust the slices with salt and pepper. Throw them into hot fat, browning first one side, then the other. Serve very hot.

Potatoes and Onions, Hashed.— Slice two potatoes to one onion. Parboil together about fifteen minutes in salted water. Pour off water, and drain. Meantime be frying some bacon. When it is done, remove it to a hot side dish, turn the vegetables into the pan, and fry them to a light brown. Then fall to, and enjoy a good thing!

Beans, Boiled.—Pick out all defective beans, and wash the rest. It is best to soak the beans over night; but if time does not permit, add one-quarter teaspoonful of baking soda to the parboiling water. In either case, start in fresh cold water, and parboil one quart of beans (for four men with hearty appetites) for one-half hour, or until one will pop open when blown upon. At the same time parboil separately one pound fat salt pork. Remove scum from beans as it rises. Drain both; place beans around pork, add two quarts boiling water, and boil slowly for two hours, or until tender. Drain, and season with salt and pepper.

It does not hurt beans to boil all day, provided boiling water is added from time to time, lest they get dry and scorch. The longer they boil the more digestible they become.

Left-over beans heated in a frying-pan with a little bacon grease have a pleasant and distinctive flavor.

Beans, Baked.— Soak and parboil as above, both the beans and the pork. Then pour off the water from the pork, gash the meat with a knife, spread half of it over the bottom of the kettle, drain the beans, pour them into the kettle, put the rest of pork on top, sprinkle not more than one-half teaspoonful of salt over the beans, pepper liberally, and if you have molasses, pour a tablespoonful over all; otherwise a tablespoonful of sugar. Hang the kettle high over the fire where it will not scorch, and bake at least two hours; or, add enough boiling water to just cover the beans, place kettle in bake-hole as directed on page 297, and bake all night, being careful that there are not enough embers with the ashes to burn the beans.

If a pail with thin lid must be used for a beanpot, cover its top with a two or three-inch layer of browse or green twigs before shoveling on the embers.

Baked beans are strong food, ideal for active men in cold weather. One can work harder and longer on pork and beans, without feeling hungry, than on any other food with which I am acquainted, save bear meat. The ingredients are compact and easy to transport; they keep indefinitely in any weather. But when one is only beginning camp life he should be careful not to overload his stomach with beans, for they are rather indigestible until you have toned up your stomach by hearty exercise in the open air.

Baked Beans for Transport.—" Cook the amount thought necessary and, when finished, pour off every last drop of water, spread them out on plates, and let them dry over a slow fire, stirring constantly. When dried they can be carried in a sack or any other receptacle, and can be prepared to be eaten within five minutes by the addition of hot water. If the weather is cold, do not dry them, but spread them out and stir around with a stick. They will freeze, and if constantly stirred will be so many individual beans, hard and frozen; they can be handled or carried like so many pebbles, and will keep indefinitely. Add hot water and, as soon as thawed out, they are ready to eat." (*Edward Ferguson.*)

VEGETABLES

Onions, Boiled.— More wholesome this way than fried or baked. Like potatoes, they should be of as uniform size as possible, for boiling. Do not boil them in an iron vessel. Put them in enough boiling salted water to cover them. Cover the kettle and boil gently, lest the onions break. They are cooked when a straw will pierce them (about an hour). If you wish them mild, boil in two or three waters. When cooked, drain and season with butter or dripping, pepper, and salt. Boiled milk, thickened, is a good sauce.

Green Corn.— If you happen to camp near a farm in the " roasting-ear " season, you are in great luck. The quickest way to roast an ear of corn is to cut off the butt of the ear closely, so that the pith of the cob is exposed, ream it out a little, impale the cob lengthwise on the end of a long hardwood stick, and turn over the coals.

To bake in the ashes: remove one outer husk, stripping off the silk, break off about an inch of the silk end, and twist end of husks tightly down over the broken end. Then bake in the ashes and embers as directed for potatoes. Time, about one hour.

To boil: prepare as above, but tie the ends of husks; this preserves the sweetness of the corn. Put in enough boiling salted water to cover the ears. Boil thirty minutes. Like potatoes, corn is injured by over-boiling. When cooked, cut off the butt and remove the shucks.

Cold boiled corn may be cut from the cob and fried, or mixed with mashed potatoes and fried.

Kedgeree.— Soak 1 pint split peas overnight; drain them, add 1 pound rice, some salt, pepper, and ½ teaspoonful ginger. Stir, and cover with 1 quart water. Stir and cook slowly until done and almost dry. Make into a mound, garnished with fried onions and sliced hard-boiled eggs.

Greens.— One who camps early in the season can add a toothsome dish, now and then, to his menu

by gathering fresh greens in the woods and marshes.*
As a salad (watercress, peppergrass, dandelion, wild mustard, sorrel, etc.): wash in cold salted water, if necessary, although this abstracts some of the flavor; dry immediately and thoroughly. Break into convenient pieces, rejecting tough stems. Prepare a simple French dressing, thus:

> 1 tablespoonful vinegar,
> 3 tablespoonfuls best olive oil,
> ½ teaspoonful salt,
> ¼ teaspoonful black pepper.

Put salt and pepper in bowl, gradually add oil, rubbing and mixing till salt is dissolved; then add by degrees the vinegar, stirring continuously one minute. In default of oil use cream and melted butter; but plain vinegar, salt, and pepper will do. Pour the dressing over the salad, turn the latter upside down, mix well, and serve.

A scalded salad is prepared in camp by cutting bacon into small dice, frying, adding vinegar, pepper, and a little salt to the grease, and pouring this, scalding hot, over the greens.

Greens may be boiled with salt pork, bacon, or other meat. To boil them separately: first soak in cold salted water for a few minutes, then drain well, and put into enough boiling salted water to cover, pressing them down until the pot is full. Cover, and boil steadily until tender, which may be from twenty minutes to an hour, depending upon kind of greens used. If the plants are a little older than they should be, parboil in water to which a little baking soda has been added; then drain, and continue boiling in plain water, salted.

Some greens are improved by chopping fine after boiling, putting in hot frying-pan with a tablespoonful of butter and some salt and pepper, and stirring until thoroughly heated.

Poke stalks are cooked like asparagus. They

---

* Nearly a hundred edible wild plants, besides mushrooms and fruits, are discussed in Volume II, under head of EDIBLE PLANTS OF THE WILDERNESS.

VEGETABLES

should not be over four inches long, and should show only a tuft of leaves at the top; if much older than this, they are unwholesome. Wash the stalks, scrape them, and lay in cold water for an hour; then tie loosely in bundles, put in a kettle of boiling water, and boil three-fourths of an hour, or until tender; drain, lay on buttered toast, dust with pepper and salt, cover with melted butter, and serve.

Jerusalem artichokes must be watched when boiling and removed as soon as tender; if left longer in the water they harden.

Dock and sorrel may be cooked like spinach: pick over and wash, drain, shake, and press out adhering water; put in kettle with one cup water, cover kettle, place over moderate fire, and steam thus twenty minutes; then drain, chop very fine, and heat in frying-pan as directed above.

Mushrooms.— Every one who camps in summer should take with him a mushroom book, such as Gibson's, Atkinson's, or Nina Marshall's. (Such a book in pocket form, with *colored* illustrations, is a desideratum.) Follow recipes in book. Mushrooms are very easy to prepare, cook quickly, and offer a great variety of flavors. The following general directions are condensed from McIlvaine's *One Thousand American Fungi:*

To Cleanse Mushrooms.— As they are found, cut loose well above attachment. Keep spore surface *down* until top is brushed clean and every particle of dirt removed from stem. If stem is hard, tough, or wormy, remove it. Do all possible cleaning in the field.

When ready to cook, wash by throwing into deep pan of water. Pass fingers quietly through them upward; let stand a moment for dirt to settle; then gather them from the water with fingers as a drain. Remove any adhering dirt with rough cloth. Thus wash in two or three waters. Lay to drain.

The largest amount of flavor is in the skin, the removal of which is seldom justifiable.

Concise Rule.— Cook in any way you can cook an oyster.

Broiling.— Use well-spread caps only. Place caps on double broiler, gills down. Broil two minutes. Turn and broil two minutes more. While hot, season with salt and pepper, butter well, especially on gill side. Serve on toast.

Frying.— Heat butter boiling hot in frying-pan. Fry five minutes. Serve on hot dish, pouring over them the sauce made by thickening the butter with a little flour.

Hunter's Toast.— Carry a vial of olive oil, or a small can of butter, and some pepper and salt mixed. Make fire of dry twigs. Split a green stick (sassafras, birch, or spicewood, is best) at one end; put mushroom in the cleft, broil, oil or butter, and eat from stick.

Camp Bake.— Cover bottom of tin plate with the caps, spore surface up. Sprinkle with salt and pepper. Place a bit of butter on each. Put another tin plate on top. Set on coals, or on a heated stone, fifteen minutes. No better baking will result in the best oven.

All mushrooms on the following list are delicious:

Coprinus comatus.	*Lactarius volemus.*
Hypholoma appendiculatum.	" *deliciosus.*
Tricholoma personatum.	*Russula alutacea.*
Boletus subaureus.	" *virescens.*
" *bovinus.*	*Cantharellus cibarius.*
" *subsanguineus.*	*Marasmius oreades.*
Clavaria botrytes.	*Hydnum repandum.*
" *cinerea*	" *Caput-Medusæ.*
" *vermicularis.*	*Morchella esculenta.*
" *inæqualis.*	" *deliciosa.*
" *pistillaris.*	

Canned Tomatoes.— To a pint of tomatoes add butter twice the size of an egg, some pepper, very little salt, and a tablespoonful of sugar. Boil about five minutes. Put some bread crumbs or toast in a dish, and pour tomatoes over them. Butter can be omitted. Some do not like sugar in tomatoes.

Canned Corn.— Same as tomatoes; but omit sugar and bread. Add a cup of milk, if you have it.

Miscellaneous Vegetables.— Since campers very seldom have any other fresh vegetables than potatoes and onions, I will not take up space with special recipes for others. The following time-table may some time be useful:

VEGETABLES

Boiling of Vegetables.

Asparagus	20 to 25 minutes
Cabbage	20 to 25 minutes
Carrots	30 to 40 minutes
Cauliflower	20 to 25 minutes
Corn (green)	15 to 20 minutes
Beans (string)	25 to 30 minutes
Beans (Lima)	30 to 35 minutes
Beans (navy, dried)	$2\frac{1}{2}$ to 4 hours
Beets	30 to 40 minutes
Onions	30 to 40 minutes
Parsnips	30 to 35 minutes
Peas (green)	20 minutes
Potatoes (new)	20 minutes
Potatoes (old)	30 to 40 minutes
Spinach	20 to 25 minutes
Turnips	30 to 35 minutes

SOUPS.— When Napoleon said that "soup makes the soldier," he meant thick, substantial soup — soup that sticks to the ribs — not mere broths or meat extracts, which are fit only for invalids or to coax an indifferent stomach. "Soup," says "Nessmuk," "requires time, and a solid basis of the right material. Venison is the basis, and the best material is the bloody part of the deer, where the bullet went through. We used to throw this away; we have learned better. Cut about four pounds of the bloody meat into convenient pieces, and wipe them as clean as possible with leaves or a damp cloth, but don't wash them. Put the meat into a five-quart kettle nearly filled with water, and raise it to a lively boiling pitch."

Here I must interfere. It is far better to bring the water gradually to a boil and then at once hang the kettle high over the fire where it will only keep up a moderate bubbling. There let it simmer at least two hours — better half a day. It is impossible to hasten the process. Furious boiling would ruin both the soup and the meat.

"Nessmuk" continues: "Have ready a three-tined fork made from a branch of birch or beech, and with this test the meat from time to time; when it parts readily from the bones, slice in a large onion. Pare six large, smooth potatoes, cut five of them into quarters, and drop them into the kettle; scrape the sixth one into the soup for thickening. Season with salt and white pepper to taste. When, by skirmishing with the wooden fork, you can fish up bones with no meat on them, the soup is cooked, and the kettle may be set aside to cool."

Any kind of game may be used in a similar way, provided that none but lean meat be used. Soup is improved by first soaking the chopped-up meat in cold water, and using this water to boil in thereafter. Soup should be skimmed for some time after it has started simmering, to remove grease and scum.

To anyone who knows *petite marmite* or *poule-au-pot,* these simple directions will seem barbarous — and so they are; but barbarism has its compensations. A really first-class soup cannot be made without a full day's previous preparation and the resources of a city grocery. Mulligatawny, for example, requires thirty-two varieties of spices and other condiments. No start can be made with any standard soup until one has a supply of "stock" made of veal or beef, mutton or poultry, by long simmering and skimming and straining.

In camp, stock can be made expeditiously by cutting one or two pounds of venison into thin slices, then into dice, cover with cold water, boil gently twenty minutes, take from the fire, skim, and strain. A tolerable substitute is Liebig's beef extract, or beef cubes, dissolved in water.

Onion, cloves, mace, celery seed, salt, and red or white pepper, are used for seasoning. Sassafras leaves, dried before the fire and powdered, make the gumbo *filé* of the creoles. Recipes for a few simple, nourishing soups, are given below:

Venison Soup.—"Put 4 or 5 lbs. of deer ribs in a bucket of water. Cook slowly until only half a bucket of 'stock' remains. Add 1 can tomatoes, ¼ cup rice, and salt to taste. Cook until these are done." (*Dr. O. M. Clay.*)

VEGETABLES

(2) Take 4 lbs. of lower leg bones of deer, or moose, caribou, sheep, goat, elk, etc., 2 lbs. of the meat, a large handful each of julienne and rice, a few pieces of pork, 1 teaspoonful of salt, pepper to taste, and 4 quarts of water. Crack the soup bones so that the marrow will run out, place in a large pot with the meat, water, and julienne, and boil slowly until the meat is shredded. Take out bones, add the rest of the ingredients, add hot water to make the desired quantity of soup, and boil until rice is cooked. (*Abercrombie.*)

Squirrel Soup.— Put the squirrels (not less than three) in a gallon of cold water, with a scant tablespoonful of salt. Cover the pot closely, bring to the bubbling point, and then simmer gently until the meat begins to be tender. Then add whatever vegetables you have. When the meat has boiled to a rag, remove the bones. Thicken the soup with a piece of butter rubbed to a smooth paste in flour. Season to taste.

Croutons for Soup.— Slice some stale bread half an inch thick, remove crust, and cut bread into half-inch dice. Fry these, a few at a time, in deep fat of the "blue smoke" temperature, until they are golden brown. Drain free from grease, and add to each plate of soup when serving. (See also page 356.)

Tomato Soup.— Take a quart can of tomatoes and a sliced onion. Stew twenty minutes. Meantime boil a quart of milk. Rub to a paste two tablespoonfuls each of flour and butter, and add to the boiling milk, stirring until it thickens. Now season the tomatoes with a teaspoonful of sugar, a little salt, and pepper. Then stir into the tomatoes one-half teaspoonful baking soda (to keep milk from curdling), add the boiling milk, stir quickly, and serve.

Bean Soup.— Boil with pork, as previously directed, until the beans are tender enough to crack open; then take out the pork and mash the beans into a paste. Return pork to kettle, add a cup of flour mixed thin with cold water, stirring it in slowly as the kettle simmers. Boil slowly an hour longer, stirring frequently so that it may not scorch. Season with little salt but plenty of pepper.

Pea Soup.— Wash well one pint of split peas, cover with cold water, and let them soak over night. In the morning put them in a kettle with close-fitting cover. Pour over them three quarts cold water, adding one-half pound lean bacon or ham cut into dice, one teaspoonful salt, and some pepper. When the soup begins to boil, skim the froth from the surface. Cook slowly three to four hours, stirring occasionally till the peas are all dissolved, and adding a little more boiling water to keep up the quantity as it boils away. Let it get quite thick. Just before serving, drop in small squares of toasted bread or biscuits, adding quickly while the bread is hot. Vegetables may be added one-half hour before the soup is done.

Turtle Soup.— Clean the turtle as directed in Chapter XV, leaving legs on, but skin them and remove the toes, as well as outer covering of shell. Place remaining parts, together with a little julienne, in fresh, hot water and boil until all the meat has left the bones. Remove bones, add hot water for required quantity of soup. Salt and pepper to taste. A tablespoonful each of sherry and brandy to each quart of liquid improves the flavor.

Condensed Soups.— Follow directions on wrapper.

Skilligalee.— The best thing in a fixed camp is the stock-pot. A large covered pot or enameled pail is reserved for this and nothing else. Into it go all the clean fag-ends of game — heads, tails, wings, feet, giblets, large bones — also the leftovers of fish, flesh, and fowl, of any and all sorts of vegetables, rice, or other cereals, macaroni, stale bread, everything edible except fat. This pot is always kept hot. Its flavors are forever changing, but ever welcome. It is always ready, day or night, for the hungry varlet who missed connections or who wants a bite between meals. No cook who values his peace of mind will fail to have skilly simmering at all hours.

CHAPTER XXII
BEVERAGES AND DESSERTS

Coffee.— To have coffee in perfection the berry must be freshly roasted and freshly ground. This can be done with frying-pan and pistol-butt; yet few but old-timers take the trouble.

There are two ways of making good coffee in an ordinary pot. (1) Put coffee in pot with cold water (one heaped tablespoonful freshly ground to one pint, or more coffee if canned ground) and hang over fire. Watch it, and when water first begins to bubble, remove pot from fire and let it stand five minutes. Settle grounds with a tablespoonful of cold water poured down spout. Do not let the coffee boil. Boiling extracts the tannin, and drives off the volatile aroma which is the most precious gift of superior berries. (2) Bring water to hard boil, remove from fire, and quickly put coffee in. Cover tightly and let steep ten minutes. A better way, when you have a seamless vessel that will stand dry heat, is to put coffee in, place over gentle fire to roast until aroma begins to rise, pour boiling water over the coffee, cover tightly, and set aside.

Tea is best made in a covered enameled pail. Leave the lid off until the water boils hard, then drop the tea in (one heaped teaspoonful to the pint is a common rule, but it depends on the strength of the brand you use), remove from the fire at once, stir it to make tea settle, cover tightly, and steep *away* from fire *four minutes by the watch.* Then strain into a separate vessel. A better way is to use a tea-ball, or put the tea in a small square

BEVERAGES AND DESSERTS

of cheesecloth, tie it up in loose bag form, and leave some string attached to remove it with.

A good deal of the aroma escapes from a teapot, but little from a covered pail.

If tea is left steeping more than five or six minutes the result is a liquor that would tan skin into leather. To boil is — well, it is like watering a rare vintage. You know what the old Colonel said: "My friend, if you put water in that wine, God'll never forgive you!"

Chocolate.— For each quart of boiling water scrape up four tablespoonfuls of chocolate. Boil until dissolved. Then add half a pint milk. Stir with a peeled stick until milk has boiled up once. Let each man sweeten his own cup.

Cocoa.— Follow directions on can.

DESSERTS.— *Dried Fruit.*— Evaporated or dried apples, apricots, peaches, prunes, etc., are misprized, under-rated, by most people from not knowing how to prepare them. The common way is to put the fruit on to stew without previous soaking, and then boil from one-half hour to two hours until it is more or less pulpy. It is then flat and insipid, besides unattractive to the eye.

There is a much better way. Soak the fruit at least over night, in clear cold water — just enough to cover — with or without spices, as you prefer. If time permits, soak it from twenty-four to thirty-six hours. This restores the fruit to its original size and flavor. It is good to eat, then, without cooking. To stew, merely simmer gently a few minutes in the water in which the fruit was soaked. This water carries much of the fruit's flavor, and is invaluable for sauce.

California prunes prepared in this way need no sugar. Dried apples and peaches have none of the rank taste by which they are unfavorably known, but resemble the canned fruit. Apricots properly soaked are especially good.

Jelly from Dried Fruit.— I was present when a Southern mountain woman did some "experiencin'," with nothing to guide her but her own wits. The result was a discovery of prime value to us campers. Here are the details — any one can follow them:

Wash one pound of evaporated apples (or common sun-dried apples of the country) in two waters. Cover with boiling water, and put them on to stew. Add boiling water as required to keep them covered. Cook until fruit is soft (about half an hour). Strain off all the juice (cheesecloth is convenient), and measure it. There will be, probably, a quart. Put this juice on the fire and add half its own measure of granulated sugar (say a scant pound — but measure it, to make sure of the proportion).

Now boil this briskly in a broad, uncovered vessel, without stirring or skimming, until the juice gets syrupy. The time varies according to quality of fruit — generally about twenty minutes after coming to a full boil. When the thickened juice begins to "flop," test it by letting a few drops drip from a spoon. When the drops thicken and adhere to the spoon, the syrup is done. There will be a little more than a pint. Pour it out. As soon as it cools it will be jelly, as good as if made from fresh fruit and much better than what is commonly sold in the stores.

The apples remaining can be spiced and used as sauce, or made into pies or turnovers, or into apple butter by beating smooth, adding a teacupful of sugar, spicing, and cooking again for fifteen or twenty minutes.

If preferred, a second run of jelly can be made from the same apples. Cover again with boiling water, stew about fifteen minutes, add sugar by measure, as before. This will take less boiling than the first juice (about seven minutes). Enough jelly will result to make nearly or quite a quart, all told, from one pound of dried apples and about one and one-half pounds of sugar.

Apricots or any other tart dried fruit can be used

BEVERAGES AND DESSERTS 381

instead of apples. Sweet fruit will not do, unless lemon juice or real apple vinegar is added.

Wild Fruits.— The time of ripening of American wild fruits is given in Volume II, under the heading EDIBLE PLANTS OF THE WILDERNESS.

Pie.— It is not to be presumed that a mere male camper can make a good pie-crust in the regular way; but it is easy to make a wholesome and very fair pie-crust in an irregular way, which is as follows: Make a glorified biscuit dough by mixing thoroughly 1 pint flour, 1 teaspoonful baking powder, ½ teaspoonful salt, rubbing in 4 heaped tablespoonfuls of lard (better still, half-and-half of butter and lard), and making into a soft dough with cold water. In doing this, observe the rules given under *Biscuit.* The above quantity is enough for a pie filling an 8 x 12 reflector pan. Roll the dough into a thin sheet, as thin as you can handle, and do the rolling as gently as you can.

From this sheet cut a piece large enough for bottom crust and lay it in the greased pan. The sheet should be big enough to lap over edge of pan. Into this put your fruit (dried fruit is previously stewed and mashed), and add sugar and spice to taste. Then, with great circumspection and becoming reverence, lay on top of all this your upper crust. Now, with your thumb, press the edges of upper and lower crust together all around, your thumb-prints leaving scallops around the edge. Trim off by running a knife around edge of pan. Then prick a number of small slits in the top crust, here and there, to give a vent to the steam when the fruit boils. Bake as you would biscuits.

Note that this dough contains baking powder, and that it will swell. Don't give the thing a name until it is baked; then, if you have made the crust too thick for a pie, call it a cobbler, or a shortcake, and the boys, instead of laughing at you, will ask for more.

Snits und Knepp.—This is a Pennsylvania-Dutch dish, and a good one for campers. Take some dried apples and soak them over night. Boil until tender. Prepare knepp as directed for potpie dough, only make a thick batter of it instead of a dough. It is best to add an egg and use no shortening. Drop the batter into the pan of stewing apples, a large spoonful at a time, not fast enough to check the boiling. Boil about ½ hour. Season with butter, sugar, and cinnamon.

Apple Dumpling.— Make a biscuit dough (see page 347) and roll out to ¼ inch thick. Peel and quarter some apples and remove the cores. Put four quarters together and cover it with a globe of dough. Put in a cloth and boil like pudding. (page 384) for 25 minutes.

To bake dumplings: roll the dough quite thin, cover as above, and bake.

Fruit Cobbler.— Make up your dough as directed under *Pie,* excepting omit baking powder, and use ½ pound of mixed butter and lard to 2 pints flour. Mix with coldest spring water, and have your hands cold. After putting under crust in greased pan, pour in scant 3 pints of fruit, which may be either fresh, canned, or evaporated (soaked as explained under *Dried Fruits*), leaving out the free juice. Cover with upper crust, bake brown, and serve with milk or pudding sauce.

Doughnuts.— Mix 1 quart of flour with 1 teaspoonful of salt, 1 tablespoonful of baking powder, and 1 pint of granulated sugar, and ½ nutmeg grated. Make a batter of this with 4 beaten eggs and enough milk to make smooth. Beat thoroughly and add enough flour to make a soft dough. Roll out into a sheet ½ inch thick and cut into rings or strips, which may be twisted into shape. Fry by completely immersing in very hot fat; turn when necessary. Drain and serve hot.

Gingerbread.— Mix 1 cup molasses, 1 tablespoonful ground ginger, ½ teaspoonful salt, ½ cup melted butter or drippings, 1 cup milk, 3 cups flour with 2 teaspoonfuls baking powder mixed in it. Bake ½ hour.

BEVERAGES AND DESSERTS 383

Cookies.— Mix 4 cups flour with 3 teaspoons baking powder and 1 cup sugar; pour into this 4 tablespoons melted butter or drippings; add 1 cup raisins and 1 teaspoon cinnamon and cloves or allspice. Mix with enough water to make of the consistency of biscuit dough. Roll out to about ½ inch thick (or thinner if raisins are omitted). Cut with top of baking powder can, and bake to a light brown.

Puddings are either baked in an oven or reflector, or boiled in a cloth bag. Baked puddings are quickest and easiest to manage. A few examples of simple puddings are given below. They may be varied indefinitely, according to materials available. Deep tin pudding pans are convenient to bake in. Snow may be substituted for eggs (see page 353).

Rice Pudding.— Mix 1 pint cold boiled rice with 1 quart milk and sugar to taste. Put in a well-greased pan, dust nutmeg or cinnamon over the top, and bake slowly one hour. Seeded raisins are an agreeable addition. Mix them in before baking. To stone them, keep them in lukewarm water during the process. A couple of eggs make the pudding richer.

Fruit Pudding.— Line a deep dish or pan, well greased, with slices of buttered bread. Then put in a layer of fruit, dusting it with sugar and dotting with small lumps of butter. Repeat these alternate layers until the dish is full, the last layer being bread. Bake ½ to ¾ hour, with moderate heat. Eat hot, with the sweet sauce given below.

Cottage Pudding.—

    1 pint flour,
    ½ pint sugar,
    ½ pint milk,
    2 heaped tablespoonfuls butter,
    1 egg,
    2 teaspoonfuls baking powder,
    Grated rind of a lemon,

Mix thoroughly the flour and baking powder. Rub the butter and sugar to a cream, add the milk and egg beaten together; then the lemon rind. Add this to the flour and mix well. Butter a pan well to prevent scorching and dredge it with flour or powdered bread-crumbs. Pour in the batter, and bake about half an hour in hot oven.

A richer pudding is made by using one-half pound butter and two eggs.

A cupful of stoned raisins, minced figs, or dates, added to the batter, converts this into a good fruit pudding. Nutmeg, cinnamon, or other flavoring may be substituted for lemon.

Batter Pudding.—

> ½ pint flour,
> 1 pint milk,
> 1 heaped tablespoonful butter,
> 6 eggs.

Beat flour and milk into a smooth batter. Then add the eggs, beaten light. Stir all well together, adding the butter in tiny lumps. Dip a clean cloth bag into hot water, dredge it with flour, pour the batter into this, tie up firmly, and put into plenty of boiling water. Keep this boiling steadily for an hour. Then dip the bag quickly in cold water and remove cloth with care not to break the pudding. Serve very hot, with a sauce.

Plain Plum Duff.—

> 1 quart flour,
> 1 heaped teaspoonful baking powder,
> 2 tablespoonfuls sugar,
> 1 ℔. seeded raisins.
> ¾ ℔. suet (or see below).

Venison suet chopped fine, or the fat of salt pork minced up, will serve. Marrow is better than either. Mix the dry ingredients intimately. Then make up with half a pint of water. Put this into a cloth bag prepared as in the preceding recipe. Since suet puddings swell considerably, the bag must be large enough to allow for this. Place in enough boiling water to cover, and do not let it check boiling until done (about two hours). Add boiling water as required to keep the bag covered. Turn the bag upside down when pudding begins to set, or the fruit will all go to the bottom; turn it around now and then to prevent scorching against sides of pot. When done, manipulate it like cottage pudding. Serve with sweet sauce.

A richer duff can be made by spicing and adding molasses, or the rind and juice of a lemon.

Sweet Sauce for Puddings.— Melt a little butter, sweeten it to taste, and flavor with grated lemon rind, nutmeg, or cinnamon.

Brandy Sauce.— Butter twice the size of an egg is to be beaten to a cream with a pint of sugar and a tablespoonful of flour. Add a gill of brandy. Set the cup in a dish of boiling water and beat until the sauce froths.

Fruit Sauce.— Boil almost any fresh fruit until it is quite soft. Squeeze it through cheesecloth, sweeten to taste, heat it, and pour the sauce over your pudding. Spices may be added during the final heating.

Hard Sauce.— Work 2 tablespoonfuls of butter with a small cupful of sugar to a cream. Flavor with a little nutmeg, lemon juice, brandy, or whatever may be your preference.

CHAPTER XXIII
COOK'S MISCELLANY

Dish Washing.— Gilbert Hamerton, in his *Painter's Camp,* dwells lovingly upon all the little details of camp life, excepting this:

5 P. M. Cease painting for the day. Dine. . . . After dinner the woeful drudgery of cleaning-up! At this period of the day am seized with a vague desire to espouse a scullery-maid, it being impossible to accommodate one in the hut without scandal, unless in the holy state of matrimony: hope no scullery-maid will pass the hut when I am engaged in washing-up, as I should be sure to make her an offer.

There is a desperately hard and disagreeable way of washing dishes, which consists, primarily, in " going for " everything alike with the same rag, and wiping grease off one dish only to smear it on the next one. There is another, an easier, and a cleaner way: First, as to the frying-pan, which generally is greasiest of all: pour it nearly full of water, place it level over the coals, and let it boil over. Then pick it up, give a quick flirt to empty it, and hang it up. Virtually it has cleaned itself, and will dry itself if let alone. Greasy dishes are scraped as clean as may be, washed with scalding water, and then wiped. An obdurate pot is cleaned by first boiling in it (if you have no soap powder) some wood ashes, the lye of which makes a sort of soap of the grease; or it may be scoured out with sand and hot water. Greasy dishes can even be cleaned without hot water, if first wiped with a handful or two of moss, which takes up the grease; use first the dirt side of the moss as a scourer, then the top. To scour greasy knives and forks, simply

COOK'S MISCELLANY

jab them once or twice into the ground. Rusty ones can be burnished by rubbing with a freshly cut potato dipped in wood ashes. The scouring rush (*Equisetum hymenale*), which grows in wet places and along banks throughout the northern hemisphere, has a gritty surface that makes an excellent swab. It is the tall, green, jointed, pipe-stem-like weed that children amuse themselves with, by pulling the joints apart. The sooty outside of a pot is readily cleaned with a bit of sod ("monkey soap").

In brief, the art of dish washing consists first in cleaning off nearly all the grease before using your dish-cloth on it. Then the cloth will be fit to use again. Dish-cloths are the supplies that first run short in an average outfit.

COOK'S MEASURES

45 drops water=1 teaspoonful=1 fluid dram.
2 teaspoonfuls=1 dessertspoonful.
4 teaspoonfuls=1 tablespoonful.
2 tablespoonfuls=1 fluidounce.
4 tablespoonfuls=1 wineglassful.
8 tablespoonfuls=1 gill.
2 gills=1 cup.
4 gills=1 pint (1 ℔. water).
2 pints=1 quart (1 ℔. flour).
4 quarts=1 gallon.
2 gallons (dry)=1 peck.
4 pecks (dry)=1 bushel.

OUTFITTER'S DATA

Baking powder .... 1 ℔.=1¼ pints.
Beans, dried .... 1 qt.=1¾ ℔s.
Coffee, roasted whole .... 1 qt.=10 oz.
Corn meal .... 1 qt.=1¼ ℔s.
Flour .... 1 qt.=1 ℔.
Macaroni .... 1 ℔.=8⅞x2⅜x2⅜ in.
Oatmeal .... 1 qt.=⅝ ℔.
Peas, split .... 1 qt.=1¾ lbs.
Rice .... 1 qt.=2 ℔s.
Salt, dry .... 1 qt.=1⅞ ℔s.
Soda crackers are about 3 times as bulky as bread, weight for weight.
Sugar, granulated .... 1 qt.=1¾ ℔s.
Tea .... 1 qt.=½ ℔.

Bacon, breakfast .... 1 flitch=5–8 lbs., average.
Salt pork .... 1 side=30–40 lbs., average.
Salt pork .... 1 belly=20 lbs., average.
Butter, closely packed...... 1 lb.=1 pint.
Butter, creamery .... 1 lb.=4⅝x2½x2½ in.
Eggs, desiccated .... 1 lb.=6x3x3 in.=4 doz. fresh.
Eggs, fresh .... 1 doz. (average)=1½ lbs.
Lard .... 3 lb. pail=5x5 in.
Lard .... 5 lb. pail=6x6 in.
Milk, evaporated .... 7 oz. can=2½x2½ in.
Milk, evaporated .... 12 oz. can=3⅜x3 in.
Milk, evaporated .... 1 lb. can=4⅜x3 in.
Apples, evaporated .... 1 lb. (14 oz.)=7⅛x4½x2 in.
Apples, evaporated .... 1 peck=6 lbs
Corn, canned .... 1 can=2¼ lbs.=4⅝x3⅜ in.
Fruit, canned, small can, same as corn.
Fruit, canned, large can, same as tomatoes.
Tomatoes, canned .... 1 can=2½ lbs.=4⅞x4⅛ in.
Lemons .... 1 doz.=2 lbs.=2 qts.
Raisins, stemmed .... 1 lb.=1⅓ pints.
Carrots .... 1 qt.=1¼ lbs.
Onions .... 1 qt.=1 lb.
Potatoes .... 1 peck=15 lbs.
Sweet potatoes.......... 1 peck=14 lbs.

A TABLE

FOR READY REFERENCE IN CHOOSING WHAT TO COOK

All recipes in this book are here grouped under *Quick, Medium,* or *Slow,* according to the time they take. Everything under *Quick* can be prepared in less than 25 minutes, and so is specially suitable for breakfast or luncheon.

The table also shows at a glance what recipes call for milk, butter, or eggs, and what do not. The following abbreviations are used:

E = Eggs required (whole or desiccated).
B = Butter required.
M = Milk required (may be evaporated or powdered).
E*= Eggs desirable, but may be omitted.
B*= Butter desirable, but other fat may be substituted.
M*= Milk desirable, but water may be substituted.
¶ = Made over from previously cooked material.

COOK'S MISCELLANY 389

QUICK
(*Under 25 minutes*)

Fresh Meat, Game.

Broiled meat, game. B.*	292
Fried meat, game	291
Chops	292
Kabobs	296
Brains, fried	306
Brains and eggs. E.	306
Liver, fried	306
Kidneys, fried	306
Milt, broiled	307
Venison sausages	307
¶Croquettes. B, E.	307
Small birds, roasted. B.*	319
¶Deviled birds. B.	319
Frog legs, broiled or fried. B.*	328

Fish.

Fish, fried	321
Fish, broiled. B.*	322
Fish, skewered	322

Shellfish.

Oysters, stewed. B, M.	329
Oysters, fried. E.	329
Oysters, scalloped. B.	330
Oysters, sauté. B.	330

Cured Meat.

Bacon, broiled, fried, toasted	332
Salt pork, broiled or fried	333
Ham, broiled or fried	333
Bacon, or ham, and eggs. E.	332
Pork fritters	333
Pork sausages	334
Slumgullion	335
Dried beef, creamed. M, B.*	335
Canned meat, heated	336

Cured or Canned Fish.

Smoked herring, toasted	337
Smoked herring, fried. B.*	337
Sprats	337
Salmon, creamed. M.	337
Salmon, scalloped. B, M.	337
Salmon on toast. B, E, M.	337
Sardines, fried. B,* E.*	338

Gravies.

Braising gravy	297
Frying gravy	302

Broiling gravy. B.* 292
Boiling gravy. B. 303
Roasting gravy 303
Beef extract gravy 303
Cream gravy. B, M. 303
Rabbit gravy 310
Bacon gravy, thin 332
Pork gravy, thick. M.* 333
Roux 302
Onion gravy 303

Eggs.
Eggs, poached (fresh). B,* E. 340
Eggs, boiled (fresh). E. 340
Eggs, fried (fresh). E. 338
Eggs, scrambled (fresh or desiccated). B,* E. 339
Omelets (fresh or desiccated). B,* E. 339
Eggs, stirred. B, E. 340

Bread.
Biscuit loaf 346
Biscuits 347
Dropped biscuits 348
Breakfast rolls. B, E, M. 348
Bannocks 344
Dough gods 351
Unleavened bread 351
French toast. E. 356
Milk toast. B, M. 356
¶Rice muffins. E, M. 362

Pancakes, etc.
Flapjacks, plain 355
Egg pancakes. E. 355
Snow pancakes 355
¶Mixed cakes 355
Corn batter cakes. E,* M.* 356
Buckwheat cakes. E,* M.* 356
Syrup 356
"Gritted" bread 354
Fried quoits 357
Fritters. B,* E, M.* 357
Dumplings. M.* 358

Porridge, etc.
¶Fried mush 360
¶Fried grits, rice 362
¶Rice with onions 362
Rolled oats 361
Breakfast cereals 362

Vegetables.
Potatoes, fried 365

COOK'S MISCELLANY

Potatoes, stewed. *B, M*.	366
¶Potato cakes. *E,* M.**	365
¶Potatoes, mashed. *B,* M.*	365
¶Potatoes, lyonnaise	366
¶Potatoes, creamed	366
¶Sweet potatoes, fried	367
Potatoes and onions, hashed	367
Green corn, roasted. *B.**	369
Greens, boiled (some kinds). *B.**	369
Mushrooms. *B*.	371
Canned tomatoes, stewed. *B.**	372
Canned corn, stewed. *B,* M.**	372

Soups.

Condensed soups	376
Tomato soup. *B, M*.	375

Beverages.

Coffee	378
Tea	378
Chocolate. *M*.	379
Cocoa. *M*.	379

Sauces.

Barbecue sauce. *B.**	296
Mustard sauce. *B*.	304
Venison sauce. *B*.	304
Broiled venison sauce. *B*.	304
Giblet sauce. *B,* M.**	316
Celery sauce. *B, M*.	320
Cranberry sauce	320
Curry sauce. *B, M.**	320
Butter sauce. *B*.	325
White sauce. *B, M*.	325
Lemon sauce. *B, M*.	325
Parsley sauce. *B.**	304
India sauce. *B, M*.	325
Sweet sauce. *B*.	385
Brandy sauce. *B*.	385
Fruit sauce	385
Hard sauce. *B*.	385
Salad dressing	370

MEDIUM.

(*25 to 45 minutes.*)

Fresh Meat, Game.

Cured venison, steamed	336
Small mammals, roasted	294
Heart, braised	306
Liver, roasted	306
Game pot pie. *B.**	307

CAMPING AND WOODCRAFT

Curry of game. B.* 308
Game pie 308
Small game, barbecued 309
Small game, fricasseed 315
Duck, roasted or baked 317
Grouse, roasted 319
Game birds, boiled 320

Fish.
Fish, baked 323
Fish, boiled. B. 324
Fish, roasted. B.* 323
Fish, planked. B.* 323
Fish, steamed 324
Fish chowder. B,* M.* 326
Fish cakes. E. 327
Fish roe 328
Eel, stewed. M. 328
Frog legs, creamed. B, M. 328

Shellfish, etc.
Clams, baked. B. 330
Clam chowder. M. 330
Crayfish, boiled 329
Crabs, deviled 331

Cured Meats.
Bacon and liver 306
Pork and hardtack 333
Corned beef hash 335
Canned meat stew 335

Cured Fish.
Salt fish, broiled 336
Codfish balls. B.* 337

Bread.
Army bread 348
Corn pone 352
Johnny-cake 352
Corn dodgers 352
Ash cake 352
Corn bread. B, E, M. 353
Corn batter bread. E, M. 353
Snow bread 353

Cereals, etc.
Rice, boiled 361
Rice, curried 362
Risotto 362
Grits, boiled 362
Macaroni, boiled 359

Vegetables.
Desiccated vegetables 363
Potatoes, boiled 364
Potatoes, steamed 365
Potatoes, baked 365
¶Potatoes *au gratin.* B, M. 366
Sweet potatoes, boiled 366
Green corn, boiled 369
Kedgeree 369
Greens, boiled (some kinds). B.* 369

Desserts.,
Pie. B.* 381
Doughnuts. E, M. 382
Snits und Knepp. B, E.* 381
Apple dumplings 382
Fruit cobbler. B. 382
Gingerbread. B,* M. 382
Cookies. B.* 383
Cottage pudding. B, E, M. 383

Sauces.
Tomato sauce. B. 359

SLOW.
(*Over 45 minutes.*)
Fresh Meat, Game.
Roasted meat, big game 294
Braised meat, big game.............................. 296
Baked meat, big game 297
Boiled meat, big game 299
Stewed meat, big game 300
Steamed meat, big game 301
Barbecued meat, big game 296
Kidneys, stewed 306
Marrow bones, boiled 307
Moose muffle, boiled 307
Tongue, boiled 307
Turkey, goose, roasted 315
Turkey, boiled 316
Jambolaya 308
Turtle, boiled 329

Cured Meat.
Lobscouse 335
Bacon, salt pork, ham, boiled 332
Ham and macaroni 360
Ham chow 334

Cured Fish.
Salt fish, boiled 336
Codfish, stewed 336

Codfish hash 337
Bread.
Sour-dough bread 349
Salt-rising bread 349
Lungwort bread 350
Porridge, etc.
Corn mush 360
Polenta 361
Macaroni, with cheese. B. 359
Macaroni, baked. B, M. 359
Spaghetti, baked 359
Rice, Spanish 362
Vegetables.
Beans, boiled 367
Beans, baked 367
Onions, boiled. B,* M.* 369
Green corn, baked 369
Greens, boiled (some kinds). B.* 369
Soups from raw materials. B.* 373
Desserts.
Dried fruit, stewed 379
Jelly from dried fruit 379
Rice pudding. E,* M. 383
Batter pudding. B, E, M. 384
Plum duff 384
Snow pudding 383

INDEX TO VOLUME I

Almanacs, 172
Ants, 220, 256
Apple dumpling, 382
Ash cake, 344, 352
Axes, 113
  Care of, 114, 115, 224

Bacon, 186
  and eggs, 332
  Boiled, 332
  Broiled, 332
  Fried, 332
  omelet, 332
  Toasted, 332
Baking bread, 342
  in a hole, 297
    ashes, 344, 352
    clay, 298
    clay oven, 345
    Dutch oven, 342
    embers, 298
    frying pan, 344
    kettle, 343
    reflector, 347
    the hide, 297
  meat, 297
  on a slab, 345
Baking powder, 346
Bandages, Triangular, 174
Bannocks, 344
Barbecuing, 296, 309
Bark as fuel, 230, 233
Bean soup, 375
Beans, 195
  Baked, 367
    and dried, 368
    with birds, 297
  Boiled, 367
Bear, Butchering, 274
  Cooking, 292, 296
Beaver tail, Cooking, 314
Bed-bugs, 256

Bed rolls, 136
Bed tick, 134
Bedding, 124
Beef extract, 199
  Gravy from, 303
Beef, Corned, 187, 334
  Hash, 335
Beef, Dried, 187
  Creamed, 335
Belts, 145
Benches, Rustic, 218
Beverages, 197, 378
Birds baked in clay, 299
  with beans, 297
  Broiled, 315
  Deviled, 319
  Fricasseed, 315
  Fried, 315
  Hanging to ripen, 282, 314
  Roasting, 317
  Small, To cook, 319
  To dress, 282
    dry, 279
    keep, 283
    ship, 283
Biscuit, 347
  Dropped, 348
  loaf, 344, 346
Bites and stings, 249, 257
Bittern, Cooking, 319
Blanket, To roll up in, 128
  To wear, 128
Blankets, 127
  Airing, 224
Blow-flies, 250, 275, 276
Boiling, 299, 324
  at high altitudes, 300
Boots, 156
  Felt, 161
Brains and eggs, 306
  Cooking, 306

INDEX

Braising, 296
Bread, 191
  Army, 348
  Baking, 342
  Corn, 352, 353
  Fried, 357
  Gritted, 352
  Lungwort, 350
  Raising in pot, 350
  Salt-rising, 349
  Snow, 353
  Sour-dough, 349
  Stale, To freshen, 347, 356
  Unleavened, 351
  Wheat, 346
Breakfast foods, 362
Breeches, 144
Broiling, 292, 322
Browse bag, 134
Buckskin jackets, 147
  moccasins, 158
Buckwheat cakes, 356
Bunks, 53
Butchering game, 264
Butter, 191
  Care of, 220
  Keeping, 191

Cakes, Mixed, 355
Calories, 181, 202
Cameras, 176
Camp conveniences, 223
  cookery, 290
  Exposure of, 216
  furniture, 53, 218
  making, 208
  pests, 241
  Privacy of, 216
  sanitation, 222
  sites, 208, 212, 216
Camp-fires, 101, 225, 230, 231
Camping, 20
  Preparations for, 207
  System in, 217
Candlesticks, Improvised, 221
Caps, 160
Capsules, 197
Carbohydrates, 179

Caribou hide, 131, 148, 158
Carryalls, 137
Catfish, To skin, 285
Celluloid varnish, 73
Centipedes, 259
Cereals, 185, 193
  Cooking, 361
  Left-over, 362
Chairs, Camp, 55
Cheese, 191
Chests, Camp, 206
Chocolate as a beverage, 379
  as food, 194
Chopping-block, 223
Chops, Cooking, 294
Chowder, Clam, 330
  Fish, 326
Chuck boxes, 207
Citric acid, 197
Clam chowder, 330
Clams, Baked, 330
  Stewed, 301
Cloth, Dyeing, 74
  Waterproofing, 72, 148
Clothes hangers, 58
  line, 224
Clothing, 138
  Colors, 143, 147, 162
  for cold weather, 162
  women, 163
Coals, To keep alive, 229
Coats, 146
  Mackinaw, 162
Cocoa, 199, 379
Codfish balls, 337
  hash, 337
  Stewed, 336
Coffee, 197
  Brewing, 378
Cold storage, 67, 220, 287
Comfort in camp, 124
Comforters, 126, 128
Compass, 168
Comrades and camp bores, 26
Condiments, 199
Cook's measures, 387
  miscellany, 387
  time-tables, 317, 373, 388
Cookers, Fireless, 66

INDEX

Cookery, Camp, 290
Cookies, 383
Cooking fires, 226
Cooking in the rain, 47
  utensils, 64, 118
  without utensils, 293, 295-299, 301, 309, 314, 315, 317, 319, 322-324, 330, 340, 344-346, 365, 369
'Coons, 263, 281
  Cooking, 312
Corn batter bread, 353
  batter cakes, 352, 356
  bread, 352, 353
  Canned, Cooking, 372
  dodgers, 352
  Green, 369
  meal, 192
  mush, 360
  pone, 352
Coots, Cooking, 318
Cot mattresses, 53
Cots, 53
Cow-bell for children, 60
Crabs, Deviled, 331
Crane, Cooking, 228
Crayfish, Cooking, 329
Crisco, 197, 292,
Croquettes, 307
Croutons, 375
Crotches, 218
Crutch, To make, 219
Curry of game, 308

Deer, Butchering, 264, 269
  Carrying on litter, 266
    pickaback, 267
  Dragging on ground, 265
  Hanging to butcher, 268, 274
  Packing on saddle, 265
  Skinning, 270
  skins, Preserving, 275
Desserts, 379
Dining place, 218
Dish washing, 386
Ditty boxes, 165
Dock, Cooking, 371
Dog trolley, 59

Dopes, Fly, 243
Dough, To mix without pan, 346
Dough-gods, 351
Doughnuts, 382
Drawers, 141
Dressing game and fish, 264
Driftwood, 239
Duck, Baked, 317
  in clay, 299
  Fish-eating, 318
  Stewed, 318
  To dress, 282, 316
Duck, Cotton, 32
Duff, Plum, 384
Dumplings, 308, 358
  Apple, 382
Dunnage bags, 164
Dutch ovens, 64
Dyeing cloth, 74

Economies, 24
Eel, Boiled, 327
  Stewed, 328
  To skin, 285
Eggs, 188
  Boiled, 340
  Desiccated, 189
    To cook, 338
  Fried, 338
  Frozen, 189
  Omelets, 339, 340
  Poached, 340
  Roasted, 340
  Scrambled, 339
  Snow as substitute for, 354
  Stirred, 340
  To pack, 189
    preserve, 189
    test, 189
Electric flashers, 173
Elk, Butchering, 273
Exposure of camp, 216
Eye glasses, 173

Fats, 179
Feet, Care of, 150
Fence, 222
Field glasses, 177
Filters, 212

Fire, Backlog, 231, 236
  Building, 235
  Camp, 225
  Cooking, 225
  Dinner, 227
  for baking, 229
  grates, 63
  Hunter's, 230
  in trench, 230, 235
    wet weather, 234
  Indian's, 232
  irons, 64, 228
  Luncheon, 226
  Precautions, 214, 234, 237, 239
  regulations, 234
  Starting in stove, 63
  Winter camp, 231
Fires, Forest, 214, 234, 239
Fireless cookers, 66
First aid, 59
  kits, 58, 174
Fish, Baked, 323
  in clay, 298
  Boiled, 300, 324
  Broiled, 294, 322
  cakes, 327
  Canned, 188
  chowder, 326
  Cooking, 321
  Creamed, 327, 337
  Cured, 188
    To cook, 336
  Fried, 321
  from muddy waters, 284, 327
  Frozen, 305
  Planked, 323
  Roasted, 323
  roe, Cooking, 328
  Salt, Cooking, 336
  Skewered, 324
  To clean, 283
    dry, 288
    keep, 286
    kill, 285
    salt, 289
    scale, 284
    ship, 288
    skin, 284
    steak, 285

Flapjacks, 355
Flashlights, 173
Fleas, 249
Flies, 222, 256
  Blood-sucking, 250, 255
  Blow, 250, 275, 276
Flies, Tent, 35, 51
Floss, Dental, 118
Flour, 192
Fly dopes, 243
Food, 178
  as a source of energy, 181
  Care of, 220, 259, 262, 263, 275, 364
  Digestibility, 185
  Nutritive values, 179, 182, 368
  Packing, 205
  Variety, 180
  Weights and measures, 387
Footwear, 150
  Rubber, 161
Fricassees, 292
Fritter batter, 358
Fritters, 357
  Pork, 333
Fritures, 197, 292, 321, 357
Frog legs, Cooking, 328
Fruit, 196
  cobbler, 382
  Dried, Cooking, 379
    Jelly from, 379
  Wild, 381
Frying, 291, 302, 321
Frying-pans, 120
Fuel, 212
  Best, 237
  Driftwood as, 239
  Hardwoods as, 236
  Softwoods as, 236, 238
Furniture, Camp, 53
  Rustic, 218

Gall-bladder, 272, 282
Game, Big, Cooking, 290
  birds. *See* Birds
  Cooking, 305
  Curry of, 308

INDEX 399

Game.— *Continued.*
　Dressing and keeping, 264
　Hanging to ripen, 274, 282, 291, 314
　pie, 308
　pot pie, 307
　Shipping small, 283
　Small, Cooking, 308
Gingerbread, 348, 382
Gloves, 160
Gnats, 255
Goggles, 173
Going light, 109
Goose, Roasted, 317
　To dress, 282
Gravy, 297, 302, 303
　Bacon, 332
　Cream, 303
　for boiled meat, 303
　roast meat, 303
　from beef extract, 303
　Onion, 303
　Pork, 333
Greens, Wild, 369
Grilling on a rock, 293
Grits, Boiled, 362
　Fried, 362
Gritted bread, 354
Groundhog, Cooking, 313
Ground sheets, 37, 107
Grouse, Baking with beans, 297
　Broiled, 319
　Roasted, 319
　To dress, 282, 283
　dry, 279
Guy frames, 46

Ham, 187
　and eggs, 333
　　macaroni, 334
　Boiled, 333
　Broiled, 333
　chow, 334
　Fried, 333
Hardtack, 191, 333, 335
Hardwoods and softwoods, 236
Hare. *See* Rabbit

Hash, Codfish, 337
　Corned beef, 335
　Potato and onion, 367
Hat-bands, 139, 160
Hatchets, 165
Hats, 159
Head nets, 160
Headwear, 159
Heart, Cooking, 306
Herrings, Smoked, Cooking, 337
Hitch, Magnus, 47
Hobnails, 154
Hogs, 222
Horn, Huntsman's, 118

Ice, 220, 287
Insect bites and stings, 249, 257
Insecticides, 247
Insects in camp, 256
　Noxious, 241

Jackets, Leather, 147
Jackknives, 167
Jambolaya, 308
Jelly from dried fruit, 379
Jerusalem artichokes, Cooking, 371
Johnny-cake, 352

Kabobs, 296
Khaki, canvas, 33
Kedgeree, 369
Kidneys, Cooking, 306
Kindling, 233
Kit bags, 165
Knickerbockers, 145
Knives, Pocket, 167
　Sheath, 166

Lanolin, 149
Lanterns, 60, 117
Lard, 197
　Larrigans, 157
Latrine, 223
Leather, To waterproof, 154
Left-overs, 307, 319, 355, 360, 362, 365, 366, 376

INDEX

Leggings, 145
Lemonade powder, 197
Lightning, 215
Liver, Cooking, 306
Lobscouse, 335

Macaroni, 193
  Baked, 359
  Boiled, 359
  with cheese, 359
Mackinaws, 147, 162
Mammals, Small, To dress, 280
Mapping, 169
Map cases, 171
Maps, 170
Marrow-bones, 307
Match, To light in wind, 234
Matchboxes, 173
Matches, To waterproof, 173
Mattresses, 53, 134
  Air, 135
Measures, Cook's, 387
Meat, Canned, 187, 336
  Stewed, 335
  Care of, 220, 275
  Cooking, 290
  Cured, To cook, 332
  Curing, 276
  Frozen, 305
  "Jerked," 277
  Salt, Boiled, 299
Medical kits, 58
Mending canvas, 40
Mice, 263
Midges, 255
Milk, Condensed, 190
  Powdered, 190
  To heat, 300
Milt (spleen), To cook, 307
Moccasins, 157
Moose, Butchering, 273
  muffle, To cook, 307
Mosquito bars, 39, 55, 74, 106
  dopes, 243
Mosquitoes, 160, 241
Mulligan (skilly), 376

Munson shoe lasts, 151
Mush, Boiled, 360
  Fried, 360
Mushrooms, Cooking, 371
  Edible, 372
Muskrat, To cook, 313
  dress, 281

Neckerchiefs, 143
"No-see-ums," 255
Nut butter, 196
Nuts, 196

Oatmeal porridge, 361
Oil, Olive, 197
Oiled cloth, 71, 73
Oilskins, 160
  Care of, 161
Omelets. *See* Eggs
Onions, 194
  Boiled, 369
Opossum. *See* 'Possum
Outfits, Individual, 112
Outfitter's data, 387
Outfitting, 23, 109
Oven, Clay, 345
  Dutch, 64
  To use, 296, 342
  Reflecting, 121
  To use, 296, 323, 347
  Sheet steel, 122
Overalls, 160
Overshirts, 142, 162
Oysters, Fried, 329
  Roasted, 330
  Sauté, 330
  Scalloped, 330
  Steamed, 301
  Stewed, 329

Pack, Indian, 267
Packing, 113, 205
Pacs, Shoe, 157
Pancakes, Corn, 352, 356
  Egg, 355
  Snow, 355
Parboiling, 300, 305
Parsly butter, 304
Pea soup, 376
Peas, 195
Pegs, To drive in tree, 220

INDEX

Personal kits, 164
Pests of the woods, 241
Photography, 176
Pie, Fruit, 381
  Game, 308
  Pot, 307
Pillows, 135
Pine knots, 233
Plasmon, 192
Plaster, Adhesive, 116
Pliers, 115
Plover, Cooking, 319
  To dress, 283
Plum duff, 384
Poisoning, Ptomaine, 188, 286
Poke shoots, Cooking, 370
Polenta, 361
Ponchos, 146, 160
Porcupine, 259
  Cooking, 313
  To dress, 313
Pork and hardtack, 333
  fritters, 333
  Salt, 187
    Boiled, 333
    Broiled, 333
    Fried, 333
Porridge, 360
'Possum, Baked, 311
  Roasted, 312
  To dress, 311
Pot pie, Game, 307
Potatoes and onions hashed, 367
  au gratin, 366
  Baked, 365
  Boiled, 364
  cakes, 365
  Creamed, 366
  Fried, 365
  Lyonnaise, 366
  Mashed, 365
  Steamed, 365
  Stewed, 366
  Sweet, Boiled, 366
    Fried, 367
Pots, 119
Pouches, 165
Privacy of camp, 216
Protective coloration, 162

Protein, 179, 185, 202
Provisions. *See* Food
Ptomaine poisoning, 188, 286
Pudding, Batter, 384
  Cottage, 383
  Fruit, 383
  Rice, 383
  sauce, 385
  Suet, 384
Punkies, 255
Puttees, 145

Quail, Cooking, 319
Quilts, 126, 129
Quoits, Fried, 357

Rabbit, Baked, 310
  Fried, 310
  Roasted, 310
  Stewed, 310
  To dress, 281, 310
Raccoon. *See* 'Coon.
Ragouts, 300
Rail, Cooking breast of, 319
Ration lists, 200
  Cruisers' and campers', 203
  U. S. Army, 200
Rats, 263
Reflectors, 121
  Baking in, 347
  Roasting in, 296, 323
Refrigerators, 67, 220, 287
Refuse, Disposal of, 222
Repair kits, 116, 161, 176
Repairs, Quick, 116
Rice, 193
  Boiled, 361
  Curried, 362
  Fried, 362
  muffins, 362
  Spanish, 362
  with onions, 362
Risotto, 362
Roasting, 294
Roasting-ears, 369
Rolls, Breakfast, 348
Roughing it, 110, 124
Route sketching, 169

Roux, 302
Rubber clothing, 160
  footwear, 161

Saccharin, 193
Salad dressing, 370
Salads, Scalded, 370
  Wild, 370
Salmon, Creamed, 337
  on toast, 337
  Scalloped, 337
Salt, 199
Sandals for wading, 157
Sanitation, 222
Sardines on toast, 338
Sauce, 303
  Brandy, 385
  Butter, 325
  Celery, 320
  Cranberry, 320
  Curry, 320
  Fruit, 385
  Giblet, 316
  Hard, 385
  India, 325
  Lemon, 325
  Mustard, 304, 326
  Pudding, 385
  Tomato, 359
  Venison, 304
  White, 325
Sausage, Pork, 334
  Venison, 307
Saws, 59
Scales, 115
Scent glands, 305, 310, 312–314
Scorpions, 257
Shade, 215
Shear lashings, 47
Shears, Tent, 47
Sheath knives, 166
Shellfish, Cooking, 329
  Steamed, 301
Shelter-cloths, 97
Shelves, 58
Shipping fish, 288
  Game, 283
Shirts, 142
  Mackinaw, 147, 162
Shoe laces, 135, 151

Shoe-pacs, 157
Shoes, 151
  Breaking in, 152
  Canvas, 159
  Care of, 152
  Waterproofed, 153
Sink, Camp, 223
Sirup, 194
  To make, 356
Skilligalee, 376
Skins, Preserving, 275
Skunk-bite, 262
Skunks, 260
Sleeping bags, 126, 129, 131, 135
Slickers, 160
Slumgullion, 335
Smudges, 256
Sneakers, 159
Snipe, Cooking, 319
  To dress, 283
Snits und Knepp, 381
Snow bread, 353
  glasses, 173
  pancakes, 355
Soap, 119, 141, 176
Socks, 142
  German, 146, 161
Soda, Substitutes for, 354
Sod-cloths, 37, 74
Sorrel, Cooking, 371
Soup, 373
  Bean, 375
  Canned, 188
  Condensed (dry), 188
  Croutons for, 375
  Pea, 376
  Squirrel, 375
  stock, 374
  Tomato, 375
  Turtle, 376
  Venison, 374
Spades, 59, 115
Spaghetti, 359
Spleen, Cooking, 307
Sprats, Cooking, 337
Spring box, 221
Springs, 210
Squirrel, Barbecued, 309
  Broiled, 309
  Fried, 309

INDEX

Squirrel.— *Continued.*
  soup, 375
  Stewed, 309
  To dress, 280
Stakes, To drive, 219
Stationery, 172
Steaming fish, 324
  meat and vegetables, 301
Stewing, 300
Stings, 249, 257
Storm set, 45
Storms, 51
Stove-pipe holes, 40
  spark arrester, 63
Stoves, Cook, 60
  Heating, 63, 79
Stove-shield, 63
Stuffing for fish, 323
  rabbit, 310
  turkey, 315
Sugar, 193
Sweaters, 147
Sweets, 193
System in camping, 217

Table for choosing what to cook, 388
Tables, Camp, 56
  Rustic, 218
Tarantulas, 258
Tarp bed-sheet, 134
Tea, 198
  Steeping, 378
Tepees, 81
Tent, Action of wind on, 51
  canopies, 36
  Care of, 40
  door, 39
    weights, 39
  flies, 35, 51
  floors, cloth, 105, 107
    wooden, 49
  furnishings, 221
  furniture, 53
  ground, 212
  hangers, 58
  making, 88, 98
  materials, heavy, 31
    light, 69, 71
  mending, 40

Tent.— *Continued.*
  on rocky or sandy ground, 50
  shears, 46, 99, 106
  tripods, 83, 104
  parrels, 93, 96
  poles, 40, 45, 47, 78, 82, 94
  rental, 41
  ropes, 34, 75
  slides, 75
  stakes and pins, 40, 43, 50, 75
  striking, 43
  trenching, 49
  ventilation, 38
  windows, 38, 74
  with side bars, 48
  workmanship, 34, 74
Tents, "A," 92
  Alpine, 94, 96
  Baker, 98
  Bell, 78
Tents, Camp-fire, 100
  Canoe, 102
  Colored, 35
  Commissary, 101
  "Compac," 103
  Conical, 78
    To pitch, 79
  "Explorer's," 106
  for fixed camps, 29
    shifting camps, 68, 76
  Frazer, 84
  George, 85
  Hudson Bay, 95
  Insect-proof, 106
  Lean-to, 98
  Light, 68
  Marquee, 84
  Miner's, 82
  Pyramidal, 81
  Ross, 96
  Royce, 85
  Second-hand, 41
  Separable shelter, 96
  Semi-pyramidal, 84
  Shelter, 96
  Sibley, 78
  Snow, 105
  Tarpaulin, 98

INDEX

Tents.— *Continued*.
  Tropical, 37
  Wall, heavy, 29
    light, 76
    To pitch, 41
  Waterproof, 34, 69
  Wedge, 92
    To pitch, 92
  Whymper, 94
Ticks, 247, 255
Time-tables, Cook's, 388
  for boiling vegetables, 373
  roasting birds, 317
Toast, French, 356
  Milk, 356
Toilet articles, 176
Tomato soup, 375
Tomatoes, 195
  Cooking, 307
Tongue, Cooking, 307
Tools, 59, 113
Trees and lightning, 215
  Neighborhood of, 214
Tropics, Pests of, 251
Trousers, 144
Trout, To clean, 283
Turkey, Boiled, 316
  Roasted, 295, 315
  Stuffing for, 316
  To dress, 282
Turtle, Cooking, 329
  Soup, 376

Underclothing, 139
Union suits, 141

Vacations, 17
Vegetables boiled with meat, 299
  Canned, 195
    Cooking, 363
    Cleaning, 363
  Dehydrated, 195, 200
    Cooking, 363
  Dried, Cooking, 363
  Fresh, 194
  Storing, 364
  Time-table for boiling, 373

Venison, Cooking, 305
  Cured, Cooking, 336
  Sauce for, 304
  sausages, 307
  soup, 374
  To cure, 276
    hang for ripening, 274, 291
    jerk, 277
    ship, 288
Vests, 148

Waders, 157, 161
Wall pockets, 58, 137
Warbles, 311
Wash-boilers, 206
Wash-stand, 222
Washing clothing, 141, 142
  dishes, 386
Watches, 169
Water, 209
  Alkaline, 210
  To clarify, 211
    cool, 212
    purify, 211
Waterfowl, To dress, 282, 316
Waterproof cloths for tents, 34, 69
  tents, 34, 69
Waterproofing cloth, 72
  leather, 154
  matches, 173
  Woolens, 148
Waterproofs, 160
Weight of game, Computing, 280
Weights and measures of food, 387
Whistles, 170
Wild, Call of the, 17
Wilderness, Charm of, 21
Wind, Action of, on tents, 51
Wolverines, 262
Women, Clothing for, 163
Woodcock, Cooking, 319

Woodchuck, Cooking, 313
Woods as fuel, 236
  Green, as fuel, 237
  hard to split, 237
  Hardwoods and softwoods, 236
  Spitfire, 237
  Uninflammable, 236
Woodsman, Qualities of, 24, 110
Wool vs. cotton, 127, 128, 140, 144
Woolens, To waterproof, 148
Wounds, Treatment of, 175

www.ingramcontent.com/pod-product-compliance
Lightning Source LLC
Chambersburg PA
CBHW021051080526
44587CB00010B/204